THE SOUL OF BASKETBALL

THE SOUL OF BASKETBALL

THE EPIC SHOWDOWN BETWEEN LeBRON, KOBE, DOC, AND DIRK THAT SAVED THE NBA

Ian Thomsen

Houghton Mifflin Harcourt
Boston   New York
2018

For information about permission to reproduce selections from this book,
write to trade.permissions@hmhco.com or to Permissions, Houghton Mifflin Harcourt
Publishing Company, 3 Park Avenue, 19th Floor, New York, New York 10016.

hmhco.com

Library of Congress Cataloging-in-Publication Data
Names: Thomsen, Ian, author.
Title: The soul of basketball : the epic showdown between LeBron, Kobe, Doc,
and Dirk that saved the NBA / Ian Thomsen.
Description: Boston : Houghton Mifflin Harcourt, 2018. | Includes index.
Identifiers: LCCN 2017050919 (print) | LCCN 2017046213 (ebook) |
ISBN 9780547746890 (ebook) | ISBN 9780547746517 (hardcover)
Subjects: LCSH: National Basketball Association — History. | Basketball —
United States — History. | James, LeBron. | Bryant, Kobe, 1978– | Rivers, Glenn. |
Nowitzki, Dirk, 1978–
Classification: LCC GV885.515.N37 (print) | LCC GV885.515.N37 T56 2018 (ebook) |
DDC 796.323/64 — dc23
LC record available at https://lccn.loc.gov/2017050919

Printed in the United States of America
DOC 10 9 8 7 6 5 4 3 2 1

For Jacqueline
Christopher
Maureen

I will not follow where the path may lead, but I will go where there is no path, and I will leave a trail.

— Muriel Strode

Jazz music explains . . . what it means to be American. Which is that it's a process. And democracy is a process. It's not always going to go your way. Sometimes you have to play that riff and listen to what somebody else is playing. Jazz believes in freedom of expression. But it also believes in people communicating with each other. A lot of times things might not work out. But there's always another time.

— Wynton Marsalis

CONTENTS

PROLOGUE: THE FAIRY TALE

So," asked the interviewer hired by LeBron James to interview him in front of a live TV audience, "does the team that you're going to, that you'll announce in a few minutes — do they know your decision?"

"Uh, they just found out," LeBron replied.

"They just found out?" Even LeBron's accomplice looked surprised.

"Yeah."

"So the other five, on pins and needles, they don't know. They'll be listening to this?"

"Right," LeBron said.

LeBron, 25 years old, was the most precious free agent of the new lucrative era that had been pioneered decades earlier by Michael Jordan. A half-dozen franchises of the National Basketball Association had convinced LeBron to consider playing for them, and the other twenty-four teams were unmistakably envious. At 6 feet 8 inches tall and more than 260 pounds, LeBron was on his way to becoming the most versatile star in the short history of the NBA. Already he had been named the NBA's Rookie of the Year, an All-Star for the ensuing six seasons and the league's Most Valuable Player the past two years.

In prime time, on national TV, LeBron was about to announce which lucky franchise would be given the opportunity to pay him more than $15 million annually.

"Do you have any doubts about your decision?"

"Um, no," LeBron said unconvincingly. "I don't have any doubts at all."

His body language betrayed his words. It appeared to be occurring to LeBron just now, on TV screens throughout America, that he was not yet everything that he was cracking himself up to be. LeBron had been hailed since adolescence as the second coming of Michael Jordan, and yet he had not come close to leading his hometown team, the Cleveland Cavaliers, to the NBA championship. That was the problem with this outlandish production, which he had created for himself. He looked anxious.

"Would you like to sleep on it a little longer, or are you ready to make this decision?"

All around the country people were yelling for LeBron to get to the point. His made-for-TV event had been on the air for close to a half hour already.

"I've slept enough," said LeBron. "Or the lack of sleep."

His curious vanity show, titled *The Decision,* was meant to take advantage of the public interest in his future. LeBron would insist that he produced his TV special to raise $2.5 million for the Boys & Girls Clubs of America, which was admirable indeed. But there was no doubt that he also viewed this reality-based infomercial as a chance to grow his own brand commercially. He paid up front for the national airtime on ESPN, and he took personal responsibility for selling the commercials and sponsorships in order to leverage his fame and extend his reach further into the entertainment mainstream.

As many as thirteen million Americans were drawn to watch *The Decision* by its promise of betrayal. Was LeBron putting his fans in Cleveland through needless angst before announcing that he would re-sign, after all, with the Cavaliers? Or, even worse, had he chosen the cruel gimmick of this self-serving TV show as a vehicle for abandoning his hometown team in favor of a more glamorous destination — the New York Knicks, the New Jersey Nets (themselves on the verge of relocating to chic Brooklyn), the Chicago Bulls, the Los Angeles Clippers, or the Miami Heat?

LeBron's decision was being driven by his desire to win at the highest level and define himself as an NBA champion. But his conceit of *The Decision* was burying that lead. LeBron, inexplicably, was taking himself out of context in order to satisfy the prime-time format of reality TV.

So why was he choosing to cast himself as the villain? The cynicism of his fiasco was inconsistent with the high-minded devotion to teamwork that he had shown throughout his brief career. Never mind the surprise announcement that he was about to make: LeBron's active participation in his own demise would emerge as the real twist of the show.

It was being broadcast from a suburban Boys & Girls Club gymnasium that had been chosen for him in Greenwich, Connecticut, an hour north of Manhattan. LeBron had grown up playing in gyms like this, and he should have felt at home amid the two-toned cinder block, the stale smells and muted echoes. But he would find no comfort here. By the time he arrived via private jet, the little gym had been taken over by LeBron's corporate partners. The warm brown glow of the basketball court was blighted by the black-curtained stage on which LeBron and his co-host sat facing each other. There were hot lights and wires and strangers everywhere, all under frenzied pressure to synchronize the details of a live broadcast that was doomed to fail. The local children who normally might have been playing in the gym had been propped up on rows of shallow bleachers to serve as the TV backdrop to LeBron, alongside a banner that read "Great Futures Start Here." The boys and girls sat in fidgeting demonstration that LeBron was doing all of this for them rather than for himself.

A dozen years earlier LeBron might have been sitting down there looking up to his hero, Michael Jordan, for inspiration and guidance. But then, Jordan surely would have known better; he never would have made the mistakes that LeBron was making now. As LeBron sat high upon the throne of a director's chair, the scene told a story all its own, of how LeBron's fame radiated out and reshaped the order of everything that mattered to him. Too late he would realize that he had hired in the cameras and microphones without knowing how to explain himself. He was exploiting his dream before he had fulfilled its promise.

The interviewer, behaving as if everything was going terrifically, smiled his big smile and said, "Are you still a nail biter?"

LeBron looked wounded. He was aware that his nervous habit, as televised in close-ups during the timeouts of Cavaliers games, was viewed as a symptom of his failure to live up to the expectations that had been shadowing him since he was 16 years old. "I have, a little bit," he said in his deep, resonant voice, trying to smile back while squeezing his long fingers into his lap. "Not of late."

"You've had everybody else biting their nails. So I guess it's time for them to stop chewing. The answer to the question everybody wants to know: LeBron, what's your decision?"

On this night of July 8, 2010, the tension within LeBron was shrinking his eyes. "In this fall —" He stopped abruptly. "This is very tough," he went on with newfound sincerity, as if suddenly asking himself what he was doing and how he had come to this strange place in his life.

But then, just as quickly, LeBron was reverting to the script. "In this fall I'm going to . . ."

• • •

LeBron had been discovered as a skinny 16-year-old with acne and long, un-managed hair who was starring for an Amateur Athletic Union (AAU) team from Akron, his hometown forty-five minutes south of Cleveland. Even then, not quite a decade before *The Decision,* LeBron had the makings of everything anyone could want in a basketball player — size, strength, athleticism, skills and vision — a point guard with a power forward's build. He was the most gifted prospect the NBA scouts had ever seen.

In those days there was nothing not to like about LeBron.

He was devoted to his mother, Gloria James, a troubled single parent who had given birth to LeBron when she was 16. He was grounded in his closest childhood relationships, and he remained loyal to those friends even as his own fame grew exponentially. He was well-spoken and intuitive. As a child LeBron had been exposed to poverty, crime and negligence, and yet his inclination was to avoid violence and steer clear of trouble. His mother and he had moved house a dozen times already when LeBron was invited to live out his fifth-grade year in the wholesome home of Frank and Pam Walker and their three children in Akron. Years later the Walkers would recall LeBron's please-and-thank-you manners, his shy personality and his desire to oblige. "He wants to be liked," Pam Walker would say. For the first time in his life, the Walkers established for him a daily schedule of homework and chores, and he embraced the discipline.

In high school he could have easily hoarded points for himself, but he wasn't one of those gifted bullies who claims to own the ball. LeBron's ideal was to share it, in the belief that he couldn't win unless his teammates won too. Their happiness made him happy.

The commercial sponsors who had done so well in the 1990s with Michael Jordan were now, in the new millennium, lusting after the teenaged LeBron as if he were the surest thing ever. Their confidence in his potential had everything to do with the revealing nature of basketball as the one sport that provided every player with the freedom to pass or shoot the ball. The intuitive nature of LeBron's playmaking — he decided whether to keep or share the ball at full speed in the flow of the game — made it impossible for him to fake the commitment to teamwork that he was expressing.

Anyone with a stake in the NBA could see that the way LeBron played basketball was an authentic demonstration of the man he wanted to become. He had the potential to surpass Michael Jordan — to marry Jordan's scoring and defensive skills with an evolved desire to create opportunities for his teammates. Bigger and stronger and every bit as athletic as Jordan, LeBron was expected to become all things to all people.

What, then, would go wrong? Why, within a decade, would LeBron go on TV to betray his own values and ambitions?

When Michael Jordan was 25, the same age as LeBron on the night of *The Decision,* he admitted to his own chronic fear that an off-court scandal would ruin the goodwill that he was building on the court. He was leveraging his talent for basketball in an unprecedented way, and he worried about all of the potential mistakes that he couldn't see coming. He had "nightmares of something terrible happening to me that would destroy a lot of people's dreams or conceptions of me," he said in 1988. "That's the biggest nightmare I live every day."

Jordan's instinct for self-preservation was the result of having assembled his portfolio of sponsorships from the ground up, piece by piece. By contrast, when LeBron came into the NBA at age 18, he was rewarded with eight-figure endorsements before he had accomplished anything of real importance in basketball. His client list appeared to have been inherited directly from Jordan.

"The mix of products was exactly the same — Coca-Cola, Nike, McDonald's," said Jordan's agent, David Falk, while noting that McDonald's had entered LeBron's stable only months before *The Decision.* "You want to say, 'Come on, change the mold. Been there, done it. Do something new.' Why can't we find a new mix, to come in and say we're going to do it differently?"

Falk continued, "People try so hard to invent the next Michael, and they'll never be able to do it. It happened with Jordan because no one was trying to make it happen. Today it doesn't happen because everyone is trying so hard to make it happen, and then it's not genuine. It has to be genuine. Seeing all of these people trying to create the next Jordan makes you want to throw up. It has to be real. It has to be genuine."

LeBron was being cast as the new Jordan, even though the two players had been raised in entirely different basketball worlds two decades apart. In 1978, when Jordan was a 15-year-old sophomore in Wilmington, North Carolina, he failed to earn a place on the varsity basketball team at Emsley A. Laney Senior High School. His heir would meet no such failure: When LeBron was a 17-year-old junior at St. Vincent–St. Mary High School in Akron, his photograph appeared on the cover of *Sports Illustrated* with a headline that introduced him as "The Chosen One."

A similar opportunity had been made available to Jordan when he was an 18-year-old incoming freshman at the University of North Carolina. *Sports Illustrated* wanted to feature Jordan on the cover with his fellow starters. But that offer was rejected by coach Dean Smith as a reward that Jordan hadn't earned. Instead the magazine's 1981–82 preview of the college season featured Smith and four of his upperclassmen — every Carolina starter *except* Jordan.

"LeBron's games in high school were shown on national TV," said Falk. "And Dean wouldn't let Michael be on the cover of *SI* because he was a freshman. Think about that." Dean Smith, Jordan's mentor, was banishing entitlement from his life; he was encouraging Jordan to reach and fight.

By the end of that season, with his team down by one point in the final thirty-two seconds of the NCAA title game, Smith would draw up a jump shot that the freshman Jordan would convert to win the national championship. Jordan would go on to become first-team All-America each of the next two seasons, as well as the consensus NCAA Player of the Year as a junior, sending him on to the 1984 Summer Olympics as America's leading amateur basketball player and eventual gold medalist. Having accomplished all that, Jordan, a 6-foot 6-inch guard, was still no better than the number three pick in the 1984 NBA draft. He sat watching as a pair of 7-footers, Akeem (who would rename himself Hakeem) Olajuwon and Sam Bowie, were chosen ahead of him.

"He came in under the radar," said Falk. "There was not a single guy in the NBA who thought Jordan was going to be that great."

The opposite was believed of LeBron. When he entered the NBA as the number one pick straight out of high school, the anticipation for his greatness was almost universal. As any teen might have done — including Jordan, had he been enticed to turn pro instead of submitting to Dean Smith for three years — LeBron embraced the hype as if it were real. Adults rich and powerful were offering him millions of dollars based on his potential, and who was young LeBron to argue? Of course he wanted to believe.

Jordan, having considered himself the underdog, was able to overdeliver. LeBron, by comparison, was introduced to the public as if his success was guaranteed.

As a Cleveland Cavalier he chose to wear number 23, which had been Jordan's original number. On his right biceps was a tattoo of a crowned lion amid the script *KING JAMES*. Across the skin of his broad back, like an oversized name sewn onto a jersey, LeBron had a tattoo based on the headline of his magazine cover from high school: *CHOSEN-1*.

"I asked him why he had that tattoo on his back and why he wouldn't want to take it off," said Pat Riley, the president of the Miami Heat, who watched *The Decision* from a restaurant in South Beach while waiting for LeBron to make his choice official. "That's just above and beyond expectations and having to prove yourself. I mean, he agreed to have somebody put that tattoo on his back. There was a part of him that believed that."

CHOSEN-1 and *KING JAMES* and 23 were more than nicknames and numbers. They were titles of inheritance, and on the court, in the ultimate sport of merit, they would emerge as obstacles for him to overcome.

Jordan did not win the NBA championship until his seventh season, when he overcame his reputation for being selfish.

By 2010 the complaint against LeBron, after his seventh season, was that he needed to play more selfishly and that he was lacking Jordan's killer instinct.

Jordan, in spite of his worst fears, would not go unscathed by scandal. His nightmares came true in the 1990s, when his habit of gambling in casinos and on golf courses led to speculation, never proved, that his brief "retirement" (resulting in a short-lived baseball career in 1993–94) had been forced on him by NBA commissioner David Stern.

And yet Jordan's audiences kept growing in America and around the world because fans could see for themselves that he had his priorities straight. Regardless of any personal flaws, it was obvious to the record numbers of viewers who watched Jordan win NBA championships in his final six full seasons with the Chicago Bulls that winning the game came first for him. That was why they didn't begrudge him his rewards. As much as he valued his money and fame, he was driven by a higher calling when he played basketball. Jordan's fans the world over were convinced that he respected the game, which was taken to mean that he respected them as well.

By contrast, when basketball fans became convinced that LeBron was trying to exploit them, which was a natural assumption based on *The Decision,* they felt compelled to question his respect for the game. The mess he made off the court began to seep onto the court. The fans' perception was giving way to a miserable reality for LeBron — and for his league.

LeBron and his generation of NBA stars had grown up revering Jordan, with dreams of building upon his legacy. But how could they ever relate to him?

Before Jordan turned pro in 1984, the NBA had been on the verge of bankruptcy. Throughout the fourteen-year span of his career, new money began pouring in, and it transformed the struggling league into a global entertainment industry. The money brimmed over and trickled down to the youth levels, changing basketball in America from top to bottom, and LeBron was among the first stars to grow up in this new world.

When Jordan was a teenager, high school coaches held the power of authority over players like him, and he had little choice but to do as he was told. When LeBron was in high school, he held the power. He and his friends decided where they would play — not only for a private high school in Akron but also for the Shooting Stars, the local team in the Amateur Athletic Union, which had been reshaped by the new money of the 1990s. The top AAU programs and tournaments were now underwritten by the sneaker companies as part of their manhunt for the next Jordan, which led, full circle, to the discovery of the teenaged LeBron.

Sponsors like Nike, Coca-Cola and McDonald's wielded new power over basketball. As professionals, Jordan and LeBron would be paid more for thirty-second commercials and other promotional agreements off the court than for their performance on the court.

In Jordan's youth there had been fewer concerns about whether the cart was being put before the horse, and maybe that was because Jordan was raised in a time when money had little to do with basketball. He wouldn't discover the world of commercials until after he was all grown up. His childhood love for the game was uncomplicated and single-minded.

LeBron, who in his senior year of high school drove a $50,000 custom-made Hummer H2, had no such advantage.

When Michael Jordan stole the ball and sank the most dramatic of all jump shots to win his farewell championship for the Chicago Bulls in 1998, it was like a fairy tale come true. His career had peaked at its very end, and his league had been saved. At that moment all things in basketball seemed possible.

In the dozen years following Jordan's retirement from the Bulls, the four biggest NBA stories were played out away from the court: In 2004 Kobe Bryant and Shaquille O'Neal were divorced as teammates of the championship Los Angeles Lakers; later that year the players of the Indiana Pacers brawled with fans in Detroit; in 2007 Tim Donaghy was exposed as a crooked referee; and in 2010 arrived *The Decision* of LeBron James.

The Decision was final proof that the NBA was not living happily ever after. There was reason to fear that the game was under threat, that off-the-court realities were overwhelming on-the-court ideals, that the dream was at the mercy of its rewards.

LeBron was sitting before the cameras at the end of a long wild-goose chase that was supposed to end with him becoming the "next Jordan." But it now appeared, on live television, that he had been sent down the wrong path. He was never meant to be what Jordan had been. Little could he know that the terms of his inheritance would hold him responsible for putting the money in its place, for affirming the NBA's higher calling and for reconnecting the American game with its soul.

As LeBron struggled to find the words to announce his decision, his destiny was coming into focus. A new basketball world, affluent and conflicted, had been handed down to him. His mission was to make sense of it.

THE SOUL OF BASKETBALL

1

THE BASTARD

No sooner did he begin to dribble the ball than the Boston Celtics were running a second defender at Kobe Bryant. He responded to their double-teaming as they hoped he would. He tried to do as Michael Jordan might have done.

It was Game 7 of the 2010 NBA Finals in Los Angeles. The Lakers and the Celtics had been meeting routinely in the championship round since 1959 — their reunions accounting for almost one-fourth of the NBA Finals over the past fifty-two years — but the tactics for this winner-take-all game did not hark back to the days of Bob Cousy versus Jerry West or Bill Russell versus Wilt Chamberlain or Larry Bird versus Magic Johnson. Instead the game plan of Boston's head coach, Doc Rivers, had led the contest in an entirely new direction. His team's defensive strategy was based on Kobe's obsession with the ghost of Jordan. It was as if the Celtics were channeling Hamlet.

"I went to Tibs," recalled Doc of his pregame conversation with defensive assistant Tom Thibodeau, "and I said, 'We've got to double-team Kobe more in this game.' We hadn't done that all series. It was a feeling I believed in my heart, that Kobe was going to do whatever he could to win the game himself. And we could not allow that to happen, because then he would — he's that good."

As his Celtics ran out to an early lead, Doc could see Kobe taking the bait. "The philosophy was the right one," Doc said. "Because he wasn't going to leave it in someone else's hands."

Instead of passing to his open teammates, Kobe kept pounding the ball stubbornly, greedily, even as the two Celtics defenders were guiding him into the least accommodating corners of the court, trapping him there as if he had followed his dribble into a dark alley, the ball thumping like a panicked heartbeat. One of Kobe's well-defended jumpers caromed wildly off the edge of the backboard. An air ball soared over the rim.

He was playing the biggest game of his life as if he were one isolated Laker against five interwoven Celtics. Kobe had never looked more vulnerable or desperate with the ball.

"You guys are working too hard," shouted coach Phil Jackson to his Lakers as they huddled during a timeout. "Relax out here and play right. You've got to get better shots. You do that by making the ball move. The ball's got to move."

Jackson was scolding the team, but his words were meant specifically for Kobe. After ten seasons in two tours with the Lakers, Jackson had learned to avoid confronting his star head-on. Everyone in the huddle grasped the larger story. They knew very well that Kobe had dreamed all his adult life of becoming his generation's Michael Jordan. That was the goal the Celtics were now daring Kobe to reach for, because they knew that it could never be.

The immediate goal for Kobe was to win this game for the fifth NBA championship of his career, which would give him one more title than his former teammate and rival Shaquille O'Neal.

"I read something that Shaq said comparing me to Anfernee Hardaway," recalled Kobe, "and how I wouldn't be able to win without him."

"Penny" Hardaway, an All-Star guard with the Orlando Magic, had reached the 1995 NBA Finals in his second season with O'Neal. After O'Neal left the Magic to join the Lakers, Hardaway was limited to one playoff series victory in eleven years.

"I take that as a challenge," Kobe said of O'Neal's comment. "You're challenging me. I will show you that I can win. I'm going to show you and I'm going to show everybody that agrees with you."

In the years following Jordan's retirement from the Bulls, the 7-foot-1 O'Neal and 6-foot-6 Kobe stepped forth as the NBA's biggest stars while leading the Lakers to the first three championships of the new millennium. O'Neal was dominating the league at age 30, forcing rivals to stockpile big men in hopes of corralling him, and Kobe was his 23-year-old complement on the perimeter.

The certainty of winning many more titles should have been enough to hold them together. But this was a complicated era defined by Jordan, whose new convoluted standard would tear O'Neal and Kobe apart.

Jordan's most startling achievement on the court had been to lead the NBA in scoring in each of his six championship seasons. This had been done only one time in the previous forty years, by Lew Alcindor (who would rename himself Kareem Abdul-Jabbar) of the Milwaukee Bucks in 1970–71. Jordan proved that a champion could be selfish and selfless at the same time, which obliterated the moral code for basketball that had been established by the Celtics in the 1950s and '60s. The Celtics were proud that none of their stars had ever won the NBA scoring title, based on the stubborn belief of their coach Red Auerbach that a hard choice had to be made — that players had to decide whether they were playing for themselves or for their team.

O'Neal would pull off the Jordan double by leading the NBA in scoring while winning his first championship in 1999–2000 alongside Kobe, who was clearly influenced by the example. And so the two Lakers each took on the challenge of picking up where Jordan had left off. Jordan had been the league's leader in every way — its biggest star commercially, its top scorer and its undefeated champion over his last six full seasons in Chicago. Nothing less would do for O'Neal and Kobe, which meant that each wanted the other to get out of the way. Instead of recognizing how much they needed each other, as the leaders of virtually all of the previous NBA championship teams had done, Kobe and O'Neal grew to view each other with suspicion. O'Neal was preventing Kobe from emulating Jordan, and vice versa.

"If you think about me having to sacrifice my game and what I can do individually — which I've shown since Shaq left — that's a very mature thing to do," Kobe said. "I'm 20, 21 years old, and I could go out there and score 35, 36 points a night. I sacrificed that to play in Phil's system and to play with Shaq. For a 20-, 21-, 22-, 23-year-old, that's not an easy thing to do. But I did it, and from that standpoint that was a very grown-up thing to do."

Those sacrifices had been normal among NBA champions until Jordan came along. O'Neal and Kobe put up with each other for five years of championship contention, until they couldn't take it any longer.

"He was going to stay and I was going to go, or he was going to go and I was going to stay," Kobe said. "One of those things had to give because I was hell-bent on proving that I could win without him."

Kobe had grown up imitating Jordan's scoring moves as well as his personal mannerisms. Early in his career Kobe spoke like Jordan in cadence and tone, with the same gestures, down to the mid-sentence flicking of his lip with his tongue. He was forever seeking advice from Jordan, though their conversations were a one-way street. "I really don't say much to him," said Kobe, "because, shit, 90 percent of the stuff I know comes from him."

In Kobe's second NBA season, when he was a 19-year-old coming off the bench for the Lakers, the fans voted him into the starting lineup of the 1998 All-Star Game at Madison Square Garden. It was billed as a showdown between Jordan, who at 34 was making his All-Star farewell as a Bull, and his anticipated heir. Jordan and Kobe were shooting guards who applied explosive athleticism to overwhelm their larger opponents. Like Jordan, whose championship career was spent entirely in Chicago, Kobe had been drafted into a large market that would give him every chance to maximize his appeal. When Kobe swiped at the ball and Jordan pulled back, it was as if the greatest star was playfully refusing to pass the torch on to his next in line.

During that season young Kobe spoke openly of wanting to win at least as many championships as Jordan. He no longer made such claims in 2010, out of respect for his role model, but the Lakers' rivals in Boston knew better. "Kobe could be chasing Michael," Doc Rivers said.

In the summer of 2003, months before his final season with O'Neal, Kobe was arrested and charged with raping a 19-year-old hotel employee in Edwards, Colorado. The accusation would be dropped when the woman refused to testify. She settled her civil suit against him after he issued a public statement of apology without admitting guilt. "Although I truly believe this encounter between us was consensual, I recognize now that she did not and does not view this incident the same way I did," wrote Kobe. "After months of reviewing discovery, listening to her attorney, and even her testimony in person, I now understand how she feels that she did not consent to this encounter."

One year later Jackson was leaving the Lakers as their head coach, and O'Neal was being traded to the Miami Heat. A tell-all book by Jackson, *The Last Season: A Team in Search of Its Soul,* was published soon thereafter. Jackson's bluntness was astonishing. "Was I surprised?" wrote Jackson of the rape allegations. "Yes, but not entirely. Kobe can be consumed with surprising anger, which he's displayed toward me and toward his teammates . . . From what I understand, the defining characteristic of Kobe's childhood was his anger."

While O'Neal was winning fifty-nine games and leading Miami to the Eastern Conference Finals in 2005, laying down the foundation for the NBA championship that he and Dwyane Wade would win one year later in the NBA Finals against the Dallas Mavericks, Kobe's Lakers were suffering through the first losing season of his career. Jackson's replacement, Rudy Tomjanovich, quit as coach three months into a five-year, $30 million contract. Kobe's Lakers failed to reach the playoffs that year, while O'Neal's Heat were thriving.

That was all it took for Kobe to decide that he wanted Jackson to return to the Lakers, even though he had betrayed numerous confidences in his best-selling book. It was a choice that many NBA stars would not have made — including Jordan, who held lifelong grudges against those who disrespected him. "I don't think he was being fair," Kobe said of Jackson's accusations, but he was able to set aside his feelings because he was focused on the bottom line. One bad year had helped him to identify his priorities. Putting up with Jackson's disloyalty was less important to Kobe than benefiting from Jackson's wisdom and expertise in the triangle offense. (It may have helped, too, that Jackson had coached Jordan to six championships in Chicago.)

"It was just a phone conversation," said Kobe of his willingness to be coached by Jackson again. "We talked briefly. If you come to me and say, 'I apologize, I'm sorry that it took place,' all right. Cool. Let's move on."

When Jackson returned to coach the Lakers for the 2005–06 season, his relationship with Kobe was no longer dysfunctional. Their partnership was now being played out on Kobe's terms.

"When Phil came back, he made it a point: I'm not going to get into any more confrontations with Kobe, at all, at any cost," said Brian Shaw, who would spend eleven years with Kobe as a teammate and assistant coach. "So Kobe pretty much got to do whatever he wanted to do, and Phil stayed away from having any more confrontations with him. And then Kobe in return got this system back that he excelled in."

Was Kobe liberated simply because his coach had decided that encouraging him was in the best interests of everyone, including the Lakers? Or had he seized this freedom because Jackson had boxed himself into a corner by sensationalizing their relationship?

"I think it was a little bit of both," said Shaw. "[For] most of the people who were on that team or were coaches on that team, the stuff that Phil was talking about in the book, they would have said, 'That's right-on.'"

With O'Neal gone, however, Jackson had no option other than to coach Kobe with the same latitude that he had provided to Jordan throughout the 1990s.

"You got to work with this guy after you said all this stuff about him," Shaw said. "But I also think Kobe matured. He was a different Kobe. By the time Phil came back, he felt like he could allow Kobe to police his own situations and have some ownership in how things were done around there, be more of a leader than when Phil first left."

By now the future was coming into focus for Kobe. The accusation of sexual assault ensured that he would never be adored to the same degree as his idol Jordan. His divorce from O'Neal and his fleeting 2006 demand to be traded from the Lakers were combining with other controversies to transform him into the NBA's edgiest star. Instead of emulating the likeability of Jordan, Kobe appeared to be following the controversial path of Jordan's adversary Isiah Thomas.

In 2008 the Lakers traded for All-Star power forward Pau Gasol, enabling Kobe to win his fourth championship one year later against the Orlando Magic. "It probably was some kind of a liberating experience for me," said Kobe about his first title without O'Neal. He responded by embracing his villainy and revealing a personality all his own. He made crude jokes in public. He swore during televised interviews. After years of behaving like Jordan's replacement, Kobe was refusing to make believe anymore.

Off the court, Kobe had given up the challenge of becoming the next Jordan commercially. On the court, however, he was doubling down on the challenge to play like Jordan. He was pushing himself and his teammates harder than Jordan ever had. Kobe the player was all business. He was obsessed with the bottom line.

"He wants to build you up," Shaw said of Kobe's relationships with his teammates. "But he doesn't want anybody to save anybody."

Shaw had been around Kobe for more than a decade. After Shaw signed with the Lakers as a 33-year-old guard in 1999, in time to win championships alongside O'Neal and Kobe in each of his final three seasons as a player, he recognized Kobe's ability to sense fear in his teammates. If Kobe saw that you were afraid, "it's over for you, whether you're the teammate or family member or whatever," said Shaw, who joined Jackson's coaching staff in 2005. Many times Shaw would try to prevent Kobe from intimidating a teammate at practice. "You're going to kill his spirit," Shaw would say to Kobe. "He can't take what you can take."

"Then he doesn't need to be out here," Kobe would reply.

"So you got to monitor that as a coach with him," explained Shaw, "because if you put weak people around him, he could destroy them. If he senses fear in you as his teammate, he's going to try to rip your throat out. He's going to try to tear your head off if he senses that you're afraid of him or you let him run you over. He's going to run your butt over, he's going to steamroll you. I know that from being around him. That's why I can challenge him on stuff when he's wrong. If you think that you're going to get into his inner circle or good graces because you're just going to let him do whatever he wants to do, even if it's to your own detriment, because 'Oh, it's Kobe, so he can go ahead and elbow me, or he can smack me'? He's going to smack the shit out of you then, if you allow him to do it. I remember I was fishing one time and I was catching sharks and stingrays. I know he loves sharks, so I texted a picture of these sharks and stingrays that I was catching and he texted me back, 'What did you do with them?' And I was like, 'I just took them off the hook and I threw them back in the water.' And I'm not going to tell you what he said that I should have done to them, but it was just his whole killer instinct."

Kobe wanted Shaw to finish off the sharks.

"Yeah," said Shaw. "He was like, 'Why let them go? It was their fault, they got caught, so they got to pay the price for getting caught.' But that's his mentality. It's through and through. He wants to beat you, and not just beat you but beat you down."

In the years following his separation from O'Neal and reunion with Jackson, Kobe was scoring as prolifically as Jordan had. And yet rarely did Kobe make the game look as easy or artistic as Jordan. When Kobe raised the ball high, it was as if he was lifting something of enormous weight, like Atlas hoisting the world. Other stars played with more grace, but with Kobe there was always a muscled tension built in, as if he wanted the fans to recognize how hard it was for him to win. Most of his peers sought to avoid altercations and conflicts, but Kobe was different. He managed his career as if he was seeking to create drama and tension, because those battles appeared to renew and strengthen him. He preyed on situations that made his rivals uncomfortable. He found strength in their uneasiness. He was willing to go further and make choices they weren't willing to make.

Kobe was earning an estimated $48 million in 2010, but the money didn't define him on the court. Whether he was training out of sight in weight rooms and practice gyms or performing in the arenas, he behaved as if he had nothing and was desperate to prove himself. Success was deepening Kobe's hunger, just as it had for Jordan.

Let one of his teammates miss two or three jumpers, and Kobe might not share the ball with him for some time. But if it were Kobe missing shot after shot after shot, as was happening in Game 7 against the Celtics in 2010, he would keep shooting. Kobe, like Jordan, did not trust his "supporting cast" nearly as much as he trusted himself.

LeBron James made his NBA debut in 2003, in the midst of Kobe's legal troubles and his dissolving partnership with O'Neal. LeBron was a "people person," Kobe surely was not, and it took little time for the NBA's sponsors to recognize the difference. Instead of Kobe, it was LeBron who became heir to Jordan's marketing empire. Every commercial advantage would be handed down to LeBron, while Kobe would serve as a kind of bastard son for whom nothing would come easily. Kobe would have to fight for everything, and he would be proud of that. He was more than willing to sacrifice popularity in order to become his generation's answer to Jordan on the court. He embraced his role as the bastard.

Kobe was only 31 as he led his Lakers through the 2010 playoffs, but almost half of his life had been spent playing above NBA rims, going up high and landing hard. In the opening round, when the Lakers were losing Games 3 and 4 at Oklahoma City to the young duo of Kevin Durant and Russell Westbrook, Kobe was limited to a combined 36 points. "I literally couldn't bend my knee," Kobe said. "After Game 4 I was confident leaving that arena because I was going to get it drained and I knew it was going to make a big difference, and we weren't going to lose again in that series." And he was right: He finished off the Thunder with 32 points in Game 6 on the road.

By Game 7 of the NBA Finals against Boston, his right knee, which had been repaired twice by surgery over the years, was swollen again. His right index finger, which had been broken in two places earlier in the season, was ravaged by arthritis; it was wrapped with athletic tape around a splint that provided barely enough support to launch the ball to the basket. Kobe had worked with an assistant coach to change his shooting stroke by resting the ball more heavily on his thumb and middle finger, so that the index finger would be aiming the ball instead of driving it. It was extraordinary for Kobe to count on winning the championship with a jump shot that had been overhauled in midseason. And yet his accommodations were taken for granted by opponents and fans, so high were the standards to which he held himself.

"Everything," Kobe would say with an extended laugh when asked whether it was his knee or his finger that had limited him in the seventh game against the Celtics. "Everything. And Boston, they'll hit you there too."

Which Celtics were slapping at his finger?

"They all do," Kobe said. "They're an old-school '80s team." Which was a compliment from Kobe, to say that they could have played in Jordan's era.

By now it appeared as though the empire of Jordan had been divided cleanly between his two heirs: Kobe was taking after Jordan on the court, competitively, and LeBron was following him off the court, commercially. Although Kobe was slammed, as always, for dominating the ball and trying to win by himself, the criticisms of LeBron were even more damning: He was accused of choosing the path of least resistance and being distracted by his fame.

Over the past year in particular the strain seemed to be getting the best of LeBron. In the early going of the 2010 playoffs, Kobe watched the canny Celtics succeed in discouraging LeBron on their way to an upset of the top-seeded Cavaliers. LeBron appeared to be defeated long before the series was over. As Kobe prepared for Game 7 against Boston, one thing was sure: He wasn't going to let the same thing happen to him.

The seventh game of the 2010 NBA Finals was played on Kobe's home floor in the Staples Center, a circular arena with nineteen thousand seats on the outskirts of Hollywood. Its court of blond wood was bathed in a soothing beige light, like a theater-in-the-round. Many of the expensive seats surrounding Kobe were filled night after night by the world's most famous actors — Denzel Washington, Dustin Hoffman, Sylvester Stallone and others, including Jack Nicholson, in his conspicuous place near the visiting team's bench.

Their fame was derived from an industry that made them look bigger than they really were. To meet one of Hollywood's leading men in person was to be disappointed by his size, as if seeing him through the lens in reverse. The opposite was true for Kobe. On television he looked small in relation to the 7-foot centers and 6-10 power forwards, but in real life Kobe towered over the film stars who sat courtside looking up at him.

In addition, Kobe's achievements had not been scripted in advance. His body was chiseled not for appearance's sake but for the sake of competition. Every Lakers game revolved around Kobe in much the same way a big-budget movie is a vehicle for its stars. But Kobe's stage was more revealing. His performance did not come to a halt with each whistle, in the way that a Hollywood director will cut short an embarrassing scene and allow the actors to gather themselves. There was no such privacy for Kobe. When the action stopped during Game 7, the fans did not take their eyes off Kobe as he strode to the bench for a timeout, his chest heaving violently.

They had been watching the development of his character for fourteen years, from the teenager to the man—fighting against authority, instigating conflict and having to learn everything the hard way—but they had never seen him looking so helpless. The pressure was robbing him of breath. Anyone in the storytelling business could see that Kobe's arc was peaking. He was going to break through, here and now, or he was going to fail.

The signs were not good. The Lakers were trailing the Celtics 49–36 deep into the third quarter, and it was all because Kobe had missed 13 of his 17 shots. Throughout Jordan's best years he had never shot the ball that poorly in a crucial game. Kobe was misfiring his team out of the championship, which was the point made by Jordan's 19-year-old son, Marcus, on Twitter when he heard the TV broadcasters likening Kobe to his father:

> NO ONE . . . And I mean NO ONE should EVER com par kobe Bryant
> to my dad an say that he is anywhere near close to my dad. He's jagging
> this game.

It was true that Jordan had never played so inefficiently in an NBA Finals game, but it was also true that he had never experienced the accumulation of pressure that was now crushing Kobe. The five decades of Lakers-Celtics history were far more burdensome than any of the Bulls' rivalries, and these Celtics in particular were more talented and clever than any opponent Jordan had faced in the Finals.

Not only was Kobe seeking his fifth NBA championship in order to separate himself from O'Neal, but he was also racing in-house to catch Magic Johnson and Abdul-Jabbar, who had won five titles with the Lakers, and he was pursuing Jordan with his six. On top of everything else, the Celtics had earned their seventeenth NBA championship at the expense of Kobe and his Lakers two years earlier, in 2008. Kobe was expected not only to get even for that humiliating defeat but also to earn L.A.'s sixteenth championship, furthering its pursuit of Boston as the NBA's winningest franchise (with its seventeen championships).

It was fair to argue that this Game 7, with all that was in play for the Lakers and Celtics, was the biggest game in the history of the league. Their feud had never been more relevant as the fourth quarter approached. These two teams had created this chance for Kobe to do something that Jordan never had done, to be part of a story that would earn him his own place in the game's collective memory, to separate himself once and for all.

And yet Kobe kept shooting, in competition with his ghost.

"He was trying so hard," said Shaw, who sat beside Kobe in the huddle. "I had to keep reminding him, 'It'll come, just let it happen.'"

Let it go, Shaw may as well have been telling him.

Hyperventilating, fighting himself, Kobe was no longer following the path laid down by Jordan. He was alone, and in his panic and pain Kobe was not able to see that his vulnerability could be a source of renewal. It could make him more accessible and ultimately more powerful. He was a teammate in need.

In the end, the other Lakers would look up to see Kobe standing on a courtside table, holding the game ball against his hip and waving his bandaged index finger as high as it could reach. It was symbolic of the distance he had traveled in the NBA, and his short time remaining.

"Kobe . . . Kobe . . . Kobe . . ."

The fans had been chanting his name midway through the fourth quarter. By then Kobe's breathing was back to normal as he leaned the length of his crooked body toward the basket for three shots from the free throw line. They weren't waiting to be entertained by him any longer. They were on their feet, drawn to him, singing to inspire him.

"MVP . . . MVP . . . MVP . . ."

They were reaching out to help Kobe as he made all three free throws. Eight minutes, 46 seconds remained in this season that had begun nine months ago. His Lakers had climbed back to within one point of the Celtics, 59–58. And now, instead of trying to pull his "supporting cast" along behind him as Jordan would have done, Kobe was being supported by his teammates. They were doing for him what he had wanted to do for them.

It was by emulating Kobe that his fellow Lakers rescued him. His longtime teammate Derek Fisher, who had entered the NBA alongside him fourteen years before, would sink the game-tying three-pointer with the authority of a defining shot by Kobe. Pau Gasol, the 7-foot All-Star from Spain, who had been derided as a "soft" European, turned into a hard-edged bastard who chased down 18 rebounds at both ends of the floor. His basket with ninety seconds to go gave the Lakers a 6-point lead. Ron Artest, known as the least reliable star in basketball, turned cold and calculating. His 20 points and 5 steals, including a three-pointer in the final minute, inspired Phil Jackson to credit him as the most valuable player of this make-or-break night. Altogether the Lakers missed 56 of their 83 shots in mimicry of Kobe's poor shooting. Their 83–79 victory over the Celtics played out like a synopsis of Kobe's long career: a wrong-footed start, reinvention, redemption.

As Kobe celebrated his fifth NBA championship, he was decisively not the player he had dreamed of becoming a dozen years earlier in his All-Star debut alongside Jordan on Broadway. How he had envied Jordan's command of the theater that night. Everywhere Jordan looked, the world was staring back at him. The game and its fans and their sponsors all appeared to be locked into the orbit of his compelling gravity, and Kobe had been locked into it, too, until now.

"It was maybe my best game," Kobe would say months later. "Because it was the proof for myself of evolution, of figuring out how to win when I'm not scoring the ball very well. How do you do that in the biggest game?"

He won by making no claim to Jordan's majesty. Kobe missed 18 of his 24 shots from the field, he scored 23 ugly points by converting just enough free throws, he chased down 15 rebounds and swept up other loose balls to overcome the fraying of his tired body and the detours of his misplaced ambitions. In this era of basketball played by millionaires, there could be no more frenzied game than this victory over the Celtics. Kobe's stubbornness had been earned throughout his years of fighting to be the player he could never be. He could never be Jordan, and from that failure he had broken free.

Never again would he be so vulnerable as in that seventh game. The insecurity that had been driving him for so long—to prove that he could win the biggest games without O'Neal, as Jordan would have won them—would be replaced by an assured, settled confidence. He was going to be his own man, looking to score because that's who he was, and seizing command on his own terms.

Michael Jordan had given birth to an age in which there could be no more Michael Jordans. This was Kobe Bryant's era now, for as long as he could hold on.

The 2010–11 season would be his farewell run with Jackson, who was postponing his retirement for one year in order to pursue a three-peat of championships with Kobe's Lakers. Kobe's unspoken responsibility, which he would discharge throughout the upcoming season, was to hold the younger stars of the so-called AAU generation to the on-the-court standards that he had learned from Jordan.

In his role as caretaker of the NBA's competitive values, Kobe's first target appeared to be LeBron, who had joined the NBA seven years after Kobe. *The Decision* would be aired within three weeks of the Lakers-Celtics' Game 7, and the basketball world was already fawning over LeBron when Kobe sent a text message to him.

"Go ahead and get another MVP, if you want," Kobe wrote with characteristic sarcasm, as reported by Kevin Ding of *Bleacher Report.* "And find the city you want to live in. But we're going to win the championship. Don't worry about it."

2

THE DECISION

The idea had dawned on Pat Riley in 2006. That was when three of the NBA's most talented friends — LeBron James, Dwyane Wade and Chris Bosh — negotiated contracts that would set them free onto the open market in the summer of 2010.

"I said this is going to be one of those opportunities in a lifetime to build a team through free agency," recalled Riley, who at that time was both coach and president of the Miami Heat. "As long as you have one of the players."

Riley had Wade, who weeks earlier had driven Miami to its first and only NBA championship with a furious comeback, at the expense of Dirk Nowitzki, the star of the Dallas Mavericks.

"From 2006 we had thought about it, in the back of our mind, that we wanted to have the opportunity to go after them," Riley said.

Bad luck and worse results pushed the idea to the front of his mind. Within two years of their championship O'Neal would be gone, Wade would be injured, and Riley's team would be finishing dead last with a record of 15-67. Instead of winning the 2008 NBA draft lottery and the rights to the number one pick, Derrick Rose, a future Most Valuable Player, Riley would be left to squander the number two pick on Michael Beasley, an immature forward who would be traded, signed or waived by a half-dozen NBA franchises (along with two teams in China) before he turned 28.

It was in 2008, after he had moved 35-year-old O'Neal to the Phoenix Suns in a midseason deal, that Riley shared his vision for free agency with Wade. "We traded Shaq, and Dwyane wanted to know, 'What are you thinking, Coach? How are we going to build this thing back to a championship team?'" recalled Riley.

The plan for the next two years, explained Riley, was to invest in short-term contracts and compete for the playoffs while breaking in Erik Spoelstra, the new head coach, who had been working his way up the Heat organization for thirteen years before being chosen by Riley to succeed him on the bench.

Per Riley's expectations, Spoelstra was able to coach the Heat into the opening round of the playoffs — but no further — while salvaging forty-three wins in 2008–09 and forty-seven the following season. Miami was filling in with temporary players on short-term contracts around Wade, which enabled Riley to clear the books for his far-fetched run at the free-agent class of 2010.

"He was getting very antsy," said Riley of Wade, who was watching his peak years pass him by. Wade had doubts about Riley's plan. "He mentioned to me, 'If you think that LeBron's going to come here, you're dreaming,'" recalled Riley. "'Not going to happen. He won't. He's different.'" Riley wasn't sure what to make of that warning. Was Wade saying that LeBron wouldn't want to team up with other stars? Did he have no interest in leaving Cleveland?

"I nodded my head," recalled Riley of his response. "I didn't know LeBron like Dwyane knew LeBron. But I could not believe that if Dwyane Wade and LeBron James and Chris Bosh could have the chance to all play together, they wouldn't want to do it."

It was a crazy plan. Who would essentially run in place for two years, setting aside almost $50 million in cap space in hopes of pursuing an unprecedented dream that was unlikely to come true? And yet Riley was undeterred. He believed that he understood the hearts of great players better than they did themselves. If only he could put himself in front of LeBron, Bosh and Wade when they became free agents in the summer of 2010, he would make them an offer they couldn't refuse.

During his management of the Heat franchise since 1995, Riley had become the modern-day equivalent of Red Auerbach, the legendary coach of the Boston Celtics who had also served as their chief executive. Like Auerbach, Riley's moral code was reliable and unyielding. In his twenty-four years of NBA coaching, Riley had led the Los Angeles Lakers and Earvin "Magic" Johnson to four championships in the 1980s to go with the Heat's lone title two decades later.

Auerbach and Riley were the most inspirational and exacting coaches of their eras. In 1981, shortly before the NBA would realize its potential as a mainstream entertainment industry, Riley was hired, at age 36, to coach the Lakers, who had already been led to one championship by Johnson. Overnight Riley became the NBA's most demanding coach, working his players tirelessly and toughening them with the backbone and fiber they would need to triumph twice against Larry Bird's Celtics. Riley reached seven NBA Finals in his first eight years with the Lakers.

"There was no doubt that in the '80s I totally got full of myself, let me tell you," Riley said. "Success has a tendency to do that. I was told by my friends a lot at the time, but I didn't realize it was happening to me."

Riley, a 6-4 swingman from upstate New York, peaked in 1966 as an All-America at the University of Kentucky. From there he played nine NBA seasons off the bench with three franchises, including six years with the Lakers. "I was an average, journeyman player, and I got the job with the Lakers as the interim head coach — they were looking for someone else."

In spite of reaching the NBA Finals in his first four seasons as their coach, Riley believed he was on his way out after losing Game 1 of the 1985 NBA Finals at Boston by 34 points in what was known as the "Memorial Day Massacre." "Had we not won the championship in '85, I probably would have gotten fired. That was the pressure I was feeling at the time," Riley said. "And then, after we beat the Celtics in Boston Garden to win that championship, there was a change in me. It happened from doing too many commercials, too many books and magazine covers and speeches, and you think you're bigger and better than everybody else. What I've learned is that your talent doesn't make you better than anybody else. I think everybody has to go through that."

He had a much easier time recognizing the impact of wealth and celebrity on his players, and his counteractions would influence the entire league. The biggest winners of the 1980s and '90s — Johnson, Bird, Isiah Thomas and Michael Jordan — would devote themselves religiously to the priorities set forth by Riley. He was a framer of their constitution, a founding father of pro basketball's modern era. The richer and more famous his Lakers became off the court, the more he demanded of them on the court.

Handsome and magnetic, Riley — in his tailored suits, his leading-man jaw set off by his combed-back hair — behaved like a star on the sideline. His ego was insatiable, and yet his priorities were blue-collar and sacrosanct. Work before play. Achievement before celebration. The same priorities would empower Jordan to transform the NBA in the 1990s, and Riley would take so much pride in the achievement of Jordan's ideals that he made a show of retiring his number 23 in Miami, even though Jordan had never played a minute for Riley or the Heat.

Riley had been introduced to Jordan at the 1984 Summer Olympics in Los Angeles, where Riley had served as protocol director for the basketball tournament. Through the rest of that decade his Lakers dominated Jordan's Bulls, but in the 1990s the Bulls won both of their playoff series against Riley's New York Knicks. And so the only semblance of a relationship between Riley and Jordan was that the former had established the standards that would be fulfilled by the latter. Riley tried to convince Commissioner David Stern to retire Jordan's number 23 in every arena throughout the league. "Like the ghost of the NBA," said Riley, who further suggested that the numbers of other transcendent stars, such as Bill Russell, Magic Johnson and Larry Bird, also be retired. "I thought it would be neat," he said, "and another way for the NBA to make a lot of money from the jerseys."

Stern didn't go for Riley's idea. Jordan didn't approve either when he heard that his number was going to be retired in Miami. "Everybody in the league was trying to give him something, and he got tired of it," Riley recalled. "He let us know he didn't want anything pregame. But after all the years of him kicking my ass, I said, 'No—I'm going to make him do this.'" So ambitious was Riley to affirm their connection in spirit that he stood alongside Jordan at the retirement ceremony on the court in Miami in 2003, minutes before Jordan would play his final game there as a 40-year-old guard who had come out of retirement for the Washington Wizards. His was the first jersey ever to be retired by Riley's franchise. It was a strange night.

"I was a little embarrassed that we didn't have Magic Johnson's number up there, but Michael was the transcendent player—along with Bill Russell," said Riley. "We darkened the lights, and he just looked up at the scoreboard and saw this video. I think he was stunned that I would do it for him, because we were mortal rivals."

"In honor of your greatness," announced Riley as he pointed up to Jordan's oversized jersey hanging high above them, "and for all you have done for the game of basketball, not only in the NBA but for all the fans around the world, we want to honor you tonight by hanging your jersey forever—number 23 from the rafters of the AmericanAirlines Arena—and no player ever again will ever wear number 23 for the Miami Heat here." He looked at Jordan and said, "You're the best."

That night Jordan scored 25 points for the farewell victory of his career. "I thought Pat was trying to get my mind thinking about all the accolades," said Jordan, "and then next thing you know I forget about the game. I said I ain't going to fall for that." And so, in their final duel, he fulfilled Riley's ideal again.

This episode became relevant years later, in the aftermath of *The Decision,* when it was reported that Riley had arranged a meeting with LeBron and Jordan in November 2009, while the Cavaliers were in Miami to play the Heat.

"I never did that," Riley said. "That's fake news. That never happened, in any way, shape or form. Never."

That meeting, according to the reports, had been meant to link Riley to Jordan historically, in order to appeal to LeBron eight months before he would become a free agent.

"I remember I got a call from Mike Fratello," said Riley of his friend, the former NBA coach who was in Miami to broadcast the Cavaliers-Heat game the following night. "He invited me to go to dinner, and Michael Jordan was in town also, so he went to the dinner. I think his fiancée was with him, and I brought my wife, Chris. Very rarely does that ever happen with me and Michael. I run into Michael in different parts of the world a lot of times, and we might have a drink together. We had a nice, quiet dinner the night before the game. I invited him to the game and he said, 'I'll only come to the game if I can sit with you.' So there we are together, and we're both talking to each other with our hands over our mouths all night so nobody can read our lips. It was just a conversation about the game and what's going on. And on the way out, he challenged me to a pool game in our players' lounge, in which I did beat him, which he didn't like, doesn't happen very often. But everybody thought that I had put them together that night, that I had brought him down to put them together. Is that what everybody thought?"

It was reported that Riley had told LeBron, during their alleged meeting, about the need for current players to appreciate Jordan.

"There was never any conversation about LeBron, or meeting, or putting them together," Riley said. "Why would Michael want to help me anyhow?"

Nor, insisted Riley, had he enlisted Wade to recruit LeBron. "I never once, never told Dwyane, 'I want you to talk to LeBron.' Never, ever," Riley said.

Wade would in fact serve as the chief recruiter of LeBron and Bosh. "If he did that, it was on his own — talk to Chris, talk to LeBron, reach out to each other once the season was over with, text each other, do whatever they do," Riley said. "He knew I was after him. He knew I was going to set up meetings with all these guys, if I could get on the list. And obviously we got on the list."

LeBron's preference would have been to stay in Cleveland and to recruit stars to come play with him there. By the night of *The Decision,* however, that hope was long gone.

The reason for his departure from the only home he had ever known could be traced back to the 2007 playoffs. That spring 22-year-old LeBron single-handedly won Game 5 of the Eastern Conference Finals at Detroit by scoring Cleveland's last 25 points in their 109–107 overtime victory. The Cavaliers would beat the Pistons once more to put LeBron into his first NBA Finals, where he would experience the first of many comeuppances: The San Antonio Spurs would sweep Cleveland in four games.

It was the fourth championship for power forward Tim Duncan and coach Gregg Popovich, who had been developing and refining their schemes in San Antonio long before the NBA had even heard of LeBron. The Spurs ran their cuts as if choreographed. They rotated and covered for one another at both ends of the floor with beautiful efficiency. They were more committed to their shared goal and far more talented from top to bottom than the Cavaliers, and they were the first team to demonstrate that LeBron, gifted as he was, was in over his head.

One year later Cleveland was being drummed out of a second-round playoff series by the Celtics. LeBron scored 45 points in Game 7 at Boston but was offset by Paul Pierce, his matchup at small forward, who scored 41 on his way to driving the Celtics to the 2008 championship. So began the trend by which selfless opponents were able to beat LeBron at his own game: The Spurs throttled him, the Celtics inundated him, and then, in the Eastern Conference Finals of 2009, in spite of the 38.5 points per game LeBron scored, his Cavaliers would have no answers for the mismatches created by the Orlando Magic around their 23-year-old center, Dwight Howard. So frustrated was LeBron that he refused to shake hands with the Magic players as they moved on to the NBA Finals, in which they would be dismissed in five games by Kobe Bryant's Lakers.

LeBron, who was meant to elevate his teammates, was being cast now as a prima donna. He was making more money off the court than anyone in the NBA, but his playoff results weren't supporting the contention that he was the game's greatest player. He was growing frustrated with the failure of the Cavaliers to pair him with a fellow star. Over his final five seasons in Cleveland only one team-mate, 6-foot 1-inch Mo Williams, a former second-round pick from the University of Alabama, would be invited to play with LeBron in the All-Star Game —and then only after injuries to two stars had opened up a spot.

The postseason collapses were inflaming fears in Cleveland that LeBron would leave in 2010 as a free agent, and so, in advance of the 2009–10 season, the Cavaliers traded for Shaquille O'Neal. He was the biggest star yet to be teamed with LeBron. He was also going to be 38 years old when the playoffs arrived. It had been four years since O'Neal had won his last championship, in Miami, as the enforcer behind Wade, and six years since his exile from Kobe's Lakers. Throughout the 2010 playoffs O'Neal would spend a majority of the games watching from the bench rather than helping LeBron on the court. It was a move of desperation to bring them together.

No star in modern times had been able to win the NBA championship with so little talent as LeBron had around him in Cleveland. Jordan, Duncan, Johnson, Bird and Thomas had each won titles with at least one peaking Hall of Famer at his side. The dearth of high-level teammates would force LeBron to average 29.4 points over the five years leading up to *The Decision,* including the 30 points per game he poured in to win the NBA scoring title in 2007–08. In spite of those numbers, it was obvious to Riley that LeBron had no interest in emulating Jordan as a scoring champion.

"I said to him, 'If you're not Magic Johnson, then I've never seen one, okay?'" recalled Riley of their conversation, which took place soon after LeBron had left Cleveland. "I said, 'Look, I don't know if you like him as a player or who you want to model yourself after, but you're him. You're Magic Johnson who wants to score too.' I can remember him not making much out of it, but he laughed a little bit."

At 6-9 Johnson had been listed as one inch taller than LeBron, who was heavier, stronger and more explosive athletically. "Earvin could really turn it on and rebound and go coast-to-coast and make plays, and kick it to threes, and take it to the post, and play the pick-and-roll—he was so unorthodox that nobody had ever come down the pike like him until LeBron did," Riley said. "The one that could really do all the things Magic could do with great force—even more force—is LeBron. He can pass and think, and he's smart and motivating. He inspires. He's fun. He's out there."

And then Riley stopped himself. He was careful not to misrepresent LeBron as just fun and games. There was a serious bottom-line approach that informed every aspect of LeBron's career.

"But this is a machine," Riley went on. "LeBron is a machine on the court and his whole life is — I think it is, but I could be wrong, I'm not privy to the inside working of it. He's got a machine that works off the court for him too."

LeBron's off-the-court payoffs had come gushing in before he played his first NBA minute in Cleveland. The $90 million Nike contract that he received as an 18-year-old piled up with his other endorsements, like loans that would come due eventually. By his seventh year with the Cavaliers he was grossing $42.8 million, as estimated by *Forbes* — and $27 million of it was coming from endorsements and royalties. The only way for him to make good on those cash advances was by winning the NBA championship.

Year by year, as LeBron failed to live up to the highest expectations of him on the court, the interest on his unpaid debts was compounding. And no one wanted to hear excuses about the failings of his teammates.

As he approached the 2009–10 season in Cleveland with O'Neal at his side, he was on the verge of earning a despicable reputation as the anti-Jordan. When the pressure grew, it would be said, young LeBron wilted.

In the early going of the 2010 playoffs, in the final seconds of the Cavaliers' opening-round triumph in five games against the Chicago Bulls, LeBron made news by missing a free throw. He shot it with his left hand.

It was known that LeBron's right elbow was bothering him, because it had been wrapped in a white elastic sleeve for the past two games. By shooting left-handed, LeBron was drawing attention to his injury just as he was bracing for round two of the playoffs against the elderly Celtics, who had finished eleven games behind his top-ranked Cavaliers during the regular season. The Celtics were huge underdogs in this series, but LeBron knew better. They had three stars who were certain to enter the Hall of Fame, as well as Rajon Rondo, their extraordinary 24-year-old point guard who had become an All-Star two months earlier. If LeBron was going to take the blame for another playoff loss to Boston, he was also going to let everyone know that he was injured in addition to being outmanned. For the next four days the news coverage in Cleveland would be focused on the health of LeBron's elbow.

The Cavaliers versus the Celtics amounted to a clashing of generations. For years LeBron had been trying to nurture a sense of community among his teammates in hopes of elevating them to his level of play. On the court before each game he would oversee a team-building ritual—a sideshow that would have been beneath Jordan, Johnson, Bird or Kobe. For several minutes the Cavaliers would carry on, hugging and slapping one another on the back and standing erect to fling military salutes at one another. "It's just getting ready for battle, getting my soldiers ready," explained LeBron. After they had made a show of dancing like boxers in front of one another while throwing shadow punches and shaking hands amid a choreography of slaps and gestures, LeBron would gather his teammates to pose for an imaginary group photo, which he would snap with an imaginary camera, and which he then would place on an imaginary stool before running over to smile alongside his team as the imaginary timer went off.

The older Celtics, glancing over from the far end of the court, thought all of this was ridiculous.

Before Game 1 of the series in which they were supposed to be finished off once and for all by the younger Cavaliers, the Celtics' 48-year-old coach, Doc Rivers, came skipping into the visitors' locker room in Cleveland, in his dress shirt and slacks, with his own imaginary camera held up in front of one unwinked eye. He half-danced around the room, stopping to take imaginary snapshots of his players. He pretended to be bowling a strike. He crossed his arms and glared around the room with bravado. He stiffened his back and saluted.

"I was doing all this shit," recalled Doc, "and they were laughing their asses off. And I said, 'Now that's some fun shit, right?' I said, 'They want to have fun. Our job is to make this no fun. To make this fucking war. To make this brutal—to make this shit hard. To make it so hard that they give in. Because you can't have fun for eighty-two games, and all of a sudden take their fun away. Then they can't function. They'll question each other, second-guess each other.' I said, 'We've got to create turmoil for them.' That's what we did."

Doc's assistant coach Tom Thibodeau, the Celtics' defensive coordinator, fine-tuned a plan to challenge the ball wherever it went. Most of the time it went to LeBron, and whenever he looked up, the Celtics wanted to have two or three defenders shaded between LeBron and the basket to dissuade him from driving. They wanted LeBron to make the correct basketball decision. They would be urging him to share the ball, because those were matchups that the Celtics could win outright. The Celtics were going to get into LeBron's lesser teammates aggressively, bumping them and playing them up tight and making them believe that this moment was bigger than they could handle. The regular season had belonged to the Cavaliers, but the Celtics were going to claim ownership of the postseason. They were going to demoralize LeBron and make him lose his last bit of faith in his teammates.

"You could see he knew he didn't have enough," said Doc of LeBron. "There was one play where we scored, he goes like this — looks around a little bit, he's looking around like . . ." Doc's arms were held out, mouth agape, eyes blank and palms raised in mimicry of the silent appeal LeBron was making in the middle of the series. "And he's right in front of our bench, he wasn't doing it for us or for anybody," said Doc. "He looked around like this, like, 'What the fuck? Who the fuck do I have on this team?' He could feel it."

When he saw LeBron standing alone in frustration, Doc turned to assistant coach Kevin Eastman and the rest of his staff on the bench and shouted, "Got him!"

"I said it right then, right in that moment," said Doc, his voice rising with the memory. "I knew we had him. I turned to Kevin and said, 'Got him! We got him!' That's a strong statement, but I felt that we were winning this. It was a neat moment for me. Usually you don't say that."

LeBron had been drafted into the NBA in 2003 as the most talented team-minded rookie anyone had ever seen; seven years later the Celtics were disconnecting him tactically from his teammates. The Celtics were fusing together defensively and spacing from one another offensively, with Pierce and Kevin Garnett hovering around their favored spots, while Ray Allen ran tireless semicircles around them and Rondo dribbled like a conductor keeping the beat, taking in the view peripherally, feeling the rhythms of the various matchups, gauging instinctively which of his future Hall of Famers should be fed or whether he should attack the space that was his to take almost any time he pleased. This was Rondo's coming out, when he established himself as the young star capable of extending the lifespan of his older teammates. In Game 4 at Boston he put together a triple-double of 29 points, 18 rebounds and 13 assists to even the series.

In Game 5 at Cleveland LeBron missed 11 of 14 shots as his own fans abandoned their arena with several minutes remaining in the blowout 120–88 loss. It was proof of the discontent that Doc had witnessed days earlier. Rondo was no match one-on-one for LeBron, and yet he was the envy of the world's most gifted star, who longed to play with so much talent around him.

The fans in Boston were confident that their Celtics would clinch the series with a win at home in Game 6. With smart-ass ingenuity they summed up what LeBron had come to represent. In the tenth minute, as he prepared to shoot a pair of free throws, he heard the jeers rising up all around the TD Garden. *"New York Knicks,"* the Boston fans were beginning to chant. *"New York Knicks."*

Even then, weeks before the announcement of his plan to broadcast *The Decision,* suspicion that LeBron would abandon Cleveland as a free agent in preference for a more glamorous market was peaking. The speculation was based on the emerging point of view that LeBron cared more about marketing than he did about winning. The chanting of the Celtics fans reflected their belief that LeBron had become more focused on his future earnings than on the game itself. They were accusing him of being a weak-minded loser who had played up his elbow injury as a shield of excuse. They were insisting, loudly, that he was using the game for his own purposes and that they, here in the birthplace of teamwork and championship basketball, had no respect for him.

They were daring him to prove them wrong, with little fear that he would or could.

"New York Knicks," they began chanting again in the second quarter.

For the Cavaliers coaches and executives, the taunts were shocking. LeBron had not yet peaked as a player, and yet the optimism about his future had veered suddenly and unexpectedly into pessimism. The team-minded star was being rebranded as a cynic, a mercenary. The commercial debts that LeBron had taken on early in his career were now eclipsing his reputation.

"New York Knicks," they were chanting ever more happily into the final minutes.

Their Celtics were up by 11 as LeBron set himself at the free throw line once more with 3 minutes, 27 seconds remaining in his Cavaliers career. He was hunched over, knees bent, staring up at the basket as if deaf to what he and everyone could plainly hear. He knew they were killing him. After a decade of portrayal as the star of tomorrow, LeBron was being held to account for the failures of today.

On television Pat Riley could see what Doc Rivers had recognized days earlier. As LeBron walked off the court in Boston and removed his Cavaliers shirt on his way to the visitors' locker room, he was acting out his frustrations.

"Seven years, banging his head against the wall," Riley said. "He got beaten again, and he just walked right off the court at the buzzer. Didn't talk to anybody.

Didn't congratulate the Celtics, and he pulled off his jersey on his way to the locker room and he just walked in. And I said, 'Man, this guy is like Michael. It took Michael seven years to win a championship. And here LeBron's had seven years, and he's banging his head against the wall.'"

For LeBron, the lessons of this latest failure were harder than any other to comprehend as he sat in the crowded visitors' locker room after the 94–85 loss. His feet were planted in a large plastic tub of ice water, his forearms crossed upon his thighs, as he hunched over to stare down at the printout of the box score lying on the pebbled surface of the floating ice. LeBron had generated a triple-double of 27 points, 19 rebounds and 10 assists. Only Williams (22 points on 18 shots) and O'Neal (11 points in 24 minutes) had joined him in double figures. The Game 6 statistics spelled out the ways that his fellow Cavaliers had let him down again.

But LeBron was not without responsibility. The pressure to do everything was bringing out the worst in him. No longer could he believe in his teammates, which for a team-minded star like him was the same as not believing in himself.

Even so, in the weeks to come LeBron would contribute to an impression of ambivalence. Before long this defeat, the worst of his life, would recede in the media's coverage of him. In hindsight, it would seem, the final buzzer had announced not his decline but rather his liberation. When he pulled off the wine-red Cavaliers jersey on his way to the locker room, it was as if the failed basketball star was turning into a commercial superhero — the greatest free agent of modern times. Here were all these rival stars throughout the NBA playoffs killing one another to earn the championship that would place them atop their world; and over there, unique to himself, LeBron was proving that whatever happened on the court was less important than the potential that he would become the world's biggest star someday. The imminence of his free agency changed the tone of the conversation so quickly from pessimism back to optimism that it was almost as if he was being rewarded for losing.

Of course the loss to the Celtics had wounded him deeply. The frenzy of the coming weeks would inspire LeBron to keep his chin up and continue trusting himself, because if the marketplace believed in his future, why shouldn't he? He couldn't allow the results of the games to bring him down. He had to keep pushing onward. It was his duty as a star, and there were bills to be paid.

• • •

Pat Riley was 65 as he approached his audacious summer of 2010. In his recruitment of LeBron, he was adapting to a generation that was in many ways foreign to him.

"I am a different animal in a world that is changing," Riley said. "I was a traditional conservative, from years back. It was how I was taught. My values were my values. And now we're dealing with nontraditional players that speak their own mind and look at you differently if you take away something that was the norm from their standpoint."

LeBron, who had been raised since adolescence to replace Jordan, was ground zero for this evolving basketball world.

"I remember a story that Lynn Merritt told me about the recruitment of LeBron back then," said Riley of LeBron's brand manager at Nike. "He actually took all of those guys, Maverick and Randy and Rich and even some of his other friends that he was really loyal to — he took them to Portland and taught them how to get into the business and what business is about." In fact Maverick Carter, who would become LeBron's business manager, interned at Nike while LeBron was still in high school. "And so from the get-go a team was put together," Riley said. "A huge company supported them very early, and that kind of stuff never happened before."

Maverick Carter, Randy Mims and Rich Paul had been friends with LeBron in Akron, and in 2005 he and they formed a company, LRMR, to manage his off-the-court businesses. LeBron's "team," as he referred to his partners, was going to be joined by Leon Rose, one of the NBA's most respected agents, to hear Riley's long-imagined proposition.

"Most coaches teach their athletes to be pure," Riley went on. "You're using the platform of basketball to win games or get recognition or earn a living — or win championships. And it's a short period of time in which you can do this, so you put all you can into this and push everything else out of your life, except your family and your friends and your health and your team."

Traditionally NBA stars had their basketball lives and their private lives. Now there was a third pillar, which had been introduced by Jordan and was being embraced by LeBron. There was the commercial life.

"And now it was okay for a player to be distracted by branding," Riley said.

It was more than okay. Dating back as far as their teenaged years, when LeBron and Bosh joined the AAU teams of their choice and traveled the country performing in tournaments that billed them as future NBA stars, the three free agents Riley was pursuing — including Wade, the late bloomer — had dreamed of a power marriage between the game they loved and the business they lusted after. The new goal, rather than keeping them separate, was to fuse them together.

Many times in recent years the Heat's social media department had reached out to the players (and the players' agents) recommending that they take down inflammatory messages posted to their public accounts. Self-inflicted controversies that never could have been generated by players in the 1980s had become the norm. Riley insisted that his players turn off and stow away their phones ninety minutes before each game and not to go back to them until the game was over. They could listen to music or study the scouting reports the Heat downloaded to iPads for each game, but no last-minute texting or posting to Twitter or Facebook was allowed.

"But I can't get in the way of where our country is going and where our world is going," Riley said. "We can't stop social media. And it's a big, big part of their life. There are teams where guys are running into the locker room at halftime and the first thing they're going right to their phones and checking their messages and sending. If you want to become punitive about it, then what you do is you start taking devices away from people: They all have to check them in at a certain place when they walk into the locker room, and they don't get them until they leave. You'd probably have quite a rebellion on your hands if somebody did that."

All of this back-and-forth with the customers had started with Jordan, pre-Internet, when his Nike silhouette told the story of a smaller player rising up to conquer the traditional giants. He had redefined the NBA by branding himself as a David against the 7-foot Goliaths. "Michael Jordan became his logo," said Riley.

Jordan's fans had connected with him as the underdog who changed the basketball world. But what was LeBron's identity? He had the medium of social media, but what was his message? What did he stand for?

This was where Riley was planning to help him.

It was the morning of July 2, 2010. Four years after the long-shot possibility had first occurred to him, Riley could be seen pacing the hallway in downtown Cleveland like an expectant father. LeBron arrived two minutes before their eleven o'clock meeting.

The small conference room on the eighth floor was catered with food and soft drinks. On one side of the table sat Leon Rose, LeBron, Maverick Carter and Randy Mims. Opposite them was the Miami team of assistant general manager Andy Elisburg, vice president of basketball operations Nick Arison, his father and Heat owner Micky Arison, Riley, Erik Spoelstra and Alonzo Mourning, a star of Miami's 2006 championship team who had retired to become Riley's vice president of player programs. "I felt very uncomfortable sitting there in the room," Riley said. "I had never sat any time when I was going to talk to my team or a player in the locker room or on the court." So he squeezed out from the table and stood with his hands on the back of the chair as he emceed the presentation.

"I started with: 'We want you to understand that we are going to make sure the main thing remains the main thing,'" Riley said. "And immediately, LeBron had a little furl in his brow. 'The main thing is to make sure the main thing remains the main thing?'"

But Carter was nodding and smiling. He recognized the term from *First Things First,* a self-help book by Stephen Covey. "It's the beginning of the book: The main thing is making sure the main thing remains the main thing," Riley told LeBron. "Now, the main thing with us is winning championships. The main thing with us is continuity and management and coaching. The main thing with us is a committed, single-proprietor owner who can make all of the decisions on winning championships, owning your own arena, building a culture that is set up for championship play. And we think you and Chris and Dwyane can do something really special."

The main thing LeBron could find in Miami, Riley was implying, was the one thing he didn't have.

And then Riley introduced Micky Arison as the financial muscle behind the main thing.

"One of the themes of the meeting was that the man says yes," said Riley, who went on to list the financial commitments that Arison had made to players in Miami over the years. "He says yes for winning. He said yes to a $125 million contract for Alonzo Mourning, and then twenty seconds later he said yes to another $105 million contract for Juwan Howard, and then for P. J. Brown and then Dan Majerle, and then Brian Grant, and then for Eddie Jones and then Shaquille O'Neal."

Miami was not nearly so large a market as New York or Chicago or Los Angeles, whose franchises were also recruiting LeBron. But Riley was making it clear that Arison, the billionaire chairman and CEO of Carnival cruise lines, would be able to make up the difference financially. Taking on the three stars, in addition to the role-players who would help them contend for championships, would eventually incur a punitive "luxury tax" that the NBA charged any franchise that paid its players far beyond the threshold of the salary cap. Arison then spoke to LeBron across the cramped conference table to personally assure him that the money would be spent.

"Any time Micky saw the window for winning — and he's smart enough as a businessman to see that — he would say yes," Riley told LeBron. "He's saying yes to you and the tax and everything else."

There were other details to be discussed about the style of play, the daily commitments, the long-term goals. For many of the specifics Riley deferred to Arison and Spoelstra, who used video to demonstrate how LeBron would fit in. As the presentations wore on, Riley reached into his briefcase and pulled out a chart as well as a small mesh bag.

"I put the bag next to me on the table," Riley said. "I pulled out another chart and put it on the table."

LeBron wasn't interested in the charts. The bag was another story.

"LeBron asked me, 'What's in there?'" Riley recalled. Riley dropped the bag in the middle of the table. "Then LeBron opened it up and spilled them all out onto the table," Riley said. "There were thirty-five different rings in there."

In 2006 the ring manufacturer Jostens had created a half-dozen models to celebrate Miami's championship. The rings that had been given to Wade and his teammates had featured 159 diamonds embedded in almost 2.5 troy ounces of white gold. Additional prototypes had been made of platinum, sterling and other precious materials. Riley had kept those models in this bag with all the other rings he had acquired throughout a half century of college and professional basketball.

"So he played with them for a while," said Riley of LeBron. "He had a smile on his face that somebody had so many. He said, 'What are these rings?' I said, 'Those are All-Star rings.'"

When Riley's Lakers ruled their conference in the 1980s, he earned invitations to coach the Western Conference in the All-Star Game eight times in nine years. The rule had since been changed to prevent one coach from dominating the event. But by then Riley had built up a stock of eight All-Star rings, and into the bag they had gone.

"I used to walk into the locker room of the Western Conference and all of the players would boo me because they'd see me every year," Riley told LeBron.

He had earned his six championship rings with the Lakers, including one as an assistant coach in 1980 and another as a backup shooting guard in 1971–72, when Jerry West and Wilt Chamberlain established NBA records for winning 33 straight games and 69 games overall, the latter to be surpassed by the 72 victories of Jordan's Bulls in 1995–96. There was the ring from Riley's 2008 induction to the Hall of Fame, and on and on. Altogether they served as both a promise and a challenge to LeBron. He was only 25, but his seven NBA seasons had flown by and his own bag was empty of the main thing. Riley knew what he was thinking.

"Part of my presentation was about superteams — teams that had won multiple championships, had been together for a long time, that had at least three what you would consider superstars that all were great players in their own right, had sacrificed points and rebounds and all of those things to win championships," Riley said. "Go all the way back and start with the Celtics in the '60s, and then go on up to 2010, and all of those championship teams had one thing in common. They had a trifecta of players that were so good together, two superstars and one star, and you can just go down the list of all the championship teams that had that. I said to him, 'It's essential. You're not going to win a championship just bringing in guys. Cleveland has tried to do everything for you. Toronto has tried to do everything for Chris. But they just could not break loose with the players they needed to be able to win a championship.'"

Amid all of this encouraging talk, Riley also brought up the burden that LeBron would be taking on. Riley had generated four championships with the Lakers in the 1980s, a seventh game in the NBA Finals with the Knicks in the 1990s, and the most recent championship with Miami in 2006. The victories of those teams had been a byproduct of their disciplined approach to teamwork.

"The one thing I said to him was: 'I know you don't want this, but you cannot and you do not want to be treated differently than anyone else,'" Riley said. "'We can't really have a double standard here.'" He explained that there would be different measures for training and conditioning, based on the ceilings for each player. "But you have to be one of fifteen," Riley told LeBron. "We have this philosophy: We will give you exactly what you need to win, but we're not going to give you everything you want. And sometimes we have to say no. And then we're going to say no. Sometimes the nos will be hard nos. And sometimes, the nos will be: 'No.' But there'll be a lot of yeses in there too."

Riley was confident that LeBron would be receptive. "On July 1 we had sent him the log-in to a website with four different segments, about thirty minutes long, of what the Heat were about — the city, our franchise, the ownership, the pursuit of championships," Riley said. "Because he had logged in, we were able to view what he went to. LeBron was very active. He looked at our presentation before we met with him more than any other free agent. He went over and over it."

By way of his conversations with LeBron, Wade and Bosh, Riley would realize that all three were worried about coming together after each had been the franchise star of his own team. They were thinking about the enduring influence of Michael Jordan, and his ghostly role in the Lakers' divorce of Kobe and O'Neal. How could they join together on the court without diminishing their commercial identities off the court?

"I think one of their biggest concerns was the egos — while everyone is getting branded and trying to get endorsements and money and all of that stuff, how is all of that going to work out?" Riley said. "There was a real discussion about it — where back in the old days, there would have never been a discussion about it. It would have just been about playing and bringing guys together."

At least they were having open discussions among themselves about this issue.

"That was important, I think," said Riley. "And then Nike, being the force that they are in this whole thing, they wanted to make sure that the platform was going to enhance LeBron and the product."

Riley understood what LeBron was trying to achieve. He recognized the main thing for LeBron better than LeBron could for himself.

"There was going to be a whole other level of expectation now that was even higher than the level of expectation during the CHOSEN-1 years," recalled Riley. And so he tried to explain explicitly what lay ahead for LeBron. "This is: You have to win now," Riley said to LeBron. "Now, you have to win. Because if you don't win, this will be an epic failure."

Dealing with the fear of this challenge was going to be crucial to his journey, Riley told LeBron.

"The word 'fear' came up," recalled Riley, for he was the one to mention it. "And both of them, Maverick and LeBron, looked at me. Like, 'Fear? Afraid of what?' They almost mocked me. This was a big decision. I was trying to tell them, 'Shit's going to hit the fan, man.' 'Afraid? Us?' They had so much confidence in what they were doing, and they were so smart in a lot of ways."

And yet LeBron had no idea of what he was about to take on. How could he know that winning a championship was going to be even harder than it seemed?

• • •

The meetings took place over a span of three days on the eighth floor of the IMG building on St. Clair Avenue, a fifteen-minute walk from the Cavaliers' arena. Fans waiting outside held up signs that read "Home," to be seen by LeBron as he drove in and out of the building each day. He visited with the New Jersey Nets and New York Knicks on Thursday, July 1; with the Heat and Los Angeles Clippers one day later; and with the Cavaliers and Bulls on the third day.

The appointment with the Heat lasted almost three hours. Riley smiled on his way out as he passed the Clippers' general manager, Neil Olshey, and their team president, Andy Roeser. They were waiting in the lobby for their presentation, which they would complete in one hour.

"When I walked by," recalled Olshey of his run-in with Riley, "I said, 'Coach, if you were a player, someone would fine you for running late.'"

Just then it occurred to Olshey that the decision had already been made.

"I saw Riles and all of them come out, and I just read it," Olshey said. Later that afternoon, by the time he was returning to the lobby to be asked by a sportswriter for his prediction, Olshey was certain of the outcome. "I said, 'He's going to Miami,'" Olshey recalled. "I said it because I knew. The only team that had positioned itself to do what Miami was able to do was Miami. I watched when Miami walked out of the room. They had him. I saw it."

Later that day Olshey spoke with his agent, Warren LeGarie, who also represented Mike D'Antoni, the coach of the Knicks. During their time with LeBron, the Knicks had detailed how he could earn $1 billion by playing in New York. And that had been their mistake: The Knicks had undervalued LeBron's integrity by assuming that the commercial opportunities would hold sway. Riley had understood better than anyone that LeBron's fulfillment off the court would depend on his happiness on the court.

"I said, 'Warren, they have no shot,'" Olshey said, meaning the Knicks. "'I'm fucking telling you, they had better go after somebody else, because they have no shot. He's going to Miami.'"

Riley agreed with Olshey. "I just felt they've got to do it," he said of LeBron, Wade and Bosh. "I could not see them not doing this. The quiet desperation of Chris and LeBron, of wanting to get to a place where there was enough talent, was important."

The main competition appeared to be coming from the Chicago Bulls, who had started preparing for their meeting with LeBron six months in advance. John

Paxson, the Bulls' executive vice president, who had won three championships in the Chicago backcourt alongside Jordan, led the recruiting team, which included Jerry Reinsdorf, the franchise owner who had paid Jordan's NBA salaries and now hoped to be responsible for LeBron's. The Bulls decided to go business casual with sport coats and no ties; LeBron had on a sweatsuit. He and his advisers were handed iPads outlining the Bulls' plan to spend their cap space on LeBron and Wade (or Bosh) to go with 21-year-old point guard Derrick Rose, who had already become an All-Star, and Joakim Noah, the two-time NCAA champion center from the University of Florida. "It looks like a video game," said LeBron of the talent lined up for him in Chicago.

Despite the strength of their offer, Paxson worried that Riley would sweep away all three free agents. "He's got an aura about him, much like Phil Jackson does," said Paxson, who had played for Jackson in Chicago. "He's always been a good salesman. He gets you to believe."

LeBron, Bosh and Wade had had the makings of a package deal ever since they entered the NBA as the number one, four and five picks, respectively, in the 2003 draft. One year later LeBron and Wade summered together in Athens as teammates (with Carmelo Anthony, the number three pick of their draft class) on the dispirited 2004 U.S. Olympic team, which lost three games and settled for the bronze medal, leading to a reorganization of USA Basketball around the leadership of Jerry Colangelo. In the 2008 Summer Olympics at Beijing, LeBron and Wade redeemed themselves with a gold medal alongside Bosh, Anthony and Kobe, the team captain, who steered his younger teammates through a tight final game against Spain. LeBron, Wade and Bosh were represented by the same agency, which had helped them negotiate the like-minded contracts that provided them with this unprecedented chance to essentially form their own roster.

"We were the only team that had $48 million of cap space," said Riley. "Someone told me that LeBron said, 'You mean they can do this? They can do this? How can they do it?' Once Leon [Rose] showed him the math — 'This is how it can be done, and you guys can all fit into these slots' — then they started to get serious."

But still Riley couldn't count on landing all of them — or any of them. And so he pursued the other stars of this rich free-agent class: Amar'e Stoudemire, Joe Johnson, Carlos Boozer, David Lee and others.

"There was a lot of nervous energy," Riley said. The NBA had allowed teams to begin speaking with free agents at midnight eastern time on July 1. Riley and the Heat had been in Los Angeles that night in order to launch the dialogue at 9 p.m. Pacific time. "We wanted to get a head start," he said. "We started in L.A. and talked to six or seven free agents out there. And then we headed to Chicago, and then to Cleveland, and then we went back to Chicago and then down to Charlotte. I remember pulling into Chicago and right behind us were two private planes. One of them was Prokhorov's plane."

Mikhail Prokhorov, 6 feet 8 inches tall, was a 45-year-old Russian oligarch who had recently purchased the New Jersey Nets. His plan was to upgrade the moribund franchise to a new arena in Brooklyn, in hopes of creating a lucrative rivalry with the Knicks. Prokhorov, like Riley, was in Chicago to meet with Wade and Bosh. He was promising to outspend everyone in order to build an NBA champion.

"There were, like, twenty SUVs," said Riley of the private hangar in Chicago. "Prokhorov came out right in front of me and got into the four cars with his contingent. This was big stuff. This was not a game to me. This was serious."

The tension and uncertainty of the situation were expressed in the form of rumors. "In the middle of free agency, after all these teams are starting to run around, we begin to hear things," Riley said. "And people behind the scenes were beginning to talk to everybody else. Somebody that was part of LeBron's family or his inner circle would talk to you. Or you would hear that C.B. was beginning to waver. Or all of a sudden, oh my God, LeBron's going to go to New York and C.B.'s going to Chicago — I'm going to be left alone. Everybody got a little bit psychotic at about the third day of free agency, about things happening."

Riley was insistent on staying in close touch with the agents. "They would be right-on with the truth, because they wanted the best for their players," said Riley. "The players looked at what we were putting together as something unique, something exciting. You were going to be the flavor of the year. You'll put pressure on everybody. What a wonderful situation. The agents, they wanted their players in the best position to win a championship and create something that was good."

A July 4 call from Leon Rose informed Riley that all three players appeared to be headed to Miami. "But there was no real commitment or confirmation," said Riley, and he resisted the urge to demand a pledge there and then. Instead he watched as Wade and Bosh continued to take meetings amid speculation that both would sign with Chicago. "They wanted to go through the process of being recruited," Riley said. "When they were talking to other teams, I felt that the most important thing for us to do was not to pressure them, because we could lose everybody. So I took that risk. I said, 'Well, if it's not those three and they decide to go somewhere else, then we've got $48 million of room. And we have Mario Chalmers and Joel Anthony.'"

Those were the only two players under contract with Miami: Chalmers, a second-round pick with two years of NBA experience, and Anthony, an undrafted center from Montreal.

It was an all-or-nothing hand of poker that Riley was playing with his franchise, with his career. What future would he and the Heat be facing if they came away from this two-year gamble empty-handed? And yet Riley was focused far more on the upside than the downside.

"I've been around for so long and been in so many competitive situations," Riley said. "There was not an arrogance or an overconfidence about this. I just felt in my gut they would have to be foolish not to become Kareem, Magic and Worthy."

Whenever the long odds of out-recruiting the rest of the NBA for all three of the top free agents threatened his confidence, Riley would refer back to the starring trios who had won most of the NBA championships over the past half century:

Bill Russell, Bob Cousy, Bill Sharman (or Tom Heinsohn)
Russell, John Havlicek, Sam Jones
Wilt Chamberlain, Hal Greer, Chet Walker
Kareem Abdul-Jabbar, Oscar Robertson, Bob Dandridge
Jerry West, Gail Goodrich, Chamberlain
Walt Frazier, Earl Monroe, Willis Reed
Havlicek, Dave Cowens, Jo Jo White
Dennis Johnson, Gus Williams, Jack Sikma
Magic Johnson, Abdul-Jabbar, James Worthy (or Jamaal Wilkes)
Larry Bird, Kevin McHale, Robert Parish
Moses Malone, Julius Erving, Andrew Toney
Isiah Thomas, Joe Dumars, Bill Laimbeer
Michael Jordan, Scottie Pippen, Horace Grant
Hakeem Olajuwon, Clyde Drexler, Robert Horry
Jordan, Pippen, Dennis Rodman
Tim Duncan, David Robinson, Sean Elliott

Shaquille O'Neal, Kobe Bryant, Glen Rice (or Horry)
Duncan, Tony Parker, Manu Ginobili
Dwyane Wade, O'Neal, Alonzo Mourning
Kevin Garnett, Paul Pierce, Ray Allen
Kobe, Pau Gasol, Lamar Odom

"Three guys," Riley had told LeBron. "You have got to have more support. You have to have another superstar next to you to win."

He had gambled the past two seasons and the years to come based on his faith in LeBron's competitive heart — that his desire to contribute to championships would offset the personal upheaval of leaving his hometown and moving to Miami, where Wade would always be the most beloved star of the Heat.

"I know how torn he was about leaving because I went through the process with him," Riley said of LeBron. "That was a courageous thing for him to do."

"Those guys ended up making a decision because they wanted to win," Paxson would say later of LeBron, Wade and Bosh. "How can you not respect that? That's what we want our league to be about, that's what we want our players to be about. We want them to be about winning."

Basketball men — NBA insiders like Riley and Paxson — were inclined to view LeBron's decision constructively. They tended to give him the benefit of the doubt because they understood what his actions were saying by the way he played and by the choice he made as a free agent. But they were in the minority. Millions of fans would be angered by LeBron, because all they had to go on were his words.

"I wasn't in agreement with it," Riley said of LeBron's plan to reveal his choice on live TV. "I said, 'Don't do this.' If he's going to do it, drive down to Dan Gilbert's office and tell him."

Rose, too, was urging a private meeting to break the bad news to Gilbert, the Cavaliers' owner. The problem, as explained to Riley, was a youth camp in LeBron's hometown to which he was already committed. "He didn't want to make an announcement and then do this Nike camp in Akron when he's already announced that he's going somewhere else," Riley said. "They had to wait until the very end to fulfill his obligations and not put him in a negative, embarrassing situation in front of all of these people in Akron."

LeBron's camp was concerned about potential violence if he were to hold a news conference or make an announcement in Cleveland. Amid fears of backlash, LeBron made the decision essentially to change the subject — to develop the TV show in order to raise money for charity. But any hope of creating goodwill was undermined by the amateurishness of the production and LeBron's failure to articulate his message.

"This is a very emotional time for me," he said during the live broadcast of *The Decision*. "I know it's emotional for the fans and also for the area. And if it was a perfect world, I would have loved to stay, because I've done so many great things for that team, they've done so many great things for me. But I feel like it's time to change."

Obviously he was nervous — he kept repeating himself. But as the show moved along, he was at least trying to present his side of the story, that he had been searching for co-stars who could help him win championships. He spoke of how Garnett, Pierce and Allen had created an environment in Boston for their teammates to become champions. "Now you see Rondo as being one of the best point guards we have in our league," LeBron said. "And Kendrick Perkins, who knows if he don't go down, what happens in the NBA Finals."

He had been paying close attention to Riley's presentation. "Since 1980, you look at all the teams that won — the Lakers teams, the Pistons teams, the Bulls teams, the Spurs teams, the Celtics teams — it's not just been one superstar that go out on the court and dominate the whole game and win an NBA championship," said LeBron, and then he went on to list the stars of those teams. "You become a superstar individually, but you become a champion as a team."

The problem was one of context. His explanations were being overwhelmed by the arrogance of the stage that he had assembled. He had put on this show as if it were a surprise birthday party that he was throwing for himself, as if he was expecting all of America to sing along and be happy for him.

But his audience was loath to collude in his exploitation of them. The final minutes of his show would be hijacked by the video of a Cavaliers fan who was seen lighting LeBron's jersey on fire and leaving it on the pavement. The flames sought out his name and number first. That image from Cleveland conveyed the anger that millions of fans throughout the country were feeling. It also triggered LeBron's defense mechanism.

His response was to scold his abandoned supporters for *their* lack of loyalty. "I had seven great years in Cleveland, and I hope the fans understand," he said.

"And maybe they won't. But I'm going to ultimately be happy with the decision I've made, and just continue to be great."

The star who had been known for his selfless play on the court looked nothing like this alter ego who was staring into the black hole of the camera to rationalize *The Decision* shamelessly and self-destructively. This LeBron was speaking non-sensically in run-on sentences that made him sound uncertain and weak.

"It had nothing to do about money for me," he said. "I could have asked Cleveland to do a sign-and-trade and I could have got the six years and got the money."

Which, actually, he was planning to do in Miami. The next day LeBron, Wade and Bosh were going to ask Riley for six-year contracts, which would require Miami to negotiate sign-and-trade deals with Cleveland and Toronto. By asking for the extra year, the stars would be forcing the Heat to relinquish assets — draft picks especially — that would limit their ability to upgrade the roster in the years ahead.

"I wanted to do what was best for LeBron James and what LeBron James is going to do to make him happy," he went on in the third person, regrettably. "Put the shoe on the other foot; the Cavs would have got rid of me at one point. Would my family burn down the organization? Of course not."

Worst of all was LeBron's ignorance of his role as savior of the forlorn city of Cleveland. He had been cast as the son of Northeast Ohio, the one chosen to help renew Cleveland amid its shuttered industrial plants, the underdog meant to bring his city its first big-league sports championship since 1964. His association with Cleveland was unique, his brand was genuine, and LeBron was too inexperienced to grasp how good he had it.

He was throwing it all away for a TV reality show. For the potential of a little more fame in advance of his championships.

Over his wretched NBA season to come, LeBron would refuse to accept that his performance on television had defined him. It was as if he believed that had not really been him on *The Decision,* as if that person on TV was someone he was pretending to be. "This is a business," he pleaded to his viewers that night, as if the misunderstanding was theirs. *The Decision* suggested that business for LeBron, at that time, was a kind of fantasy world in which he portrayed himself superficially and one-dimensionally for show and for profit.

It was as if there were two LeBrons. The likeable star who would rather pass than shoot was LeBron in his original form. The villain of *The Decision* was a TV character who could never have enough money and attention.

On the court, he was true. Off the court, he was exploiting his own best qualities.

"Guys in this league can change their mind," Riley said. On the night of *The Decision,* as he and his wife, Chris, walked from their home to meet Micky Arison at a table for ten at Red, the Steakhouse, in Miami Beach, Riley was confident but not assured. Wade and Bosh had revealed one day earlier that they would be signing with the Heat, and anonymously sourced reports insisted that LeBron was planning to join them. But LeBron had not said publicly what he was planning to do.

"I was in Rome during the World Cup," said Riley of an overseas trip he had taken with Chris in 1990, "and when Italy was playing, there was not one person on the street, nothing. Cars weren't going, everybody was watching that game. And in South Beach everybody was watching this announcement."

Riley had already finished his dinner when the restaurant went quiet.

"I'm going to take my talents to South Beach and join the Miami Heat," announced LeBron. He had borrowed that phrase from 17-year-old Kobe Bryant, who at a 1996 press conference in his high school gym in Ardmore, Pennsylvania, had declared: "I have decided to skip college and take my talent to the NBA."

LeBron's announcement was met with a groan from a small audience of Knicks fans gathered just outside the Boys & Girls Club gym where *The Decision* was taking place. The response could be heard on TV, and it unsettled LeBron. His eyes half-closed.

In Miami the reaction was different. "When he said that, I yelped," said Riley. "I fist-bumped Micky and ran outside and I could hear across South Beach everybody cheering. It was a really incredible experience."

Instantly he was on the phone to Rose, firming up LeBron's itinerary before launching himself into the hundreds of details, big and small, that would have to be finalized over the next several days.

"That night at three in the morning we met him at the airport," Riley said. "He had two private charters come in, and I brought a lot of people down, family and everything. They got off the plane, and I remember walking right up to LeBron. He was worn-out. He was just worn-out. He almost had tears in his eyes."

By then LeBron and his camp were aware of the response by Cavaliers owner Dan Gilbert, who had publicly savaged LeBron. "It really stung hard with them," Riley said. "LeBron just gave me a big hug and he slumped. And I just remember how heavy this was for all of them. It wasn't like they were smiling and happy to be in Miami. They had just broken the chain of his life in Akron, and it took tremendous guts to do that. I hear it from players all the time: 'I'm a grown-ass man, treat me as such.' Well, he made a grown-ass decision by doing that."

Riley had recruited arguably the most talented player in the history of basketball. Now he and his organization were liable for transforming LeBron's potential into championships. That responsibility was going to be more difficult than any recruiting pitch. But Riley was able to commiserate.

"We shared a lot of common things," he said. "My career at the beginning was nothing but pressure, period. My first nine years as a coach were like his first eight as a player. We were expected to win, and we did win; he was expected to win because he was the CHOSEN-1. He became so disenchanted with himself, in not being able to deliver for Akron or Cleveland, that he had to go — he simply had to go and try something else.

"While I was happy and celebrating, I just knew how much pain he was in. It was a real poignant moment at the airport. There wasn't a lot of joy. They were exhausted, they were fatigued, they had made the decision of a lifetime, and I don't think anybody really got that part of it. The media just went to work on him and crucified him. But that's what happens — it happened with Michael — and when it does, you live up to your greatness by showing people that you made the right decision."

Riley wasn't aware of just how bad the previous evening had been for LeBron. The response was spreading by word of mouth across social media and talk radio. He would have been criticized for leaving Cleveland under any circumstances, but the way LeBron left gave credibility to the criticism. He had cast himself as a young, entitled egomaniac — and he wasn't done yet.

"The vehicle that he took to announce it smacked of, I think, to everybody, 'This is all about me,'" Riley said. "But he did something that in this country you have the right to do. Nobody owns you. He had given them everything that he could give them. It never turned into what he really wanted, a championship, and for him to do that, he was probably going to have to make a change."

On that morning after, the symbolism of *The Decision* meant little to Riley. He was consumed with filling out a roster that could win the championship that season.

Riley had been planning to sign LeBron and Bosh to five-year deals, which was the maximum allowed for departing free agents. Their insistence on a sixth year put Riley in the uncomfortable position of having to negotiate with the Cavaliers one day after *The Decision*. "There wasn't a lot of pleasantry exchanged," said Riley. The Cavaliers agreed to sign LeBron to a six-year contract before trading him to the Heat in exchange for two picks in the first round and another two in the second round. The sign-and-trade with the Toronto Raptors for Bosh cost Miami another couple of first-rounders.

"We actually had them all in the office with their families and their representatives, everybody was happy, and the last thing you want to do is say, 'We're not going to make these sign-and-trades,' and get in some kind of argument," said Riley. "Henry Thomas [Wade's and Bosh's agent] said, 'My guys are worth it.' I said, 'I don't want them walking into my office saying that we can't get any trades to acquire young guys.' Those picks could have bolstered the youth of our roster."

At the same time, the three stars were willing to reduce their annual salaries on behalf of a more talented complement of role-players. LeBron wanted to play with Mike Miller, a free-agent shooter, forcing him, Wade and Bosh to give up close to $3 million between them. "I said, 'If we get Mike Miller, then we can't give you the max,'" Riley said. "They said they would split $45 million." The number shrank further when Wade convinced LeBron and Bosh to make room for forward Udonis Haslem to re-sign with Miami.

"We had seven players right off the bat, and then everyone was calling us," Riley recalled. "'Do you want [Juwan] Howard at the minimum?' We got [Zydrunas] Ilgauskas at the minimum. We got Eddie House at the minimum. Before you know it, we were able to fill out a veteran, competitive roster for that first year."

Later that season, Mike Bibby, a former number two pick known for his clutch shooting, would surrender his guaranteed salary of $6.2 million with the Washington Wizards in order to sign a minimum contract with the Heat. "These were guys that were willing to sacrifice money to win," Riley said.

After two years of hoarding cap space, the Heat were negotiating and dispensing all the money in a matter of hours. The three stars signed their six-year contracts while dressed in the Heat uniforms that they would wear to a public celebration of their arrival minutes later. While the players and their families were escorted downstairs for the celebration, Riley squared away the remaining details of what had been his most promising twenty-four hours in Miami.

"Then I said to Micky, 'Let's go down and enjoy this press conference,'" Riley recalled. "When I got there, I couldn't believe there were eighteen thousand people in the arena."

The Heat had organized welcomings for other big stars in previous years, but this pep rally was doomed to play out differently.

"It was the same thing we did with Shaquille," Riley said. "Shaquille showed up in a big diesel, an eighteen-wheeler, and walked up the steps of the arena. There were thousands of fans there for him, and he soaked everybody with a squirt gun and guaranteed everyone he was going to bring a championship to Miami, which he did. Nobody was saying anything about that. It was fun. It was Shaq. It was great."

O'Neal, a likeable three-time champion, was just promising to do what he had done before. LeBron, America's new villain, would be making promises that he could never keep.

"Dwyane said to me, 'Let's do something bigger than what Shaq did. Let's do something bigger than that,'" recalled Riley. In turn, Riley had assigned the Heat's business manager to "do something nice and classy."

Two years earlier, Riley had foreseen the new marketplace of free agency and the opportunity to connect with its young empowered stars. It was as if he had opened a door without realizing all that was coming in.

Thousands of fans ran through the gates of the AmericanAirlines Arena and down the aisles — first come, first served — for the occasion of LeBron's arrival. By the time Riley and Arison made it downstairs, another ten thousand who couldn't gain entry were gathered in the afternoon heat outside. *The Decision* had heightened the demand for admittance beyond expectations.

"I knew there was going to be something, but I didn't envision that," Riley said. "It was my fault. It's all on me."

Cheerleaders in their tight white outfits danced as the arena shook like a thumping nightclub. Glamorized highlights of Bosh, LeBron and Wade were shown on the large screens above the court. And then, amid bursts of white smoke, a hidden platform at one end of the arena was elevated hydraulically to reveal the backsides of the three stars standing shoulder to shoulder in their white Heat uniforms. All at once they turned to face their screaming fans. Wade, the 6-4 guard, was smiling naturally, because this was his NBA home and these were his people. Bosh, the slim 6-10 power forward, gasped with surprise. But LeBron was on guard; he glanced aside to see how his new teammates were reacting before his own smile broke out, as if he were reading the defense before attacking. On the court his instincts were sound; here, not so much.

"You always want to put yourself in the best position possible to be able to win," declared 28-year-old Wade to the audience as he and his new teammates sat up onstage on high stools. "And having the opportunity to team up with, you know" — Wade paused to think about what he was going to say, which only made it worse when he said it — "arguably the best trio to ever play the game of basketball, is amazing."

The best trio to ever play. He was saying this of LeBron, who had never won a championship; Bosh, a five-time All-Star who at 26 had never won a playoff series; and himself, a six-time All-Star who had won just a single title in his seven NBA seasons. Many NBA trios — including Johnson, Abdul-Jabbar and Worthy, who had won three titles for Riley's Lakers — were superior.

When it was LeBron's turn he said, "The way we're going to challenge each other to get better in practice, once the game starts, I mean, it's going to be easy."

Winning was going to be easy, LeBron was saying.

"We know you guys are going to enjoy the sun and the fun and all the spoils of South Florida," said the moderator for the sake of the crowd. "But we also know you three kings came down here to win championships."

LeBron was shaking his head as he said, "Absolutely."

"Not one," said the moderator, as if a single championship wouldn't do.

"Not two," said LeBron, his glowing white headband shaking back and forth like a collapsed halo.

"LeBron, tell us about that," said the moderator, but LeBron needed no prompting. "Not two," went on LeBron, his voice hiking up, "not three, not four, not five." Wade was laughing. "Not six, not seven," LeBron went on, and Bosh, who alone had maintained his decorum, was laughing now too. "Hey!" said LeBron, holding the long wireless microphone at the top of its throat like a performing artist. "And when I say that" — now he was shouting over the laughing roars of his new audience — "when I say that, I really believe it. I'm not just up here blowing smoke at none of these fans, because that's not what I'm about. I'm about business. And we believe we can win multiple championships if we take care of business and do it the right way."

The dawning of a new day had failed to improve LeBron's hindsight or insight. He was operating so far afield from his own instincts — claiming arrogance, when he had to be insecure following his recent loss in Boston; pretending to be a guarantor of championships in spite of his own healthy doubts — that he was casting himself now as a flimflam artist. He was selling the same promises down here in Miami that he had abandoned up in Cleveland. Did he not think his creditors were going to catch up with him? His alienated supporters in Northeast Ohio were astounded by LeBron's serial failure to recognize the damage he was inflicting on himself. And yet, from the point of view that had led LeBron into this mess, there was a soothing logic to his behavior. His hype had made him more famous and richer than most of the NBA's accomplished champions, and so, when the pressure surged, LeBron knew of no better way to react. Investing in the promise of a better tomorrow had become his go-to move.

Riley would blame himself for not overseeing the details of the rally — the questions that would be asked, the hydraulic stage that had been installed for an upcoming concert, the unnecessary use of white smoke. "It threw gasoline on the fire," Riley said. "It did ring of some hubris on our part that was not planned."

Just as LeBron had been surprised by the backlash of *The Decision*, so too would Riley be stunned the next day. "I just think the euphoria of that moment and what all three of them had done had got to them," he said. "The serotonin level was going high. Some of the things that were said, I think they would take it back and be a little more humble if they could, and probably the same for us as an organization. But once it got going I was not going up on the stage to throw them off." He laughed and said, "How would that have been? I would have been booed out of the arena by eighteen thousand people."

What was especially damning about this sequel to *The Decision* was that it appeared to betray Riley's dearest competitive values. The hard-driven Riley of the 1980s would not have enabled his players to declare victory before they had won so much as a game in preseason together. The Riley of those days would have emphasized the humility necessary to play championship basketball, and he never would have provided a platform for them to revel like champions before they deserved the right.

At that time, when Riley was laying down a point of view for his Lakers and their rivals that enabled them to make sense of the NBA's emerging commercial world, they had been able to manage their celebrity by trial and error. But the old dynamics no longer held sway in the socially networked world. In 2010 every action by a player or coach could be met by an equal or greater reaction.

Riley didn't blame his team's business department for tapping into the euphoria. The Heat franchise, launched in 1988, was essentially three years younger than LeBron. Pro basketball was still establishing itself in Miami. The arrival of the three stars provided this unprecedented opportunity to connect the franchise with its customers.

"I think if I had paid more attention to exactly how we were going to introduce them, a press conference would have been enough," Riley said. "If I had to do that one over again, we would have modified it and made it a little more sane. It was crazy."

The long-pursued dream of finding a replacement for Michael Jordan had been exposed overnight as folly. The off-the-court world that had been pioneered and commanded by Jordan was now threatening to overwhelm and demoralize his heir.

"It really is bizarre how the whole thing turned out," Riley said. "I've been part of this league for fifty years, been in a lot of different situations that would create controversy or not, and celebrations, and good stories and bad stories. But this one was over-the-top on the negative towards LeBron, way over-the-top on the negative. And there was no way that we could actually help him, other than go through it with him."

All the fans had ever wanted from their stars was to be inspired by them, but now in LeBron they saw someone who was daring to take advantage of them instead. And so the same kinds of people who had cheered for Jordan would now be going out of their way to boo his heir.

LeBron's new teammates and coaches, as gathered together by Riley, would be focused on seeing him through this crisis. Riley was counting on their ideals to renew and fulfill LeBron's best intentions. But there were also fans by the millions who were convinced — by LeBron himself — that he was the enemy of all that Jordan had believed in.

Which was the real LeBron?

3

THE GAME

Opening night of the 2010–11 season was approaching, and David Stern, the NBA commissioner for twenty-seven years, knew that he was going to be on the wrong side of the country. While most of his constituency was focused on the game in Boston, where LeBron James would be making his Miami Heat debut, Stern's plan was to launch the new season in Los Angeles by handing out championship rings from the 2010 NBA Finals to Kobe Bryant's team. In the dozen years since the reign of Michael Jordan, there had been no player, coach or franchise more accomplished than Kobe, Phil Jackson or their Lakers, who had earned their latest title while pushing the NBA's ultimate rivalry to a seventh game. But *The Decision* had turned all of that into yesterday's immaterial news.

The negative energies whirling around LeBron were especially frustrating to Stern because he had seen the whole mess building for a long while. That was why he had tried so hard to prevent *The Decision* from taking place. "It was terrible," Stern would say. "It was terrible on its own. It is fair to say that we knew it was going to be terrible, and we tried very hard for it not to happen."

One such day of reflection found Stern in a small conference room adjacent to his office at the NBA's headquarters fifteen floors above Manhattan. On the wall behind him, looking over his shoulder, were portraits of his predecessors, of which there were only three: Maurice Podoloff, who had been hired as "president" of the new league nine months after World War II; Walter Kennedy, who had taken over in 1963 and changed his title to commissioner, in line with the more established leagues of American football and baseball; and Larry O'Brien, the former director of John F. Kennedy's presidential campaign, who went on to become the NBA's commissioner in 1975, three years after his office at the Watergate complex had been burglarized by Richard Nixon's operatives. The three paintings had been commissioned by Stern after his own elevation to commissioner in 1984. It was one of many gestures meant by Stern to provide his insecure young league with a sense of its own gravity. He joked that he was never going to see his eyeglasses and gray parted haircut lurking from this wall: Stern had ruled that his portrait would not be joining those of Podoloff, Kennedy and O'Brien as long as he was alive.

At 68 Stern remained curious and combative. Sitting across the long conference table from him was the NBA's deputy commissioner, Adam Silver, who had been nominated by Stern to replace him sometime in the near future. Many in the NBA were already looking forward to that day, because Silver, at 48, was more accommodating and less belligerent than Stern. The contrast between him and his eventual successor appeared to amuse Stern, who could remember when he was the fresh young leader known for building consensus.

Tiresome familiarity in combination with the demands of big business had drawn attention to Stern's less endearing inclination to bully and berate. In the self-defeating case of LeBron, however, Stern's powers had failed to dissuade the young NBA star from recasting himself as a shameless rogue.

"We made our concerns known," said Silver of the attempts by the league office to prevent *The Decision* from airing. "Ultimately that was LeBron's decision, and that was ESPN's decision to cover him in that fashion. But it's water under the bridge."

Silver was trying to change the subject, but Stern would let neither himself nor his deputy off the hook. "Okay," said Stern, his voice rising. "I am on record — go back and check it — as saying publicly it was ill-conceived, poorly executed and badly produced. And that caused some of my partners to say, 'How come you're saying bad things about us?'"

Those partners included ESPN, which was paying Stern's league $485 million for the rights to broadcast NBA games in 2010–11.

"It caused some colleagues to cringe too," said Silver, apparently referring to himself.

"Yes," agreed Stern, nodding across the table to Silver. "That's okay. We felt it and we expressed it, beforehand and after. And we also dealt with Dan Gilbert, who was imprudent."

Stern had deflated Gilbert, the owner of the Cavaliers, with a $100,000 fine for his efforts to destroy LeBron's reputation in the late-night hours after *The*

Decision. In an emotional public email addressed to Cavaliers fans, Gilbert had referred to LeBron as "our former hero," "narcissistic," "cowardly" and "heartless," to be followed that night by an interview with the Associated Press in which Gilbert accused LeBron of being a "quitter" during the recent playoff loss to the Celtics. All of these slurs were cast five days after the owner had tried to recruit LeBron with an animated video detailing the love Gilbert and his franchise had for LeBron as a person. Such were Gilbert's imprudences.

The Cavaliers hired a law firm to investigate Miami's recruitment of LeBron, but no action would be taken by Stern on allegations that the Heat had violated the NBA's tampering rules, which applied to teams but not to players. Along those lines the commissioner could not make sense of the accusations that Wade, LeBron and Bosh had "conspired" to play together. "What the heck is that all about?" said Stern. "These are guys that can get traded at a moment's notice if they don't have a no-trade clause. We send them to a team in the draft, we set up a series of rules that makes it profitable for them to stay at that team, and then at some given number of years — seven years in their case — they decide to go play for somebody else."

Having been unable to head off the damage of *The Decision* and the ensuing rally in Miami, Stern was left to acknowledge that there was only so much a commissioner could do in this checks-and-balances world. "This is not a monolithic organization. There are thirty enterprises," he said of the NBA's thirty individually owned teams, "and four-hundred-plus players, and all kinds of agents and marketers. So we are left to herd. And respond. And make the best out of all these circumstances."

"I would only say, and not defensively at all," added Silver, "part of the attraction of sports, of this community, is the fact that it is real. It's not like what is called 'reality programming.'"

"We're reality on the court, and we're reality off the court, okay?" said Stern, as if repeating a fact of life that he wished were not always so. "And people are fascinated by both aspects of it."

Stern had tried to stop ESPN from abetting LeBron in his self-destruction. More pleas of warning had been made to LeBron and his young marketing team from Akron, who ignored the NBA in deference to the advice they were receiving from Ari Emanuel, the powerful Hollywood agent who had helped pull together the deal to televise *The Decision,* along with Jim Gray, who had served as its emcee. In the months afterward, Stern would engage in philosophical arguments with Silver over the values of *The Decision*. He would warn his deputy against being "too nice" about a show that had turned into "a comedy of errors." Silver, in turn, would remind Stern that for all of the criticism ESPN had received for its amateurish production, the network remained proud of the high rating it delivered after two years of speculation about LeBron's future.

Above all else, the commissioner had come away wishing that he could somehow prevent the NBA's new marketplace from intruding on and obscuring the game. "In a perfect world," said Stern of the perpetual free-agent gossip that had drummed up interest for *The Decision,* "I would have frozen the period of speculation to the very two weeks after the Finals." And yet Stern also would admit that the focus on LeBron leading up to *The Decision* had not been without its benefits. It had generated two years of noisy hype that the NBA could not have manufactured otherwise. It had created interest, in the way that the scandal of a Hollywood star drives up the box office. Even so, Stern was ambivalent. "I intellectually knew that all of the speculation about LeBron was getting us inches and feet that we would not otherwise get," he said. "But I didn't have a gut reaction in that direction. My reaction was that it detracted from the game."

Then again, the games weren't the draw they used to be. The NBA still had not come up with a winning identity to fill the space left by Jordan.

"You can't regulate anything these days," Stern said of *The Decision.* "Whatever happens, we shouldn't be the people that generate it."

The first step, Stern knew, was for young stars like LeBron to do their most influential work on the court. For the sake of the NBA's future, the focus needed to return to the game.

When Stern was elevated to commissioner in February 1984, nine months before Jordan would make his debut with the Chicago Bulls, the survival of pro basketball was not assured. Less than two years earlier, the *Boston Globe* had published a five-day series forecasting the death of the NBA, based on the widely held premise that the league relied on too many black players and an unsustainable financial model that was pushing several teams toward bankruptcy. Playoff games were being aired on tape delay, at 11:30 p.m., as late as 1986. Three years later CBS was relinquishing its national TV rights in the belief that the NBA would fall into decline without the rivalry of Magic Johnson and Larry Bird, according to Dick Ebersol, who as the new president of NBC Sports stepped forward to become Stern's TV partner just as Jordan was launching his run of championships.

A quarter century later, in the negative light of *The Decision,* Stern was routinely criticized for his role in commercializing the game — for converting the sport into a mainstream entertainment.

By then, of course, every league in America had negotiated similar trade-offs: Major League Baseball had been dumbed down by the enhanced home-run hitters of its steroid era, while the National Football League's clunky old style of handing the ball up the middle had been replaced by the slick passing offenses that made for great TV. Many of Stern's critics had benefited from the NBA's transformation — including his own players and team owners, who came across like millionaires complaining amid their caviar and champagne.

Many of them were too young or new to professional basketball to account for the doomsday that Stern had been helping to avert since the late 1970s, when he served as the top aide to Larry O'Brien. Stern would never forget the hard years that preceded the opulence, and in that sense he was like a child of the Great Depression.

"One of the things we always say behind closed doors is, no matter what happens, we are the 'black sport,'" Stern said. "That's just a given."

It was a sobering reality, especially since his rival leagues in America — the NFL and MLB — had developed identities all their own that transcended race. And yet, dating back to his 1966 hiring as outside counsel to the NBA in his first year out of Columbia Law School, Stern had rejected the prevailing view that pro basketball would be ruined by its dependence on African American players. Even in those early years when there appeared to be no commercial future for a league of black stars, Stern believed that the NBA was destined to survive and thrive.

Then came the collapse of the Berlin Wall, the end of the Cold War and the opening of new markets around the world; the dawning of digital television and the Internet; and the export of the 1992 Dream Team. The landscape had shifted, and the NBA, endangered for so long, was an unexpected beneficiary of the new world order.

The celebration was short-lived, however. Money had saddled the NBA with a new set of problems in the years of Jordan's absence. The newfound wealth of the league — with revenues rising to a record $4 billion in 2010 — had resulted in a greedy standoff between the team owners and the players, who couldn't agree on how to share their fortune. Then there was LeBron's celebrity run amok, which had convinced him to sell off his good name in the interest of reality TV.

More than a quarter century ago, Stern's urgent mandate had been to deliver more money and larger audiences to his starving league. That mission had been accomplished, and then some, during the Jordan era. The problem, emerging just now in this age of unprecedented prosperity, was that the NBA had failed to come up with a new mission. There had to be something more valuable than money and TV ratings.

What was the NBA's higher calling?

The NBA's rival leagues — MLB and the NFL — had recognized their own symbolism for some time. Baseball was the national pastime, the game of summer that makes time stand still. Football was a race against time in the pursuit of territory, the game of military precision and gladiatorial values.

Baseball was peace.

Football was war.

But what was basketball? What was the meaning of the NBA? What was the story that its players were acting out on the court?

This failure of identity had real consequences. In 2004, when Ron Artest of the Indiana Pacers incited a brawl with Detroit Pistons fans in the stands, Stern was faced with endlessly replayed news footage showing black players and white fans in combat at an NBA game. "You're coming out of a place where people have the freedom to say in the '80s or late '70s that you could never be successful because you're too black and America won't accept blacks," said Stern, for whom the incident served as a reminder that all of the NBA's impressive financial gains had not changed the old prevailing point of view. Reactions to the brawl were coded, but racism was there all the same. As soon as whites and blacks are in conflict, noted Stern, "the use of the words 'thug' and 'punk' suddenly becomes permissive."

When black players of the NFL or MLB were caught in embarrassing or incriminating scandals, those incidents didn't define the leagues racially because Americans understood what those sports were all about — they knew intuitively that baseball was peace and football was war. But when a black basketball player was in trouble, the public response often focused on race, with no means for changing the subject. There was no higher calling. Even after all of Jordan's gains, the NBA was still America's "black sport."

The NBA was seventy-seven years younger than MLB, twenty-six years younger than the NFL and four years younger than its own commissioner. It was the little brother of the other major sports leagues, and in this season of 2010–11 — in response to its issues of greed, celebrity and race — it was desperate for an epiphany of self-recognition.

From his earliest years as commissioner, when he was being told that the future was dire, Stern looked forward to his visits to the foreign frontiers of basketball. Not only was he able to explore opportunities and relationships on behalf of the NBA, but he could also separate himself from the business-first parochialism of America and view his league from the refreshing perspective of distance. He realized that basketball lovers in Europe, South America and beyond saw the same promise that he saw. They didn't view the NBA as the "black sport," or even as a vehicle for making money.

To them the NBA was theater, improvised and unpredictable, which played out the ideals of America — a melting pot of freedoms in which players of all colors and cultures took up the chance to fulfill themselves while helping others to do the same, at breakneck speed: All for one and one for all. That ideal was exported to Barcelona in 1992 by the Dream Team of Michael Jordan, who headlined the first Olympic basketball team from the United States to feature NBA stars.

Why did basketball spread and grow so quickly around the world? The answer had everything to do with the ideals of its inventor, James Naismith, an immigrant from Canada whose parents had emigrated from Scotland. In 1891, in Springfield, Massachusetts, Naismith responded to the public need for a team sport to be played indoors in winter, and along the way he created a game that was symbolic of the New World: In "basket ball," he decided, the same rules would apply to all of the players, and everyone would have equal access to the ball.

This is why the American game grew organically on every continent: Basketball was the sport of merit.

Throughout the 1980s the NBA's young chief was invigorated by the idealism that greeted him overseas. Stern the romantic capitalist longed for a new identity for his league that would eclipse borders, a niche that would be comprehensive, a message to inspire anyone, anywhere. He became the commissioner of wanderlust — forever jetting off to Europe, to China, to India, to South America and

Africa, in search of answers to questions he was just beginning to phrase. He was all over the map, literally and ambitiously.

The end of the Cold War awakened in Stern a revolutionary vision. When Jordan, an African American, became the most popular team athlete around the globe, Stern moved to create a new basketball world. In comparison with the conservative commissioners of American football and baseball, Stern appeared to be scattered, impulsive and even somewhat delusional in imagining that his little league, which had survived on the edge of bankruptcy for most of its short life, could one day network the entire planet.

Around the world, basketball had risen to become the number two team sport (behind soccer). In America, however, the NBA was mired at number three (behind the NFL and MLB).

The irony of Stern's domestic predicament was that his rival sports in America weren't truly American. Baseball was descended from cricket and other ancient games. American football was a next-generation version of rugby and soccer.

In baseball and football, the players were not seen as being equal. In baseball the pitcher was endowed with special powers that separated him from his teammates. The same was true for the quarterback in football.

Rules that enabled some players to have more importance than others did not exist in the equal-opportunity world of basketball. In every game of basketball, the most important player was the best player. In the 1960s that was Celtics center Bill Russell, and in the 1990s it was Bulls guard Michael Jordan. In the new millennium, in spite of his off-the-court troubles in 2010, the best player was destined to be LeBron James, a forward who would embrace the freedoms of basketball by mastering every skill of the game.

For American fans who grew up loving the traditional sports of football and baseball, the inherent mystery of basketball was why the best players were so dominant. Russell, Jordan, Magic Johnson and Larry Bird had much greater influence over the NBA than the greatest players in baseball and football had over their leagues. The reason was obvious. NBA stars were able to make the most of their talent because their sport was based on merit. The rules encouraged them to play both ends of the court without limitation. They were liberated by their freedoms. May the best man win.

Baseball, in which every player waited in line for his turn at bat, and football, in which players were lined up like pieces on a chessboard, were drawn from the Old World desire to place limits on what people could do and who they could become. These games were like fantasies that recalled a simpler time of authority and submission, when order was enforced, people did as they were told, and the world made sense.

This was what Stern was up against in the 1980s. His competitors, the NFL and MLB, provided fans with a respite from their daily lives. Baseball and football games were escapes from reality.

The NBA, by comparison, offered no such escape. The NBA reflected the realities of life in America. With no rules to separate one group from another, and all players having the same rights and privileges, the messiness of the ongoing American experiment — of race and culture and generations and individuality and greed — was being acted out on the courts of the NBA night after night.

In basketball, by and large, the winning teammates were those who chose, by their own free will, to embrace their differences as strengths that could elevate and propel their team. The players who didn't show respect for one another tended to be losers.

In America, where freedoms are often taken for granted, the theater of the NBA was often frustrating. Elsewhere, however, it was inspiring.

By 2010 there were two basketball worlds. There was basketball in America, where the sport was run like a business. And then there was basketball everywhere else, where the laws of profit and loss were not yet all-powerful. On the foreign frontiers, basketball was seen as being more valuable than a business.

As Stern looked ahead to the 2010–11 NBA season, he could see no end to the bickering over money. The owners of teams in the NBA's smaller markets — franchises like the San Antonio Spurs, Indiana Pacers and Charlotte Bobcats (which was owned and operated by 47-year-old Michael Jordan) — wanted big-city franchises like the Los Angeles Lakers and New York Knicks to share income from their local TV broadcasts and other revenue sources. The Lakers were negotiating a twenty-year deal to televise their games in Los Angeles for a reported $200 million per year — ten times more than the Miami Heat received for their local broadcasts. Most of the small-market teams were losing money, said Adam Silver, and altogether the NBA was projecting losses of $1 billion over three years. Stern wanted the wealthy teams to share with the less wealthy ones in order to improve competition throughout the league and elevate the business for everyone.

It was a hard sell because, at the very same time, Stern was also trying to convince the owners and players to negotiate a new collective bargaining agreement. The NBA was raking in more money annually than the gross domestic product of at least forty-two countries — including Cape Verde and Dominica, which had sent players to the NBA — but the four hundred or so NBA players and the owners of the thirty teams could not agree on how to divvy it up.

The league's economic framework was unsustainable, the owners and players were polarized, and their negotiations to find a way forward were in gridlock. The players refused to accept the facts of financial ruin as set forth by the owners, and the owners responded to the stubborn negotiating stance of the players with equal cynicism. Prosperity was making them all miserable.

Back in the 1980s, when no one could imagine so much wealth ever being generated by the "black sport," the owners and players had been far more understanding of each other. In those days common ground was easier to find because the fear of bankruptcy endangered everyone equally. The owners asked for a ceiling on player salaries, and in return the players were guaranteed a fixed annual percentage of the NBA's revenues. That was how the first salary cap in pro sports was conceived by the young, consensus-building Stern.

After the two sides had shaken hands on that deal, the NBA players insisted on an unprecedented drug-testing policy for cocaine and other recreational drugs, in hopes of restoring the good health and reputation of their league. "The union wanted it to be that if you were caught, you would be banned for life," said Russ Granik, the former NBA deputy commissioner who worked alongside Stern in the 1980s. "It was really our side and David who were saying, 'Aren't you entitled to some mercy? Maybe they can turn their life around. We'll call it a lifetime ban, but let's give them an opportunity to be reinstated.' It was the opposite of how people might have thought that [policy] came about."

By 2010 the shared instinct for survival was gone. Neither the players nor the owners were of any mind to seek common ground. Their tendency instead was to view anyone of authority, especially Stern, as an adversary. A number of them had grown to detest Stern because he claimed so much power and lorded it over them like an emperor. Instead of recognizing the need to invest in their shared league, the players and the owners were competing to grab their own dividends — to cash in before someone else could beat them to it.

As the commissioner approached the end of his long reign, he could see no other option than to lock out the players at the end of the 2010–11 season — a shutdown of league operations amid a worldwide recession, no less — in order to force a reasonable conversation between two groups that were refusing to acknowledge their need for each other. They were facing their second lockout since Jordan's last NBA Finals appearance, in 1998.

Stern had come in as a consensus builder in a failing league, and now, even as his players and owners were swimming in a pool of money that was deeper than ever, he was going to be treated as a bullying dictator on his way out.

"If you've been doing something for forty-five years," Stern would say of his association with the NBA, "or you've been doing this job I am in for twenty-eight years, you know you have the ability to at least delude yourself into thinking that you're doing what's best for the group. And then you take every shot that you can take. And what are they going to do? Other than fire me? I'm not running for reelection."

Stern was confident that he and Silver would eventually coerce financial agreements between the players and the team owners, and also between teams in the larger and smaller markets. But a balancing of the books was not going to resolve the missing link of identity that was feeding the inevitable lockout as well as the crisis of LeBron.

Who were the people of the NBA? What did their community stand for? What did they want to become? Such issues were beyond Stern's control. In this league that was of, by and for the players, only they could answer those questions. Who among them would be able to put the money back into perspective and renew the game's ideals?

In the midst of *The Decision*, relatively little attention was being paid to another expensive free-agent agreement that had been reached in Texas a few days earlier. It had gone without saying that the Dallas Mavericks were going to re-sign power forward Dirk Nowitzki to a contract that would guarantee him $80 million for the next four seasons. Dirk had played for the Mavericks since he had arrived in the United States as a 20-year-old from Würzburg, Germany, in 1999, the year after Jordan's retirement from the Bulls.

"I started playing when I was about 13, which was 1991," said Dirk. The Dream Team had arrived in Europe one year later. "I was a big Charles Barkley fan," Dirk went on. "Not a lot of people know that, but he's the reason why I started wearing number 14, because he wore 14 in the Olympics." Years later, when Dirk came to the Mavericks, Robert Pack was wearing number 14. "So I just flipped the numbers," said Dirk, who had been wearing number 41 in Dallas ever since.

Like LeBron, Dirk had accepted a slightly discounted salary in order to help his team surround him with better talent. Unlike LeBron, Dirk had not sought competing offers on the open market.

The goal that mattered to Dirk more than any other was the NBA championship. He was 32 and already more accomplished than he ever could have imagined coming from the other side of the ocean. All of his awards and rewards left him feeling hungrier for what he didn't have. If he was meant to win the championship, it was going to be in Dallas, his adopted home.

The Mavericks had been confident of retaining their biggest star as Dirk approached free agency in July 2010. But they also saw the fuss that was being made over LeBron and others on the free-agent market, and they wanted to make certain that Dirk wasn't feeling taken for granted. So the Mavericks arranged for hundreds of employees and fans to greet him at the Dallas/Fort Worth airport when he landed from Germany to negotiate his new contract with the help of his longtime mentor, Holger Geschwindner. When Dirk heard of the reception, he told the team he was changing his plans. He booked another flight in order to arrive late at night and avoid the celebration.

"I didn't want a big spectacle at the airport," Dirk would say later. "The circus —that was never my thing, you know?"

4

THE TRADITION

It was July 2010, and Doc Rivers could not get over his team's loss one month earlier in Los Angeles. His six years of coaching the Boston Celtics boiled down to two games against Kobe Bryant's Lakers. There was Game 6 of the 2008 NBA Finals, which Doc's Celtics won, and Game 7 of the 2010 NBA Finals, which they lost.

"I think about it all the time," Doc said of the Game 7 loss in Los Angeles. "I think about that far more than I think about the Game 6 that we won — I don't remember that. But I can replay every play of Game 7."

Of course he was exaggerating. In 2008 the Celtics had earned their seventeenth championship — only the New York Yankees had more among the American professional football, baseball and basketball leagues — and Doc, when pressed, could recite all kinds of details from the biggest victory of his life.

The Celtics had been pulling away from the Lakers since the second quarter, and their fans were celebrating the impending 131–92 victory, when Tom Thibodeau, the Celtics' defensive coach, approached his boss on the sideline.

"I hate that Tibs has this over me," said Doc. "We had our starters in, it was four minutes left, we were beating the shit out of them. So Tibs walks over and says, 'Are you going to sub? I think we got this.'"

Doc laughed at the memory. "And I was like, shit, I'd seen Kobe too many times. With five minutes left, that's too much time for Kobe," said Doc. "But you don't do the math at that point, even though you're up 40."

For most of his life Doc had been obsessed with his unrealized dream of winning the NBA championship, first as a player who failed to experience the NBA

Finals in thirteen seasons with four teams, and then as head coach of the Orlando Magic, whose run of devastating injuries prevented them from winning a playoff series during his five seasons there. After Doc took control of the Celtics in 2004, the lows of his first four years in Boston threatened to overwhelm him. When his ultimate triumph arrived at age 46, he expected to be transformed. "You would think you won the title, it would quench your thirst," he said. "But to me I don't think it did anything, and that surprised me. I thought, 'Boy, once I win — *ahhh.*' But I wanted to win just as bad the next year. I don't think it did anything at all."

By contrast, the loss of the seventh game in 2010 followed him everywhere. He was haunted routinely by it; though not so much by the devastating knee injury that sidelined his starting center, Kendrick Perkins, because bad luck is beyond anyone's control. What Doc couldn't stop dwelling on were the plays his team could have and should have made to win the game. At any moment they would pop up in his mind like a computer virus, freezing him in his recent past. "It's just little shit," he said.

He found himself focusing on his team's response to a shoulder injury suffered by Paul Pierce, the Celtics' All-Star forward, that forced him to the bench for a brief time in the third quarter. "Paul goes out with that little stinger he had, and they made the 9–2 run in that little two-and-a-half-minute period."

There were the baskets by Ron Artest — "We should have defended them better" — and Derek Fisher's rainbow three-pointer against Rajon Rondo to tie the score with six minutes remaining. "We told the guys, Rondo in particular, all the time, 'You've got to close all the way out, you can't close halfway out.'

"There was a foul Kobe should have picked up — an extra foul — and they would have had to sub him out," Doc went on. "There were a couple of foul calls that hurt us that I thought were bullshit calls. You remember the game was a physical game, and then all of a sudden they went to a touch-foul game? The game went from a completely physical basketball game the first half, then all of a sudden in the third quarter they were calling touch fouls. It was like the game had changed, the way it was being called. That bugged me, that you could see that. That affected us. Because obviously, it's easy to say, we could have had two."

Two championships, he meant.

In the end, the difference was the play of Kobe himself. "I give him credit, he made a couple of great passes," Doc said. "And I'm still pissed because I think we could've gotten out to them." With a little over a minute remaining, Kobe went up as if to shoot over a Boston double-team—but instead passed to Artest for his three-pointer over Pierce, to put the Lakers ahead 79–73. "We didn't close out completely," Doc said.

The gloom lifted that summer, thankfully, when the 2010–11 NBA schedule came out. Doc and his players were rejuvenated by the news that they would be opening the season at home against the sensationalized Heat of LeBron James, Dwyane Wade and Chris Bosh. Miami's arrogance would galvanize Boston and inspire its stars to renew their commitment to teamwork in its most traditional form, as set forth a half century earlier by coach Red Auerbach and his generous star, Bill Russell. Instead of dwelling on the title that had been taken from them by their oldest rivals in Los Angeles, Boston's trio of Pierce, Kevin Garnett and Ray Allen found themselves looking forward to a new type of rivalry. For Pierce, the longest-serving Celtic, who would be matched up against LeBron, the Celtic Way itself was under attack.

"It's like they had been given something that they hadn't earned," said Doc of LeBron and the Heat. "And I thought that offended our guys."

For many years LeBron had been the best small forward in the Eastern Conference, and Pierce had been second best. And yet Pierce's Celtics had beaten LeBron's Cavaliers when it mattered—in Game 7 of the 2008 conference semifinals, and then on opening night of the following season, when Pierce cried while accepting the championship trophy and raising the seventeenth banner in the TD Garden. "I said, 'Oh jeez, we're done,'" said Doc. Then LeBron came out from the visitors' locker room, and Pierce's tear ducts tightened like fists. He outscored LeBron 27–22, and the Celtics won by 5.

One year later LeBron was opening the 2009–10 season in Cleveland amid tremendous hope—to be crushed, ominously, by yet another loss to Pierce's Celtics. And then came the defeat in the final game of the Cavaliers' 2010 postseason at Boston, the loss that provoked LeBron to take his talents to Miami. Pierce, more than any other player, had broken LeBron's heart and chased him away.

Weeks later Pierce could not believe what he was seeing in Miami, where LeBron and his new teammates were celebrating in the theatrical smoke of their summer pep rally. "I was sitting there watching," said Pierce, "and I was like, 'What is this?' It looked like they just won the NBA Finals, and they're talking about winning all these championships that they haven't won yet. They acted like they won something."

Pierce understood their ambitions. He had been in LeBron's sneakers three years earlier, when Pierce was the high-scoring All-Star who hadn't come close to winning the championship. Then, in the summer of 2007, the Celtics had made blockbuster trades for Allen, the All-Star shooting guard of the Seattle SuperSonics, and Garnett, the former league MVP of the Minnesota Timberwolves.

Instead of predicting an easy path forward, as LeBron had done at his premature celebration in Miami, the new Celtics regarded one another with humility. Allen was 32, Garnett was 31 and Pierce was 30. Their time in the NBA was already growing short, and there were no visions of five, six or seven titles. Their experience had taught them how difficult one championship would be.

"We went through the same thing, kind of," Pierce said of the Heat's instant rise into contention. "A lot of people had us on magazine covers and anointed us when we all got together, and I remember somebody in the papers saying, 'They're on the cover of the magazine, but they ain't won nothing.' But we knew that. We didn't celebrate."

As surprised as Pierce was that the rally had happened on Pat Riley's watch, he was not inclined to hold Riley accountable. "He has a chance to get the best player in the league—what is he going to say?" Pierce said of Riley. "This is a new generation."

Pierce viewed himself, Garnett and Allen as leaders of the older generation —Kobe's generation—which had made them less vulnerable to the influences of the AAU and social media and the commercial expectations that had been so alluring to LeBron (as well as to their own young point guard Rondo). Recognizing their willingness to push everything else to the side in order to win a championship together, Doc asked his three stars to meet with him weeks before training camp opened. They were standing with their coach on Huntington Avenue in Boston when an amphibious duck boat—empty of passengers—pulled up in front of the building. After the three players had joined Doc on board, he explained that they would be following the route of the championship parade that was theirs to earn. The four of them spent the ride through Boston holding on around hard turns, taking in the views and working up their plan of sacrifices and vows that would ultimately line these streets with hundreds of thousands of celebrating fans at the end of the season.

"That was the best thing that happened," Pierce said. "Doc told us his expectations of us, and it was fun, all of us sitting down together and talking about it."

Nine months later Pierce was back in the duck boat, smoking a cigar in emulation of Red Auerbach and following the route as envisioned by Doc. At least Pierce assumed it was the same route.

"The parade was such a blur, I didn't even know what direction we were going in," Pierce said. "I was puffing the cigar, and the next thing I know I went underneath and threw up. I got really sick, I got light-headed and dizzy, and I sat under for a good ten to fifteen minutes."

The first duck boat ride had been their version of the rally in Miami, except they had conducted theirs in private. Out of respect for one another and the difficulty of their mission, they would keep their preseason parade secret until they qualified for the NBA Finals.

"I loved our relationship, how we talked all the time," said Pierce, who had been waiting his entire basketball life for teammates like Garnett and Allen. "We knew we had to sacrifice. I knew I wasn't going to average 25 or even 20 points, and I was ready for that. I had a chance to play with other great players. I'm doing what I got to do."

In doing that, Pierce fulfilled his ambition to join the long list of Celtics champions — led by Bill Russell, John Havlicek and Larry Bird — who had made the most of their careers by sacrificing their own games. Pierce had come to see that success in basketball was a less-is-more paradox. That was why he was so insulted by the preseason shenanigans in Miami. LeBron was expecting to dethrone the Celtics without showing any respect for how hard it had been for them to renew their championship tradition.

Pierce was more than captain of the NBA's winningest franchise; he was also the only active Celtics player with a direct connection to Red Auerbach. Their relationship had begun at a charity event in the summer of 1998, not long after the Celtics had drafted Pierce in the first round. "I was like, 'That's Red,'" said Pierce. "And he called me right over."

Auerbach was in semiretirement, but he knew all about Pierce, a 19-year-old small forward who had been first-team All-America as a junior at the University of Kansas before sliding inexplicably from the top of the 1998 NBA draft. Rick Pitino, who was beginning year two of a hopeless four-year run as the Celtics' coach and team president, had wanted to choose Dirk Nowitzki with the number ten pick that year. But when Dirk was taken off the board at number nine as part of a prearranged trade that would send him from the Milwaukee Bucks to the

Dallas Mavericks, the Celtics were grateful to find Pierce waiting for them. That had been the longest hour for Pierce, sitting at the draft in Vancouver, British Columbia, in his beige striped suit as one losing team after another passed him by. He was too young to imagine the benefits he would derive from the Celtics and Auerbach, the godfather of the NBA, who in the 1950s and '60s had laid the foundations for professional basketball.

"He sat on this couch and he just started talking to me, like, 'I watched you at Kansas,'" Pierce remembered. "It was unbelievable to me that he even knew me."

By then Auerbach had become the NBA's Yoda. He looked entirely foreign in the world he had created. Auerbach was shorter than 5 foot 10, with a rounded belly and whitewalls of hair framing his bald head. Not quite 81, he had another eight years of life in him. He was inhaling from his trademark cigar in those days before smoking had been banned indoors, and he had a slow, contemplative way of explaining the Celtics tradition that enabled Pierce to piece together, little by little, a championship timeline of four decades that began with Russell in the mid-1950s, was renewed around Havlicek in the 1970s and continued with Bird in the 1980s. By way of these stories the old man was introducing Pierce, as he sat uncomfortably in an armchair, to his own potential. There was something about Auerbach's tempo that provided those in whom he was invested the space to think things through and understand the truth of what he was saying, even as the words came forth unevenly between the clouds of smoke.

Auerbach was living proof of the NBA's youth relative to the other sports leagues in America. John McGraw, the first great manager in baseball, and Knute Rockne, the coach who set forth the values that would define American football, had been dead for more than sixty years. But here, before Pierce, with hints of freshly cremated tobacco staining his shirt, was the man who had established the laws of teamwork in basketball.

"This is one of the most legendary coaches sitting down talking to me for the next forty-five minutes and giving me a piece of his mind on how he followed my career and what it means to be a Celtic," Pierce said. "He wanted me to understand the players that had been through here, how they wore the jersey with pride, and it wasn't about the individual and the name on the back. It was about winning and how to help carry on the tradition. He had so many stories about when he coached and how they did it and how they played, and you're sitting there in awe and soaking it all in, especially being so young. It's like, man, I wish

I could have recorded it now, you know? If the era when I first came in was like now, with the iPhones and the video, I could have recorded it so I could look back on it."

Auerbach would not have appreciated the iPhone. The memories he was sharing with Pierce were meant to be kept close, like a family secret. Pierce would be his final protégé, and Auerbach's slow cadence was meant to discover, point by point, whether Pierce grasped his meaning. He spoke not to be recorded, but to be understood.

There would be many more memories for Pierce as he matured in the organization, slowly and unsteadily, in spite of his own impatience and stubbornness. Russell would take him out to dinner. Tom Heinsohn, the former championship player and coach of the Celtics who was now broadcasting their games courtside near the Celtics' bench, would engage Pierce in heart-to-hearts. "I think they really saw something in me, even though I was on losing teams," Pierce said of the old Celtics who sought him out, one after another. Bird. Havlicek. Bob Cousy. Dave Cowens. Jo Jo White. They were growing more comfortable around him, treating him less like a project and more like their equal.

"I just loved seeing them at the games," Pierce said. "You don't see that around other franchises, the great players of the past. I remember players from other teams would be like, 'Damn, y'all got Havlicek around here, y'all got Cousy. It must be sweet just having those guys around, just coming to practice.' I always liked to listen to their stories, and how was it when they played, how was they in the locker room, how was they off the court, did they hang, what type of partying or what type of trouble they got into. It was not as documented back then as it is now. Everything we do is Twittered, everything is. So that's why it was always good to talk to them."

A fundamental truth of Pierce's determination was made public, almost tragically, in his third NBA season, in the months after he was stabbed nearly to death in the early morning hours at a nightclub in Boston. He had been speaking briefly with a young woman when he was attacked from behind by a group of men who smashed a champagne bottle over his head. They stabbed him six times in the face and five more between his shoulders. The expensive leather jacket Pierce was wearing provided a shell that kept the tip of the knife just short of his heart, and that was the difference between a senseless death and the fulfillment that Auerbach envisioned in him.

"I remember seeing a psychiatrist shortly after," he said. "I saw her for two days and I was, like, 'I can't do this.' That's why I always found myself going to the gym in the morning, at night. I was always in the gym after. This is my therapy, I needed to be out here, this is the only thing that was going to get my mind off of this stuff. Here I was free from thinking about it and everything that's happened to me, and it helped me not think about the pain."

Twenty-five days after his stabbing, Pierce was playing in a preseason game in Rockford, Illinois, against the Chicago Bulls. The Celtics weren't going to make the playoffs that year, and Pierce was weakened by his trauma, yet he played in all eighty-two games while averaging 25.3 points per game, a 30 percent increase over his second season. He dared the older, stronger opponents to take him on. "I wore a vest to a lot of the games, and I remember I took my first charge and Pitino was like, 'You need to be careful with that,'" he said. "It was like I fit the mold of a true Celtic. When I look back and see Larry out there with his bad back, or guys hobbling down the floor playing through the pain — I was like that. I wanted to be out there."

Pierce had grown up in a poor neighborhood of Los Angeles, near the "Fabulous" Forum, where he would see the Lakers in the parking lot before and after their games. He loved Magic Johnson and hated the Celtics, and he never could have imagined all of the times he would find himself staring into Bird's wooden eyes as he walked slow laps around him in the upstairs of the Celtics' arena, in a concourse shared with the Sports Museum. Pierce said, "They got the statue of him" — frozen in his artwork crouch, eyes on the distant rim, ready to go up. "He's a lot smoother than me," continued Pierce, who tended to follow through on his shot as if throwing a dart. "The way he shoots looks like perfect form almost."

In his early years in Boston, Pierce carried himself as if torn between emulating Bird and emulating Jordan, who won his championships while leading the NBA in scoring. Even as Pierce's best years were slipping away, the old Celtics encouraged him to think of himself as a champion, as if faith would put a ring on his finger someday.

The executives of other NBA teams would tiptoe around their millionaire stars, afraid to antagonize them after a tough loss. But Auerbach was from the time before players could leave as free agents. "The one thing I always respected about Red, he always spoke his mind," Pierce said. "I remember there would be times he'd come in after the game, good or bad, he was going to tell me how he felt about my play and the team.

"He was like, 'You played terrible,'" Pierce continued. "He would come in and tell you exactly how he felt. But I respected that. He'd tell you what you'd need to do better. He really followed the game."

The Celtic Way was becoming irrelevant in the post-Jordan NBA. Pitino, who lost faith in his own decisions while making trade after trade, resigned abruptly in 2001 with a record of 102-146 — the worst of any Celtics coach with at least three years on the job. The following year the franchise was sold for $360 million to a large partnership headed by private equity millionaires. To manage their front office, they hired former Celtics All-Star guard Danny Ainge, who in the 1980s had won two championships alongside Bird, and Ainge in turn hired Doc Rivers to be the new coach.

Doc's thirteen-year career as an NBA point guard began in the 1980s in Atlanta, where his Hawks won at least fifty games for four straight seasons without ever winning a playoff series against Bird's (and Ainge's) Celtics. Doc wanted in on the Celtics' winning history, dormant though it had become. He had a deep need to renew that tradition, for the franchise and for himself.

When Doc arrived in 2004, Pierce was a 27-year-old All-Star whose teams had gone 219-241 while winning three playoff series in six seasons. He was like so many from Kobe's generation who had grown up idolizing Jordan. "A lot of people labeled me as selfish, but I was like, who do y'all want me to pass the ball to?" said Pierce. "Look at the teams I'm playing on. People couldn't see the type of game I always wanted to play because I was on so many bad teams. So I had to do what I had to do, just to keep us at least respectable. I didn't want to play on teams where I had to score 30, 40 points a night just for us to have a chance — not to win, but just to have a chance of winning. That's not what I wanted. I wanted to show people that I can be a strong defender, I can be a good passer, I can score, and I can do other things in my game. But I had to carry this load because of our teams."

That approach was undermining Doc's hopes of renewing the Celtics tradition. He encouraged Pierce to sprint with his teammates (instead of walking up the floor as if the game revolved around him) and to share the ball in faith that they would provide him with better looks at the basket than he could create by himself. Doc was evangelizing Auerbach's traditional values to a player whose generation had moved beyond them. The old Celtics watching from the stands or on TV could see that Doc was in the right, and that he was losing the argument.

"I remember being so frustrated and walking out of the huddles talking about trading me," said Pierce, who could be seen muttering to himself. "Sometimes he would snatch me out of the game. I would be upset with him and saying that to him. I would go through the motions sometimes in practice because I didn't like the stuff we were doing or I was frustrated with the moves. It was good days and bad days.

"He took me out of the game when he felt I wasn't doing right. That was one of the first times that had happened to me. I remember one time I didn't run on the break. He was like, 'Run! Run!' I didn't run, and he took me out. Why the hell you taking me out, man? Don't be taking me out of the game. The game was a close game, three minutes to go. And then he put me back in and it was late and I hit a crucial three — and I pointed at him, don't you be taking me out of the game!" Pierce laughed as if he couldn't believe he was describing himself. "I remember that."

As successful as Jordan had been in proving that an African American in the "black sport" could become the most popular and profitable athlete around the world, his gains had not been as important as those of Bill Russell.

Russell's achievements transcended money and fame. Off the court he was a leader of the civil rights movement of the 1960s, and on the court he joined with Auerbach to establish a culture for racial equality within pro basketball. The Celtics became the first NBA team to select a black player in the NBA draft (Chuck Cooper, in 1950), the first to start five black players (in 1964) and the first to hire a black head coach (Russell, in 1966, whom Auerbach chose as his replacement to serve as player-coach). All of these moves were validated by the eleven championships Russell won during his thirteen seasons in Boston. The Celtics' emphasis on merit at the expense of race would not have been so influential if they hadn't proved, by their annual celebrations, that theirs was the right way.

In those days there was no free agency for stars like Russell. Auerbach had absolute authority, but he refused to wield it. His players worked earnestly on behalf of the team because Auerbach created partnerships with them.

"What made our team so different — and why so many of the players got into coaching — was the whole system was built on communication," said Heinsohn, who won eight championships as a teammate of Russell's (and would earn another two as head coach of the Celtics in the 1970s). During practice Auerbach might suggest a change in strategy. He then encouraged his players to make suggestions, and together they would work up the new plan.

"It would be a tight game with two minutes to go, and we would end up winning the game," Heinsohn went on. "Everybody thought that Red was a basketball genius because we were winning the game. And really what happened was, he would call timeout, and he would say, 'Has anybody got anything?' And you were expected to tell him how they were playing you and could you get open on such and such a move. So he was not designing plays, but listening to the players, who told him what they thought they could do. Which was brilliant. Because then you were making a commitment to make it work in front of your teammates."

While other teams were wasting their energy on power struggles and quarreling over who was in charge, the Celtics were pulling altogether in the same direction. Russell's vision of a society based on merit and equal rights was acted out by his teams with inspiring consistency.

A half century later, the financial dynamic had been flipped upside down. Now the stars of the NBA had authority over their coaches. But the same dynamic held true: Players who created honorable partnerships with their coaches held the ultimate advantage.

Doc had established a worthy alliance with Pierce by their third season together. By then, however, they felt isolated from the rest of the team. Ainge had been rebuilding with immature prospects, and the 2006–07 Celtics were among the worst teams in the league. When Doc visited his players in their locker room, he was like a tamer entering a den of lions. They held the ultimate power — the eighteen games in a row they lost were proof of that — and yet his job was to make them believe he had authority over them, in spite of their guaranteed contracts.

Like Pierce, Doc leaned on the alumni. He wrote letters inviting every retired Celtic to attend practices or games, at home or on the road, in hopes of infusing him and his team with the old community spirit. In particular Doc relied on Heinsohn, who as the Celtics' TV analyst traveled on the team charter. When their plane landed in suburban Boston, Doc would give Heinsohn a lift to his car. "He would say, 'Hang in there, kid, hang in there. You're a hell of a coach, kid.' He just kept saying it all the time," recalled Doc. "'I'm telling you, I know what a coach is, you're a hell of a coach. Don't let them get to you. I think you're thinking about quitting. Do not quit.' He was so important to me. I really believe, without that, I walk in one day and I quit. Losing with the team we had — we had a bunch of nimrods at times — I mean, when you feel like you can't do things . . ."

If he had been coaching for any other franchise, Rivers said, he would have walked away. Because the losing was killing him. "That stuff, to me, I don't think you get that anywhere else," said Rivers of his support from Heinsohn and other Celtics champions. "Anywhere else."

Before Ainge could find the kind of players that Doc could transform into champions, he first had to assemble his own team of scouts, analysts and advisers. By 2006 he had put together the NBA's most eclectic front office, which enabled him to discover Rondo.

With his unusual hires, Ainge was pursuing a traditional agenda: He was replicating the old Celtics front office from the era when Auerbach did everything himself. There were three areas in particular he was addressing. First there was an eye for talent, as possessed by scouts like Chris Wallace, Leo Papile and young Ryan McDonough, who traveled everywhere to see players in person. Then there was the statistical breakdown of each player's strengths and the potential for those strengths to be fitted together in the most efficient way, which was the role taken on by the data-driven analyst Mike Zarren. Finally there was the intuitive understanding of the players as human beings, which was the domain of Jon Niednagel, who was known throughout the NBA as "the Brain Doctor." Auerbach had been able to do all of this on his own, without scouts, spreadsheets or brain typing. Ainge, a highly skilled athlete who had stopped playing major league baseball for the Toronto Blue Jays when he was drafted by Auerbach in 1982, was trying to replicate Auerbach's genius by parsing out his talents among a variety of specialists.

The original discovery of Rondo was made by McDonough, who had no basketball experience when the Celtics hired him in 2003. His access to the team had been provided by his father, Will McDonough, a star sportswriter at the *Boston Globe*, who had been close friends with Auerbach. Ryan McDonough learned to scout first by studying college games on video, and then by attending those games in person.

In 2004, eighteen months before Auerbach's death, McDonough escorted Red to the University of Maryland to scout the Jordan Brand Classic, a high school all-star game that Michael Jordan hosted every year. McDonough guided Auerbach along by the arm as several volunteers hovered about to show them to their courtside seats. Thirteen of the twenty players in that game would go on to play in the NBA, including Dwight Howard, LaMarcus Aldridge and Al Jefferson. Among them was Rajon Rondo, a long-armed 6-foot 1-inch guard from Louisville who was headed to the University of Kentucky. "He liked Rondo," said McDonough. "Red wouldn't say a whole lot, he wouldn't gush about players, but he said, 'Keep an eye on him.' Good advice."

McDonough's appreciation for Rondo would be affirmed by Zarren, who was among the first data analysts to be hired by an NBA team. In the year before the 2006 draft, the Celtics had Rondo rated among the top four players likely to turn pro, based on his exceptional production in many phases of the game apart from shooting. "When we looked at the modeling work, Rondo was near the top of the list — and he was a name no one was talking about," said Zarren. "If you looked at the mock drafts in November of that year, he was in the forties."

Zarren has a law degree from Harvard University and an economics degree from the University of Chicago, where he studied under Steven Levitt, one of the authors of *Freakonomics*. He could have become rich by way of a career in finance or the law, but more important than salary to Zarren was his allegiance to the Celtics. He grew up in Boston as a huge fan of Kevin McHale. Ainge hired Zarren on the suggestion of Daryl Morey, who, in those years before he was named general manager of the Houston Rockets, was splitting his time between the business and basketball offices of the Celtics. As Zarren worked his way up to assistant general manager (a title he shared in 2010–11 with McDonough), he and his father continued to attend games together, sitting in the cheap seats. For the first several years, the fans sitting nearby didn't appear to realize that Zarren, wearing his satiny green Celtics jacket, was helping to discover and acquire the very players he was cheering on like a maniac.

As it became clear that Rondo was meeting the high standards of McDonough and Zarren on the court and in the spreadsheets, Ainge consulted with Niednagel for another point of view. The Brain Doctor had insight into the wiring of Rondo's personality.

"I think people misconstrue sometimes with Jon," said Ainge. "He's not always [helping us in] picking the best players, but Jon can help us understand who those players are — like, who we're getting: Do we want to put up with this? This guy has some talent, but here's some things you're going to have to deal with? Without even knowing all of their background, without even knowing their family history, but just watching their tendencies on the court, he has a great way to read people."

Niednagel had grown familiar with Rondo's potential by studying his mannerisms — the patterns of his blinking, the way he moved and spoke and interacted on and off the court. Those traits are crucial in Niednagel's field of expertise, known as brain typing. "It is the single greatest determinant for why people do what they do," said Niednagel, who headed the Brain Type Institute in Thornfield, Missouri.

The Brain Doctor's own profile had been heightened in 1998 when he was hired by the San Diego Chargers to help them prepare for the NFL draft. The Chargers were planning to use the number two pick for Peyton Manning or Ryan Leaf, the top two quarterbacks on the board. Niednagel told the Chargers to hope that Manning would be available, because his brain type was ideal for an NFL quarterback, the same as that of Johnny Unitas, Joe Namath, Joe Montana and Brett Favre. Under no circumstances should they choose Leaf, he warned, because Leaf was wired to respond negatively to pressure — his view of the field would shrink. The Indianapolis Colts used the number one pick on Manning, who became one of the great quarterbacks of all time, while the Chargers ignored the Brain Doctor's analysis and not only picked Leaf but also paid him an $11.25 million signing bonus. Three years later they were waiving Leaf, who had won only four games while throwing thirteen touchdown passes and thirty-three interceptions.

When Ainge was coaching with Phoenix in the 1990s, Niednagel implored the Suns to draft Kobe Bryant and Tracy McGrady, who would be chosen number nine overall by the Toronto Raptors' president Isiah Thomas. (We all know what happened to Kobe.) McGrady would lead the league in scoring twice while making the All-NBA Teams eight times. "He told us that Tracy was the closest thing to Michael Jordan he'd seen in fifteen years," recalled Ainge. "We spent the whole next year trying to trade for Tracy."

Zarren, the Celtics' numbers guru, was predisposed to be skeptical. Yet as uncertain as he was of Niednagel's methodology, he was a true believer in the Brain Doctor's diagnoses. "He's right all the time," Zarren said. "It's shocking how good he is at what he does, . . . and that's all that matters at the end of the day."

The Brain Doctor's point of view was based on the work of Carl Jung, the founder of analytical psychology, and Katharine Cook Briggs and Isabel Briggs

Myers, whose Myers-Briggs Type Indicator was drawn from the theory that there are sixteen brain types. Niednagel believed that brain types are a reflection of wiring, and that people are born with traits that help define who they are and what they might achieve. The best wiring for basketball is ISTP — introverted, sensing, thinking, perceiving — the brain type of Michael Jordan, Larry Bird, Jerry West, Bill Walton, Hakeem Olajuwon, John Stockton, Shaquille O'Neal and Doc Rivers.

Rondo's brain type is close, ISFP — introverted, sensing, feeling, perceiving. He is a feeler, rather than a thinker. "They have the greatest motor skills, but inside that brain is an emotional being," Niednagel said of players with this brain type. "They are very team-oriented, but they're also the most fragile. I remember telling Danny, 'He'll never be a rocket scientist, he'll always be emotional, but if he's mentored right, he could be highly productive.'"

Niednagel also warned Ainge that there would likely be friction between Doc and Rondo. Whereas Doc had the same wiring as O'Neal, Rondo was similar to Kobe.

Ainge believed that Rondo was the most valuable secret of the 2006 draft. But he was not the Celtics' priority. Ainge had zeroed in on Brandon Roy, a 6-foot 6-inch senior guard from the University of Washington. "He was my number one guy," said Ainge. "I had him rated number one in that whole draft, and we were going to get him with the seventh pick."

Then the Celtics' chief medical officer, Dr. Brian McKeon, reviewed Roy's extensive medical history and warned Ainge to stay away. "He's another great Paul Pierce, coming up in the wings," said Ainge. "And so imagine how hard that was to hear: 'Well, you know, this guy is going to have issues, Danny; he's had a foot surgery in college, he's had a knee surgery on the left knee, he's got knee surgery on the right knee . . . He's going to be able to play in the NBA, but he's going to have maintenance issues from the day you get him.'"

Which was exactly what happened with Roy in his brief career with the Portland Trail Blazers. He was an NBA star from the beginning — Rookie of the Year in 2006–07, an All-Star in his third, fourth and fifth seasons. And then, shortly after being re-signed to a five-year contract, he was forced to retire because of chronic knee problems. He was 27 years old, and Portland owed him $82 million, fully guaranteed.

The Blazers had been able to acquire Roy because Ainge, on the morning of the 2006 draft, had sent them the number seven pick as part of a trade that enabled the Celtics to lessen their burden of guaranteed contracts by $30 million in the years to come. It was the big-business reality that Auerbach had rarely faced: Ainge was weakening the Celtics in order to enhance their budget down the road.

The one consolation to Ainge was that no one else appeared to be interested in his second-favorite player. Pick after pick went by in the first round, and no one was claiming Rondo, who had played out of position as a sophomore at the University of Kentucky while arguing repeatedly with coach Tubby Smith. Wyc Grousbeck, the Celtics' principal owner, who appreciated the $30 million sacrifice Ainge had absorbed for the long-term health of the franchise, gave Ainge the go-ahead to acquire Rondo. And so Ainge and his staff made urgent calls to rival teams until the Phoenix Suns agreed to trade their number twenty-one pick to the Celtics in exchange for a pick owned by Boston in the 2007 draft. The Suns had salary cap issues of their own, and they didn't want to spend first-round money that season. When the Knicks spent the number twenty pick on Renaldo Balkman, enabling Boston to complete the trade for Rondo, a cheer rang out from the conference room in which the Celtics' owners, front office and coaches were running their draft.

Among them were two skeptics. The first was Papile, assistant director of basketball operations and the oldest of Ainge's scouts, who had doubts about Rondo's character based on his well-known troubles at Kentucky. The other was Doc, who was most disturbed by Rondo's poor shooting form. "I didn't think he could play," said Doc, "because no one would have to guard him." So unreliable was his shooting, argued Doc, that defenders would leave Rondo and double-team Pierce. Anyone could see Rondo's weakness: He shot the ball like a waiter balancing a tray of food on his flattened hand.

"Danny and Ryan McDonough really sold it, and I didn't see it," admitted Doc. "Fucking kid can't even shoot at all. How is he going to run point in this league? That was my first thing. And then he's such a loner and the leadership part of it —when we first got him, I didn't like him at all. When I saw him in the summer league and at our practices, I was like, 'Holy shit, I would never guard him.' What I didn't see was his IQ —and he has a great feel and all that —because he didn't give that to us early. We had to get that out of him.

"But that was Danny. Danny liked Rondo in the middle of the season. I remember he walked in my office one day and said, 'You've got to watch this kid, you've got to watch this tape.' Danny saw Rondo early, and he was sold. So that's pretty good eyes."

While Portland was celebrating its short-term success with Brandon Roy, the Celtics were losing fifty-eight games with their mercurial rookie, Rondo.

Doc worried that he was failing. His $5 million salary didn't shield him from the losses or help him find peace. He had always slept better when his family was in the house with him, but while he was coaching in Boston, his wife, Kris, remained behind in Orlando so that their four children could grow up in a stable home far away from the public criticism that was building around their father. At night Doc would lie in bed awake, reliving the losses and doubting whether he could convince younger-than-ever millionaires to invest in the long-term goal of winning an NBA championship in Boston.

Following that miserable 2006–07 season, the Celtics' immediate goal was to perform well in the draft in order to bring in another teenager with one of the top picks. Pierce wanted no part of that strategy. He was experiencing what LeBron would feel three years later — a desperate need to play with stars — and he was planning to ask for a trade.

If the Celtics had come away with the number one or two pick in the 2007 draft, LeBron would have had no rival in the Eastern Conference to prevent him and his Cavaliers from reaching the NBA Finals, and he might never have left Cleveland. But the Ping-Pong balls went the other way, leaving the Celtics with the number five pick, and just like that their outlook changed. Ainge packaged the draft pick into the trade for Ray Allen. The lure of Pierce and Allen enabled the Celtics to bring Kevin Garnett to Boston in a second move.

Three years after the Jordan-inspired divorce of Kobe and O'Neal in Los Angeles, the pendulum had swung back the other way in Boston. It was as if the NBA was experiencing its first steps out of the darkness of the post-Jordan years. In the name of the Celtics, the franchise that had established the league standards for teamwork on defense, selflessness on offense and the devout pursuit of championships above individual needs, the old stars would renew the best traditions while making their stand against the new AAU generation.

Over their first three years together, Garnett, Pierce and Allen would stop LeBron from having his way in Cleveland. They would beat Chris Bosh and his Toronto Raptors eleven times in twelve meetings. They would open the 2010 playoffs by knocking out Dwyane Wade's Heat in five games.

Later, when Riley was courting LeBron, he laid out a long, detailed history of championship trios. But the opponent that ran LeBron out of Cleveland was the Celtics. If he was ever going to win a championship, he would need to beat them. LeBron, Wade and Bosh were united in Miami because they wanted to do what Pierce, Allen and Garnett had done in Boston.

"Now you're seeing all these superstars want to play together," said Pierce of the Miami trio. "This is the formula. After they saw us all come together, and the way we unselfishly played together, they were feeling like, 'Okay, we can do that too.' And I honestly believe us coming together really changed the league."

At the end of his tenth year in Boston, on the night they throttled Kobe's Lakers to win the seventeenth banner for the Celtics, the Most Valuable Player award of the NBA Finals went to Paul Pierce. That same night he invited all of the Celtics — teammates, owners, coaches, staff, everybody — to celebrate in his large house near the team's practice facility in the Boston suburbs. The party was just beginning when he was told that his 2-month-old daughter, Prianna, had a fever and needed to be taken to the hospital. She had been brought to the game that night and been caught up in the crowd and the excitement of the victory.

"I was upset that she was in all of that," said Pierce. "It was three in the morning, and I had to go to the hospital. Everybody was at my house celebrating, and I had to leave. We was in the hospital room with her. It was unreal. Like, 'Damn, I wish I could be out.' But this is the most important thing."

Instead of behaving like a kid for a few rowdy days, as he'd always imagined he would, Pierce was spending his first two nights as NBA champion at the hospital watching over his baby daughter's recovery from her fever. His celebration was sobering. He had hours of quiet to dwell on his gratitude for Doc's mentoring, on how his own father had not been there for him in Los Angeles, on how a fan of Pat Riley's Lakers could grow up to revive the values of Red Auerbach's Celtics. He thought about how much more there was to winning the championship than he ever realized during those long years when he had been in no position to win. He thought about how some of the worst times in his career had ultimately brought his dream to life. He watched over his daughter and thought with love about how she had become his priority.

He also found himself growing excited for the future. The assumption in 2007 had been that the Celtics might be able to squeeze three good years from Pierce, Garnett and Allen before their old age would do them in. But at the end of their first championship season together, Pierce was stubborn in his optimism. As he thought about the trades for Allen and Garnett that had transformed him and his franchise, Pierce recalled how both the SuperSonics and the Timberwolves had pushed hard to acquire one young Celtic in particular. In both cases the trades had been called off for a time, as Seattle and Minnesota had threatened to back away entirely. But Danny Ainge had not relented. In the end he had renewed the Celtic Way without surrendering Rondo.

The arena in downtown Boston for the opening night of LeBron's debut with the Miami Heat was like a vaudeville theater from another age. The order of the pregame introductions had been left to the discretion of Eddie Palladino, the Celtics' public address announcer, and he called out LeBron first in order to give the fans more time to boo him on this night of extraordinary anticipation. They jeered LeBron with each mention of his name or touch of the ball, and they heckled when one of LeBron's passes was caught by a fan after Wade had cut the wrong way. Every mistake LeBron made was punished with taunting laughter, and every good play by a Celtic was cheered with a belligerence meant for LeBron.

This first game would flash by like a strobe — there would be eighty-one more to be played in the regular season, and another twenty-one in the playoffs for one of these teams. And yet the scalpers in Boston were getting up to $2,000 for a single ticket to LeBron's debut. This opening game of the 2010–11 season was a bigger draw than LeBron's loss in Game 6 of the playoffs had been five months earlier.

With Rondo probing to create shots for his older teammates, the Celtics and their fans took enormous joy in limiting Miami to 9 first-quarter points on their way to a 19-point Boston advantage later in the half. "Overrated!" chanted the fans while flaunting their 83–72 lead into the final four minutes.

But there was more fight in LeBron than he had shown the previous spring. He and Wade ran Miami back to within 3 points, 83–80, muting the arena with seventy seconds to go. Doc managed the ensuing timeout like a revival minister as he urged his players to show faith in the Celtic Way. "If we make the next pass," promised their coach, "the ball will find the open guy."

From the right corner Allen drove the baseline on his way to feeding Pierce at the top of the key. There, in a show of patience befitting his age, Pierce held fast with the ball: He was waiting not only for a second defender to converge on him, but also for Allen to sprint from the basket to the left corner, inches from the Heat's bench, where he spun to catch the return pass from Pierce while corkscrewing up one of his signature three-pointers before LeBron could arrive defensively. And that was that.

After the 88–80 loss LeBron looked relieved to be finished with this night in the city that continued to haunt him. "Rome wasn't built in a day," he said, which jibed not at all with the predictions he had made a few months earlier.

LeBron had failed to learn from the Celtics, as far as Pierce could see, and his actions were proof that he and his teammates didn't know the first thing about the Celtics' ongoing mission. All of their cheap preseason talk revealed their ignorance of how hard it had been for Pierce and his teammates, with the forbearance of their coach, to transition from dreaming of championships to behaving like champions. It required a fragile dynamic to uphold the values of Auerbach in this uneasy era of ridiculous money and conflicted priorities. The Celtics' understanding of what they knew combined with everything LeBron didn't know to leave Pierce and his teammates feeling both confident and indignant.

And yet, for all of their hard-earned pride, there was no doubting that the Celtics were, for the first time, envious of LeBron. With Wade, 28, and Bosh, 26, LeBron's new team in Miami was driven by an energy and athleticism that Boston no longer possessed. Pierce was 33, Garnett was 34, and Allen was 35, and their new starting center was 38-year-old Shaquille O'Neal, who was filling in while Kendrick Perkins recovered from knee surgery. The elderly Celtics were more dependent than ever on the young legs of Rondo, their explosive 24-year-old point guard. Essentially, they were counting on Rondo to side with the older generation against his own.

If LeBron's intention was to form his own trio of championship stars and beat the Celtics at their own game, Pierce was going to insist that LeBron understand the power of teamwork in full. Two weeks after their opening-night win in Boston, the Celtics flew to Miami and beat the Heat 112–107. Rondo had 16 assists, Allen made his first 7 three-pointers on his way to 35 points, and Pierce added 25 efficient points with 16 shots.

The Celtics were on their way to a 23-4 start and an early three-and-a-half-game lead over the Heat. After winning in Miami, Pierce couldn't wait to stick it to LeBron via Twitter. "It's been a pleasure to bring my talents to south beach," he tweeted, "now on to Memphis."

5

THE ENTREPRENEUR

On the eve of their opening practice in 2010, at a private dinner coach Rick Carlisle made a speech to his Dallas Mavericks players about the NBA championship, the ultimate goal, which none of them had achieved. Carlisle, who was not known for inspiring oratory, wanted them to stop dwelling on the team's five-year run of playoff losses and to instead view the upcoming season as an entirely new opportunity. To that end he reintroduced the players to one another as if to make the new year feel fresh. He began by focusing on 32-year-old Dirk Nowitzki, the Most Valuable Player of the 2006–07 season, who had averaged 22.9 points per game in a dozen years with the Mavericks since emigrating from Germany. "He's a 7-footer who changed the game," said Carlisle of Dirk's ability, unprecedented among big men, to shoot from a variety of distances.

The coach worked his way down through a roster brimming with experienced stars all seeking the same thing: Jason Kidd, the 37-year-old point guard who was already assured of reaching the Hall of Fame; Shawn Marion, the 32-year-old forward who had played in four All-Star Games; Jason Terry, the undersized 33-year-old trash-talking guard who had been chosen as the NBA's best player off the bench two seasons earlier; Tyson Chandler, 28, the former number two draft pick who had survived a chronic big-toe injury that had threatened his career and who would provide the defensive leadership the Mavericks had always lacked; Caron Butler, 30, the two-time All-Star forward of enormous character who had settled in as the Mavericks' number two scorer after Dirk.

Down this list of personalities the coach went until, at the end, he was staring at Brian Cardinal, 33, a 6-foot 8-inch forward who had not been assured of making the team.

"And I'm like, 'Fuck,'" said Cardinal.

As much as Cardinal longed to play for a contender like the Mavericks, he was just as worried that Dirk and Kidd would want nothing to do with him. Throughout his ten seasons with five NBA teams, Cardinal had earned a reputation for harassing stars like Dirk by endlessly poking and swiping at the ball, shouldering them away from where they wanted to go and sliding in front of them for high-impact collisions. "They'll love the way you play," Carlisle had told him dismissively, in part because Dirk and Kidd would no longer have to play against him.

"So he gets to me," said Cardinal of his coach's speech the night before training camp, "and he's like, 'And Cardinal . . . Did anybody see this guy play in college? He plays his nuts off. He got a $40 million contract or whatever it was.'"

The next day, as they began preparing for the 2010–11 season, Cardinal was paired with Dirk to shoot free throws. True to form, the role-player with the nonguaranteed contract was giving the franchise star a hard time.

"Oh, man," said Cardinal with earnest sarcasm, "I'm shooting with the 7-footer that changed the game of basketball. This is awesome!"

They were going back and forth, with other players and staffers joining in, when someone brought up Carlisle's reference from the night before: "Cardinal . . . Did anybody see this guy play in college?"

"Yeah," said Dirk, looking accusingly at Cardinal, "what did you even average in college?"

Cardinal stared back with a straight face.

"Four and two," he said.

"What?" said Dirk.

"Yeah," insisted Cardinal. "Four points, two boards."

In fact Cardinal had averaged 12 points and 5.7 rebounds at Purdue, where he became the only player ever to earn the program's awards for "Mr. Hustle" and "Courage" four years in a row. But Dirk was from Germany. He knew little of college basketball and nothing of Brian Cardinal, and he was laughing hysterically at his new teammate's anemic production when Cardinal finally interrupted him. "Bro, I'm kidding," said Cardinal, shaking his head. "I'm kidding."

Cardinal would make the final roster, and throughout the season he would see Dirk working out after practice with his mentor, Holger Geschwindner, who would fly over from Germany for days or weeks at a time to fine-tune his protégé's jump shot. Together they would identify and correct the smallest details amid a routine of gymnastic fakes and pivots that tested Dirk's sense of balance.

But there was more to their one-on-one sessions than spinning the ball through the basket. By focusing on Dirk's shooting stroke, Holger was helping him learn how to channel the pressures that were unique to his role as franchise star of the Mavericks.

While the NBA's American stars tended to be vocal in their leadership — telling teammates what to do while creating an aura of self-confidence meant to elevate the team — Cardinal could see that Dirk's way was to lead the Mavericks by example. He was going to demand the most of himself, and when his team was losing, he would hold himself accountable for the loss. It was the most selfless approach to leadership that Cardinal had ever seen. He wondered how someone as humble as Dirk could expect so much of himself.

As the Mavericks grew closer together that season, the newcomer at the end of the bench was going to realize how much he had in common with the leading star. Cardinal, like Dirk, had grown up with no vision of the NBA career he would eventually pursue — never mind the expectations that would threaten to demoralize both of them.

Cardinal had been raised in a small town near the University of Illinois, where he would assist his father, the athletic trainer for the men's basketball team there, by slicing orange wedges for the Illini and arranging their chairs in the locker room. In 2000 he was picked in the second round of the NBA draft by the Detroit Pistons, and just when he thought his time in basketball had run out, he not only made the Golden State Warriors' roster, but he also earned regular minutes while averaging almost 10 points per game in 2003–04. From out of nowhere he had created a market for himself as a free agent. He was a self-starter, an instigator, a hustler that every coach should love. That summer his wife, Danielle, came out of a friend's wedding to find her husband still on the phone in the church parking lot, having agreed minutes earlier to a contract with the Memphis Grizzlies worth more than $36 million over the next six years. It was better than winning the lottery because Cardinal's windfall had been earned, though he couldn't quite explain how.

An established star like Dirk knew full well that he was expected to provide a return on the team's exorbitant investment in him. But Cardinal had no idea what he was taking on. He had never thought much about the demands that come with big NBA money, because he had never imagined having it. What could be worse than the pressure of his preseason trial with the Warriors, when he needed to make shots in order to extend his career? If anything, figured Cardinal, the guaranteed income of his new contract would liberate him from the stress.

Cardinal didn't consider the other side of the coin until his second season with Memphis, when he missed twenty-eight games between surgery on one knee and soreness in the other. Over the following years his production plummeted, and insinuations arose that he was "stealing" the team's money. In 2008 his contract was packaged into a trade that sent him to the Minnesota Timberwolves, who then forwarded his contract in a subsequent deal to the New York Knicks. Immediately Cardinal's newest team phoned his agent with instructions for him to stay put: The Knicks' preference was to pay him *not* to play for the remaining months of his contract.

"I get banged up a little bit, so I'm trying to come back from my knee, and things happen," Cardinal said. "You get defined by your contract, and then certain teams want you but they say, 'We'd love to have you, but you make six million bucks, and we can't afford that.' So then you're stuck in a great financial position, but it stinks because you're not playing, and you're not respected."

When that big contract expired in the summer of 2010, he was grateful on two counts — for the savings that had set up his young family for life, and for the burden that had been lifted. It was an entirely new kind of liberation for him not to be paid that outrageous money anymore. He was driven to redefine himself — if it wasn't already too late. He longed to be a constructive teammate instead of a blight on the team's budget.

In the beginning, the idea was for Cardinal to make his career at the expense of the NBA stars who seemed to have all the advantages — talent, money, celebrity. But he knew better now. His job in Dallas was to provide support for his starring teammates, and in particular to empathize with Dirk. Living with the highest possible expectations wasn't as easy as Dirk made it look.

When Cardinal would phone home to Indiana, where Danielle was pregnant with their third child, he would describe a world that was unlike his other NBA experiences. Dirk, the best player, didn't want to be a star, but the owner of the team did. One day Cardinal was passing through the locker room, which was adjacent to a large weight-lifting area within a den of red-brick walls designed to make the players feel at home, when he nodded to Mark Cuban, the team's 52-year-old owner.

"Hey, Cubes," said Cardinal, who was 33.

"Hey, Dad," answered Cuban.

Cardinal stopped, with a grin, turned around and said, "Why the hell are you calling me Dad?"

"Because you look old enough to be my dad," said Cuban, with a jutting grin that flattened his face and all but shut his eyes.

Cuban maintained a higher profile than any other owner in the NBA. To stay buff he lifted weights and did an hour of cardio every day, multitasking by giving interviews to reporters before home games from a stair-climbing machine, the sweat dripping off him as he gasped between sentences. From his seat near the team bench he would shout at anyone who happened to be in the game, including his own players. "If guys are screwing up on the court, he will let you know," said Cardinal. "I remember him stopping me one time when I was walking over to the huddle and he was like, 'You've got to talk! You've got to communicate —talk on defense!' And I'm thinking, 'Did Cuban just stop me ten feet from the huddle?'"

He was notorious for yelling at opposing players and referees, whether to point out infractions that were going uncalled or to heckle them just for the fun of it. During the previous season he had admitted to crying out across the court at the Celtics' Rasheed Wallace, "Rasheed, you're fatter than me!"

"I believe it on all counts — that he was fatter than him, and that he would yell it," said Cardinal.

There were other times when Cuban's anger would hang over the Mavericks like a foul gas. "Sometimes when you're sitting on the bench and the court's right here and you're looking at the court and he yells something, you're just like, 'Oh, God, I am not going to turn around,'" Cardinal said. "Because he's sitting right over there. And you're just like, 'Oh, God, did he just say that?'"

"Everyone's on the bench, you just start looking at your feet," said Casey Smith, the Mavericks' athletic trainer. "And you're like, 'Don't make eye contact. Just let this go away as quickly as possible.'"

Having to endure his rants was a small price to pay for all the benefits of playing for Cuban. "It's a love-hate thing," said Cardinal, and for perspective he referred to his own recent past. "You want to get paid like a superstar, but you don't want the pressure of a superstar; you want a passionate owner, but you don't want him to talk right at you when you screw up? You can't have one without the other. So I would much rather have somebody that's passionate, that's going to give you all the resources that you need to be successful, and I'll take some of the criticism that I'm going to get. Because it might be deserving, and you know he cares."

Cuban showered the Mavericks with luxuries that were either upgraded from what other teams provided or introduced by him to the NBA: a first-class plane, the best hotels, a dietician to provide healthy food at practices and games. He outfitted each player's locker with high-tech toys and ergonomic chairs. He tried installing cameras at the top of the arena to snap photographs of the defense — a trick he learned from the NFL, though it turned out the Mavericks coaches didn't have time during the games to study them. The Mavericks became the first team to do full cardiac workups of the players. Cuban was the first owner to hire a staff of development coaches to spend extra time teaching on-the-court skills to young players who had been lured prematurely out of college, an advancement that was ridiculed initially and then mimicked by every franchise. The Mavericks believed they had the best support staff in the NBA, replete with "life coaches" to lead by the hand the new generation of immature players who didn't know how to open a checking account or arrange for insurance and the other necessities of adult life. Dirk had been one of those lost souls when he had arrived from Germany the year before Cuban bought the team. The Mavericks traveled with their own massage therapist, and a portable MRI machine joined them on the road for playoff games. That machine would accrue a lot of mileage: In Cuban's first full season of ownership they would win fifty-three games in the regular season and reach the second round of the postseason, launching a run of eleven straight years with fifty or more victories.

"This is a little thing, but the towels were a brilliant idea," said Keith Grant, the assistant general manager who had been with the Mavericks for all but four months of their thirty-year existence. "These nice, fluffy towels: He put our logos on them, and it made an impression on the other teams. You never knew, somewhere down the road, where this guy would want to play in Dallas, because of what we were trying to build. The changes we made here, visionary-wise, were unbelievable."

Cuban was also the NBA's most polarizing owner. Opponents and their fans denounced him as a wannabe who sought attention at the expense of his team and the league. In some arenas, claimed Cuban, he would time his ruckuses in order to incite the fans to rain down boos on him while one of the home team's players was shooting free throws. His own players tended to respect Cuban's self-aggrandizing agenda, which included becoming famous, having fun and bringing out the best in them. "There are a lot of owners who might not even live in the same city that you're in," said Cardinal. "Don't even know that you're playing that night."

The investments that Cuban made in the welfare and productivity of his players enhanced his credibility with them. Much more than a hanger-on, he insisted on being a partner in their pursuit of the championship. He was paying in excess of $86 million in salaries to his players in 2010–11, more than any other team in the NBA except the champion Los Angeles Lakers and the Orlando Magic, and all of the extras he provided had contributed to losses totaling well over $100 million since his impulsive decision to buy into the NBA a decade earlier. The players recognized that he was giving them every advantage, and he was around them constantly to make sure he received their best efforts in return. He knew more about the team he owned than the opposing owners knew about their teams.

"The big difference is, being that I'm so close to everything that's going around, you can't bullshit me," Cuban said. "In other situations" — and here he was referring to the traditional ownership model in pro sports — "you're depending three levels back on what your G.M. says, and then maybe you go in and hear what some players say, and then maybe you go in and your coach tells you something different. It's hard for everybody to have the same perspective for the short term and the long term because they want to keep their jobs. So I've been able to keep my eye on the long term and the short term and balance things out from there. If I hear something, chances are I've seen it. And that's not to say I've caught everything, because I haven't. But there's no way you're going to be able to tell me one thing and then do another — and when you do, I see it and I catch it. Unless you're there, you're not going to see all this stuff that destroys chemistry, that makes things bad."

When Cuban bought the Mavericks in 2000, he had been phenomenally rich for nine months. Coach Don Nelson and his son/assistant Donnie Nelson assumed that the young Internet billionaire would fire them instantly. They knew nothing of Cuban's background: that he was the grandson of Russian Jewish immigrants named Chabenisky (whose family name had been simplified at Ellis Island), that he was the son of a car upholsterer in Pittsburgh named Norton Cuban, that after graduating from Indiana University in 1981 he had moved to Dallas to live with friends as the sixth man in a three-bedroom apartment, sleeping on the couch or the floor and keeping his few possessions piled in a corner. At nightclubs he and his friends would each buy a twelve-dollar bottle of Freixenet champagne, tear off the label and drink from the bottle in order to avoid picking up bar tabs they couldn't afford. "Of course the next day was hell," recalled Cuban in his e-book, *How to Win at the Sport of Business,* "but since when was I responsible enough to care about a hangover?"

By day he sold computers, leading to several start-up companies and culminating, in 1999, with his sale of the online radio company Broadcast.com to Yahoo! for $5.7 billion. Cuban's personal windfall of more than $1 billion enabled him to purchase a majority stake in the Mavericks for $285 million from Ross Perot Jr., the son of the former presidential candidate.

The Mavericks had not had a winning season in ten years when Cuban — 6 feet 3 inches tall, athletic, with floppy black hair — made an authentic first impression by walking into their offices in a T-shirt, jeans and sneakers. It was their losing streak that had helped attract Cuban to the Mavericks. "The building was half-empty," he said. "There was no energy. No excitement. I thought to myself that I could do a better job than this. It's pretty typical to this day, if I walk into a business that I think is mismanaged, to think through what I would do differently."

Cuban insisted that everyone call him Mark, and by 2001 he was going out of his way to separate himself from the traditional sports owners when he sat on the baseline edge of the court like a team ball boy during a Mavericks game at Minnesota. "They said it wasn't fitting for an owner to sit there," he explained of the $100,000 fine he received for not watching from a chair like a grown-up.

Rival general managers would realize that Cuban was unlike their teams' owners when he began calling them about trades. He left the evaluation of talent up to the Nelsons and their staff, but once they decided who should play for the Mavericks, Cuban was in the middle of the dealmaking. "I told Nellie that if I was going to be able to help him and provide him money, I was going to have to be actively involved in everything — from trades to draft picks," said Cuban. "I think all G.M.s were surprised to get a call from an owner. And I'm sure all of them called Nellie to make sure I wasn't crazy and that I was serious."

Learning how to acquire players was simple. More fascinating to Cuban was the riddle of the NBA's traditional business model. "I had to figure out what the product was," he said. "Everyone thought they were selling basketball."

Everyone was wrong, he informed his employees in the early days of his ownership. "We were selling fun," he said. "We had eight-dollar tickets, and that was cheaper than going to the movies or going to McDonald's, yet our experience was far more fun and unique."

A majority of the game tickets were much more expensive than eight dollars, of course, and so Cuban set out to create demand by changing the way the Mavericks sold their product. "They always highlighted the other team's best player," said Cuban, who told the marketing department to stop focusing on the arrival of Kobe Bryant or Tim Duncan, for example. Instead he ordered them to sell customers on a night of unpredictable fun, while warning that anyone who emphasized the team's wins and losses would be fired.

Cuban was a difficult, demanding boss behind the scenes, but in public he was the most accommodating owner in sports. He encouraged customers to email him personally with suggestions to improve their experience and the franchise overall, and he acted on dozens of their ideas. His public-address announcer would rally fans to stand up and yell, which was also unusual, and during time-outs Cuban would treat them to hilarious videos created in-house, including one comparing Shaquille O'Neal to the cartoon character Fat Albert, for which Cuban was fined $25,000 by the league office. (There would be many more fines.)

Franchises like the Boston Celtics had their own timeless approach to basketball that they were forever seeking to update, as if they were refitting a classic 1960s Mustang with more efficient horsepower and the newest airbags. Cuban had no blueprints to go by. He was operating a team that had little history of success in a state famous for football and baseball; his best player wasn't even American; and Carlisle was the only decisionmaker among his coaching staff or front office who had played in the NBA. The new owner of the aptly named Mavericks was systematically reinventing the business of professional basketball ownership, deciding with each step of his education whether the old way should be replaced by a new, better way. It was the equivalent of entering an auto race by building his car — a hybrid of various technologies — from scratch.

He was an innovator competing in a world of traditions. "I thought I had a huge advantage because everyone else did it the same way," Cuban said. "When everyone seems to be doing things the same way, that is not the way to win."

It was extraordinary for a newcomer to have earned so much credibility in an NBA locker room. Cuban had been around pro sports for only eleven years, leaving him with less NBA experience than many of his players and most of his employees. He was a computer geek who as a season-ticket holder in Dallas had earned a bad reputation among the Mavericks players for yelling at them from his courtside seat — sometimes encouragingly, sometimes not.

On the eve of his purchase, Cuban happened to be in a bar in Dallas when he saw Dirk. "I know I'm going to be his boss the very next day; he has no idea," recalled Cuban. "So I walk up to him and say, 'Yo, let me buy you a beer.' He just looks at me. Shakes his head. Walks away."

Cuban would tell this story to an arena filled with Mavericks fans at the end of the 2010–11 season.

"The next day I walk in," Cuban went on, "and I'm supposed to get introduced to the team. I walk up and I look at him, and he just shakes his head."

In the early weeks of the new season, in the Dallas locker room, another story would provide additional perspective on Dirk. This story was about Michael Jordan, in the final season of his comeback with the Washington Wizards.

As their team president and minority owner, Jordan had been unable to transform the young Wizards. So he had put himself back in uniform in order to show the AAU generation firsthand how to be professional. One day at practice Jordan pointed to a young teammate and said, "I want you in my group." The teammate was Brian Cardinal, 25, who could not believe he had been chosen by Jordan. Since joining the Wizards weeks earlier, Cardinal had daydreamed of the lengthy give-and-take he was planning to have with the NBA's greatest player, but he'd never built up the nerve. "I was scared to death to say anything," Cardinal said.

He hadn't even played in an NBA game alongside Jordan (Cardinal would get only fifteen minutes on the court that season), which was why it meant so much to him when he was picked from the crowd of teammates to run the three-man weave with Jordan and the 38-year-old big man Charles Oakley. It all happened so fast — *I want you in my group* — and then they were running the floor and sharing the ball like equals.

"Unbelievable," Cardinal was saying to his new teammates in the Mavericks' locker room. "It's awesome. I make the layups and I'm thinking, 'This is my shot. I'm going to show him that I can play.' I don't know why in a three-man weave that anybody would think that you could show anything. But we did it, we went down and back and made layups."

The ball was zipping between them as they began their final lap. He handed the ball to Jordan, who passed it to Oakley, who relayed it ahead to Cardinal, and as Cardinal handed off the ball one last time, he leaned in too close around the back of Jordan's leg.

"I'm running as fast as I can," said Cardinal, "and I hear a huge thud. *BOOM.* And I'm thinking — it happened behind me — I'm like, 'Sweet God, please tell me that I did not trip M.J.'"

He turned and sprinted back to the crowd that was gathering around Jordan, who was 39 years old and sprawled flat on his back. At this point in the retelling, Cardinal was interrupted by one of his Mavericks teammates.

"That was *you?*" said Brendan Haywood, who had been the 23-year-old starting center for the Wizards in 2002–03.

Haywood could recall in horrifying detail the domino effect of Jordan's arms and legs flailing for balance on his long way down. But he had not remembered that Cardinal had been responsible. Which, from Cardinal's point of view, made the story even more hilarious. He was used to being forgotten.

As he leaned into the crowd that had gathered around Jordan, Cardinal with enormous sincerity said, "M.J., you okay? Are you all right?" Cardinal could feel Oakley staring at him murderously. The Wizards' trainer had also come running over and said, "M.J., you okay? You okay?"

Jordan propped himself up to glare at Cardinal. "He starts yelling at me every name in the book," Cardinal recalled. "And I'm like, 'Oh my God, did I just do this?'"

As he looked around to see Dirk and his other new teammates laughing along with him, Cardinal found himself thinking about the differences between Dirk and Jordan. Dirk, more so than any other franchise star, was one of the guys. He rejected the perks of off-the-court endorsements, because he had no need for the extra money and little interest in grabbing attention for himself.

Another quality that separated Dirk from Jordan was his reluctance to tell teammates and others in the organization what to do. It was not just that Dirk felt too much respect for his peers and colleagues to be throwing his weight around. He also did not appear to view himself as a leader.

If the Mavericks were going to win the championship, that would have to change. Dirk would need to find a touch of Michael Jordan in himself.

In his first six years Cuban made ownership look easy while winning 340 games in the regular season and eight rounds in the playoffs. A growing number of

NBA owners ridiculed him as a young know-it-all who'd had the dumb luck to buy the Mavericks just as their youthful trio of Dirk, Steve Nash and Michael Finley were blooming into stardom.

"They spend a lot of time criticizing, nitpicking, calling the league 20, 30 times a day," Bill Davidson, the 84-year-old owner of the Detroit Pistons, complained of Cuban and James Dolan, the impetuous owner of the New York Knicks, in a 2007 interview with the *Detroit Free Press*. "Ridiculous things. I'm the one person who can speak up — and has spoken up — and tell these people that they're just wrong."

Davidson lit into Cuban at an owners' meeting, as Cuban remembered it, "telling me that I had never done anything good for this league and that I had gotten lucky with the internet stock thing, and something to the effect that I was an embarrassment. David Stern stepped in to quiet him, and I remember starting off a response by calling him the name of another old-time owner."

It could not have soothed tensions for Cuban to refer to Davidson, a billionaire who had won three NBA championships, by the wrong name.

"I just didn't know the guy's name," insisted Cuban. "I wasn't being flip. It wasn't intentional. I just didn't know his name."

Whereas his rivals tended to see pro sports as a secretive society of sacred traditions, Cuban viewed the NBA as an entertainment industry that needed to evolve. The reason attendance was climbing in Dallas was because the Mavericks had lured in customers who hadn't previously been basketball fans. Cuban couldn't understand why the other owners wouldn't put aside their differences and see it his way.

"Anytime someone tried to 'put me in my place' it just made me mad and motivated me," recalled Cuban in an email. "It started when they interviewed me to qualify me as an owner — something, by the way, the full Board Of Governors hasn't done since. I remember the guy from the Knicks, Dave Checketts, asking me if I was going to be 'like that other owner from Dallas.'" The implication being that Cuban would emulate Jerry Jones, the maverick owner of the NFL's Dallas Cowboys. "I told him straight up that 'I hope so. Winning and creating new sources of revenues for his team and the league is something I hope to emulate.'"

The rift between Cuban and the league grew over his public attempts to upgrade and modernize NBA refereeing. "It is key to the integrity of the game, and it's the focal point around which fans question our integrity," explained Cuban, whose approach to NBA ownership had been drawn from his previous life as a fan. "I was very vocal about the officiating when I was a season-ticket holder, and now that so much was at stake I got even more vocal."

In the opening month of his first full NBA season, he was fined $5,000, then $15,000, then $25,000 over a span of nine days for comments he made about the refereeing to reporters and to the referees themselves. He was fined an NBA-record $250,000 for freeze-framing a scoreboard replay of a missed goaltending call that would have tied the game with twelve seconds remaining. (Eventually all NBA teams would be permitted to showcase refereeing mistakes without penalty.) He was fined $100,000 and suspended for one game for yelling at the referees and gesturing with his hands around his throat. The following season came the mother of all fines — $500,000 for publicly criticizing Ed Rush, the NBA's head of officiating. "Ed Rush might have been a great ref, but I wouldn't hire him to manage a Dairy Queen," said Cuban in 2002. "His interest is not in the integrity of the game or improving the officiating."

Cuban's larger complaint was that the referees as a group lacked oversight, training and accountability. By now he had begun to hire interns to create a database of referees' calls in order to identify trends in subjectivity.

"I was all over the league when Mr. Rush was published in a magazine saying that the first two minutes were not to be officiated the same as the last two minutes," Cuban would explain years later by email. "I was killing [league officers] Stu Jackson and Joel Litvin and Russ Granik with emails asking where in the rule book this was stated. I was killing them with stats and information that they didn't even have . . .

"The biggest issue I had was with management competence," Cuban went on. "Just because you were a good salesperson doesn't make you a good sales manager, any more than being a good ref makes you a professional manager of officials. My feeling was that until they brought in someone from the outside who was a professional manager, there was going to be cronyism and more."

Cuban's complaints were drawing attention, but he wasn't the only team executive who was investigating the referees.

"When I was coaching, we did a tremendous amount of research on officials' calls," said Miami Heat president Pat Riley. "Every single call that an official made in every game, we would chart. After twenty or thirty games with one official, you could get a tendency on the things that he would call — travels, hand-checks — and we especially would chart the kinds of calls they would make prior to getting into the penalty versus the calls they would make after you were in the penalty, and fourth-quarter calls."

In the midst of Miami's postseason rivalry with New York, when the Knicks were knocking out the Heat in three successive winner-take-all games through 2000, Riley's analytics indicated that four NBA referees were making calls that favored the Knicks close to ninety percent of the time in the fourth quarter. "I went up to New York with videotapes — compare-and-contrast videos — and I said, 'You tell me about this foul with New York, this foul with us,'" he recalled. "They said, 'You're right, but we can't control the emotions of an official during the course of the game.' They didn't like the fact that I brought the names up to them. But these were analytics. There was no coincidence in these analytics."

Commissioner David Stern believed that complaining about the referees in public damaged the integrity of the game. Now he had to deal with an outsider, in Cuban, the NBA's first "millennial" owner in spirit, who insisted — loudly — that silence was even more destructive.

Cuban's NBA fines drew attention to the fundamental problem he was trying to fix, and so he claimed to be happy to pay them — as well as make a charitable contribution in the amount of each fine. After insisting that Rush wasn't qualified to manage a Dairy Queen, Cuban took the further step of making amends to Dairy Queen: He spent one morning working at a franchise in suburban Dallas, where a thousand customers lined up to have him serve them ice cream in front of a dozen TV news cameras.

"I remember being in Phoenix and having one of the refs just glare at me, then fuck us on a call," said Cuban. His fellow owners believed Cuban's whistle-blowing was doing harm to their league, but he would not relent from his insistence that the NBA was oblivious to the potential scandal that was looming. "I always felt that one of the biggest problems the league had were that fans always thought the refs tried to influence the outcome of games," Cuban wrote. "I thought the only way to disprove it was to get the facts. Most owners disagreed with me."

The NBA upgraded its oversight of officiating, though never to the standards demanded by Cuban. To his critics within and outside the league, he acted as if he had all the answers. He was the braggart who was making his success look easy, as if outsmarting everyone else. Don Nelson resigned and was replaced by Avery Johnson, a rookie coach who had retired as a player one year earlier, and the team continued to show improvement. First Finley and then Nash were cast aside, and yet the Mavericks went deeper into the playoffs even as the roster grew younger.

By 2006 Cuban had emerged as the cocky, inexperienced owner of a surprising team that was less than an hour away, by the game clock, from winning the NBA championship. His Mavericks were leading 89–76 with 6 minutes, 34 seconds remaining in Game 3 of the NBA Finals in Miami — putting the Heat on the brink of a 3–0 deficit, from which no NBA team had ever recovered. Then 24-year-old Dwyane Wade exploded to score 12 of Miami's final 22 points to steal the 98–96 win.

Over the concluding two games, as if to punish Cuban for his foresight, Wade would sink almost as many free throws as the entire Mavericks team.

Dallas was up by a point in Game 5 at Miami when Wade received two free throws for a foul charged against Dirk with one second remaining in overtime. No sooner had the horn sounded on that crushing loss than Cuban was running onto the court to yell at a referee. From there he would turn and glare maniacally at Stern, who was sitting in the stands, and then he would use profanities in his complaints to reporters. Cuban would be fined $250,000 for all of that.

"I think," said Stern the next day, "the pressure of his first Finals may be getting to him."

The Mavericks of Mark Cuban, who had stood one and one-eighth games short of winning the championship, would lose four games in a row. The officiating was not entirely to blame for their squandering of the '06 Finals, from Cuban's point of view, but it had played a demoralizing role. The loss left Cuban to wonder whether he could ever recover his enthusiasm for the NBA. Over the year that followed, he thought hard about selling the Mavericks.

His criticisms of NBA officiating had been affirmed on the biggest stage, he believed, and at his expense. One year later Cuban's trust in the league would be restored by way of a most unlikely source — Tim Donaghy, the crooked referee who resigned from the league in 2007 while being investigated for betting on games he had officiated over the previous two seasons.

"I knew there were issues before the scandal broke," recalled Cuban in an email. "I didn't know he was gambling, but I was told by multiple people that he was a timebomb waiting to go off, and I told the league. My big question came in a game in February of his last year when he actually pushed Biedrins out of the lane rather than call a defensive three-seconds which helped change the outcome of a game."

It came out that Donaghy had tapped Golden State Warriors center Andris Biedrins on the hip in an apparent stab at affecting the point spread. Donaghy's fifteen-month prison sentence served to endorse Cuban's concerns about the oversight of referees. Stern responded to the most threatening scandal of his administration by hiring Ronald Johnson, a retired two-star U.S. Army general, to overhaul referee operations. "Things never really changed until they brought in Ron Johnson," said Cuban. "He brought professional management techniques, something the group never had before."

Thereafter Cuban's appraisals were taken more seriously. His rivals grew increasingly appreciative of his point of view, especially as Davidson's generation gave way to younger owners who paid escalating prices for their teams and demanded a return on their investments. One like-minded owner was Michael Jordan, the president of the Charlotte Bobcats, who bought out Robert Johnson in 2010. By then Cuban was being fined less and asked more often for his opinions on all matters of the NBA, including the ongoing negotiations for a new collective bargaining agreement.

"We always took our complaints about the officiating behind the scenes because the NBA could come down hard on us — suspend me for ten games, fine me a million dollars," Riley said. "Mark as an owner has done well in bringing it really public and not worrying about the consequences. So I commend him for that."

The increasing respect for Cuban had something to do with the difficulties his team was experiencing in the playoffs. After their devastating loss in the 2006 Finals, the Mavericks had been unable to bounce back. That loss had flattened their arc. They were recast as an underperforming team, which would win at least fifty games before losing all but one of their postseason series over the next four years. No longer could Cuban offend his peers as a know-it-all based on the success of the Mavericks, because it was clear that his team did not have all the answers. Riley's Heat had humbled him.

"Mark is an extrovert," Riley said. "When he bought the Mavericks, they were not very good, and his personality alone took them to another level. He was very public in making the franchise relevant, and Mark had to be the one to drive that point."

In the years after the Mavericks' collapse in Miami, Cuban would turn over his roster and coaching staff. But he would not let go of his star. The Mavericks were an outside-the-box franchise, through and through, and Dirk was their embodiment on the court. He was a rags-to-riches entrepreneur like Cuban, minus the arrogance.

"We can already say that Tyson Chandler is the best center in the history of the Dallas Mavericks," said Cuban while dining at the bar of a dark, empty New Orleans restaurant around the corner from Bourbon Street on a Tuesday night in November 2010. A large flat-screen TV colored his chicken quesadilla in a variety of shades as he rooted for the visiting New York Knicks to beat the Denver Nuggets, on account of Denver being a rival of Dallas in the Western Conference. The Nuggets had reached the Western Conference Finals as recently as 2009, but they were likely to fall out of contention this season because their All-Star forward Carmelo Anthony had demanded a trade — to the Knicks, in fact, who on this night were beaten by Anthony's 26 points. It was turning into a big public mess for the Nuggets, and Cuban was happy to have put such controversies behind him.

When Cuban was finished with supper, he went for a walk along Bourbon Street, popping into bars to look for a place that played acceptable music. As he made his way down the street, an occasional stranger would do a double take, shout out his name or say hello. "It's mainly because of *Dancing with the Stars*," he explained with a big smile. Years earlier, after five weeks on the show, Cuban had been voted off for his performance of a samba to the theme of *I Dream of Jeannie*.

One night later, not far from Bourbon Street in the New Orleans Arena, the mood of Cuban's Mavericks was focused and edgy. It was the tenth game of the year, and yet they were playing as if the playoffs were at stake. Two nights earlier, in Dallas, the young New Orleans Hornets had suffered their first loss of the season, and as the two teams met in the rematch, Cuban was yelling and accusing and cheering near his team's bench. The game revolved around a power forwards' duel between Dirk and David West, the fiery 30-year-old fellow All-Star from New Jersey, whose Hornets opened the second half with an extended 29–9 run. His team's performance had angered Dirk, who responded by scoring on West and celebrating with a raised fist and a mocking grin. Soon Dirk was screaming again as he scored while falling away, and then, upon earning an offensive foul for bulldozing West out of the low post, Dirk turned and walked straight at West as the two yelled at each other. With 8.7 seconds remaining, Dirk up-faked and drove for a layup to pull his Mavericks to within a point, 98–97. Jason Kidd stole the ensuing inbounds pass, enabling Carlisle to diagram a last-second play for Dirk, but West knocked away Dirk's dribble near the three-point line before he could attempt the final shot.

It was an enervating loss, to be followed by another one two nights later to the visiting Chicago Bulls despite Dirk's 36 points. The bulk of his NBA career was behind him, but Dirk was attacking this opening month as if he'd accomplished nothing — as if he hadn't made the All-NBA Teams for the past nine years, as if he hadn't played in the last eight All-Star Games, as if there weren't an MVP trophy with his name on it at his parents' home in Germany.

Dirk had exceeded all of the expectations that had greeted him as a 20-year-old NBA rookie, but he didn't want to hear about it. "I'll be proud of myself when my career is over," he said as he signed autographs for fans who were waiting for him and other players behind a short barricade on the loading dock of the New Orleans Arena. "Right now I'm still chasing my dream, so I'm not really slowing down or thinking about anything. I want to get my goal. I don't want to retire not having a ring, so that's really my focus in basketball. For at least four more years I want to leave it out there like I always have and we'll see how far we can go."

He was pursuing those next four years as if they represented the final four minutes of a winner-take-all game in the NBA Finals. He could not afford to dwell sentimentally on how far he had come; all that concerned him was the time he had left to finish what he had started so long ago, when he had no idea what he was getting into.

Dirk was trying to become the first immigrant to lead an NBA team to the championship. It was true that in both 1994 and 1995, amid Michael Jordan's brief "retirement" to play minor league baseball, the Houston Rockets had been led through the NBA Finals by Hakeem Olajuwon, a 7-foot center from Lagos, Nigeria, whose exquisite low-post footwork was drawn from his childhood love for soccer. Unlike Dirk, however, Olajuwon had been indoctrinated for three years at the University of Houston in the program of "Phi Slama Jama," as Olajuwon's high-flying teammates referred to themselves. Houston had provided him with the most celebrated American training ground, culminating in three NCAA Final Fours. Olajuwon was already a household name when he became the number one pick of the 1984 NBA draft, two spots ahead of Jordan.

Dirk, by comparison, had entered the NBA with zero understanding of American basketball. America itself had been a mystery to him. His successes, and the corresponding elevation of his own goals with each year, had surprised him.

To watch Dirk play was to recognize that his aim, at first, was to be proficient in basketball. There was very little in Dirk's game that appeared natural or meant to be. American stars like Jordan, Kobe and LeBron tended to be extraordinary athletes — as if they had been born with a running start — whereas Dirk's moves were choreographed, complicated, and slow-forming by comparison, as his long torso and arms swung around to catch up with the squeaky pivoting of his feet. Everything he did had a look of rehearsal to it, as if he had been raised to keep count of the tempo under his breath, like an awkward teen in a dance studio. That he appeared to maintain control of his balance — even as he staggered and twirled to leap away from the basket, or raised one knee high for the creation of space between himself and the defender — was proof of the hard work he had put in to make the unnatural feel natural to him.

He was 7 feet tall with dark blond hair that framed his long, blank face and preserved his privacy like a scarf. He was quick to smile and make strangers feel at home, and yet his own insecurities were rarely expressed. He was perfectly fluent in English, his second language, his vocabulary strong, his German accent soft and deferential. He was a good listener when approached by fans and a surprising jokester among teammates, especially the newcomers like Brian Cardinal, who could not believe the extent to which he tried to make them feel comfortable, unlike many American stars who responded to competition by staking out their own territory.

The greatest American players claimed ownership of the NBA with a sense of destiny, as if their championships were meant to be. While Dwyane Wade was attacking the basket as if it belonged to him and no one else in the 2006 Finals, Dirk was set back on his heels, unable to conjure up the same ruthless self-belief.

The source of Dirk's strength was his innate humility, born of doubting himself. "I'm a very negative guy," he said. "It's a German thing. My mom is like that, so I got it a little from her. I think that attitude always kept me in the gym. If I would have a bad game when I was young, sometimes I stayed after games and shot or worked out; or the next day, I'm like, 'I'm the worst player ever. I've got to be in the gym, I've got to train, I've got to do cardio, I've got to lift, I've got to shoot.' It just always made me work hard, because I'm always the hardest on myself, and I think that negative side, it worked good for me. Over the years, then, you try to tweak stuff, and be more positive here and there after games, and try to forget a little quicker."

The Mavericks' director of sport psychology, Don Kalkstein, helped with those tweaks, beginning with Dirk's preparation shortly before each game. Kalkstein would rebound the ball for Dirk while Brad Davis, the Mavericks' player development coach, put Dirk through his pregame warmup, and in the early years of Dirk's career those preparations were agonizing. "Some of these shootarounds right before the game would last until Dirk felt comfortable, and that sometimes would take a long time," said Kalkstein. "From the neophyte's eye you would say, 'He's making his shots.' But he didn't feel comfortable."

Dirk would stay on the court shooting and shooting and shooting for close to a half hour, in the misplaced hope that his warmup might carry him through the game. Kalkstein and Davis would engage in small talk with Dirk in order to distract him from the pressure he was feeling to compete with the Americans. He needed to develop the faith that his hard work would translate into results.

"Dirk has gotten older and he's changed," Kalkstein said. "He has the ability to accept that 'I might not feel just right now, but that doesn't mean I'm not going to feel just right later.' Where, when he was younger, paranoia would set in, and he would make sure that he felt the way he needed to feel at that particular time, or it may not carry over into the game."

As the Mavericks' postseason losses mounted following their collapse in the 2006 Finals, Cuban continued to invest in the organization. He hired a full-time statistical analyst, Roland Beech, and rehired Kalkstein, who had left Dallas for a short time to work for the Boston Red Sox; the team made room for both of them to sit on the bench alongside the more traditional coaches. Despite all that he was spending to ease the strain on his players by way of coaching and life training and number crunching and brain shrinking and all the other upgrades he had made over the years, Cuban was aware that these layers of assistance were intensifying the pressure on Dirk to hold up his end of the equation. Cuban knew that Dirk's job was the most important one of all. Dirk himself behaved as if he was no more significant than anyone else, in his belief that the work of every employee was crucial to the team. But Dirk also realized, as did all of his colleagues in Dallas, that their failure or success would depend on his shooting of the ball in the crucial sequences of the most important games, and especially in the final seconds.

The $17,278,618 salary that Dirk was paid in 2010–11 added to the expectations, because everyone — the fans who paid exorbitantly for their tickets, the broadcast partners who were liable for enormous rights fees, the journalists who found every star lacking in comparison with Jordan — saw fit to demand satisfaction of the highest order. A high return was expected because Dirk was guaranteed so much. And then, with the clock ticking down, the happiness of everyone who depended on him hinged on the touch and the spin that Dirk applied to a ball nine inches in diameter on its high arcing path to a circle eighteen inches across and as far as twenty or more feet away.

The pressure to carry an NBA team, in this era of a price tag attached to everything, threatened to be all-consuming. The Mavericks needed Dirk to feel that pressure. They needed Dirk, in a constructive way, to embrace and absorb the expectations that were bearing down on him. They believed — all of them, from Cuban on down — that his anxiety could incite and transform him into the leader who could turn their contending team into a champion.

In the privacy of their locker room after one game in 2010–11, Dirk lost his temper and yelled at a teammate, and Carlisle didn't like it. "Rick called him out," said Casey Smith. "And someone else spoke up and said, 'No, it's his team. If that's the way he feels, he needs to say it.' They see how much pressure is on him for us to win. And they see how he gets killed." Smith referred back to a 2009 playoff loss to the Denver Nuggets in which Dirk averaged 34.4 points, 11.6 rebounds and 4 assists over the five games, and yet was blamed once again for a failure to lead. "Still his fault," said Smith. "And he's fine with it. So it's his team, and everybody knows it's his team."

It was because of their belief in Dirk as a person that they believed he could transform the pressure into a force for good: that he could be propelled by the fires that threatened to devour him. They recognized, too, that the next crucial step would be for Dirk to wrest leadership of the team away from Cuban.

Their collapse in the 2006 NBA Finals had shown that Cuban's powers of influence could lead them only so far. Cuban could not compel his players to win the championship any more than Stern could heal, by dictate, the fundamental problem of his league's identity. Real change had to develop from the ground up. The Mavericks' dream of winning the NBA championship would have to be finished by Dirk, with the ball in his hands, against the best homegrown Americans.

And then, one night during the 2010–11 season, the team turned the corner. There was a possession that ended badly because Dirk had passed when he should have shot. The Mavericks lost the ball, the other team scored, and Cuban screamed impulsively at Dirk to do better. He had yelled at all of his players a thousand different ways, but this time, as Dirk prepared to inbound the ball, he responded.

In that moment of quiet in the arena, without so much as a glance in the direction of Cuban sitting on the far side of the court, Dirk passed the ball back into play with one hand as he pulled out his mouth guard with the other and shouted:

"SHUT THE FUCK UP!"

On the bench they were all looking down at their feet again. But this time the words weren't coming from the owner. His teammates and coaches grasped the larger meaning.

Dirk was ready.

Dirk himself was beginning to think that this might finally be the year for his dream to come true. The Mavericks were playing tremendous defense around Chandler, which was uniting them in a way Dirk had never experienced. "In November I was like, 'Yeah, this might actually work,'" said Dirk. "We had a really good November and December, and I think we were playing some of the best basketball I have seen in the Mavericks."

They were on their way to recovering the ground that had been lost five seasons earlier in Miami when Dirk, just after Christmas, suffered a knee injury that would sideline him for three weeks. On the first day of 2011 Caron Butler, the starter at small forward, also went down with a knee injury, which would end his season. The team went on to lose nine of eleven games over the span of three depressing weeks, and with just three months separating them from another likely failure in the playoffs, there was once more no reason to think of the Mavericks as contenders for the NBA championship.

6

THE ALL-STAR

The 2011 All-Star Game was being played in Los Angeles at the Staples Center, in a climate of elegant fraternity. The NBA's greatest players were taking it easy on one another in order to help everyone look greater — with one hostile exception.

This was Kobe Bryant's home court, and he was defending it. He was competing as if the clock had been turned back three decades, to a time when the shorts were shorter and the All-Stars were fiercer. "You kind of expect it," said Doc Rivers, who was coaching the Eastern Conference team against Kobe's Western Conference All-Stars. "He went for it early."

By the end of the opening quarter Kobe had already begun to distance himself from his peers, and in particular from his Eastern rival Dwyane Wade of the Miami Heat. The NBA Finals were not quite four months away, and Kobe was investing in the groundwork. He posted up Wade to convert a turnaround jumper. He drove along the curb of the baseline for a two-handed dunk. In one of their chases downcourt Wade reached out to keep a hand on Kobe, who replied by slapping back at him blindly, like a stiff-arming tailback. At the three-point line Kobe pulled up to knock down a shot before Wade could contest. At the other end of the court he baited Wade to drive, then reached around behind to tap the ball free.

It was no coincidence that Kobe was doing this against the opponent he was most likely to guard if the Lakers were to meet the Heat for the championship in June. Wade, who had entered the NBA seven years after Kobe, was every bit as competitive as Kobe outside the setting of the NBA's All-Star Weekend. But the venue made no difference to Kobe.

His performance was worthy of those years when the All-Star Game was a proving ground for Jordan, Bird and Johnson. It was as if Kobe was trying to conjure up the 1980s — when, in the second quarter of the 2011 game, my cellphone buzzed. Isiah Thomas was calling.

I was able to guess the reason for his call, and it had nothing to do with Kobe's ruthlessness. But the timing was apt all the same, because Kobe was fighting in the same way that Thomas had fought a quarter century earlier, when the All-Stars were so ruthless that Thomas would be accused of "freezing out" Jordan.

Jordan was a 21-year-old NBA rookie when he was limited to 7 points and fewer shot attempts than any of his fellow Eastern Conference starters in the 1985 All-Star Game. Twenty-three years later, in his Hall of Fame induction speech in Springfield, Massachusetts, Jordan would go out of his way to identify Thomas, his Eastern Conference teammate, as a possible co-conspirator with Magic Johnson and George Gervin, who as members of the Western Conference team had supposedly colluded with Thomas to diminish Jordan in his All-Star debut.

"They say it was a so-called 'freeze-out' in my rookie season," said Jordan from the Hall of Fame podium as he glared at Thomas sitting near the stage. "I wouldn't have never guessed . . . but you gave me the motivation to say, You know what? Evidently I haven't proved enough to these guys. I've got to prove to these guys that I deserve what I got at this level. From that point forward I wanted to prove to you — Magic, Larry, George, everybody — that I deserved to be on this level as much as anybody else."

Thomas was amazed.

"I wish somebody would just watch the game," Thomas would say months later. "You'll see it isn't true."

The story had been perpetuated by Dr. Charles Tucker — an agent associated with Thomas, Johnson and Gervin — who told reporters after the 1985 game that Jordan's fellow All-Stars had "decided to teach him a lesson." Jordan was a rookie, and there is no doubt that many NBA stars were envious of the personalized Nike shoe deal and other endorsements that were already distancing Jordan from the rest of them commercially. But would they risk losing the game just to indulge their jealousy?

A review of the game would provide no indication that Jordan had been sabotaged or limited in any way by Thomas. During his twenty-two minutes on the court, Jordan would receive seven passes in the run of play (not including routine inbounds passes), and four of them were delivered by Thomas, including an attempted alley-oop lob that was knocked away by a defender at the rim. Jordan was neither demanding the ball nor fighting to get open in his rookie All-Star Game, and there was no hint of animosity or resentment, as Thomas received numerous passes from Jordan in return.

Thomas's reputation as a villain of the NBA's most compelling era would be launched that day by the accusations that he had masterminded the freeze-out of Jordan. But his role in the supposed conspiracy made no sense to him. At that time Thomas was an undersized 23-year-old point guard with one series of playoff experience, and he didn't see how he could have been expected to dictate strategy to the older stars who had been winning championships and carrying the league.

"Before the game would start, Bird, [Kevin] McHale, [Robert] Parish — they really had a thing, like, 'We're going to beat the West's ass.' That was in the locker room they were saying that," said Thomas of the Celtics stars, who at that time were the reigning NBA champions. "And you went at the game like, 'Okay, we're going to dominate you.'"

Decades later Thomas was watching a DVD of the 1985 All-Star Game when, at the end of the first half, Jordan attempted to drive to the basket. He was slammed hard in the face, the ball was knocked loose, and Jordan staggered away, head down, holding his jaw.

"In the All-Star Game nowadays they let you go lay that up," Thomas said. "Back then? Shit, them guys coming." He watched a replay of Larry Nance, a 6-10 power forward from the Phoenix Suns, arriving in slow motion to prevent Jordan's layup. "He just got hit in the mouth," said Thomas. "That's how you played back then, and it ain't nobody getting up and breaking up a fight because of it. He got hit in the mouth in an All-Star Game."

More provocative than any myth of a freeze-out was the hostility displayed by the biggest stars of the NBA's most entertaining era. The West would win 140–129, and yet the high-scoring All-Star Game of 1985 produced few dunks. Jordan was not being singled out for punishment: The defenders of both teams refused to surrender easy baskets to anybody. The offensive firepower was the result of teamwork and skills. "The guys were that good," said Thomas. "When you got these kinds of players out there, everybody's making the right read, everybody's making the right play, so there's not a whole lot of 'Let's get that guy the basketball, and he's going to do something good with it.'"

This was nothing like the All-Star Games of LeBron's generation, in which he and his rivals would step aside defensively as if holding a door open for one another. To be dunked on was viewed as emasculating by many players of the new millennium, and safer therefore not to contest the dunk at all. By contrast, Jordan had played in a glorious time of outright competition, in which the unchallenged dunk would have been viewed as cowardice — a sabotaging of the NBA's high standards.

The 1985 All-Star Game was played in the NFL's Hoosier Dome in Indianapolis as a kind of homecoming for Bird, the Indiana legend. More than forty-three thousand fans were there in spite of a heavy snowstorm, and even then Bird's rivals had no interest in yielding the stage to him. The local hero was shifting over to defend the rim in the second half when Adrian Dantley of the Utah Jazz drove the lane and elbowed Bird hard across the nose. Bird went down like a fighter who hadn't seen the punch coming. Blood was dribbling like a weak fountain off his chin as he sat on the bench, tipping back his head while a trainer stuffed gauze up his broken nose and into his mouth. Within minutes Bird returned to the game in his white, blood-spattered jersey.

"Adrian Dantley cheap-shotted me," Bird would say years later. He warned Dantley that afternoon that he was going to get him back.

Two years later, in the third quarter of Game 7 of the Eastern Conference Finals in the old Boston Garden, Dantley suffered a concussion when he collided headfirst with his Detroit Pistons teammate Vinnie Johnson while diving for a loose ball. That accident would hospitalize Dantley and contribute to the 117–114 loss that prevented Isiah Thomas's Pistons from reaching the NBA Finals. Millions of fans watching that afternoon were focused on the larger impact of Dantley's collision on the race to the NBA championship, but Bird was thinking about something else entirely as he walked over to the crowd of players and medical staff that had gathered on the court around Dantley, who was sprawled on his back in delirious pain.

"Remember that? He was really hurt," Bird would recall. "I looked in there and said, 'Got you back.'"

So vicious was the 1985 All-Star Game that when a collision with his friend Magic Johnson forced Thomas to play the second half with a heavy bandage around his hamstring, the 6-9 Johnson exploited the injury by attacking Thomas repeatedly. Even Julius Erving, the elegant champion who was about to turn 35, was brought down hard when Nance, a first-time All-Star, blocked his attempted dunk from behind. "Look how big everybody is, that's how the league was back then," said Thomas. "So there I am, I'm running my little ass."

Thomas, 6-1, was rubbing his palms together as his best days ran back and forth across the screen. "When I watch basketball, I'm always like this," he said, looking down at his clammy hands. "It's like a conditioned response, like Pavlov's dog."

Thomas was a person of respect among the modern generation of NBA stars. One year after the death of his revered mother, Mary Thomas, in 2010, many of the biggest names in basketball played an exhibition game in Miami to benefit Mary's Court Foundation, which had been created by Thomas and his wife, Lynn Kendall. It was like an unofficial All-Star Game in his honor: The players included LeBron, Wade, Chris Bosh, Carmelo Anthony, Kevin Durant, Chris Paul, Rajon Rondo, Russell Westbrook, James Harden, Jamal Crawford, John Wall and Rudy Gay.

The story of Isiah Thomas's childhood was known throughout the NBA. It was the subject of a 1989 Emmy-winning movie, *A Mother's Courage: The Mary Thomas Story*, which was shown routinely to students in urban classrooms. Thomas had been raised on the West Side of Chicago as the youngest of nine children. Born in 1961, he was beginning grade school when the violent new culture of addictive drugs flooded into his neighborhood. Among the future generations of American inner-city stars who would inherit leadership of the NBA, Thomas would be viewed as a kind of pioneer — the first of their kind to survive a world that was changing for the worse.

"The Vice Lords basically started in our neighborhood," said Thomas of the street gang that claimed, in its early years, to incorporate social change into its agenda. "The Black Panthers came to the neighborhood, Martin Luther King came to the neighborhood, and my mom interacted with all of them. She marched, she was in the civil rights. All the good thoughts that was going on in terms of desegregation, voting rights, education — all that stuff was happening on the West Side of Chicago.

"And then drugs came into the neighborhood. And it was like my mother said: She knew about alcohol, she knew about marijuana and stuff like that, but when heroin came into our neighborhood right after Vietnam, there was no education for that. And it literally wiped everybody out. It devastated families. It probably had the effect of the napalm bomb just dropped in the community. All the spirit, all the consciousness, all the good thoughts, it turned into this ugly thing that you see today. Gangs. Violence."

By then Thomas's father had moved out of their house. There were days when his mother would walk to work for the lack of bus fare. She and her children were living hand to mouth, with little in hand.

"I remember the first time I had a gun put to my head," Thomas said. "I was in sixth grade and I was shining shoes on Mayfield and Madison at the pool hall. And that was how we made money, we'd go shine shoes at different places. The shoe-shine booth was right by the door and he walked in, put the gun to my head and said 'Nobody move.' And this guy was shooting pool, that's who they were after. They had an umbrella case and in the umbrella case there was a pipe and they beat the shit out of him. It was three guys: the guy who had the gun to my head and two others. I shit my pants. When that type of fear hits you, you just lose everything. And I lost everything. I went to the bathroom and kind of cleaned up, and everybody just kind of went back to doing what they do."

Another day he was playing basketball on an outdoor court that was sloped — uphill toward one basket, downhill toward the other — when a gun was fired. "We were on the low end, so I heard the gunshots behind me as you were going upcourt," he said. "Everybody just took off running and people scattered, and they say when they start shooting you're supposed to hit the ground. So there was a car there and I dived up under the car. Remember they used to have those low tailpipes? Well, the tailpipe was hot. I'm laying up under the tailpipe, and as I raised up it scarred my back just a little bit, so I had to arch; and I'm hiding from the tailpipe, and the guy gets shot and he goes down right in front of me. I'm looking at him but I can't do anything. I'm up under the car and he's laying right in front of me. I don't know if he died or not."

His aggressive style of basketball was influenced by his neighborhood. "You definitely learned how to trust your instincts," he said. "I had to walk outside every day and I had to be able to look at a guy a block away and decide if he was going to let me walk by, if he was going to rob me, or kill me. And if I made the wrong decision on that guy it was over. And you had to learn how to trust that feeling, and you couldn't afford to be wrong."

Thomas learned to view his surroundings in terms of strength and weakness. "We were in a fight just about every day," he said, laughing, "until you got to be the guy that nobody fucked with." To avoid a fight was to express weakness. When he was 12 he was playing pickup basketball at the Boys' Club with a teammate who would rob him of his bus fare after every game. "For like two weeks this guy robbed me every day," he said. "As soon as we got done playing, everybody would break off and we would walk outside. As soon as I walked outside he would be standing there: 'Give me your money.'" Thomas tried to point out that they were teammates, that they had been passing and setting screens for each other and tapping at each other running back up the court. "'Fuck that, give me your money.'" One day an older player told Thomas that he should resist because his robber didn't know how to fight. "So he asked me for my money and I'm like, 'No, man, I ain't giving you my money today,'" said Thomas. "He hit me so hard. I mean he hit me in my chest so hard. But after that, for whatever reason, I never fought him back, but he just stopped robbing me."

When he would share these stories with the modern-day NBA stars, Thomas would point out that the values of the inner city had degraded since his childhood, and that in some ways it was worse for them than it had been for him.

"Now they shoot — they just shoot you," he said. "Back then when I was growing up, every contest was about let's fight and let's make it a fair fight. Everybody would make a circle and best man wins. Nobody was jumping in, and if you was getting your ass kicked, you lost that day, you had to go home and get better."

He became aware of drugs when he was 7 or 8 years old. "I won't say his name because he's still alive," said Thomas, "but I remember he was the starting center — he and my brother played [at] St. Philip High School — and he gets to shaking, and he's OD'ing, and we had to drag him outside the house so he wouldn't die in the house."

Mary Thomas moved her family to a different house practically every year. "My mom would get apartments and houses in different names and just ruin everybody's credit," he said, laughing. "So my brothers had bad credit, my sisters had bad credit. Good thing there was nine of us. I mean, everybody had bad credit because my mom had a house in everybody's name and we couldn't pay the rent. And back then they used to set you out. If you couldn't pay the rent, they would literally come in your house and take your furniture and set it out on the street. They can't do that anymore. Well, I remember coming home from school, I'm walking with my friends, and we walking by my house and the furniture's outside and they laughed, 'Oh somebody got set out! Somebody got set out!' 'Oh look at their shit all out in the street!' And you can't say it's your house. So you're like, 'Oh yeah, man, somebody got set out, can you believe that shit? Somebody got set out!' So you end up walking by your house, and then the guys they go and pick over the stuff. 'Oh yeah, I'm going to take this, I'm going to take this.' So they start stealing from you. From you. But you can't say 'that's mine.' Which is fucked-up. Which is really fucked-up."

In later years it would become a cliché to refer to basketball as an escape for young men from the inner city — a kind of hollow fact repeated so often as to numb its meaning. As far as Thomas was concerned, there was nothing cliché about it. He used basketball to manage the hunger of growing up in a home without food.

"There's a thing they call endorphins and adrenaline, and you get addicted to those because they are like drugs. They take away hunger, they take away pain," he said. "Now that I'm older, I understand it. When I was playing I would ask the same question: During a game I wasn't hungry, but right after a game I was starving. But now you get more educated about your body and everything else, you understand adrenaline and endorphins kick in and it takes away all that stuff.

"Playing basketball in a lot of ways became my way of self-medicating. That was the place where you went to get happy. The place where you found peace. It was your drug."

The parents of Isiah Lord Thomas III were from Mississippi, and his father, his namesake, didn't like to see Thomas playing basketball. "You got to remember where they came from, their understanding of entertainment and sport," said Thomas. "He didn't believe that basketball was a viable option. He thought that we should strictly be focused on education, and 'this basketball thing,' he called it, basically you just entertaining for the white man. And I can understand where he was coming from. Now that I understand the history of sport, entertainment, slaves, how they were pitted against each other to entertain — that's where he was coming from. And that's basically how he viewed sports for the African American. 'That's beneath you,' and he would say it. 'I'm not going to support that.' He came to one of my basketball games my senior year, and he stayed for a half and left. I saw him walk out of the door.

"I understood, because where he was coming from and where he viewed it in his perception, of sports, entertainment . . ." Thomas paused in the gathering of his thoughts. He was being careful. "That was his view. I was a kid who just liked playing. I didn't have those historical views or perception that he brought. Nor did my family. Like all my brothers, we all played, and my mother took us to the games and everything else. As a black male in that society, at that time, his perception was just totally different than what was happening in the present.

"My mother came to every game. My mother was like, 'Hey, look, you like playing, I like watching you play, the games are entertaining, you're good at it.' I like basketball like my mom liked basketball. She didn't buy into his perspective or his perception, although we as a family totally respected it. Because he did educate us on how and why he was thinking and feeling the way he thought and felt."

His parents would speak to him and his siblings about the larger context of slavery. "That was a weekly conversation in our household," Thomas said. "We talked about all facets of it. Why education was denied, colonization: all that stuff we were deeply educated in from their point of view and their perspective. Never about hate. Never was it you got to hate the white man for doing this. It was just an understanding of the system that you're living in, how you have to work within that system. You don't necessarily have to believe. But you have to work. You have to get an A on this paper. You don't have to believe this paper, but you have to get an A on it."

He remembered his father as having worked as an engineer at the International Harvester plant in Chicago. "When he was in the household we were living large," said Thomas. "There was food every day, everybody was going to school. It was good family structure. And all of that ended when I was 6.

"He couldn't get the promotion because, at that time, so the story goes, he would have been one of the first black foremans there. And they brought in a guy underneath him, a white fellow that he had to train, and then they promoted the guy over him. When they promoted him, he hit the roof. Called bullshit. And they fired him. And when he lost his job, you didn't know it at the time, but now that you know it, and what it's all about, he sat at the window for like six straight months in his pajamas, just sitting looking out the window. Who knew what depression was then? We know it now when we see it. And then he just spiraled, he really spiraled. Then drugs and everything started happening with my brothers. I think if I was to look back on it, I would say that the shame that he was under and probably felt made him leave. Not being able to face that or do anything about it."

His suffering reached the point that Mary Thomas could abide it no longer. "She was a fighter," said Thomas. "My dad named her Joe Louis, that was her nickname. She kicked him out. That's how that went. He didn't say, 'Oh, hell, I'm leaving.' She kicked him out. She was like, 'Look, as they say, either shit or get off the pot, because we got some work to do here.' But at that time no one knew his frame of mind."

He took a job driving a truck. Thomas would see him now and then. By 1986 he had moved back into Mary Thomas's home because he had cancer. "He died in my mother's bed," said Thomas. "My mother took care of him the last year that he was sick."

By then Thomas had established himself as a star in the NBA, and he had repeatedly offered money to his father. "An amazing thing is that my dad died not taking one penny from me," said Thomas. "I offered to pay his rent. I offered to buy him cars. My father never would take one penny from me. 'No, that's your money.' I used to take it personal when he wouldn't take money from me. But I can look now and I see what happens in other families with money and everything else. My father was down-and-out and he wouldn't take a dime from me. I'm probably the only NBA player that can say that—or one of, at least in my situation."

Thomas never believed he was among the best young players in his neighborhood. He didn't become a strong ballhandler until years after the Harlem Globetrotters had run a clinic at the Boys' Club and shown him how to pat at the ball and control it close to the floor. "If you ever see that tape of me playing against Portland, where I'm dribbling the ball real low and I spin—that's Marques Haynes and Curly Neal," said Thomas.

He was rejected by other private schools, in their belief that he was too small, before he was offered a scholarship to attend St. Joseph High School in the suburbs. Every morning he would be out the door at 5:15 a.m. to take four buses and a train to school, and he would return home after 10:30 each night. The school was racially divided: Thomas was one of the few black students at St. Joseph, and he fought routinely with other boys during his freshman year. But he was never uncomfortable with the environment, he insisted, "because I could fight."

He anticipated a big payoff in the late 1970s when he was a star high school senior who was being recruited to play college basketball. "I was getting offered cars, money and everything. And we wanted all those things—I wanted them, my brothers wanted them," he said. "I mean we was down for it. And I never forget this one college recruiter came to our house and he had a briefcase. Opened up the briefcase and he said, 'In this briefcase is $50,000 cash.' So my brother's like, 'Yeah, Junior!' We like, 'Yeah, we going to this school!'

"That scene went on for about a minute. And my mother sat there, and she closed the briefcase. Hit the two things. Pushed it back to the gentleman and said, 'My son is not for sale.' And we was like, 'Yeah, yeah, yes! We for sale!'"

Mary Thomas's sons didn't dare say out loud what they were thinking. They sat quietly and let their body language sulk for them. "She's Joe Louis, remember," said Thomas. "We were all there: My brothers and everyone was part of my whole recruiting process."

The recruiter walked out with his $50,000 briefcase and left the Thomas family to their home without money or food.

"So now it's time for the lesson," he said. "Of course we don't want to hear this lesson. You're sitting there, starving. No food. It's like, well, how we going to eat tonight? This conversation is good, but it ain't doing nothing for this" — he slapped at his flat stomach for effect. Then he paused, to give respect to the memory of his mother, who was about to speak to her children. "So she goes, 'There was a time where all of us were bought and sold. And there's no price that I will ever accept for you.'"

He didn't want to hear her lecturing then, as hungry as he was. "But now that I'm older," he said, "how lucky was I?"

When Indiana University coach Bobby Knight arrived at the Thomas home, he and Mary Thomas hit it off immediately. "He said, 'Mrs. Thomas, I'm offering your son three things. I guarantee you that he will go to school every day and be educated, he'll be a gentleman, and I'll teach him to play basketball as well as I can. Other than that, that's all I'm offering. I don't know if your son can really play for me. But I can guarantee you that he will be educated, he'll be a gentleman, and everything I know about the game I'll teach him.'"

Mary Thomas was impressed, but her son was not. "Who wants to play for this guy? I didn't want to play for him," said Thomas. "So him and my mom, they got to talking and everything. And my mom asked him, she said, 'In Indiana, right outside of Bloomington, there's a place called Martinsville and it's the home of the KKK. Who is going to protect my baby from them?' Coach Knight was great. He goes, 'If we're winning, they'll protect him.'"

When Thomas was finished laughing, he went on with the story. "My mom laughed," he said. "My brothers didn't. No, my brothers were like, 'That shit ain't funny. That's some bullshit.'"

As a sophomore Thomas would lead Indiana to the 1981 NCAA championship, and by the end of the decade he would become the smallest player ever to serve as the biggest star of an NBA championship team while leading the Detroit Pistons through the NBA Finals in both 1989 and 1990. Another two decades later, the NBA would grow less threatening to players of his size — enabling the Celtics' skinny 6-1 guard Rajon Rondo to become a star — but the progress came too late for Thomas. His career, like his life, was defined by conflict.

He was the NBA Rookie of the Year; he played in a dozen consecutive All-Star Games through 1993; he was a Hall of Famer and voted among the NBA's fifty greatest players. But he was also blackballed from the 1992 Dream Team out of personal spite, not only by Jordan, who could not forgive Thomas for his behavior in the vicious rivalry between Chicago and Detroit that ultimately hardened the Bulls and enabled them to become champions, but also by Magic Johnson, who believed that his close friend had spread rumors that Johnson was bisexual after he was diagnosed in 1991 with HIV, the virus that causes AIDS. Thomas denied that accusation, insisting that he was especially sensitive to these issues because his brother Gregory had contracted HIV before Johnson's diagnosis. (Gregory Thomas would die of AIDS in 2004.)

In spite of his size Thomas was rarely appreciated as the underdog. Instead he was vilified for controversies spun from his rivalries with Jordan, Johnson and Bird during the NBA's golden era spanning the 1980s and '90s. Among them, Bird alone maintained empathy for Thomas. Bird had grown up poor in Indiana and was scarred by the suicide of his father, while Jordan and Johnson had been raised in two-parent working-class homes.

"The only thing I ever said about Isiah — I couldn't believe what he did to Magic," said Bird in reference to the question of Johnson's sexuality. "That's their business, but I don't care; if I have one of my best friends forever, I could never do that to him, even if I thought it, you know? I just couldn't do that. But everybody's got their own issues, and do things the way they do them. But I've always liked Isiah. I never had any problem with Isiah."

Dispute and scandal followed Thomas everywhere he went in the NBA, whether on the court or in franchise management. The New York Knicks went 141-241 during his five seasons as team president through 2007–08, a disheartening period that included a sexual harassment lawsuit brought by Anucha Browne Sanders, who in 2006 was fired as vice president of marketing by the Knicks. One year later she was awarded a judgment of $11.6 million by a jury of four women and three men. The jury held Madison Square Garden and its chairman, James Dolan, responsible, with $6 million of the award attributed to the hostile work environment that Thomas had created.

And so two public perspectives of Thomas developed in parallel. The mainstream view focused on the stories of his misconduct, casting him as a cutthroat who didn't respect the structured rules of the NBA society to which he had graduated from the West Side of Chicago. The less common view, held by many of the younger NBA stars who were raised in neighborhoods similar to his, focused on how far Thomas had come and what he had been able to achieve in spite of the frightening odds piled up against him like walls for him to climb.

Carmelo Anthony was one of those young NBA stars who related to Thomas. When Anthony was growing up in Baltimore, the only examples of success within his neighborhood were the drug dealers. "My role model was people on the corner of my block," said Anthony. "Whoever was making money. Money to me back then was somebody making five hundred dollars, a thousand dollars, two thousand dollars — that was people who I looked up to. There wasn't no Fortune 500 companies or NBA players. We didn't have no NBA players when I grew up."

Emulation, like politics, was local. "They're successful," said Anthony of the drug dealers. "Whether you see them in the cars, you see them with the French clothes on. That's what we wanted; that's what I wanted. I want to be like him. I want that."

He wanted what they owned, but he didn't want a life like theirs. They were fighting to protect a corner of land that wasn't worth dying for. He wanted to escape the neighborhood rather than own it. "I knew that what they had, they wasn't getting it the right way," he said. "So I knew that. I wasn't going down like that." How did he know better? "I'm with them, I'm out there with them every day."

The rags-to-riches assumption would be that Anthony clung to basketball with the long-shot goal of playing his way off the streets. The truth is that neither he nor Thomas was able to envision his own upside. Instead of dreaming his way out of poverty, Anthony was discovered and claimed by the marketplace of basketball, as if he were the winner of an extraordinary lottery.

"I was playing basketball, but it was for the fun of it," he said. "Everybody in my neighborhood was playing, but it wasn't nothing serious. Then I went to high school. My freshman year I got cut from varsities. Then I was like, 'Forget basketball, I don't need to play no more. I don't want to play.' My sophomore year I got cut again, I didn't play varsity, and after that I was like, 'I don't need this no more, I don't need basketball.' I ain't played most of my ninth-grade year; most of tenth-grade year I ain't played basketball — I played pickup. I'm just talking about I didn't take it as serious."

The game he loved was baseball, and he was also learning to play football when, with no warning, he was graced by his genes in a way that Thomas never was: Anthony grew almost half a foot, resulting in his unanticipated identification as a basketball prodigy. Within three years he was the go-to scorer of the NCAA champion Syracuse University and the number three pick in the 2003 NBA draft — two spots behind LeBron, two ahead of Wade. The marketplace had airlifted him away to the NBA, where as a 6-foot 8-inch forward in 2010–11 he was receiving a salary of $17,149,243, with the money guaranteed whether he was able to play in every game or not.

Stars with Anthony's background were among those rare beneficiaries of the all-or-nothing world in which they had been raised. It was a world that made little sense to them. The world that was outraged by LeBron's behavior in *The Decision* was the same world that did not appear to be troubled by the violence and poverty to which LeBron had been subjected as a child in Akron. It was a world that encouraged players like LeBron, Anthony and Wade to look up to Isiah Thomas as an achiever rather than a disappointment, because their own experiences had taught them how far he had come. They saw the mistakes Thomas would make in the larger context. To them it was miraculous not only that they had survived their upbringing, but also that they were now on top of a world that only a few years earlier cared so little about them and whether or not they succumbed to hunger and stray bullets. As survivors, they appreciated as no one else could the Dickensian miracle of their survival. No one but they and their friends, their people, appeared to recognize the paradox of wealth and poverty that spanned their short lives, and the insanity of it all drew the stars of LeBron's generation together in the way that war makes brothers of soldiers. All they could do was make the best of their bizarre lives, because there was little hope for change. The worst neighborhoods of inner-city America had been black holes of drug-ridden poverty since the earliest days of Isiah Thomas, and he was approaching 50 now.

Two days after his broadcast of *The Decision*, and the day after the rally in Miami, LeBron showed up in New York to attend the celebrity wedding of Anthony to TV personality and actress La La Vásquez, to be detailed by a crew of roaming cameras and broadcast across six episodes of the VH1 reality show *La La's Full Court Wedding*. On his way into the reception LeBron was jeered by New Yorkers angry with him for shunning the Knicks. Inside, when guests were invited to toast the bride and groom, LeBron stood up and changed the subject to himself.

"If you want any chance against us in Miami," he joked to Anthony, "you'd better team up with Stoud in New York."

LeBron was referring to All-Star power forward Amar'e Stoudemire, a free agent who had agreed to a contract with the Knicks shortly after they had failed to land LeBron. LeBron's close friend Chris Paul, the All-Star point guard of the New Orleans Hornets, saw LeBron's toast and raised it: Paul announced that he and Anthony would indeed be forming their own Big Three with Stoudemire at Madison Square Garden. That set off a new series of toasts throughout the hall that encouraged Anthony, a 26-year-old All-Star small forward, to leave the Denver Nuggets in order to come "home" to New York — where he and his siblings had been raised in the Red Hook projects of Brooklyn until he was 8 years old, at which time their single mother moved them to Baltimore.

Sitting among the 320 guests at the reception and absorbing these aftershocks of *The Decision* were the Nuggets' owner, Stan Kroenke, and his son, Josh, the team's president. It was a wedding unlike any they had attended. Not only was it a made-for-TV event, but many of the toasts were focused less on the happy couple and more on how Anthony should escape his obligations in Denver. After the Kroenkes had sat through a number of humiliating statements about their team, word was relayed to their table that Anthony wanted Stan Kroenke to stand up and make a toast that would let everyone know of his and Josh's presence, in order to put a stop to their embarrassment. The Kroenkes' experience would contribute to a new idea spreading among the NBA owners that *The Decision* had ignited a quiet rebellion in which stars like Anthony were happy to continue receiving huge salaries from their employers while at the same time plotting against them.

For all of this talk of a potential move to New York, Anthony still owed one more expensive season to the Nuggets. He was their player, but not for long. In the month after his wedding, Anthony met formally with Josh Kroenke to confirm that he wanted to be moved to a franchise in a big market, with the Knicks at the top of his list. The Nuggets were certain that Anthony's trade demand had been inspired by *The Decision* and LeBron's inciting toast.

Months later it would further bemuse the Kroenkes to know that in their own arena, less than an hour after the Nuggets had clobbered the Heat by 28 points, LeBron and Wade stood in the hallway outside the locker rooms huddling quietly with Anthony, whose trade demand continued to be the biggest story in Denver. It was clear that the three of them wanted to be seen meeting in conspiracy. The two stars of Miami wanted it known that Anthony wasn't isolated by the controversy of his desire to play in a larger market and that he had their support. They believed that he wasn't a villain for wanting to leave Denver, in the same way that LeBron wasn't the evil person he was being made out to be. The bond uniting these three stars transcended their allegiances to the teams that were leasing their talent. They viewed all of this from a perspective of survival and triumph that could not be understood unless you came from their neighborhoods.

Five weeks after that meeting in Denver, LeBron, Wade, Anthony and their fellow players of the sixtieth NBA All-Star Game were gathered in a large makeshift dressing room following their practices in Los Angeles. It was the day before they would all appear on Kobe's court to play together; they were now awaiting the arrival of Commissioner David Stern. He was meaning to speak to them about their ongoing negotiations with the owners for a new collective bargaining agreement, which were at a standstill and likely to result in a lockout of the players after the season.

Stern was late. At last he came into the room with a cluster of league officers. There was a table in the center of the room, and Stern made a show of walking around it to mark off his territory, then pausing to glance at the ceiling as if gathering his thoughts. When he began to speak, it was to remind the players of how long and successfully he had worked on their behalf, of how the NBA had been viewed (before many of them had been born) as a league with no future because of its reliance on black players, and of how today these same players were the highest paid in any league throughout the world.

It was true that Stern had liberated them in all kinds of ways to become wealthy and famous. In 2001, fatigued by the defensive trends of the NBA, which had been launched in the 1980s by Isiah Thomas's "Bad Boys" Pistons and furthered by Pat Riley's hardheaded teams in New York and Miami, Stern put together a special rules committee headed by Jerry Colangelo, owner of the Phoenix Suns, with the goal of speeding up the game and allowing zone defenses to be used for the first time in the NBA. Many teams fought against Stern's autocratic rewriting of the rule book, because they had invested a lot of guaranteed money in defensive-minded players. But Stern, with the backing of his committee, pushed through the changes, with the results being that scoring increased, the pace grew more entertaining, and the game became increasingly universal and egalitarian. The new rules favored speed over size, which empowered smaller players like

Rajon Rondo and his rival Chris Paul to become All-Stars without fear of the hard intimidating fouls that had left thick scars around Isiah Thomas's eyes.

Stern had followed the example of professional basketball in Europe, where the game was defined less by the size of the players and more by their skills. The All-Stars in this room had been rewarded by his desire to open the NBA up to the largest audience and the most diverse pool of talent. These gains had been achieved even as the commissioner had silenced debate and dissent among those owners and players who were obsessed with short-term gains at the expense of long-term investments.

The money they were making had been earned on his watch, Stern was reminding the players that afternoon in Los Angeles, and if only he had wrapped it up then and there, he might have had a constructive impact on the negotiations. But Stern kept talking. He could not help himself. Maybe by now he had so much power that he couldn't rein himself in, or maybe his respect for the players' emerging leverage incited him to respond in kind. In any case he kept talking, making unseemly allusions to knowing where all the bodies had been buried along the way, like a leader who had grown used to not being interrupted, until he realized too late that these players for whom he had achieved so much were no longer listening to him. They were beginning to pull on their coats and gather their gear even as he continued his lecturing, and some of them were even making small talk among themselves in competition with him. It was some time after Stern heard more than the sound of his own voice that he stopped, said his abrupt goodbyes and walked out.

The Carmelo Anthony negotiations between Denver and rival teams would go on for six months. The bartering was managed by a 40-year-old retired player from Nigeria named Masai Ujiri, who had been hired as the new general manager of the Nuggets shortly after Anthony had tendered his request to be traded.

Having fallen in love with the game as a 13-year-old in the ancient Nigerian city of Zaria, Ujiri, a 6-foot 4-inch guard, had immigrated to Bismarck, North Dakota, for two culturally (and meteorologically) shocking years of junior college, to be followed by a half-dozen seasons in which he played professionally in Europe's smaller leagues for no more than $5,000 per month. In those days his ultimate goal was to become an NBA scout who would travel back home to Africa in hopes of discovering young players who could live out their dreams in

America. Instead he had networked his way up through the NBA to earn management control of Denver's roster. It was an amazing story.

All of the rival negotiators were hoping to fleece Ujiri. Some of them expressed condescending pity for him, telling reporters how sorry they were to see his new career being sabotaged by one of the NBA's best young players. Ujiri expressed nothing but gratitude for their sympathy. He had a young face, an easy smile and a rhythmical Nigerian accent that extended his vowels, and if his peers were patronizing, he would take no offense. He did not mind being underestimated.

Ujiri viewed the trade demand of Anthony as an opportunity to retrieve assets that would enable him to reinvent the Nuggets. Of course he didn't want to let go of his biggest star, and he would keep trying to change Anthony's mind with the understanding that he couldn't possibly get equal value in return for him. At the same time, Ujiri wasn't going to allow the departure of Anthony to ruin his franchise in the way that the loss of LeBron was burying the Cavaliers, who were plummeting to last place in their conference.

This was the job of his dreams, to run his own team in the NBA, and now that he had it, there was no feeling sorry for himself. At night he would wait for his fiancée to fall asleep in their five-story Denver townhouse and then sneak downstairs to plot strategy and return emails at three or four in the morning. "I have to get it out before I feel good about myself," he said of his work. "I won't be able to sleep until I get it out."

Ujiri was able to grasp Anthony's perspective of wanting to play on a bigger stage; it was for the same kind of goal that he had devoted years to working around the clock, apart from the four hours of sleep he needed each night, to earn this opportunity he had now in the NBA. "Carmelo's mind was set with what he wanted, and do you blame him for that?" said Ujiri. "I don't."

He would hear complaints that Anthony's trade demand was a warning to NBA owners that they were losing their leverage against the players, but Ujiri didn't see it that way either. In addition to his negotiations with the Knicks, Ujiri was pursuing offers from the New Jersey Nets, the Dallas Mavericks, the Houston Rockets, the Los Angeles Lakers and other teams in the belief that Anthony would agree to a three-year contract extension worth $65 million with any large-market team that acquired him. The financial terms of that extension were likely to be reduced at the end of the season, after Stern made good on his threat to lock out the players, and Anthony had acknowledged that his priority was to get the money while he could.

Regardless of *The Decision* or Anthony's demands, Ujiri believed that the NBA owners were always going to maintain power because they controlled the money. During the lockout, there would be tensions over the semantics of "ownership" and whether the players were "owned." But in the end, what Stan Kroenke of the Nuggets and James Dolan of the Knicks really owned was the money that the players wanted.

During his job interview to become general manager of the Nuggets, Ujiri had told Josh Kroenke that the trade for Anthony needed to be turned into a bidding war between the Nets and Knicks, because they were rivals within the New York market who both needed Anthony and couldn't bear to see the other team claim him. Ujiri also warned Anthony that if he wanted to play for the Knicks, he would need to make things right with the Kroenkes. The story of their humiliation at the wedding had become public, positioning the Kroenkes in the middle of the larger negotiating standoff between the players and the owners. Ujiri wanted Anthony to understand that he was a partner with the Kroenkes in this business, and that he needed to be sensitive to the difficult position in which they had been placed.

"I said, 'Melo, I think you really need to apologize to the Kroenkes,'" recalled Ujiri. "I said, 'I think you need to talk to them and say, "Hey, it wasn't the way I thought it would be; people were drinking a little bit, and even then people should not talk like that." And apologize and take responsibility for it.' I said to him, 'Melo, we're trying to make this thing easy on everybody. I don't know which way it will go. I couldn't tell you where you will be traded to. But I could tell you one thing: Let's make good steps, and this is a good step to make.'"

In this way Ujiri was trying to protect his team's owner as well as the player who wanted to leave. Anthony would apologize to the Kroenkes by text message. It wasn't the face-to-face statement that Ujiri was seeking, but it was important nonetheless, because the Kroenkes liked Anthony very much, and they had been wounded by the events at the wedding and his ensuing demand to be traded.

On the day before the All-Star Game in Los Angeles, Knicks owner James Dolan met with Anthony; his agent, Leon Rose; Josh Kroenke; and Ujiri. In that meeting Ujiri declared that the Nuggets were considering trading Anthony to the Nets; the accompanying silence of Anthony and his agent served as tacit affirmation that Anthony would be willing to sign an extension with the Nets if they acquired him. Dolan responded by increasing the Knicks' offer, though it was still not to Ujiri's liking.

The next morning, hours before the All-Star Game, I called Ujiri's cellphone. I had developed a long-standing relationship with him in my job as a writer for *Sports Illustrated,* and so, on the condition that I tell no one, he explained that the best potential outcome for his team would be to send Anthony to the Knicks. The problem, as he saw it then, was that the Knicks' proposal wasn't convincing. The Nets were offering four first-round picks in addition to rookie power forward Derrick Favors, who had been the number three pick in the draft; All-Star point guard Devin Harris; rookie guard Ben Uzoh; and Troy Murphy, whose contract was expiring. That trade would leave the Nuggets with young talent and cap space with which to rebuild for the long term. "If you're trying to break it down and go completely younger and rebuild, then you go with the New Jersey route," Ujiri said. "If you are trying to reload and get good talent and find the upside on some kids, then the Knicks' deal is the one you want."

The Knicks' deal was built around a trio of established young players: small forward Danilo Gallinari, point guard Raymond Felton and small forward Wilson Chandler, in addition to a pair of second-round picks and a future first-rounder. There was no potential for receiving a new franchise star from the Knicks. If the Nuggets wanted to gamble on discovering the next Carmelo Anthony, they would bet on Favors, the draft picks and the cap space to be gained from the Nets. Ujiri preferred the bird-in-the-hand offer of the Knicks, whose young role-players could be plugged into the Nuggets' rotation to keep them in the playoffs for the next several years, despite the absence of a marquee star like Anthony. But the offers were so competitive that Ujiri wasn't sure which one the Kroenkes would prefer, especially since it would be natural for any NBA owner not to send Anthony to the Knicks in order to avoid the appearance of surrender.

"That is why the big kid in New York has to be in it," said Ujiri.

The big kid was Timofey Mozgov, a 7-foot 1-inch undrafted center from Russia who had no potential to become a star. He had not joined the NBA until the summer of Anthony's wedding, as a 24-year-old rookie who signed with the Knicks for $3.6 million. Mozgov was averaging 13.5 minutes and 4 points per game as a rookie for the Knicks, and only in the larger context of these trade talks could a benchwarmer like him have been seen as a difference maker: His inclusion might convince the Kroenkes to side with the offer from the Knicks.

After we hung up, I found myself thinking about Isiah Thomas. I called back to ask Ujiri for his permission to run this information by Thomas.

Thomas was living in Miami, where he had become the men's basketball coach at Florida International University in 2009, after leaving the Knicks. I told him of the competing offers, and that the Knicks might lose Anthony to the Nets unless they included Mozgov. He listened and then said, bluntly, that he wanted no part of the negotiations. I had called him in the belief that he would want to know the status of the trade talks, on behalf of his ongoing friendship with Dolan. Thomas and I had been sharing information for years; he had provided me with insight into the new generation of AAU players who were seizing control of the NBA, and I believed he would be interested in hearing about Anthony.

But Thomas was gun-shy. It had been three years since his departure from the Knicks, and he was still being criticized in New York as if he had never left. He said he didn't know Ujiri, and the last thing he needed was to have it leaked that he was involved in the talks for Anthony. He made it clear that he no longer had any authority within the Knicks organization, which meant he had everything to lose and nothing to gain. Thomas could see how this would play out: The trade with the Knicks would collapse, word would get out of his involvement, and he would be the scapegoat. "I don't want anything to do with it," he said.

I explained why I had assumed that he would be interested in hearing about the negotiations. Anthony had stuck his neck out to force a trade to New York, and if the trade was doomed to fall apart because the Knicks weren't willing to include a back-end player like Mozgov, it wouldn't only be Anthony who would be furious. Anthony's fellow NBA stars — his close friends — would be angry with the Knicks, too, and it would become more difficult than ever for them to recruit another star in the years to come. The future of the Knicks mattered not at all to me, but I figured it would be important to Thomas. He said he agreed with my point of view, as I knew he would, since he had helped me to understand this dynamic over several years of conversations.

Thomas thanked me for the call and then insisted that he was going to keep out of it. His goal was to get on with his own life. If the Knicks were going to make the trade, let them figure it out.

Hours later the All-Star Game tipped off, and from the start it was clear what was at stake among the players. They were focused on demonstrating that they were in charge of their league. They treated the ball as if it were a microphone being passed among show-business friends at a benefit concert. They were expressing fraternity with one another — and solidarity against the franchise owners.

The NBA stars of LeBron's generation likened themselves to the marquee actors and actresses who attracted the attention and sold the tickets and powered the Hollywood film industry. In that light these stars were approaching the collective bargaining negotiations with Stern and his owners as if they were in a battle for the ownership of basketball itself. What gave team owners the right to seize half or more of the revenues in an industry that was driven by its performing artists? "I mean, artists don't give up 50 percent of their revenues," Rajon Rondo, the Celtics' All-Star guard, would complain to the *Boston Herald* while pursuing the entertainment analogy. "There's no business model for what they want us to do."

Rondo was citing a false example. The NBA players as a group were, in fact, receiving a greater share of the revenues than their peers in music or the movies. In Hollywood the casts of the biggest blockbusters were obviously receiving less than 50 percent of the revenues. *Harry Potter and the Deathly Hallows: Part 1* had grossed almost $1 billion globally in 2010, but its actors had not earned anything close to $500 million. Daniel Radcliffe, the star of the movie, had been paid $25 million in 2010, according to *Forbes*.

In the music industry one-third of the gross ticket sales from concerts was being passed on to musical artists like Beyoncé or Bon Jovi, according to analysts from *Forbes* and *Billboard*. The rest of the money helped pay for all kinds of investments in the shows — infrastructure, marketing, travel and so on — that in turn helped make the artists seem larger than life and therefore worthy of the highest prices and acclaim. Money had to be spent in order to be generated.

The same dynamic existed to serve the NBA players, who never would have been earning the average annual salary of $5.15 million if not for the thousands of associates in a variety of fields whose everyday work elevated the league. The players were going to be reminded soon enough of the diverse basketball economy that made them rich and famous: During the lockout of 2011, when they would attempt to stage their own exhibition games, the events they hosted would be amateurish, low-quality affairs that diminished the players' value, as surely would occur if Jack Nicholson or Denzel Washington abruptly consented to appear in low-budget B movies.

From the All-Stars' point of view, the long weekend in Los Angeles was their version of the Academy Awards. They used the All-Star Game to stage a show that featured them as they saw themselves. When a player made a run at the basket, his peers tended to step out of the way and let him have it. They lobbed alley-oop passes to one another at the expense of the competition between the teams. Before the opening tip, three fellow starters of the Eastern Conference joined with LeBron to mimic his pregame routine of tossing handfuls of talcum powder into the air to form a white cloud above the courtside table — even though two of those players were employed by teams that were competing against him. All of this revealed the extent to which money and fame had changed their point of view. Jordan, through no fault of his own, had created a world in which his heirs no longer feared being hit in the mouth at an All-Star Game.

The only star who was openly objecting to these displays of mutual affection was Kobe Bryant. Something more immediate was driving him. He was greedy for every advantage he could grab, as if even this game might help him win the championship at the expense of his rivals.

After fifteen NBA seasons, Kobe's will to win was more powerful and galvanizing than the players' unified stance. He high-fived his Lakers teammate Pau Gasol and exhorted a Kevin Durant three-pointer with a shout of "Let's go, Kevin!" He yelled for teammates to cover Wade in transition, and he shouted instructions to his rebounders when he realized one of his own jump shots was veering left. While the East was at the free throw line, he muttered something to Dwight Howard and Wade, and they did not laugh in response.

The game peaked in the third quarter when LeBron committed a turnover and chased the ball as it was relayed ahead to Kobe, who looked over his shoulder as if daring a challenge. As he chased the smaller, older champion, LeBron was suddenly focused on creating an image of his own: He was going to slap away the dunk and raise questions about Kobe's age and ability to finish. Kobe gathered and rose to the basket, feeling the heat and breath of LeBron hovering behind him — but he dunked quickly, not one of those showy tomahawk extravaganzas that define All-Star Games. He dunked like a lizard's tongue snapping at its prey. Four large hands were around the rim, but the ball was gone. On their way back up the floor Kobe was laughing with LeBron. It was laughter with an edge.

Kobe was showing his younger rivals that they were missing the point of the game. There was no need to prove the power of their union, not here at least. They were the owners of this moment, and a moment like this was more valuable than money. It was to connect themselves to moments like this that the newest owners were spending hundreds of millions of dollars to buy their way into the NBA.

The owners had the money.

The players had something more valuable than money.

Kobe was a ruthless scorekeeper. He demanded every dollar he could take from every negotiation. But now he was engaged by a deeper ruthlessness. To play in this game, on this stage, was more valuable than any handshake deal. There were hundreds of millions of people the world over who wished they could have the opportunity that Kobe was fulfilling now, and the envious included many of the NBA's richest team owners, who would have traded some or all of their fortunes to be the All-Star that Kobe had become. Kobe understood, because the day was coming soon when he would be off the court with them, watching someone else play this game that enabled him to understand who he was and who he could be.

Time would be set aside later for negotiating with the owners. What Kobe was doing now was transcendent. Everything else was business.

The West converted Kobe's leadership into a 148–143 victory as he scored 37 points to win his fourth All-Star Most Valuable Player award, equaling the NBA record of Bob Pettit, a Hall of Famer who had retired in 1965. Afterward his rivals tried to laugh at Kobe's expense, as if he was guilty of taking the game too seriously.

"You could tell from the start he wanted to get the MVP," said Stoudemire of the Knicks. "He was not passing the ball at all. That's Kobe."

"That's how Kobe is," said Chris Bosh of the Heat. "I've seen him play kids hard."

What else were they going to say? Kobe had hijacked their group statement.

I was watching the second quarter from the press section of the Staples Center when my phone buzzed with a call from Isiah Thomas. "Well, I passed on the information," he said, without saying to whom it had been passed. "Now we'll see what happens."

I told him about the old-school lessons Kobe was sharing with LeBron, and Thomas laughed. "That's what he does," Thomas said.

The next morning the news broke that Timofey Mozgov had been included in the Knicks' offer to Denver. That night the trade was completed. Carmelo Anthony was moving to New York, and Isiah Thomas was not, for this one time, the villain.

7

THE TRADE

In Boston, a short time before the All-Star Game, the Celtics were visited by the Mavericks, Lakers and Heat over a span of ten days. They lost their game against Dallas in the final five seconds when Dirk Nowitzki fumbled the ball near the basket before rescuing it back out to Jason Kidd for a three-pointer, flipping Boston's one-point advantage into an eventual 101–97 defeat.

Next the Celtics were beaten 92–86 by the Lakers on 20 second-half points by Kobe Bryant, who took no small joy from winning in Boston while also ruining the big night of Ray Allen, a longtime rival. Allen, the Celtics' 35-year-old shooting guard, made a pair of shots in the opening quarter to break the NBA record of 2,560 three-pointers, which had been held by Reggie Miller of the Indiana Pacers. The Boston fans were standing in celebration when Allen, the number five pick of the 1996 NBA draft, was approached at midcourt by Kobe, who had been picked eight spots later. As Kobe bumped fists halfheartedly with Allen after all of the other congratulations had been offered, Doc laughed to himself. "You know they hate each other," said Doc, still smiling days later. "I was like, wow, that was hard."

Doc believed the competitive hostility between Kobe and Allen to be a wonderful thing. Rivalries like theirs distanced them from the generation of LeBron James, whose stars tended to be friendly with one another.

In spite of their losses, the Celtics were cheered by the recent return of Kendrick Perkins, who had recovered from knee surgery earlier than expected. In one of his first games back, Perkins stood up to the Orlando Magic's powerful young All-Star Dwight Howard while reminding Doc how much his team had missed its headstrong center. "Dwight hits him with an elbow, hits him with another one—and Perk just stands there," said Doc. "And I was like, 'Holy shit! This is awesome.' And I even said that at halftime, I said: 'That is toughness! Toughness is somebody hitting you in the face; you're looking at them and laughing and walking away. That's a tough motherfucker.'"

Perkins was 26 but carried himself as if he had nothing in common with LeBron's AAU generation. He worried not at all about his unimpressive career averages of 6.4 points and 6.0 rebounds, because his job as he and his coach saw it was to establish Boston as the most aggressive old-school team in the championship race. Both Paul Pierce and Doc were convinced that the Celtics would have beaten the Lakers in Game 7 of the 2010 NBA Finals if not for Perkins's injury in Game 6. But team president Danny Ainge disagreed: He insisted that the absence of Perkins had been more than offset by the production of backup center Rasheed Wallace, who generated 11 points, 8 rebounds, 2 assists and 2 blocks in thirty-six minutes while starting Game 7. "It would have been nice to have Perk come off the bench, but Rasheed was playing great," said Ainge, who was convinced that Wallace's offense had given the Celtics their best chance to win.

Three days after their loss to Kobe's Lakers, the Celtics were beating LeBron's Heat 85–82, thanks to a surprising 15 points from Perkins. Doc was aware that he valued the intimidating leadership of Perkins more than Ainge did. The Heat missed 17 of their 35 shots from the paint and made only 3 of 16 three-pointers as the Celtics extended their defense around Perkins.

The Celtics were 3-0 against Miami and feeling good about their chances of bullying past the Heat in the playoffs now that Perkins was back on his feet. "Perk is the perfect instigator," said Doc, invoking the favorite term of Red Auerbach. "The best day in Perk's life was when he read in *Sports Illustrated* that he was the most overrated, hated player." In a 2009 poll of 190 NBA players who were asked, "Which NBA player thinks he's a lot better than he really is?" the two leading vote-getters were Perkins and DeShawn Stevenson, who had since become the starting small forward of the Mavericks. "I bet he has that framed," Doc said of Perkins. "The players were saying it to try to piss Perk off and say, 'You ain't that good.' Perk took it and said, 'This is great!' For him, it was like, 'I'm under your skin. You're thinking about me, you motherfuckers!' That's Perk."

While Perkins had strengthened them up front, the Celtics had been weakened on the perimeter. Tony Allen, their best midsized defender, had moved to Memphis as a free agent shortly after *The Decision*. More recently, 6-foot 6-inch Marquis Daniels, Paul Pierce's backup at small forward, had suffered a frightening spinal-cord injury that would result in surgery. The NBA trade deadline was eleven days away, and Daniels was waiting to undergo surgery. His absence was going to force Boston to pursue help on the wing.

"We have to," said Doc as he sat behind his office desk the day before that February win against Miami. "We're not going to win without it. We're just not big enough against LeBron. We're going to get somebody."

Because his Celtics had earned the best record in their conference at midseason, Doc was named coach of the Eastern Conference for the 2011 All-Star Game. His twelve-man roster, as selected by the fans and the Eastern Conference coaches, included four of his own players — every Celtics starter except Perkins.

Doc was confident in his ability to coach stars of every personality type. He had devoted his basketball life to relating to his teammates, his opponents and the players he coached from their points of view. As a point guard from the NBA's greatest generation, he had sought to inspire Hall of Fame teammates such as Dominique Wilkins and Patrick Ewing to upset opponents like Larry Bird and Michael Jordan, but they had always fallen short. As a young coach in Orlando, he had dreamed of recruiting Tim Duncan to play with Grant Hill, but he wound up instead with young Tracy McGrady, who had been unable to carry the injury-depleted Magic. Now that he was coaching Kevin Garnett in Boston, Doc finally had access to that rare star who was capable of leading his team to the NBA championship.

"The superstars are the easiest guys to coach," Doc said. "They play because of something other than the money. It's the average player and the below-average player that's chasing the money. Those are the guys that are tough, because you're trying to get them to buy into a role, to be a winner — but they're trying to make their careers."

The suspicion among millions of fans that LeBron was interested mainly in wealth and fame, based on the unpleasantness of *The Decision,* was not shared by his associates and rivals within the NBA. LeBron never behaved on the court like someone who was playing for the money. But there was reason to wonder if the negative reflection that followed him everywhere was diminishing his play, like a curse on his spirit.

"For the great ones it's never been about the money," Doc reiterated. "It's about the chase of whatever they're chasing. It's an unending pursuit. Coach-wise it's the same way. You're coaching to win, it's just unending, at least for me."

Doc's obsession with identity was at the heart of his approach. In his vocation to understand the greatest players, he was also trying to discover the best in himself. One of his most helpful insights had come from Mike Krzyzewski, who since 2005 had been coaching the men's World Championship and Olympic teams of USA Basketball in addition to his NCAA team at Duke University, where Doc's son Austin, the nation's top recruit, had committed to play basketball as a freshman in 2011–12.

"Coach K said this to me: 'The one thing about all those guys is that they live very, very lonely lives,'" Doc said. "I'm talking about Michael and Kobe and LeBron. I think the guys at the very top have lived in isolation, self-imposed. As high school kids, when everybody was partying, they were at the gym. By themselves. You become a college star, your teammates don't love you because they're trying to make it too. They act like they love you, but there's jealousies. And there's parental jealousies, from the other kids' parents. No matter what anybody else says, it's there. So when they go out somewhere, they don't really want Michael to come along because he's going to get all of the attention. They'd rather go with nine other players where they're all the stars. People like attention, and they don't like not getting it. So then Michael's alone again. Kobe's alone again. And the NBA is the same way. They go out sometimes, the stars, but most of the time they don't want to go out too much. I think being on that level, you live a lot of your life in isolation. I don't care how many friends they have — at the end of the day they're by themselves a lot. And they wouldn't trade it for the world. Because this is what they want."

What did they want, exactly? If not money or fame, what were they seeking?

Doc looked away, as if the question applied to him. "I would love to know what they're actually after," he said. "I bet they can't answer."

Doc was known throughout the NBA as a people person. In public settings he showed respect to all comers while appearing to be tuned-in and quick-minded and endlessly energetic. During his long walks through downtown Boston he would routinely engage with fans, stopping for photos and laughing at their jokes. But there was a high-maintenance aspect to him that the public couldn't see. It was draining to be "on" at all times, and so on the road he rarely dined out with his coaching staff, preferring instead to think things through in his room and recharge his energy.

"I want to win," he said. "I want to win every game, but I can't tell you what I'm after . . . I don't know what I want."

By some cosmic coincidence, Doc was coaching the modern-day version of Bill Russell, a half century later, in Garnett. So selfless was Garnett that Doc would have to plead with him to shoot the ball more often. During the playoff series against LeBron's Cavaliers in 2010, Doc emphasized the need for Garnett to shoot 20 times per game in order to exploit his matchup. Pierce would spend the entire round repeating the mantra. "Twenty shots," Pierce would repeat in Garnett's presence day after day. "Twenty shots. Twenty shots." What was impressive to Doc was that Pierce was bound to sacrifice some of his own shots for Garnett. (Garnett wound up averaging only 16 shots per game, though he did shoot more often than his teammates.)

Doc believed that Garnett could have scored more points than Jordan if that had been his goal. "All that stuff is beneath him, it really is," Doc said. "I've never had more problems giving somebody a game ball or presenting somebody with an award than Kevin Garnett. You give him anything, he just flings it out of shame. You'll never notice, but whenever it's a Kevin award, it's announced during a timeout, and while we're in the huddle, so he doesn't have to acknowledge it. Whenever it's an anybody-else award, we present it at halftime, or before the game, in front of the crowd. It's no coincidence. We'll know he's going to say, 'It'll throw me off my game. I don't want to think about all that shit.' That's what he always says: 'That shit.'"

His attitude was like a firewall he put up in protection of his performance on the court.

"That's what he thinks it is, it's shit," Doc went on. "And it's really cool. And it's not fake, and that's what you love about it. It's genuine. Some of the guys can tell you in the league exactly what they've done. I guarantee you, if you ask Kevin where do you rank in rebounds and assists, you'll get: 'I don't know; get the fuck out of here with that shit.' That would be his answer: 'Who the fuck cares? I'm trying to play, I'm trying to win right now.' That's his thought."

Doc's job, as he saw it, went deeper than designing plays to free up an open jump shot. He set out to strengthen the Celtics by drawing from his own life experiences. The more he succeeded in mentoring players like Pierce and Rajon Rondo, who had both been raised without a father, the more gratitude Doc felt for his own upbringing. He was coaching in Boston during the final two years of Red Auerbach's life, and in that brief time he saw much in common between the founding father of the Celtic Way and his own father.

"They were similar as people," said Doc. "My father was a hard, tough, great guy. He was a father for the whole neighborhood, coached the Little League team. We won the Little League championship — 9-year-old, 10-year-old, 11-year-old, 12-year-old — and everybody played, every game. If it was a one-run game and the kid hadn't gotten in, he came in. I remember sometimes, he had to take me out or whatever, and I'm pissed because we'll lose this game; and we still won. I used to laugh: 'I don't know how we're winning if we're playing everybody and the other team is only playing their nine guys.' So in that way he was a nice guy; and the other way, if the parents said anything to him, he'd tell them to go fuck themselves. 'I'm the fucking coach.' He was just a tough man; nobody fucked with him. He was strong, 6-4, great athlete. The folklore of Grady Rivers in Maywood is amazing. Great track guy. Great baseball player, great basketball player. He was one of the first black athletes to get a scholarship, I think it was Western Kentucky. Maybe he was the first; and then he had to go to the war, hurt his hand. He was just a tough, tough guy."

Grady Rivers attended all of Doc's games, and Doc liked to tell the Celtics players about the time he played basketball for his grade school team in Maywood, Illinois, in the western suburbs of Chicago. When Doc came home, his father said, "How did you play today?"

Doc gave his father a strange look and said, "I had 67 points."

"How many fouls you have?"

"Two," answered Doc.

"You had two fouls, and you think you played hard? How can you have two fouls in a basketball game? You get five, right?"

"Yeah," his son said.

"And he said, 'And you only had two,'" recalled Doc, laughing. "That's what he said, and I'm thinking, 'What the fuck? I just scored 67 points.' But in his mind you didn't push the envelope, because if you don't get to four fouls — he always said that — then you left something on the table. That was his warped way of thinking. And there's actually some truth to it. In high school it was the same way, every single game: 'How many fouls did you have tonight?' That was his question, and you knew you had to give that answer. He just wanted you to push the envelope, every day in life. That was his thing."

His father was a Chicago cop, and young Glenn Rivers (who would be nicknamed Doc in high school, when he was seen wearing a Dr. J shirt to a summer basketball camp) would stop by the holding cells to taunt the inmates ("Hey, what the fuck are you guys doing? You'll be in here for a long time, buddy!") on his visits to the precinct to see his father. Late at night he would beg to ride the beat for an hour with Lieutenant Rivers, who would drop his son at home before responding to danger of any kind. "Can you imagine today, somebody riding around with their son in the car? You'd go to jail," Doc said. "But it was awesome, watching him deal with people."

Grady Rivers rarely praised his two sons to their face, even as he bragged about Doc and his older brother, Grady Jr., to his friends. "A good day for me was being at the barbershop," Doc said. "The barber goes, 'Boy, your father was just talking about you.' And you'd try to juice the barber: 'What was he saying?' 'How good he thinks you are,' and stuff like that. He'd never tell you that, which I think is interesting. But you knew it; he just wouldn't say it."

There was a trick to being hard on people in a constructive way, as Doc learned from Auerbach as well as his father. "That's why I spent as much time with Red as I could," said Doc. "Red's biggest thing is the loyalty of his players. I didn't appreciate it, because I thought the Celtics thought they were better than everybody else, and different. When you get in here and you see it, you see that they *are* different. I've never seen the loyalty that K. C. Jones and Tommy Heinsohn have for Cousy and Russell. Usually there's jealousies. 'Oh, he wasn't that good.' 'Dominique could play, but he could never . . .' I guarantee you, if you took half the Heat out, they'll tell you a story: 'Man, LeBron's an asshole . . .' They're going to put themselves up at some point. But you don't ever hear the backbiting here. You never hear it. I've been here all these years, and I've never heard bad stories about ex-teammates. It's just the most remarkable thing.

"That's all Red Auerbach — it's all Red Auerbach. You can see how abrasive he could be, how he had his own way in thinking, and yet he had this love, too, at the same time. And that's how my dad was. My dad, people didn't fuck with my dad."

His father was 76 when he died in Chicago in 2007, one year after the death of Auerbach. The stories at the funeral made Doc laugh through his tears. "The one lady said, 'Grady wanted to be cremated, but we were concerned with all the alcohol that he consumed that he would blow up the entire church,'" said Doc. At the funeral it was like seeing a complex diagram of community involvement brought to life as his father was laid to rest.

"I didn't get to see him pass away, I wasn't with him, and that just killed me," said Doc. "That really bothered me, because he was never sick." In October 2007 Doc was in Rome, where the Celtics were training in advance of two preseason games overseas, when he received news that his father had been hospitalized. But his father's condition was good, Doc was told, and so there was no need to rush home. Weeks later, on the eve of their second game of the regular season, in Toronto, the phone woke Doc with the worst news.

"It's pitch-black in my room, so I don't know what time it was," he said. The Celtics were beginning what would be the best year of their basketball lives, the head coach included, and that morning Doc shared the news with his players. "I gave them a long speech about my father, and you could see Kevin and all of them all broken up," said Doc, who had flown back to Chicago before his Celtics beat the Raptors in overtime. Then I went back and forth." He was flying back home to Chicago, returning to his team as needed, then back to Chicago again. "After the funeral, I remember saying, 'Okay, where are we going to dinner?' My mom said, 'Going to dinner? You are getting on the plane and going to coach your team.' I was like, 'No, I need to be here.' 'You need to go coach your team. That's what you need to do. You need to go do your job,' she said. 'That's what your dad would do. You want to honor your dad? You go do your job. You go do your job all year.' That was my mom's message."

That night at the game in New Jersey, which his Celtics won on their way to an 7-0 start, Doc wore the same suit he had worn to the funeral.

Over the next summer he considered resigning from the Celtics, because he didn't know whether he had the energy for it. Garnett and Pierce knew they were on the verge of losing him. But every summer was like that with Doc: He didn't want to commit to coaching them unless his heart was with them.

In 1994, in the early weeks of his third and final season as a point guard with the New York Knicks, 33-year-old Doc and coach Pat Riley could be heard yelling at each other, while Jeff Van Gundy and Riley's other assistants listened on the other side of the office door. Their arguing went back to the previous season, when Riley had refused to activate Doc, who was in the last stage of his recovery from knee surgery, for the playoffs. The Knicks had gone on to surrender a 3–2 lead in the 1994 NBA Finals, with their last two losses coming by a total of 8 points.

"I made a huge mistake," acknowledged Riley years later. "When we ended up in the Finals, he was ready to play, and I could see the daggers in his eyes looking at me. He was a competitor like I'd never been around. Maybe with Doc we could have won Game 6 or 7."

But Riley was in no mood to concede the following November, not after Doc had gone over Riley's head and asked team president Dave Checketts for his release from the Knicks. Days later, Riley called Doc to inform him, more calmly, that the release had been granted. Doc would now be free to sign with San Antonio for his final two NBA seasons. It was during their farewell chat that Riley provided Doc with the bottom line on his future. "He was the first guy to literally say it: He said, 'You're going to coach,'" said Doc. "I remember saying, 'I'll never fucking coach.'"

Doc's plan, when he was finished playing, was to enjoy a civilized retirement as a TV broadcaster.

"You're going to coach," insisted Riley, as Doc remembered it. "You are a fray guy. You have to be in the fray. You need it. It's what gives you life, it's what gives you energy. You're competitive: You're too fucking competitive and driven to not be in the fray."

"For me," answered Doc, unable to recognize that his simmering anger was affirming Riley's point of view, "the broadcasting business is in the fray."

"Not for you," said Riley. "Broadcasting is in the fray for the guy who grew up wanting to be a broadcaster. But not for you. It's not in the fray for you."

Doc broadcast NBA games for the cable network TNT following his retirement from the Spurs in 1996, and whenever he happened to run into Riley — who by now was coaching the Miami Heat, with full authority over the roster — his old coach would pick up where he had left off: "You miss the fray? You miss the fray, you don't want to say it!"

Within three years Doc was agreeing with Riley. When he was hired to coach Orlando in 1999, he quickly earned a reputation as one of the league's great motivational speakers. Ever since then, his basketball lessons had been laced with references to a higher calling, because what his teams were doing here was expressive of the larger world out there.

"Pat Riley is an inspiration of all that," Doc said. "Of all the coaches, I don't know who is the best at Xs and Os, or who runs the best practice; all I know is that guy made you want to win. There was no agendas, you just wanted to win, and you bought in. If you can get your team to do that . . ."

If he could convince his team to buy in during the upcoming 2011 playoffs, Pat Riley's protégé believed his Celtics could knock out Riley's Heat.

Doc was able to empathize with his players by channeling his own life experiences. In 1982, his junior year at Marquette University, Doc fell in love with his future wife, Kris Campion, a blond commuting student who had been dating one of Doc's white teammates. Doc is African American, and his season that year was consumed by the prevailing racism directed toward him and Kris. "I saw Bill Russell do an interview on TV, and the trophy that he has sitting in his house, the Olympian Award, where you're voted the best amateur athlete — I was voted that that summer," Doc said. "That's how dominant I was. So now I can't even play, my focus is all fucked-up."

In 1983 he was chosen in the second round of the NBA draft by the Atlanta Hawks, who never would have been able to acquire Doc with a pick as low as number thirty-one if not for the love of his life. "That taught me a lot later about focus and distractions," he said.

Young players like Perkins and Rondo were forever coming Doc's way, and their issues always transcended basketball. How could he help them? Everyone who reached the NBA was self-obsessed — so many thousands of hours spent alone in gyms and weight rooms, and in their own heads dreaming up what was to come — and Doc's goal was to widen their point of view, to adapt and share with teammates that narrow focus.

On Martin Luther King Day he would recite in the locker room the story of Rosa Parks sitting in the front of the bus. Whatever could have convinced her of her power to make a difference? *You have to believe when no one else believes.*

Lean into problems, he would tell his players. *Don't run away from them.* "When you're in a white-water raft, if you're about to get out of control, you don't go to the middle," Doc would explain. "You lean into the water with your oars to get your balance."

He who angers you, owns you.

He urged his players to recognize the hidden meanings of their own words. If a player complained that he wasn't getting enough shots, he was actually admitting that he didn't care so much about the needs of his team. *There is what you say,* Doc would tell them, *and then there is what you are really saying.*

Nothing good happens after midnight, he would warn them, quoting his father.

It's not who is right; it's we have to get it right.

Applause waits for success.

One of his assistant coaches, Kevin Eastman, heard so many of these sayings that he began to keep a file on his computer that he called "Docisms." Every time he heard Doc provide inspirational advice, he would add it to the list.

"We may have one leader, we may have two leaders," Doc said one day, "but

I damn well know this: You've got to lead or get the hell out of the way. *Because there cannot be wishy-washy leaders.*" The players and coaches figured that Doc was referring to Rondo there.

Doc, like Riley, cloaked his messages with style. What he said was as important as how he said it. Before each game, assistant coach Lawrence Frank would spend three minutes reviewing the assignments for the defensive end of the floor, and then assistant coach Armond Hill would do the same for the offensive end. And then it would be Doc's turn to speak from the green sheet of paper he carried into each game, written in his own hand in black ink. He liked to prepare these talks while sitting in a sunlit room, unlike his role model: The iconic image of Riley in Miami was of a single lamp lit in his otherwise dark office, as he sat with his cup of coffee, sketching in blue ink on blue cardboard stock the inspiring messages that had recruited LeBron.

Doc's messaging went beyond speeches. In the Celtics' practice facility, amid the sixteen banners that were hung like tapestries, there was an empty space on the wall. Doc arranged to have a light aimed at that space, where a seventeenth banner needed to be placed. "The light couldn't be cut off — even at night it never went off," he said. "The light stayed on that entire year. Rondo came back a lot at night to work out, and he said it was real cool because you walked into the gym and there was that one light on."

After they won their championship, Doc presided over a ceremony in the practice gym. "We put the banner there in that space and had a little celebration and turned the light off. The guys loved it," he said. "And then they came back for camp, and now there's a blank banner there with the light on it again. Because now we needed another banner." When the Celtics worked on their exhausting defensive drills, Doc ordered the offensive players to play with their backs to the blank banner so that the defenders would always be facing it. The importance of the symbolism became apparent one day when Garnett, exhausted and streaming with sweat at the end of a hard practice, looked up from his defensive stance to see the blank banner. He slapped his hands hard on the floor and redoubled his efforts, and if not for the knee injury he suffered later that season, the empty banner might very well have been replaced with number eighteen.

In early 2010, after the Celtics had finished off a regular-season victory against the Lakers in Los Angeles while Kobe was sidelined by a sprained ankle, Doc turned to Eastman with a frown and said, "I think our guys are a little too giddy.

It's too early to be this happy." Moments later, in the visitors' locker room, Doc congratulated them for winning—then announced abruptly that they needed to make more than a verbal investment in the season. "I want $100 from everybody in the room, right now," he said, and everyone was scrambling to come up with $100; if someone didn't have it, a teammate or colleague fronted it for him. There were twenty-eight people in the room, and Doc held up their $2,800 in a wad of bills and said, "Guys, what we're going to do is we're going to hide this money, this investment that you have just given me. It's a small investment, I understand, but it's an investment. And we're going to hide it in this locker room because we will be back in June. We *will* be back here in June, and when we play the first game here at the Staples Center, we're going to walk into this locker room, we're going to get our $2,800, and we're going to fucking kick their ass." When they returned four months later for the 2010 NBA Finals, Doc reached up and recovered the $2,800, hidden atop one of the tiles in the ceiling, and like a prophet he passed out the money.

What Doc was seeking, what he was really seeking, were the clues that would deepen his understanding of the game's profound mysteries. There are two kinds of exploration in basketball: The search around the world for talent, for that next Jordan or Kobe or LeBron who is capable of elevating the game; and then there is the search for the meaning of the game, which is discussed far less often. The search within, to unlock one's own heart on behalf of the team and the game itself —this was Doc's obsession. He was using basketball to help his players understand who they were and how they could help one another, because it had to be their idea. He could not force teamwork upon them. They had to believe in it, and dream of it, in order to win the championship.

In February 2011, in the final minutes before the NBA trade deadline, Ainge dealt Perkins and backup guard Nate Robinson to the Oklahoma City Thunder for small forward Jeff Green, backup center Nenad Krstic, a first-round draft pick and cash.

"I've worried for the last three years: When things are not going well for us, the combination of Rondo and Perk on the floor is not great," said Ainge. "It makes us very offensively challenged. We've lost games because of our offensive droughts. We'll go eleven possessions without scoring, and it's just not a good combination. It's the combination of people sagging off Rajon, and the fact that

Perk is not a great above-the-rim guy: He's not a great catch-and-finish player or shooter. I've felt like we've been able to cover up that weakness with the Big Three and their special play."

Perkins had an embraceable personality and brittle hands; with Rondo it was the other way around. Their friendship was the closest that Rondo had on the team, and at times they fought like brothers. When Perkins inevitably fumbled one of Rondo's spectacular passes, they could be seen yelling at each other as they hurried back on defense.

The one quality they shared, apart from being the youngest Celtics starters by far, was that they were lousy shooters. They were offset by the exceptional shooting of Pierce, Allen and Garnett, whose ages were forcing Ainge to start planning for their departures. When the Hall of Famers were gone, Ainge believed, he could rebuild around one non-shooter. But he couldn't live with two.

"It was hard to invest going forward and building around the combination," Ainge said of Rondo and Perkins. As traumatic as the loss of Perkins would be for his teammates, Ainge believed this trade would bring the Celtics closer to another championship. Green, who was 6 feet 9 inches tall and 24 years old, would provide the size, athleticism and youth the Celtics would need against LeBron. "We're adding a starting-quality player to come in and give minutes, which we have never had," said Ainge.

He was also convinced that the Celtics were better with Shaquille O'Neal, who had started at center over the first three months, than with Perkins. "It gave me confidence to make the Perkins trade because of how well Shaq was playing — how well our team was playing when Shaq was on the court, I should say," said Ainge. "Whether Shaq scored 4 points or 16 points, it didn't seem to matter: Our team offense was thriving in the first forty games Shaq was playing. And then defensively when Shaq was on the court, we didn't take a step back at all."

A study by the Celtics' data guru, Mike Zarren, revealed that opponents had taken 10 percent fewer shots at the rim when O'Neal was playing than when he was out of the lineup. Perkins was more effective defending against the midrange shot from twelve to seventeen feet, but overall Boston's defense was superior around O'Neal because fewer shots were being attempted near the basket, where opponents converted at a rate of 70 percent whether O'Neal or Perkins was in the game.

Ainge was trying to accomplish two goals: improve their championship hopes immediately while also receiving value in exchange for Perkins for the long term.

Doc knew that Perkins, who would enter free agency that summer, was likely playing his final year with the Celtics, because he had already turned down a proposal of $22 million over four years, which Ainge was willing to pay in spite of Perkins's challenges offensively. "I could not go forward with nine to ten million a year, which is what I thought it would be," Ainge said. Soon after, Perkins would sign an extension with the Thunder worth almost $33 million over four years.

The trade acknowledged that LeBron's obsession with the Celtics had become mutual. Over the weeks ahead, it would become clear that Perkins had pushed too hard to recover from knee surgery ahead of schedule, and he would suffer related injuries that would limit his effectiveness with Oklahoma City for the remainder of the season. "His knee was fucked-up, and even if he had played, Perk wouldn't have been great," acknowledged Doc. "The one thing you can say with the trade: Perk's value had never been higher, and we traded him at apex. Now, that doesn't mean you should trade him . . ."

A big part of Ainge's calculus depended on the recovery of O'Neal, about to turn 39, who had been sidelined by a chronic Achilles tendon injury just as Perkins was settling back into the rotation. "I never disagreed, I never agreed; I was always back and forth," Doc said of his conversations with Ainge about Perkins. "And then at the end he said, 'You've got to trust me on this.' And I do."

In Miami, however, the response was celebratory: LeBron and his teammates were surprised and encouraged that the menacing obstacle of Perkins had been removed. "Oh, there's no doubt," said Doc of the Heat's reaction. "Trading Perk opened the door up for people to believe: 'We can beat them; now they're soft, now they just took away Kevin's protector.' And that's what that did."

"It showed there was a little of the mercenary there on their part," said Riley, who agreed with Doc that the Celtics would have won the 2010 NBA Finals if Perkins had been healthy. "When you have a contender, you keep that team together until it proves to you after four or five years in a row that the core players don't work anymore. Until then, you can add to it, but you don't subtract. They lost a big piece in making that deal. We were not unhappy with that trade."

Pierce would spend the remaining three months of the season second-guessing the trade. "He brought a swagger to our defense," said Pierce. "Him and Kevin —that was intimidating for teams to play against. People didn't like that: Perk snarling at them after blocking a shot, or setting a hard pick on them, or when they come back they know they are going to get hit. That was our swagger. That was our presence. Our team was a tough-as-nails team, and we would beat you up and we were intimidating. That was a mental edge that we had on everybody, and it was like we gave that up."

The 7.3 points and 8.1 rebounds per game that Perkins had produced in a dozen games for Boston since his quick return from surgery would be easy enough to replace, Pierce acknowledged. But there was no restoring the leadership of their old-school center, who had been 22 when Kevin Garnett was acquired by Boston. No teammate would be influenced more by Garnett than Perkins, who over the ensuing four years became more direct and confrontational with opponents (and fellow Celtics) than Garnett himself. Neither the Lakers nor the Heat, nor any other current rival, was ever so certain of its own identity as the Celtics were of theirs, and it was because Perkins had become the 6-foot-10, 280-pound manifestation of Garnett's point of view, the teammate who practiced what Garnett preached.

"Sometimes when you're a G.M., you look at talent more than chemistry issues," said Pierce. "You're upstairs, you don't know what's going on in this locker room, you don't know what's going on on the bus, that's the stuff you don't understand. You just kind of see from afar: 'Well, he's better than him . . . Well, the numbers are this and this when he's on the court . . .' But you don't see the value in the chemistry, and that's huge."

What was revealing was how little Pierce was able to empathize with Ainge, in spite of their parallel responsibilities. When Pierce missed a win-or-lose shot at the buzzer, he expected everyone to take into account the variables — a strong-arming by the defense, maybe, or a mistake in the running of the play, or a foul uncalled, or simply a bobble, stumble or some other understandable mishap. Those were the risks Pierce took on as a star.

Another set of variables affected Ainge when he committed to a trade — the salary cap, the strengths and weaknesses of rival contenders, the needs of his own team now and in future, the opinions of his owners and staff and coaches and best players — and then there were the questions of public opinion, of what the fans and the media were going to make of it. All of these influences swirled around Ainge as if he were facing a last-second shot, with altogether greater consequences. There was no algorithm to ease the decisionmaker. Every move was made (or not made) on a case-by-case basis, under pressure and always in a hurry. Each trade came down to Ainge's best informed guess in the same way that no two shots by Pierce could ever be identical.

◄ LeBron's high school games were televised nationally in affirmation of his popularity and potential. *Al Tielemans / Sports Illustrated / Getty Images*

▲ After *Sports Illustrated* introduced 16-year-old LeBron as "The Chosen One," he embraced his new identity. *Jesse D. Garrabrant / NBAE / Getty Images*

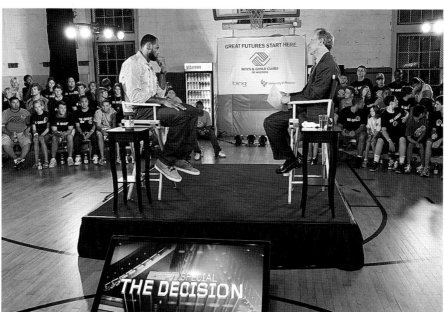

▲ With *The Decision*, the savior of the NBA recast himself as its villain. *Larry Busacca / Getty Images for Estabrook Group*

◀ LeBron appeared anxious and apprehensive throughout *The Decision*. *Larry Busacca / Getty Images for Estabrook Group*

▶ One day after *The Decision*, the Heat's new trio of Dwyane Wade, Chris Bosh, and LeBron celebrated future championships in Miami before they'd even played a game together. *Gustavo Caballero / WireImage / Getty Images*

◀ Heat president Pat Riley (right, with coach Erik Spoelstra) assembled the plan to recruit LeBron and transform him into an eventual champion. *Doug Benc / Getty Images*

◀ After celebrating his breakthrough championship in 2008, Celtics coach Doc Rivers was intent on winning again in Boston. *Jesse D. Garrabrant / NBAE / Getty Images*

▶ Kobe Bryant celebrated his victory in Game 7 of the 2010 NBA Finals at the expense of Doc Rivers (right).
Mark J. Terrill / AP Photo

◀ Spurs coach Gregg Popovich created a championship program around foreign-born stars like Manu Ginobili and Tim Duncan. *Glenn James / NBAE / Getty Images*

▶ Commissioner David Stern (right) and his future successor, Adam Silver, were dealing with an NBA labor impasse as well as the crisis of LeBron. *Henny Ray Abrams / AP Photo*

◄ When Mavericks owner Mark Cuban lost his temper, his employees had no choice but to look the other way. *Bob Rosato* / Sports Illustrated / *Getty Images*

► Young Dirk loved basketball but feared his inevitable move to the NBA. *Holger Sauer / Getty Images*

◄ Holger Geschwindner choreographed and fine-tuned all of Dirk's moves.
Andrew D. Bernstein / NBAE / Getty Images

► The pain of his 2007 MVP award created a moment of truth for Dirk. *Matt Slocum / AP Photo*

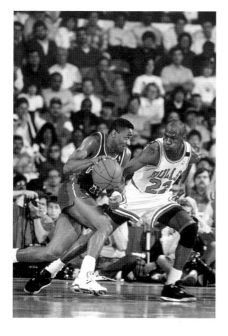

◀ Years after his bitter rivalry with Michael Jordan, Isiah Thomas emerged as a pioneer for LeBron's generation. *Manny Millan* / Sports Illustrated / *Getty Images*

▶ Who would define the next generation—Kobe or LeBron? *Mike Ehrmann / Getty Images*

▲ In all venues Kobe was determined to uphold the NBA's highest competitive standards.
John W. McDonough / Sports Illustrated / *Getty Images*

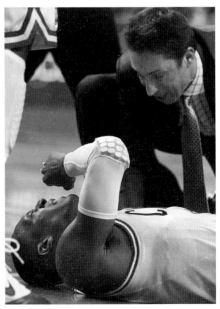

◀ Two decades after he was drafted by Red Auerbach, Danny Ainge was seeking to renew Auerbach's traditions. *Paul Benoit / AP Photo*

▼ After the trade of Kendrick Perkins, Doc was leaning on young point guard Rajon Rondo more than ever. *Nam Y. Huh / AP Photo*

▲ A Celtics physician resets Rondo's dislocated left elbow on the court. *Elsa / Getty Images*

▲ The Lakers were stunned when their contentious run ended in Dallas.
Greg Nelson / Sports Illustrated / *Getty Images*

▼ The NBA Finals changed when Wade and LeBron celebrated prematurely in the fourth quarter of Game 2. *Greg Nelson* / Sports Illustrated / *Getty Images*

▼ Joey Crawford (second from left) huddled with fellow referees Mike Callahan and Bill Kennedy in Game 5 of the NBA Finals—to the frustration of Dallas coach Rick Carlisle. *Mike Ehrmann / Getty Images*

▲ The Heat knew they had to stop Dirk in the 2011 NBA Finals—but how? *Andrew D. Bernsteinm / NBAE / Getty Images*

▲ Holger's two-decade partnership with Dirk was about to pay off for him. *Andrew D. Bernstein / NBAE / Getty Images*

▼ Their post-Finals press conference was nothing like the rally that LeBron and Wade had led eleven months earlier.
Greg Nelson / Sports Illustrated / *Getty Images*

▲ Point guard Jason Kidd, a champion at age 38, turned out to be the perfect complement to Dirk.
Mike Ehrmann / *Getty Images*

▲ A victory for Dallas, for the NBA and for the basketball world. *Greg Nelson* / Sports Illustrated / *Getty Images*

Ainge took risks that few of his rival NBA executives were willing to take, in their fear of a backlash if a trade was scored as a failure. He had not been afraid to take the last shot as a player, and he wasn't afraid now in the front office. But Pierce couldn't relate, because he had never been the team president.

All the same, Pierce wished the business influences could have been set aside until after the season. "We had the best record in the East; the way we were playing, let's finish this up and see what happens," Pierce said of Perkins's impending free agency. "Maybe in the summer Perk had to do what he had to do, and the Celtics had to do what they had to do. But I thought maybe we should have finished that out."

On the day after the 2011 All-Star Game, three days before the trade deadline, Doc and his four All-Stars flew north to Oakland, where they reunited with Perkins and the rest of the Celtics to beat the Golden State Warriors. From there they traveled on to Denver. Their game against the Nuggets was scheduled to take place several hours after the deadline. There had been no public rumors of any deal, but on the eve of the deadline Ainge called Doc to warn him of something big in the works: There was a chance, said Ainge, that the Celtics could receive James Harden from Oklahoma City in a trade for Perkins.

Doc didn't want to give up Perkins, but neither he nor his star players could argue against the potential deal as he discussed it with them that afternoon. Harden, a 6-foot 5-inch guard in his second NBA season, was viewed as a future star. He was going to average a modest 12.2 points in 2010–11 while coming off the bench to complement Kevin Durant and Russell Westbrook, who would each earn MVP awards in the years ahead. Harden's blend of skills and athleticism was spectacular, and Sam Presti, the general manager of the Thunder, had refused to let go of him over several weeks of probing by Ainge. On the morning of the trade deadline, Ainge finally accepted no as the final answer and called Doc to inform him that the talks were dead.

"So I grab Perk before shootaround and tell him, 'Hey, I know you've heard a lot of stuff, it looks like we're safe,'" said Doc.

Later that morning, while the Celtics were in the middle of their brief walk-through at the Nuggets' arena, Jeff Twiss, the Celtics' vice president of media relations, approached Doc on the court to say quietly that Ainge needed him on the phone immediately. Doc walked off the court and out through the players' tunnel, where he received the stunning news. The negotiations with Presti had resumed on a different path, and the approaching deadline had forced Ainge to make a quick decision. Perkins was gone.

As Doc walked back onto the court, he could feel the players staring at him. They knew something was happening to their team. Doc waited until they had returned to the hotel before speaking with Perkins. Then Doc called his four stars to tell them the news. Pierce and Garnett let it be known that they didn't like the trade.

"Me and Kevin were real sour on that," said Pierce. "To give up on Perk, that hurt." It hit home as they tried to console Perkins. "He was crying," Pierce said. "It was tough on me talking to him. I really didn't know what to tell him. I tried to lift up his spirit, but he was a mess. He couldn't believe it."

That night, in the visitors' locker room in Denver, Doc looked around at his players and struggled to find words. Perkins had been a 19-year-old backup center when Doc came to the Celtics, and Doc could not count the many hours they had spent talking about all kinds of things. He had taken enormous pride in the transformation of Perkins, who had grown up to embody the Celtic Way. In an industry defined by money and attention and ever-escalating pressures, it was rare to find players who were focused on the needs of the team. "We're going to miss him," said Doc in the locker room before the game, and everything he had written out on his green sheet of paper made no sense as his voice shook and the tears filled his eyes. Some of his players were crying. It was like a funeral, in the sense that they were realizing what they had shared through nearly four years of championship contention, and that it was never going to be the same.

"And I started thinking, 'We're going to get our ass blown out,'" Doc recalled. "That's the only day I think I've ever been somewhat unprofessional, because it was very difficult for me to emotionally coach. And I am an emotional coach."

They lost 89–75 that night in Denver, but by the next day Doc was refusing to indulge his emotions any longer. He had an urgent assignment: The playoffs were just two months away, and he needed to incorporate the new Celtics while holding his mainstays together. The Perkins trade, driven as it was by business realities, was threatening the investment in teamwork that had defined their franchise in all of its times of success. For Rondo, charged with quarterbacking a remodeled team, the loss of his one close friend left him feeling more isolated than ever.

But Ainge drew hope from Rondo — from his blend of youth and experience, from his easy bursts of athleticism and old-school approach to sharing the ball, and from the coming-of-age fact that his teammates were depending on him after so many years of helping him along.

"In the last thirty years — in my career since the '80s — there's only been one team that's won a championship without a 'great player,' and that's Detroit," said Ainge in reference to the 2003–04 Pistons, who had won the championship without a dominant offensive star. "So we're trying to do it like Detroit, I would say. That's our only choice right now — we'd like to get five or six or seven pieces, because Paul's not going to score 41 in a Game 7, most likely, against LeBron; and K.G. is not the best defensive player on the planet right now. Rondo is the most special of our players. He's the one that has the ability to take it to a special level, more than anyone else on our team."

8

THE ODYSSEY

MIAMI: *November 22, 2010*

Miami was foreign to LeBron James. It was unnaturally warm when he drove or bicycled the half-dozen miles to work each morning from Coconut Grove, the neighborhood in which he and his family had settled, not far from the high-rise where Isiah Thomas was living in his exile from the NBA.

The Heat practices, held downtown in a corner of the large AmericanAirlines Arena overlooking Biscayne Bay, complied with the demands of team president Pat Riley. Every day LeBron's jersey had to be tucked in, with assistant coach Keith Askins roaming the facility to point out any loose shirttails. Padded knee braces were mandatory at practice, to encourage all-out effort while minimizing injury. There was the same monotonous running of laps around the court with hands clasped overhead each and every day. Body fat was measured on Mondays, even during the playoffs.

"His first year, he was mid-260s and about 8 to 9 percent body fat," Riley said of LeBron. "I thought he was a little bit heavy, and I asked him, 'What if you got down to 250? Think about it. It's 18 pounds. Let's go and get an 18-pound weight right now and run around the court in it.' I think there might have been one day we put a 10- or 15-pound weight jacket on him and had him run around in it. 'What if you thought about getting to 250 and down to under 6 percent body fat? Speed and quickness, it would be better for your knees, you could jump a little bit higher.' He just smiled at me and said, 'Coach, I'm fine. I'm in great shape.'"

Riley wasn't going to argue with him. Through his first eight seasons, including that initial year with the Heat, LeBron played in 627 of his teams' 656 regular-season games (while averaging 40.1 minutes) in addition to all 92 playoff games. By year two in Miami, he would slim down to the mid-250s, and by the time he entered the back end of his career, surmised Riley, LeBron had reached 250. "His weight is from his waist down," Riley said. "He's got a linebacker's butt and a fullback's thighs and hamstrings. His explosiveness is from his knees up to his hips and his core. He can afford to get really thin up in his chest and stomach and shoulders and arms — that's where you can lose ten pounds."

There was more to Riley's weight obsession than bringing out the best in LeBron. It was also about creating an environment in which LeBron could eventually triumph.

"I'll never forget what Kareem Abdul-Jabbar said to me before my very first game as coach of the Lakers," said Riley, who had taken over early in the 1981-82 season. He was only two years older than Abdul-Jabbar — they had played against each other in high school — and when he began by encouraging his star center to express leadership, Abdul-Jabbar turned the tables. "He said, 'Look, Pat, you know me. I'm going to come and play every night as hard as I can, give you everything I can, because I have great pride. I know what my position is in the league,'" recalled Riley. "He said, 'What I'd like you to do is keep everybody else in shape and keep them on track and keep them going. And then I don't have to worry about doing it.'

"I'll never forget those words. And so when LeBron came, I just knew I had to do that for him. Even though he might have had his own regimen, I was going to keep everybody else on the right track and in shape. They may not have had the talent that he respected and that he needed to win, but he knew they were going to be in shape, they were going to be mentally ready, be part of the team, and that would help him win the championship. That's what the superstars want. They don't want chaos. They don't want a negative locker room. They don't want crises all the time. They don't want players bitching about minutes. They want to make sure all those other things are taken care of, and they don't want to do it. That's why great players want to go to organizations where that stuff is coherent from the standpoint of wanting to win and be a championship culture. You don't want to waste your time and lose another year because you're with an organization that's not going to make other players accountable to help you become successful."

But LeBron was not going to be successful overnight. In the weight room he would be handed a sheet of assignments detailing how much and how often to lift per day, and when he was done, there was to be no loitering. It was move in and move out. Play had given way to work.

"Players should want a routine every single day," Riley said. "Not chaos — not twenty-five other people around the locker room, the weight room, the players' lounge, every day at practice. When you're a basketball player and you have just two hours in practice or in a game, and that's the entire amount of time you have in a day, you've got to get it right. We're not stringent on it, and we've backed off. Because if I was still coaching? Forget it. It would be like being in the military. But I'm not. And so I'm not going to put that kind of thought on Spoelstra. But for LeBron, [the requirements] weren't harsh. They were just different.

"He had a hard time with all of that stuff in the beginning. But I remember saying to him, 'Maybe this is the one thing you missed. Maybe you didn't have this in Cleveland. Maybe this is all you need. Just give it a try.'"

LeBron's everyday lifestyle, which had revolved around his tastes and whims in Cleveland, was supplanted by Riley's insistence on winning habits. The goal for LeBron in the new millennium would be the same it had been for Magic Johnson in the 1980s. "You practice every single day through repetition," Riley said. "Same words, same terminology, same time, same place, same things. Repetition, repetition, repetition. Process, process, process, to get things right. And once you've disciplined yourself to a plan, it is a big breakthrough for fifteen guys to take great pride in something that might be a little bit difficult or uncomfortable for them. And then, when you leave, you were privileged to have been part of it because you learned something different."

The differences for LeBron were everywhere. His advisers — among his closest friends from childhood — were no longer escorting him onto the team plane, which was another jarring change from Cleveland, where the Cavaliers had feared the consequences of making LeBron unhappy. "This is a business trip," Riley said. "Back in the '80s with the Lakers, the players came to me and said, 'We don't want our families to travel.' Once you allow one or two to come, then you've got friends and cousins and parents coming. It doesn't become a hardcore basketball team trying to go kick ass on the road. It becomes sort of a traveling party."

LeBron had given up the uniform number 23 that he had worn in Cleveland in the belief — no doubt resulting from a conversation with Riley — that Jordan's number should be retired throughout the NBA. He was wearing number 6 out of respect for his second-favorite player, Julius Erving.

More charitable appearances were assigned to the players of the Heat than had been expected in Cleveland. "We had more team functions and parties to get everybody integrated," said Riley. As much as LeBron was aware of his own need for structure and discipline, it wasn't easy to yield to Riley's "covenants" on top of all of the negative pressure he had brought upon himself with *The Decision*.

The Miami principles that were alien to LeBron were taken in stride by Dwyane Wade, who accepted the tedium and devotion as fees that had to be paid for his membership in the high society of championship basketball. His eight years with Riley had delivered one title already, and by example Wade was guiding LeBron toward the promise of many more. The underlying message was that Wade was the leader of this team, which amounted to an entirely new perspective for LeBron.

Over the course of the 2010–11 season LeBron would spend less time altogether at Miami's practice facility than he had spent at Cleveland's, where he used to show up early and make himself at home. In Miami he did not appear so comfy: He would arrive for practice on time and leave after his requirements had been met. "He never once came up to me and said something about the coaching or the training or any of that stuff," Riley said. By no means was he breaking the rules or flouting authority. LeBron was doing all that was asked of him, and that was the difference here: He wasn't calling the shots anymore. It was as if his failures in Cleveland had stripped him of his rank and privileges.

In the opening month of the season the Heat players were gathered to watch an ESPN documentary of the notorious football program at the University of Miami, and its implication was clear. The Miami Hurricanes had been able to win several NCAA championships — in spite of their controversial behavior and the national backlash to it — because the players had embraced their role as the villains of college football. The reason this message would backfire on the Heat was that LeBron, as responsible as he was for his new team's vilification, wanted no part of playing the villain. His popularity among consumers was in free fall: Only 14 percent of Americans viewed him in a positive light, and in the category of most disliked NBA players LeBron ranked behind only Kobe Bryant. "Instead of his change to the Heat being seen as the best way he can win a championship," said Henry Schafer, executive vice president of the Q Scores Company, "many have looked at it and how he chose to announce it as a selfish move."

LeBron had lost no sponsors as a result of *The Decision*, and his $34 million in off-the-court earnings continued to lead the league. At the same time, the hatred that he was experiencing didn't propel him to prove everyone wrong so much as it appeared to weaken him. The good-or-evil question of his identity was distracting and draining, and it knocked him back on his heels. After the screening of the documentary, the Heat were crushed 93–77 on their home floor by the Indiana Pacers.

They lost again at the end of that week in Dallas to drop to 9-8 for the young season. It was during that fourth loss in five games that LeBron bumped shoulders with coach Erik Spoelstra in an incident that made national news. A timeout had been called, and while Spoelstra was walking onto the court, glancing the other way like an exiting subway passenger, LeBron rammed into his shoulder as the players approached their bench. LeBron and Spoelstra were both stubborn and frustrated, and wanting the other to step aside. "That, to me, was nothing," said Riley. "I mean, God, I used to charge out on the court and meet players and grab them by their chest, by their jersey."

Doc Rivers and Paul Pierce had had their public differences in Boston, but at least they had been given room to breathe. LeBron was under heavy media surveillance, to the gratification of the large national audience that rooted for his failure and cheered his every embarrassment. After their Thanksgiving weekend loss to the Mavericks, the Miami players held a long private meeting in the visitors' locker room, to be followed two days later by an ESPN report that cited their supposed unhappiness with Spoelstra. "If anything, he's been too tough on them," said a league source who was quoted anonymously. "Everybody knows LeBron is playful and likes to joke around, but Spoelstra told him in front of the whole team that he has to get more serious. The players couldn't believe it. They feel like Spoelstra's not letting them be themselves."

The source of the report was clearly someone complaining on behalf of Le-Bron. "Anybody inside of his 'family' that may have made those kinds of accusations early in the process — before we'd played twenty games — just didn't understand the dynamics of really building this team," Riley said.

The day after the Heat's loss in Dallas, Riley asked LeBron, Wade and Bosh to meet him in his office for ten minutes. He asked how things were progressing. "They just said, 'We're not feeling it,' or something like that," Riley said. "We talked about the typical things that we have to do, have patience and all of that stuff. And I remember LeBron looking at me, and he said, 'Don't you ever get the itch?' I said, 'The itch for what?' He said, 'The itch to coach again?' I said, 'No, I don't have the itch.' He didn't ask any more questions, and I didn't offer any more answers. But I know what it meant, and I always go back and wonder about what he was thinking at that time. He walked out scratching his leg like it was itching."

During the Heat's recruiting pitch to LeBron in Cleveland, a similar question had been raised. "They wanted to know what was going to happen with Erik," Riley said. "They wondered if I was going to be coaching. I said, 'Look, Erik is the head coach, that's it. I support him. I'm not interested in coaching.' The thought was in their mind at times that maybe I would come back and coach, I think. But I was truly done, I didn't want to get back into it, and Erik is a hell of a coach. He was coming off two good playoff years, but he had not been coaching three superstars. And then with the whole LeBron effect, it would have been a tough transition for any head coach with two years of experience."

LeBron's own choices had led him to this miserable time in his life. He had been cast originally as the NBA's protagonist — the new star crusading for more teamwork in basketball — but now he had become the antagonist. He was the antihero, infamous, a negative force who elicited cynical reactions. He was allowing the environment to define him, when it was supposed to be the other way around.

"He's got a very human side to him," Riley said. "There are a lot of human qualities. He tries to show great strength and be stronger than he is. He's not the easiest player to manage. But he's above and beyond what a coach would want. He's competitive. He's in shape. He's world-class. He wants to win.

"He's got all of the other stuff in his celestial world," Riley said of LeBron's off-the-court interests. "But he wants to win more than anything. He needs to win."

There was an odd powerlessness to this phenom who could do more with a basketball than anyone in the brief history of the American game. LeBron had emerged as the one to whom things happened, a victim of forces that he had been expected to command. LeBron had everything going for him — talent, money, fame, youth — but he had no home. He spent the first six weeks of the 2010–11 season pacing back and forth across the court and country, anxiously and without purpose, until the night he returned to the Miami locker room after an easy victory over the Detroit Pistons. A warning had been scrawled on the whiteboard:

Snow 20's

This was the game LeBron had been dreading. He and his new teammates were going to shower and dress and take a bus to the airport for their flight to Cleveland. He was returning to his former home, with no hope of making things right.

CLEVELAND: *December 2, 2010*

As the team plane approached Cleveland, the conversation on board grew quiet. The Heat players, coaches and staff recognized the trouble into which they were being drawn. They also knew that LeBron was worthy of their efforts to help him — that they would all benefit if only he could find his way. "This family, his new family, has his back and loves him truly and dearly," Wade told reporters in the Miami locker room before taking off for Cleveland. He was holding his teammates accountable for his own investment and belief in LeBron. "It's a special game for our brother."

The Heat recognized that the loathing they faced in other arenas had been relatively harmless. Even in Boston there had been a sense of humor, as if the fans meant to boo and taunt for three hours and then go home and forget all about LeBron until next time. What he and his teammates were about to experience in Cleveland was something else entirely.

LeBron had been loved in Cleveland, and that love had been exploited and used as leverage by him for the sake of his TV show. Throughout his seven seasons at home he had encouraged his fans to believe in him — until that one night when he had decided that he had no use for them anymore. He had made a lot of people in Northeast Ohio feel foolish for their support of him.

There was talk among the players, when LeBron was out of earshot, of the hostility they were feeling in Cleveland, even from the staff of the hotel where they were staying absent LeBron. "At the airport there was a car that took him to his house in Akron," Riley explained. "He did not go to the team hotel."

That night a story was put out to reporters that LeBron's friends had been barred from their former parking spots at the Quicken Loans Arena, named after the Internet mortgage company founded by Cavaliers owner Dan Gilbert. It was a night of hurt feelings.

In the visitors' locker room the Heat could hear LeBron's enemies roaring from their seats as if daring him to come out and show his face. Riley had stayed home in the belief that his presence would inflame them further. He had talked to LeBron about his own return to New York six months after his 1995 departure from the Knicks, to whom he had faxed his letter of resignation after winning fifty-five games and losing in the second round of the playoffs. "Gutless" had been the headline on the back page of the *New York Post* the next day.

"I was 'Pat the Rat,' 'Benedict Arnold' — absolute hatred," said Riley, who had left to become coach and president of the seven-year-old Heat franchise in Miami. "They had sent letters to my wife, called out my kids in school. Death threats are scary, and they were real — they were there. When I went back to New York for the game, I had the same kind of anxiety. I was walking down the corridor in the back of Madison Square Garden and they had a camera right on the locker room door when I walked out, and I could hear this thunder of boos before I had even gotten to the court.

"They saw me walking down the hallway and they were just waiting to pounce on me," Riley said. "I was a little bit hammish about it, but I went to the middle of the court and I waved my arms to everybody to bring it on. I couldn't wait to get out of there."

It was the same now in Cleveland. The noise penetrated the locker room's thick walls, and then it increased and sharpened as LeBron and his teammates dashed single file onto the court. LeBron was trying to mask his feelings, but he was no good at it. A clenched smile was frozen in place as he warmed up on the court; he wanted to appear relaxed, but the muscles around his eyes would not give. During *The Decision* he had looked anxious, and now he looked afraid. There were extra security officers everywhere. Among themselves his teammates had agreed that they were going to jump on and pummel anyone who came near to threatening LeBron. Wade was right: They were in this together.

The implicit threat of physical violence was offset, almost comically, by the arrivals of some Cleveland celebrities, which were broadcast on the arena's huge video screens: the TV actor and game-show host Drew Carey, who was a native of Cleveland; the Cleveland Indians' designated hitter, Travis Hafner; and retired Cleveland Browns quarterback Bernie Kosar, as well as many current Browns players. The loudest greeting was for Gilbert, who had criticized LeBron and accused him of quitting on his team and his fans.

For as long as LeBron had played in this arena, he had been responsible for its environment — for its optimism when he won, for its disappointment when he lost, and now for this volcanic anger. In other cities he would appear to ignore the enemy crowd and not take their jeering personally; but for this night he needed to focus on his enemies in order to fortify himself against them. He could not allow them to break him down and defeat him. In 1995 Riley's rebuilding Heat had been clobbered 89–70 in his return to New York, which did not reflect on him personally. But the circumstances were different for LeBron. He could not allow Cleveland to define him as a weak-minded loser. The fans were asserting themselves in spite of LeBron, and he needed to spite them back.

This was the night when LeBron would begin to realize that he was not isolated. He and his teammates went to the bench for their final instructions from Spoelstra. It was too loud for the coach's words to be heard. They waited in their huddle around him as he appeared to scribble a play on a small erasable whiteboard. He turned the whiteboard to face them and it read:

BAND OF BROTHERS

This was the same message that had been written on the larger whiteboard in the visitors' locker room earlier that evening. It was the title of a book telling the World War II story of the soldiers of Easy Company, written by the historian Stephen Ambrose, who drew the title from a speech in Shakespeare's *Henry V*:

> *From this day to the ending of the world,*
> *. . . we in it shall be remembered —*
> *We few, we happy few, we band of brothers*

Later in the season, following the All-Star break, LeBron and his teammates would return to Miami to find quotes from *Band of Brothers* framed on the walls of their locker room. This was the other side of the Riley Way: The discipline, focus and grinding work were meant to bond LeBron and his teammates in pursuit of a goal that elevated them all.

Now, at the scorers' table in Cleveland moments before the game, the booing intensified as LeBron — in emulation of Riley's "hammish" return to New York — defiantly tossed up handfuls of talcum powder to create a brief cloud of white, a shtick that for years had caused fans to rain approval on him. Were his fingers trembling?

The first goal of his teammates and coaches was to make sure LeBron didn't lose. No matter how well or poorly he played, this was the game he had to win. The Heat had decided to focus their attack on Mo Williams, the point guard who was Cleveland's most important and emotional player. Immediately after tip-off Wade intercepted Williams for a breakaway dunk, and then the Heat blitzed Williams on a pick-and-roll to force a timeout. When play resumed, the Heat backed off Williams and encouraged him to attempt and miss a long jump shot. The game was only one minute old, and Williams was already well on his way to a futile night of 2-for-8 shooting with 4 turnovers.

At the other end of the floor LeBron was sinking his first jump shot. He fed Wade for a couple of scores going to the basket, he blocked the shot of 7-footer Ryan Hollins, and he scored or assisted on all of Miami's final 16 points of the first quarter, giving them a 31–23 lead. Miami's advantage was up to 19 points at halftime, and by the third quarter LeBron's channeled anxiety was giving way to euphoria. He made 10 of 12 shots for 24 points in that quarter alone, and for the game he totaled 38 points with 8 assists and no turnovers.

This was the first sign of the star he would become by way of the repetitive process. "I don't think you could have a game like he had unless there was some kind of real calmness there inside of him," Riley said. "It showed how great he can compartmentalize and play."

But then there was the other side of LeBron. After making shot after shot, he kept running past the Cavaliers' bench, yelling taunts at his former teammates and grabbing at the shirt he had chosen at the expense of theirs. Before this game, with a couple of exceptions, the Cleveland players had refused to acknowledge LeBron, but now, instead of ignoring them in return, he was taking the low road.

So frustrated was Cavaliers center Anderson Varejao, a young Brazilian who had loved LeBron during their six years together, that he finished one skirmish by yanking off LeBron's headband and tossing it aside like the crown of a king he no longer recognized. This passive-aggressive tack by LeBron would be the norm throughout his first regular season away from Cleveland: He would have his way against the opponents he could bully, but the better teams would stand up against him.

LeBron's fears of facing up to *The Decision* had given way to an assertive 118–90 victory. That result, and the overall record of 19-63 that the hopeless Cavaliers would earn in his absence that season, would confirm that LeBron had made the right choice in leaving. Later in December Cleveland would launch an NBA-record twenty-six-game losing streak that would not end until February. The way he had left had been beneath him, but his desire for more talented teammates was unimpeachable. "The year before, they had the best record in the NBA," Boston coach Doc Rivers said of the Cavaliers. "Think about that. They had the best record in the NBA, and then he leaves, they keep everybody else, and they're the worst team in the NBA. That's just an amazing thing."

When Michael Jordan quit the Chicago Bulls abruptly in 1993 in order to play minor league baseball, they won fifty-five games without him the following season. Without LeBron, however, the mediocrity of the Cavaliers players was revealed. "People don't realize how great he is," said Doc.

But his talent was not at issue. It was his behavior and his priorities that the fans were intent on defeating.

He put on a false show from the bench throughout the fourth quarter of his homecoming, conversing with teammates as if everything was normal, and pointing to faces in the crowd as if he was happy to be back. In the meantime a battery was being thrown onto the court, thirty-six signs and shirts were being confiscated, four fans were being ejected and another placed under arrest, and fourteen security officers were guarding the Miami bench. At the end of the game they formed a human tunnel to protect the players and staff on their way to the locker room. By then, of course, most of the fans, including Dan Gilbert, had been gone from the arena for some time.

"I have the utmost respect for this franchise," said LeBron afterward, "the utmost respect for these fans." And that was all true — now. He respected them now that he realized the extent of their power, now that his treatment of them had incited a national revolt against him. But now was too late.

INDIANAPOLIS: *February 15, 2011*

When LeBron played against the Indiana Pacers in downtown Indianapolis, he could glance beyond the court to see the godfather of basketball's heartland, Pacers president Larry Bird, staring back from his seat in the lower corner of the stands.

Bird was the John Wayne of the NBA: He stood by and defended the principles of his own code, and so far he had kept his opinions of LeBron to himself.

Michael Jordan and Magic Johnson had second-guessed LeBron for conspiring with his rivals, Wade and Chris Bosh, instead of trying to beat them. Bird, surprisingly, took a more sympathetic view.

It helped that Bird had been dealing with LeBron's generation in his management of the Pacers, who were still recovering from their devastating 2004 brawl in Detroit. They were rebuilding with young players like 20-year-old Lance Stephenson, a 6-foot 5-inch rookie guard who had been a teenaged AAU star while growing up in Brooklyn. Stephenson's premature fame had been based on the precedent set by LeBron.

"He's very immature," Bird said. "He's really working on it though, he's really trying. I get killed around here in the press because I say Lance is our best basketball player, and they all get pissed off. But they look at the game different than I do. He's the only guy that can make a play out there that nobody else can make. The fucking kid is good; he bullies people because he's so strong. He might be an asshole out there, but he's our best basketball player."

Stephenson's $750,000 salary made him the lowest-paid Pacer in 2010–11, and he would play in only twelve games as a rookie. Even so he was alienating teammates by refusing to accept his place at the bottom of the hierarchy while insisting he was a better player than his performances showed. In his day Bird might have had little use for such an entitled teammate. But times had changed, and Bird recognized the upside in helping Stephenson rise above his upbringing.

By the time Stephenson was 15, a courtside announcer at a summer tournament had nicknamed him "Born Ready." Throughout his junior year of high school the online reality show *Born Ready* was being produced around him, and, much like LeBron, he had his media nickname, "Born Ready," tattooed on his right biceps. "It's all over the league," said Bird of the entitlement expressed by young players. He had nonetheless gambled a second-round pick on the teenager, even though Stephenson had been the victim of a great fraud. No one, not even Bird himself, ever was born ready.

Stephenson's family had viewed him as their savior since he was a teenager. "His dad runs around here like a little kid," Bird said. "His mom's the only one that's got a maturity about her. His dad's a great guy, but shit, he's playing his life through Lance. I say, 'You can't be his friend. You got to be his dad.'"

Bird told a story of how the older Pacers followed tradition by demanding that the rookies bring in doughnuts each morning. "Which is stupid," said Bird. "And Lance didn't do it one day, and them guys down there were pissed. So I was down there and I said, 'Lance, they've been doing this for years, and I know it's stupid but . . .'

"He goes, 'Hey, look.' He goes, 'Mr. Bird, I just want to tell you. Coaches used to get *my* doughnuts.'"

It was easy to imagine: The AAU coach knew that if he didn't bring doughnuts, Born Ready was going to find someone else not only to bring them but also to ask if they should have jelly in them.

"I believe it too," said Bird, grinning. "Pretty good line, wasn't it?"

Bird's ongoing mission to rebuild the Pacers was eating away at the wealth of his experience and perspective. As hard as things had become for LeBron, at least he was winning games and positioning himself for a shot at the championship. The real pain, from where Bird sat, was to enter a season with little or no hope of winning. These were the hardest years that Bird had ever endured in basketball. Throughout high school, college and the NBA, he never had a losing season. He had been the NBA's Most Valuable Player three straight years and Coach of the Year once, and he had played or coached in six NBA Finals while winning three of them. Now the Pacers were in the midst of their third straight losing season under his control. Worse, they were losing by his design.

As the leader of a small-market franchise with no access to a free agent like LeBron, Bird's only hope was to rebuild by drafting and developing young players. The Pacers were in the final season of their three-year plan to reach the playoffs, which Bird had imposed in no small part because he couldn't stand losing. "I told my staff, 'Look, it's going to be rough, but I'm here, I'll take the blows,'" Bird said. "We had people starting to doubt on the inside, and they were frustrated. Well, what do you think about me? I never been through nothing like this."

In his familiar seat in Indianapolis, in an arena of red brick and dark green steel that raised memories of the romantic Indiana gyms in which boys like him played while growing up, Bird found himself studying LeBron with empathy and envy while the fans booed. On this particular night LeBron was bullying Bird's Pacers as the Heat ran out to a 41–17 lead in the opening quarter. "I tell you," said Bird, "when he comes in here, I just sit there and watch him the whole time."

His eyes followed LeBron wherever he went on the court, with the ball or without. "The whole time," said Bird. "How he moves, where he's at. I never seen nothing like that. Michael's great, Magic was great. This kid's different. He's different — the way he plays, and the power. He's got it all, man."

Bird could relate to LeBron's unselfishness and vision on the floor, which had defined Bird and his rival Magic Johnson. But neither he nor Johnson could identify with LeBron's athleticism and strength. How must it be to play this game without physical limitations? He recognized his own software in LeBron, but the hardware was something else entirely.

"He's the one guy that I can watch play basketball all day long," said Bird. "Because he's got a couple things I didn't have: jumping ability, which I never thought was that big of a thing in our league, and he's got that speed. That's the first thing I noticed about Jordan, how quick he was, how he could cut down passing lanes. You see him three foot behind a guy and you make the entry pass — he's already in there. You always had to watch them guys, especially when you're a passer, because they can get there and get a hand on it. LeBron's the same way. You can't beat that quickness in basketball."

Bird could not imagine entering the NBA straight out of high school as LeBron (or Stephenson) had done. "I would have never thought about coming in this league at 19 or 20," he said. "Ain't no way." As a 22-year-old at Indiana State he had been reclusive, not wanting to be drawn into discussions of his divorce when he was younger, his father's suicide or other private issues that were weighing on him. So he could understand how LeBron had lost his way after so many years of public scrutiny.

"I didn't get mad at him for going down there," Bird said of LeBron's move to Miami. "It hurt a lot of people's feelings, but shit, it's his life, it's his game." Bird recognized that what LeBron had done wasn't as damaging as the way he had done it. "He's just a kid, you know?" Bird went on. "I mean, come on. We all make stupid mistakes. I made a million of them, so what the hell."

Bird was raised poor, and surely he grew up wishing for more. And yet he wasn't jealous of the AAU world that cast teenagers like LeBron and Stephenson as future millionaires, with all the attendant pressures. Bird had grown up playing basketball innocently as the game he loved, not as the business that might house, clothe and feed his parents, siblings and friends. Even so, in spite of those off-the-court demands, LeBron's unselfishness with the ball had remained uncorrupted, which was why Bird had refused the advice of his general manager, David Morway, to acquire the Cavaliers' young forward J. J. Hickson and others who had played with LeBron in Cleveland. "Morway was trying to get me to trade for them, but I ain't taking any of them fucking guys up there," said Bird. "I said, 'You don't understand, son, them guys playing with LeBron James look a hell of a lot better than what they are.'

"LeBron James is as good as anyone I ever seen. His problem now is I think that he's waiting around and seeing what he might have to do. Dwyane will do something spectacular, and it's 'Well, maybe I should go back to him . . .'" Bird shook his head. "You got to play off reaction and feel."

That was how LeBron had played the night of his homecoming in Cleveland, when the pressure had squeezed away the questions and doubts. For that one game he had been single-minded. Somehow he needed to replicate that focus within himself — without the strain of twenty thousand people screaming for his head.

"You got to see what you got to do, and it doesn't matter who's out there," Bird went on. "You see an opening, you got to take it. I think he'll get that, because he's just so good."

All the same, Bird was told, his support for LeBron was surprising. Here was Larry Bird, who maxed out his talent, showing reverence for an unfulfilled star who had yet to win the championship.

"You can't get a better basketball player than him," Bird argued. "There ain't none out there. For years it was Kobe — Kobe doing this, Kobe doing that — and Kobe has always been one of my favorites. But I watch LeBron play, and he's got the speed, he's got the power, he can score, he can rebound, he can dribble, he's got the whole package. He's going to have his day. Guys like that, they ain't going through this league without winning it."

For a small-market team like the Pacers, one championship seemed practically beyond reach; for LeBron, however, one was not going to do. To win no more than one would be to fall short of the expectations he had set forth at his rally in Miami.

"The hype," said Bird. "They put so much on him that a world championship might not be enough."

On the night of Miami's visit to Indianapolis, the Pacers' field house was sold out for only the fifth time that season, and the reason the fans had bought every last ticket was to boo LeBron. Bird sat in the stands among them, watching LeBron silently while the paying customers cheered for their own team almost as an afterthought. They wanted to see LeBron lose, and their wish appeared to be coming true as the young Pacers worked themselves back into the game, taking the lead into the fourth quarter.

But the depth of the Pacers' bench could not offset the talents of Wade, Bosh and LeBron, who amassed 90 points between them. The game was tied midway through the fourth quarter when LeBron found himself trapped and off-balance after dribbling into the top of the key. LeBron was facing toward Bird when, cradling the ball in his left hand, he impulsively tossed it underhand, high off the glass, and with three long strides outleaped everyone to finish his self-made alley-oop with a right-handed dunk. It was the same kind of ingenuity that had defined Bird three decades earlier, and it was escalated by a burst that made Bird shake his head. It was as if a next-generation version of himself had leaped off the stage.

LeBron scored the next two baskets more routinely to put away the 110–103 victory for Miami. The loss dropped the Pacers to 24-29, with two months remaining in Bird's three-year plan.

Bird was finding the market limitations on his franchise to be much harder to manage than his own physical limitations had been. He had become the world's best player with the Boston Celtics. Now, in Indianapolis, he came to work every day knowing that a star like LeBron was beyond his reach.

After the Heat's victory over the Pacers, LeBron would catch the team flight to Toronto, where the next night another twenty thousand angry fans would be waiting for him. In Indiana, however, after LeBron moved on, the Pacers' retro gym would return to normal. Bird's field house would once again be half-empty as he sat and waited for the slow growth of his young players. How he missed the circus.

9

THE HIGHER CALLING

In March 2011 the Miami Heat were in the midst of a five-game losing streak, their worst of the season, when their bus pulled up to the AT&T Center in San Antonio for LeBron's latest match with the Spurs. "We don't want to hear anything about that it takes a long time for championship teams to be built," Spoelstra was saying to a crowd of reporters two hours before the game.

One night earlier, the front-running Heat had suffered their most embarrassing loss at home, where they had allowed the Orlando Magic to recover from a 24-point deficit in the third quarter. Now San Antonio was going to pick up where the Magic had left off: The Spurs would bury LeBron's new team with 8 three-pointers and a 24-point deficit in the first quarter. "It's over," Duncan could be seen mouthing to himself after a timeout had been called in the opening minutes by Miami.

That reaction was unusual for someone so understated as Duncan, but the ultimate outcome was familiar to LeBron. In 2007 the Spurs' sweep of the Cavaliers in the NBA Finals showed him that the highest standard of teamwork was harder to achieve than he realized. Over the past four years LeBron had lost eight of ten games against the Spurs, who had been led by the same quartet — power forward Tim Duncan, point guard Tony Parker, sixth man Manu Ginobili and coach Gregg Popovich — since LeBron's senior year of high school. Their 125–95 clobbering of Miami would be their twenty-second straight victory at home, a franchise record, and would leave them with the best record in the NBA at 51-11. "It's just better when the best teams come in here and you can really lock in and see what we have," said Duncan that night.

Ten years earlier, Duncan had gone through his own free-agency decision. He was the LeBron of his day, a 24-year-old who had already won one championship (with two MVP awards on the way), and in the summer of 2000 he was expected to take his talents to Florida and the Orlando Magic.

At that time the chief recruiter of the Magic was Doc Rivers, who had recently finished his debut season by being recognized as NBA Coach of the Year. Doc's plan was to sign Duncan along with 27-year-old All-Star small forward Grant Hill from the Detroit Pistons and, if the room could be found, 21-year-old swingman Tracy McGrady from the Toronto Raptors. Doc and his general manager, John Gabriel, the reigning NBA Executive of the Year, were attempting the same coup that Riley would execute nearby in Miami one decade later. At the end of his visit to Florida in July 2000, Duncan told Doc that he wanted to come to Orlando, but first he needed to return to San Antonio in order to talk it over with Popovich. That was a bad sign, Doc knew. "Once they leave," he said, "you're not getting them."

The crisis of his star's impending freedom would become an opportunity for Popovich, who was 51, to deepen his alliance with Duncan. For three years they had been bound together by Duncan's rookie contract, but now they would be extending their relationship by Duncan's choice. He would be committing to their partnership — which meant that Duncan would be responsible for making it work.

"I think our relationship grew stronger. Well, I know it did," said Popovich of their talks in the summer of 2000. "Because we were both — and this is a huge key — we were both totally, totally honest in every single respect. Even if I was going to lose him, or even if he was going to hurt my feelings by leaving, it didn't matter. We were still going to lay it all out there."

They debated the potential for Duncan to win championships in Orlando alongside Hill and Doc. A move to Florida would bring Duncan closer to the Caribbean, where he was born and raised, as well as to North Carolina, where his father was living. Their talks in Popovich's backyard went on into the early morning, long after Duncan's wife, Amy, had gone inside the house to sit with Popovich's wife, Erin. Duncan and Popovich were both concerned about the future of the Spurs without David Robinson, the former MVP center who in 1999 had helped Duncan win the championship. Robinson was about to turn 35, and his production was in decline.

"There were some real reasons why Timmy might go," Popovich was saying a decade later. "David was in his later years, and he wasn't 'David' anymore. He was — well, he was pretty much like Tim is now; he's not at the peak of his performance anymore. David was on the other side of performance and still playing, so there were a lot of things to think about.

"We'd sit there and we'd get to the point where it's like being slaphappy. I'd say, 'Okay, there's a guarantee, sure you're going to win there — so go! Yeah, that's fine, we'll be fine here.' That kind of thing. And he'd say, 'David's getting older, what are you guys going to do? Who are you going to bring in?' We'd joke with each other, but then we would lay it on the line. And I'd say, 'Timmy, I can't guarantee. I don't know if we're going to win a championship. Hell, I didn't know — did I know, did you know we were going to win in '99? Did I know? I didn't know. It just happened. Are we going to win again? Maybe not. I can't guarantee it.'"

When it was LeBron's turn to decide whether to leave Cleveland, there was no Popovich in whom he could trust. Following LeBron's farewell loss in Game 6 at Boston, the Cavaliers imploded: Coach Mike Brown was fired, general manager Danny Ferry resigned, and in the span of five days owner Dan Gilbert went from recruiting LeBron like a son to razing him like a divorced son-in-law. Gilbert's savaging of LeBron was proof that their relationship was nothing like the one that was being sealed in 2000 between Duncan and Popovich. LeBron, who had no mentor in Cleveland, felt no need to personally inform Gilbert of his decision because their relationship had not deepened beyond the legal contract that tied them together. Gilbert should have seen it coming: LeBron had stopped replying to Gilbert's voicemails and text messages years earlier.

"And so it was just like that, back and forth, but we sat there together," Popovich went on. "It wasn't like he was with his agent, and I'm calling, and we're doing the separate kind of baloney. We did it together. Just figuring out what would be best, and he came to me one day and he said . . . what a jerk . . . he goes, 'Yeah, I'm going to Orlando.'"

A long-held breath.

"And I just, I just stared at him, and about five seconds later, then he smiled and he said, 'I had to do that.'

"'You asshole. You had to do that.'

"But that's Timmy. He just wanted to screw with me. And I do the same thing with him. But the relationship grew stronger because of it."

Popovich, who had final say over basketball decisions in San Antonio, was by no means a typical NBA coach or team president. An Indianan from Merrillville, a suburb of Chicago, he was a 1970 graduate of the Air Force Academy, where he played point guard while aspiring to become a Cold War spy. He majored in Soviet studies and learned to speak Russian, and his five-year military commitment led him on tours of Eastern Europe and Russia with an Armed Forces Sports basketball team. Maybe he spied for his country during those trips, and maybe he didn't. In either case he wouldn't say. Spies rarely do.

For six years he was an assistant coach at Air Force, and then in 1979 became head basketball coach at Pomona-Pitzer Athletics, a joint program between Pomona College and Pitzer College in Claremont, California, where his first team went 2-22. He spent seven years there, living with his wife and children in the dorm and eating in the cafeteria for one school year. Two years after he had won the Southern California Intercollegiate Athletic Conference with a record of 16-12, Spurs head coach Larry Brown hired him as an assistant. His success over the next two decades enabled him to buy a vineyard in Oregon, and the drudgery of long road trips was offset by the expensive staff dinners he looked forward to planning (and paying for) in North America's best restaurants. While visiting Paris in 2007 to attend the wedding of Tony Parker and the American actress Eva Longoria, he dined with his former player Sean Elliott at the acclaimed restaurant Le Taillevent, where Popovich spent more than $5,000 on a 1959 bottle of Château d'Yquem, a sweet dessert wine.

Much like Commissioner David Stern, Popovich was drawn to the points of view he had discovered in his travels throughout the larger basketball world. "I wanted foreign players badly," he said.

Popovich already had one in Duncan. In spite of his U.S. citizenship, Duncan tended to think of himself as an international player, because he viewed the game and its business differently than the typical American star. He was the last of the top NBA draft choices to attend four years of college, remaining at Wake Forest even though he would have been the number one pick after his junior year. His mother died of breast cancer when he was 13, and one of her last wishes had been that he and his two sisters graduate from college.

Duncan grew up as a swimmer on St. Croix in the U.S. Virgin Islands, and in 1989 Hurricane Hugo destroyed the only Olympic-sized swimming pool on the island. Duncan preferred not to swim in the ocean, out of respect for the sharks, and so in the ninth grade he began to play basketball. As Popovich saw it, Duncan's isolation from the AAU system sheltered him from viewing himself as a millionaire-to-be. "He never imagined success in the basketball world," Popovich said. "He was never coddled and never picked and never traveled across the country with this AAU camp and that camp and the other camp and told how great he was. He was outside of all of that, so it never infected him."

Popovich set out to build the team around Duncan as if he were the tree at the center of a garden. The Spurs' scouting department, led by R. C. Buford, the general manager who had been working for Popovich since 1994, would search for like-minded talent in the professional club systems of Europe and South America, where the best players signed professional contracts in their early teens and practiced twice a day. They attended high school even as they served their apprenticeships among the grown men who starred for the clubs. Tony Parker of France, Manu Ginobili of Argentina and eight other immigrants would play for the Spurs in the first decade of the new millennium. The NBA's goal internationally was to export its business around the world, but Popovich's focus was on importing the foreign idealism of basketball.

"They're all like clones in a sense that they're selfless and they have a passion to win and they really enjoy each other's success," said Popovich. "These foreign kids, we've all seen it in the last ten to fifteen years, how well they play together and what kind of team ball they play, how they move without the ball, how they pass the ball. It's bred into them from day one, and very few of them, if any, are coddled. They don't demand, expect or feel they're entitled. And that's a huge psychological, emotional sort of a milieu for a coach to work with."

It was as if a grand exchange was in the works: In return for the players' investment in the team, Popovich would help bring out the best in them as individuals. Because he believed so devoutly in this higher calling of basketball, he was able to express it in every aspect of his life.

In July 2006, in New York City, a lone man came in out of the rain and sat at the bar of a small Italian restaurant to order dinner. The place was empty in the early evening of midweek. "The manager in the kitchen calls me over and says, 'Do you know who that is?'" said the bartender, Mary Margaret O'Hara, a 26-year-old American. The manager, a young immigrant from basketball-mad Serbia, whispered to her that the customer was Gregg Popovich.

When his meal arrived she congratulated him on the Spurs' recently concluded season. "He looked a little surprised to be recognized," O'Hara said. Or perhaps he was wounded: His most talented team had been upset weeks earlier, in overtime, in Game 7 of the Western Conference Finals by Dirk Nowitzki's Mavericks. It had been Popovich's most painful loss thus far.

Popovich ordered the most expensive bottle on the menu, a $160 Super Tuscan, and chatted with O'Hara as he sat at the bar and dined on grilled monkfish with saffron. He mentioned briefly, for the manager's sake, that his mother was Croatian and his father was Serbian; he spoke of his wife and their children, a son and a daughter. O'Hara said that she had a cousin who was a teacher in San Antonio, and that one of the Spurs players had recently visited the classroom on behalf of a charity.

"I said, 'You just finished your season. Why are you here?' He says, 'I have a routine when I finish the season. I go to my favorite place in the world where nobody knows me.' He said he spends a week in New York, he goes by himself and he disconnects like a nobody, he feels completely like a nobody," O'Hara said. "This is his routine every year, whether he wins or loses."

She described the conversation as one of those unanticipated revelations of life's priorities and ambitions, a lesson that success doesn't have to express itself egotistically. Here was a celebrity who had achieved the fame that so many people yearn for and yet he wanted no part of it. He drank his glass of wine, and along with a large tip he left the rest of the bottle for O'Hara and her co-workers to share.

"I'd often say to my friends, guess who I met? And they were impressed I had met him," she said. "But with him I was impressed because I met a very famous person and he was totally normal. I had met famous actors in the restaurant a lot, but nobody was as friendly as he was. It's memorable for me; it sounds a little bit like a fantasy. Imagine it's early summer, I'm working in New York, in Greenwich Village, there's nobody in the restaurant, a downpour begins and it looks like we aren't going to get anybody in, and literally two minutes later walks in a man, and he spends a couple of hours with us and he makes us happy. He shared his meal with us."

The importance of this lone encounter was reflected in the details of her memory five years later. She told Popovich that she had lived in Albania and Italy, and that she was fluent in Italian and Spanish. "He was sociable and friendly, not gregarious, but he knew how to ask questions," she said. "He was the loveliest person, and not in an overly fatherly way he was trying to help me find some direction. He was listening to my story, and I really liked that he was trying to help me understand you can be doing other things. We were talking and he said, 'So what the hell are you doing working as a bartender in a restaurant?' And the truth of it is I should have been doing other things."

Mary Margaret O'Hara decided to earn a master's degree in international affairs. She was recalling the dinner of Popovich by phone from Madrid, where she was a schoolteacher and an English translator of Italian and Spanish. "I've been here almost three years," she said. "I have to say I am pretty happy."

Throughout the 2010–11 season the NBA was constipated by the failed contract negotiations between the owners and players. Among the divisions was the fear that money was buying power for the biggest teams, that, the way things were going, the smaller markets could never compete with the big-city destinations.

The Spurs had defied that worrisome trend by becoming the only small-market team to win an NBA championship since 1980. Over the past three decades all of the championships — except the four earned by San Antonio, which ranked among the ten least populated NBA cities — had been hoarded by the dozen most populated markets in America.

San Antonio would never be able to compete commercially with the bigger teams. So Popovich changed the terms. In addition to the measurable qualities of size, athleticism, shooting and other skills, the Spurs made a priority of character and fiber. "By 'character,' I don't mean a guy had to be an Eagle Scout when he was growing up," Popovich said. "It means he really is over himself. He really doesn't give one damn about personal accomplishments in the sense of stats or awards. That it's about the group, it's not about me. When you talk to kids, you can tell that pretty quickly — you can tell if they have a sense of humor, if they're selfless, if they understand priorities.

"If anything was even close to being equal," he went on, in reference to two potential draft picks who might be similar athletically, "we were going to go with that guy who we felt had the fiber — he needed to have the fiber, the competitiveness, so that he wanted to hurt after a loss, so he'd go home feeling bad and staying up that night because it bothers you. There are a lot of people it doesn't really bother, they can just move on. So those two things for sure I wanted to bring to the program, even if it hurt sometimes."

By now, at age 62, Popovich was becoming known for the crotchety interviews he gave to sideline reporters during nationally televised games. He considered their questions to be an intrusion, in the way that some people regard TV and cellphones to be distractions at the dinner table. He held sacred the team's privacy as coaches and players who were united by their singular goal, the NBA championship, and his vigilance created a false impression of arrogance — as if the normal rules did not apply to the Spurs, as if they were better than everybody else.

In fact the Spurs did not believe in their own superiority. It was because of their humility that they were so devoted, understanding that nothing less than teamwork would give them a chance against the rivals they respected. When the Spurs were slumping, Duncan, Parker and Ginobili didn't lash out like other stars. Instead they took on their failures personally, as if these shortcomings were all their fault. They dwelled on their own imperfections. It was no coincidence that Dirk Nowitzki had the same response, because he shared their point of view.

The obsession with discovering the next Michael Jordan was based on a cynical assumption that the NBA had peaked in the 1990s, as if nothing could be better than the past. The Spurs held to a different point of view. They believed that teamwork was the way forward. Stars like Duncan and Dirk behaved as if money was another statistic in their box scores. It was an important statistic — they weren't chumps — but they had faith that the money would come as long as they were focused on winning the games.

While rival stars throughout the NBA were jealous of LeBron's money and celebrity, Duncan tended to feel sympathy for him. "I'm definitely glad I don't have that kind of pressure on me," Duncan would later say of LeBron. "Absolutely."

"It's about honesty," said Popovich. "If the players know you're going to tell them the whole truth and nothing but the truth, you'd be amazed what you can get out of them and what kind of trust you can develop. But you've got to be ready for the other side of it. Like, 'No, we're not going to do that.' 'No, I don't think we can do that in your contract.' 'No, that's not going to happen.' 'No, we're not staying overnight there.' Why? 'Because I just don't think it's right and because of this and this.' 'Well, I disagree with you.' 'Well it's too bad, we're doing it anyway.' Now they know who you are. Now they know what to expect. It doesn't change day to day. You don't have to blow smoke. You don't have to remember what you told them four days ago to try to get them to do X, Y or Z, because they already know what you're going to say every time. So you know what the rules are, what the parameters are, what the priorities are, how we're going to get there. And then everybody does it. But if it's changing and you have to play games constantly to get things done, it's just not going to happen."

So now, in this season of 2010–11, Popovich was dealing with the downside of honesty. In spite of the Spurs' league-leading record, he was having to be honest with Duncan, who would turn 35 during the playoffs and was no longer the everyday star of the team that had been assembled in reflection of him. He would contribute 13.4 points per game that season, the worst production of his career, and he was playing fewer than thirty minutes per night. For as long as anyone could remember, the Spurs had triumphed by playing the ball through Duncan near the basket, but now Popovich was turning them into a perimeter-based team that depended on 28-year-old Parker, 33-year-old Ginobili and others to attack from the three-point line. Their defense, always Duncan's strength, was no longer as strong as in their championship years, which meant they needed to score in bigger numbers.

"You've got to be honest with him, that 'You're not doing this the same, so we've got to do this. This isn't working the same.' And there's some times he doesn't want to hear it from me," Popovich said of Duncan. "There are some times he's part hurt, part angry that I might say a certain thing, that 'You can't do that, you can't get away with that anymore, you're going to have to do such and such.' And then as you say it, because I think it's the truth, then he has his reaction or his feeling. And then that night or the next day at practice, that's what we go and do. And if he feels differently, he'll tell me."

Popovich was making their exchanges sound matter-of-fact and perfunctory, when in truth they were at least as difficult for him as for Duncan. There was more to them than the relationship of player and coach. The end of their working life together was approaching with sudden clarity, and Popovich's feelings were complicated. He knew he had to lessen his team's reliance on Duncan. He also knew the Spurs had to make a final push to win another title, because who knew how much longer Duncan might be able to contribute? More than anything, Popovich was confronted with feelings of devotion and compassion, for here was a naturally gifted star whose gifts were in decline. He was working harder than ever for poorer results. As much as he had valued Duncan's achievements at their peak, Popovich valued these diminished results more.

"I have such a respect for the integrity that he plays with in the game," Popovich said, glancing away as he spoke. "People will never know what he does all summer long so he can continue to play. Sometimes I wonder, 'Should he play?' I look at that knee, I look at that leg, and I wonder. You see him, he walks and it doesn't extend. Then the things that he goes through and the swimming and the boxing to keep his body trim — you know his body fat is unbelievable — and to keep his aerobic base all during the year, and then he works on that leg to get extension, to try to get as much extension as he can. And then we spend the year to try to keep him there and not let it deteriorate, and I see him in the games and he'll try to do something that maybe he was able to do, and now it didn't work out, and I can just see the frustration in his face. And that's when I really respect him. Because he doesn't cry, he doesn't moan, he just gets down on the other end. He just keeps trying to do it the best he possibly can. But certain things he can't do the same, as we all know, and no player can as we get older. And that gives me more respect for him than when you watched him before and he would just do what he did and you'd go, 'Wow!'"

He took a breath.

"Okay, you did that," Popovich went on. "But now that you don't have those abilities, and you're still trying to do it the best way you can and not cry and moan, and 'I wish this' or 'If only' . . . it just never comes out of his lips."

Three weeks remained in the regular season when Duncan attempted a jump shot and landed on the foot of an opposing defender. He lay awkwardly on the court, grasping his left foot in anguish, until he was helped off the floor to the locker room. He would miss the next four games, and the Spurs would lose all of them.

For close to five months they had been the best team in the NBA, and up until Duncan's injury the Spurs' best players had remained healthy. Now that Duncan was gone, they couldn't score enough to make up for their weakened defense. A large-market rival like the Dallas Mavericks could afford a season-ending injury to one of their most productive players, Caron Butler, because they were spending a total of $87 million on the salaries of their deep roster. But the small-market Spurs could not survive without the contributions of Duncan, in whom they were investing more than one-fourth of their $70 million budget for players that season.

In the final, meaningless game of the regular season, Manu Ginobili was running around a Duncan screen when his non-shooting arm was pinned between Duncan and Grant Hill of the Phoenix Suns. Ginobili's right elbow was dislocated, and his arm was fractured. He would miss the opening game of the 2011 playoffs before playing the remaining five games with a heavy brace around his elbow.

"I knew we were done," Popovich admitted later. The Spurs were the number one seed in the West, and their playoffs were ended before they'd begun. "When I realized that he couldn't even play in the first game and probably shouldn't have played after that, it was no way," he said. "My heart went in my feet."

Their misfortune overwhelmed Popovich. He dwelled on all their years of hard work and how few more chances Duncan might have, and he watched Ginobili shoot free throws one-handed during their doomed series against the Memphis Grizzlies because he couldn't raise his broken arm.

"To have that happen the very last game of the season was just incredible," said Popovich. "And you know the way I got through it? I think by the time I got on the bus I told myself, 'Quit your crying. Things go for you or things go against you.'"

For the sake of his own perspective he came up with this Faustian bargain: "The basketball gods will make Manu healthy," he said. "But you have to take Tim Duncan away from that draft. You didn't get him."

He was forcing himself to zero in on the good luck that had enabled a 2-22 coach from Pomona-Pitzer to win four NBA championships.

All of a sudden this is how Popovich was scolding himself, in those hours after Ginobili's injury: "'You think everything's supposed to go your way in life? Is it all supposed to go your way? What kind of asshole are you, you think you deserve everything go your way? You think there aren't like nine thousand other coaches that would like to have Tim Duncan on their team? You think Rick Pitino would like to have Tim Duncan in Boston when he was the G.M. and he called me and said, "Hey, I'll trade you anything, let me know what you want." You think he'd like to have Duncan? I think so.'"

Their season had ended weeks earlier, and Popovich was looking ahead to the time when Duncan would no longer be his partner. He was thinking about Jerry Sloan of the Utah Jazz, who for eighteen years coached Karl Malone and John Stockton. Since 2003, when Stockton retired and Malone moved on to the Lakers for one last run in vain at the NBA championship, Sloan had been rebuilding his program with young players.

"Yeah, we want to try to keep it going," Popovich said of following Sloan's example. "When those guys left and he started it up all over again, I think most people thought that thing was dead, and 'What the hell are they going to do after those two? It's dead. There's no way.' And they continued to play the exact same way, with success, with wins, with quality, with pride — it's just inspiring to see that."

There was, of course, another kind of lesson built into Sloan's story. In February, shortly before the 2011 All-Star Game, Sloan had been driven to retire after a series of disagreements with his young All-Star point guard Deron Williams, who showed little interest in deferring to the higher calling. As Popovich moved to rebuild his program, the traits of character and fiber would be ever more important, and he would travel far and near to find them.

10

THE IMMIGRANT

The third quarter was ending as Brandon Roy pulled up for a three-pointer.

He was nearing the end of his brief All-Star career in Portland, as was foreseen five years earlier by the Celtics' doctor in Boston. Roy's knees had given out abruptly, as if they were twice as old as the rest of him. His production had collapsed, his minutes had been slashed, and now, in Game 4 of the opening round of the 2011 NBA playoffs, his Portland Trail Blazers were being clobbered by Dirk Nowitzki's visiting Dallas Mavericks.

Roy watched his long jump shot ricochet hard back and forth within the rim, popping up to kiss the glass before tightroping along the iron and falling through the net. The response was explosive. For Dirk, it was a familiar start to another postseason failure. The Blazers were trailing by 18 points entering the fourth quarter, and yet their fans believed in the omen of that shot. Their belief was expressed ever more loudly as his teammates and then Roy himself sank shot after shot. He had been born, raised and schooled three hours to the north, marrying Roy with his fans organically as Dirk never could be married with Dallas.

There would be more jumpers and post-ups as the circuit of energy spun faster and stronger. The spiritual influence of the fans was real. Throughout the season that influence had set upon LeBron James, draining him of his power. In Portland it was empowering Roy, making him feel younger.

For Dirk, the end of the fourth quarter was like a recurring playoff nightmare played out beyond his reach: From the far side of the lane he ran helplessly at the ball as Roy banked in the winning shot thirty-nine seconds from the end. Instead of the Mavericks returning to Dallas with a 3–1 lead, the series was now even after their collapse and 84–82 loss. Roy had scored 21 points over his final dozen minutes for one of the most impressive comebacks in postseason history.

Dirk was a lonesome figure as he and his teammates left the stage for Roy to celebrate with the fans. Losses like this one once again focused the blame on Dirk because, as the Mavericks' biggest star, he was held most responsible for their ongoing run of playoff failures. "It's such an American mentality," his German mentor, Holger Geschwindner, would say. Ever since his arrival in the NBA, Dirk had been the outsider in every way — nationality, culture, race, language, even his style of play and the mentoring relationship he maintained with Holger.

These thirteen seasons away from home had intensified Dirk's need to belong — to experience the connected energy that renewed Roy's authority. In 2008, when Dirk finally qualified for the Olympics after years of trying, he couldn't stop crying on the court or in the locker room, for reasons too deep for him to explain. When he carried his national flag into the opening ceremony of the Olympics in Beijing as leader of the German delegation, he grinned like the boy he had been before he met Holger. It had been more difficult than any of his rival American stars could realize for Dirk to leave behind the people and place he loved in order to pursue his NBA dream, which was always evolving and unlikely ever to come true. There had been many times when he had asked himself why he was playing in this hostile league and for what larger cause he had abandoned his home and happiness.

Now, in 2011, Dirk was 32 years old. He was used to managing the loneliness and isolation, and the despair of losses like this one in Portland. As the Mavericks showered and dressed quietly, they waited for inspiration from Dirk of the kind wielded by Roy.

"He's not the verbal leader that you want sometimes," said Brian Cardinal, who along with Jason Kidd had been urging Dirk to speak up. At times like this over the course of the season, they had pulled Dirk aside to plead with him: "You've got to say something."

But there was nothing to be said. The next evening, back in Dallas, he and Holger would be in the gym by themselves, preparing for Game 5 the following day.

Dirk's American teammates were incapable of empathizing with him — of grasping his desire to provide leadership, to tap into the spiritual energy that Brandon Roy claimed as a birthright. After all these years Dirk had developed his own punishing response to these losses: He embraced his humiliation, he held himself to account more harshly than he blamed his teammates, and he did everything he could to live up to the demands he made of himself. The only response he knew was to revert to the method in which he had been grounded years ago and thousands of miles away. It was a ritual that had governed the second half of his life — the half that began when Holger discovered him.

Holger flips open the laptop to tap into the computing power and graphics that were not yet available in the 1990s, when he began to help Dirk discover his potential. At 66 Holger has mastered the newest technologies in order to create a visual language for his ideas. He clicks open the sophisticated program that he has refined over the years. On the screen is a lanky stick figure meant to resemble Dirk in profile as he shoots the basketball. Holger commands the stick man to release his jump shot, and what happens next is as natural as the reaction of a still pond to the impact of a heavy stone. A wave of energy begins around the feet and ankles, and that energy surges through the bending knees in a smooth, shivering wave up through the body's segments, culminating in the spinning of the ball away from the tips of the man's fingers. Which is exactly the way Dirk has been taught to shoot, his right hand flicking naturally, like a wave turning over on the shoreline.

"Coming from a soccer country," says Holger of himself, "I make sure everything I tell is not my opinion." The computer animation is meant to neutralize his German accent and his foreign point of view. It has been designed to withstand the scrutiny of American basketball coaches, "the little gods over here," as Holger calls them. His program takes into account every variable he can imagine — the length of the feet, the forearm and the upper arm, and all such relevant measurements and weights necessary to the laws of physics. He has even accounted for the resistance of air, he says: "On a long shot it makes a huge difference."

Holger manipulates the stick figure as if toying with a puppet's strings. When the ball comes out of Dirk's hand on a flatter line, it is less likely to find its way down through the basket. The higher the arc, the more routinely he scores.

Dirk would transform the coding of this theory into something natural and smooth: the elbow here, knees bent like so, chin raised squarely, mouth open, fingers splayed to touch the ball there and there and there. "Holger wants him to breathe at a certain time," said Casey Smith, the Mavericks' athletic trainer. "None of it is left to circumstances. It's all thought through."

In the beginning Holger tried to build a lesson plan for Dirk from the biographies and how-to manuals of the NBA's greatest coaches and stars. Then he realized that their approaches could not be replicated. Their shooting styles and the paths of their careers could not be refitted to Dirk's unprecedented specifications.

So he approached Dirk's shooting as if it were a scientific experiment. Holger took into account the size of the ball in relation to the size and height of the basket, the pressure exerted on the ball by the shooter's fingertips. To broaden his perspective he investigated the fine touch applied by pianists and violinists to their instruments, in pursuit of a shooting form that could be duplicated in a variety of conditions as played out in his modeling, first with pencil and paper and later with a computer. "Figuring it out," he said, "you know the most precise, or the smallest amount of, pressure you can [apply to] direct the ball in anger or in pleasure. And if you know that, you can figure out where is the point where you can make the most mistakes, and the ball still goes in; and if you have that, then you can take riskier shots."

The idea was to create a shooting stroke that would score baskets with consistency in spite of the frantic collisions and pace of the game. Dirk would not have the luxury of a golfer who can stand over every putt with the same measured form, or of a batter who can pose in the same stance, or of a pianist or violinist seated upright in a pitch-quiet hall. Dirk would be chasing and jumping and fighting for his balance against American players dead set on intimidating him physically and emotionally. Dirk's shooting stroke would have to account for shortness of breath and imperfections of balance and fear of failure. Could Dirk do in the real world what the stick man was doing in Holger's imagination? Could the theory of succeeding in American basketball be brought to life?

Holger dreamed and worked in a small German castle near Bamberg, in the Free State of Bavaria. His original sketches and calculations in pencil were in the spirit of Leonardo da Vinci's drawings. He wished to make sense of the American sport scientifically in order to liberate its natural beauty. "What I love about the game is you do not shoot to a goalie and try to kill the guy," he said, comparing Old World soccer with New World basketball. "So you have to be a sensitive shot. I like the combination between the physical strength, the power, the ability to move and all that stuff, and the elegance of the shooting."

He would encourage Dirk to be elegant and strong, powerful yet sensitive, and to think his way through his doubts, knowing when to quiet his thoughts and play intuitively with trust. He wanted for Dirk to be endlessly generous and curious in all aspects of his young life, so that those qualities would be expressed in the way he played basketball. Long before his discovery of Dirk, Holger had studied the paradox of how basketball was taught in America, where the best young athletes were compelled routinely to focus on the game at the expense of their higher education. It made no sense to Holger that players should attend school in order to concentrate on basketball. He believed it should be the other way around. Basketball was an expression of values and disciplines and science that transcended the game. The player who was ignorant of those larger lessons was also going to be ignorant in his play. He might be able to zero in on doing one or two things well, but he would be unable to adapt as the needs of his team changed within each game and throughout his career.

When Dirk and Holger first met, Dirk had been thinking about dropping out of school in order to focus on basketball. Holger said no. "When I started working with Holger, the first thing he said was 'You're going to finish high school,'" recalled Dirk. Holger arranged for tutors to work with him in math and chemistry. When Dirk didn't feel like practicing, Holger would put the ball away, pull out a chess board and teach him how to think. "If you want to be a good player," said Holger, "you have to learn how to learn."

All of Holger's theories were tested on the court under real conditions. "Science has a big advantage: It can be proved to everybody," he said. "So if we started coming from a soccer country, where basketball is almost nothing, we had to find a way — how can we catch up or even go ahead?" From the beginning he recognized that Dirk would be competing against a horde of skeptics in America who would question his German background and his unprecedented style of play. "It's a crazy idea," Holger said, "but put it in and check it out, and if the calculation does not work, forget it. And that is the best control. We put down what we wanted to achieve, how it can be done, and then we prove whether or not we are right or wrong. We go step by step, and through research and development it's pretty much up the ladder."

Dirk proved to be a quick learner, which inspired Holger to deepen the theory while keeping his protégé engaged. Dirk's progress was measured by his performance in scrimmages against American teams traveling through Europe, as well as by his appearances with the German national team. All the while Holger remained sensitive to potential setbacks. "We never put him against the Soviets during the Cold War because of the shark pool," said Holger, wary that they would try to kill the spirit of a rising Western star.

Holger was constantly gauging the outcomes as he looked for new ways to develop Dirk's talents. "We tested it, and if I had the feeling we could get it done, so we did it," Holger said of each experimental step. "Otherwise, we tried to find a step in between. The key is, it ends with the carrot. If the carrot is too far away, you lose everything."

The carrot, as dangled by the NBA, led Dirk across the ocean in 1999. His ability to make shots was the vehicle to achieve his dream. "I said, 'Okay, if there's a 7-footer who could shoot, we could change the game,'" said Holger, who wasn't seeking to revolutionize basketball in America, just change the likely perception of Dirk. "So we concentrated on shooting."

In Germany he trained Dirk and more than a dozen other German teenagers in what Holger called his Institute of Applied Nonsense. Holger wore the focused expression of a serious person, but with bright eyes reminiscent of Eugène Boch's in the famous painting by Vincent Van Gogh — eyes that sparkled like the starry night — and he refused to drum the joy out of basketball. Instead of weight lifting, which he considered a travesty for young athletes, Holger would have his players row on the lake for several hours in the morning. In the afternoon and evening there would be instruction in basketball, and at night they would sleep on the wood floor of the gym, as if seeking to be at one with the game's nature.

Dirk remembers an experiment one afternoon at the rowing camp. The players were lined up in front of an older American of African descent who was playing jazz on a saxophone. Holger walked among the players, urging them in German to perform basketball moves to the rhythms of the music. He was marrying two of the New World's most inspiring inventions, jazz and basketball. Who in America was trying anything like this?

The saxophonist was Ernie Butler, an African American soldier from Indianapolis who was stationed in West Germany during the 1950s. In his off-hours he played jazz in the nightclubs there and basketball in the small gyms of the semipro league. Butler struck up a friendship with Holger after he watched the 17-year-old score 102 points in a game. So impressed was Butler that he offered to drive the extra half hour back and forth to Holger's boarding school so that Holger could practice with Butler's team in Giessen.

"There was a period where all the black soldiers in Bavaria would come on Saturday to Munich," said Butler. "There was a gym there, and guys would have these pickup games. We'd go out Saturday night to hit the bars and discos, and

Sunday we'd meet again at the gym. It was really like the old days in Indiana where all the guys would come together and play. I encouraged my German team to get into that because it would help them improve their game, but they either shied away or didn't feel comfortable. A couple guys came but they would sit up in the bleachers. But Holger? He had no problem saying, 'Okay, I have next game,' even though these were all black guys. And he was not just saying it — he would go and play like a maniac."

Butler believed that Holger had come along at the wrong time, before the NBA was ready to admit players from Europe into the league. "Had he been born a few years later, he would have been one of the first guys from Europe to go play in America," said Butler. "I think I'm being realistic when I say that." One thing was certain: If Holger had been given any chance to play in the NBA, he would have seized it without fear.

In 1955, when Holger was 10 years old, his parents sent him to the Paul-Gerhardt-Schule, a boarding school in Laubach named after a composer of German hymns. There, in the hours between their lessons, Holger and his classmates were taught to play basketball by the headmaster, Theo Clausen, who had won a scholarship in 1934–35 to the International YMCA College (now Springfield College) in Springfield, Massachusetts, where James Naismith had invented basketball forty-three years earlier. Clausen met at least twice with Naismith — once when Naismith returned to Springfield to receive an award, and again the following summer in Berlin, where basketball was making its debut at the 1936 Olympic Games. Naismith was invited to toss the opening jump ball.

Like Holger's father, Clausen was ordered to fight for Germany on the Russian front during World War II. After the war Clausen served as the first coach of the West German national team, based on his access to basketball at its very source. "He was one of those teachers — you are lucky if you run into him, because he loved his kids; he was really a great guy," said Holger. He remembered Clausen showing a movie of the NBA champion Boston Celtics. The images of Bob Cousy and Bill Russell inspired Holger to imagine beyond the limits of his German basketball upbringing.

The game consumed Holger, and yet there was so much more to him than his love for basketball. He started his own version of Benjamin Franklin's Junto, a club in which friends from various fields would make presentations about their careers in medicine, journalism, the arts and other areas of interest. (Ernie Butler spoke to the club on race relations in the United States.) When Holger was named captain of the West German basketball team for the 1972 Olympic Games in Munich, he pursued his interest in astrology by asking each of the opposing players for his date, time and place of birth. "He went back and did all of their horoscopes," said Butler. "He came to me and said, 'Ernie, I have bad news.' He said, 'The Americans are going to lose.'"

It was meant to happen, insisted Holger, and twice in the game for the gold medal between the United States and the Soviet Union, the officials put three seconds back on the game clock. On their third try, the Soviet team scored the game-winning basket to upset the Americans 50–49. That breakthrough created hope for players around the world that they, too, might compete with the Americans someday.

Holger was the German Jack Kerouac — traveling with a teammate and their girlfriends through the Soviet Union from Moscow through Siberia; hiking Mount Fujiyama in Japan and swimming off Hawaii; buying a broken-down UPS truck in California, repairing it and then driving it across the United States, picking up hitchhikers along the way. Holger and his companion, Elle, spent another year of exploration hitchhiking throughout the United States. One night during a trip through the Sahara, two men with guns approached his tent. He offered them coffee and talked his way out of trouble. Lesson learned? "Be as nice as possible, and get out of there as quick as possible," he said. "It's correct to be scared, but somehow it's a big advantage not to know where the danger is."

Holger had established himself as a project manager known for solving a diversity of problems — whether it was helping a German woman who was losing money on her farm in Louisiana because of false billings and phony paperwork, or designing a series of ski lifts in Spain — when he first saw Dirk as a 15-year-old playing for his local club in Würzburg, Germany. Holger had recently retired from playing basketball at age 47, and as Ernie Butler had done for him, so did Holger offer Dirk the chance to train with him several times a week. It did not occur to Dirk that this peculiar middle-aged German was two degrees of separation from James Naismith.

Dirk was a naturally gifted athlete in tennis and team handball, the sport of his father, who played internationally for Germany. Jörg-Werner Nowitzki, who ran his own business painting houses, had the impression that basketball was for women — in part because his 5-foot 10-inch wife, Helga, had played for the German national team. "Basketball was known as a noncontact sport," said Silke Nowitzki, Dirk's older sister, who also grew up playing the American game.

Within a year it became obvious that Dirk could do what Holger could not — reach the NBA — as long as he was willing to commit to the adventure in full. "I don't want to hear it from the parents; I want to hear it from his answer," said Holger. "If he wants it, I can try to help. But he has to want it."

In April 1998 Dirk was focused on leading his small club, DJK Würzburg, out of the second division and up to the highest tier of German basketball when Holger announced, with no warning, that they must travel immediately to America. Dirk had been invited to the Nike Hoop Summit, an all-star game in which a team of teenaged internationals would take on the best American high school players. "I said, 'Dirk, tomorrow we fly to San Antonio,'" recalled Holger, who had kept his plans secret in order to save Dirk from the distraction.

The local newspapers were killing Holger for his sabotage of the Würzburg X-Rays, so named because Wilhelm Röntgen had discovered the X-ray in his laboratory at the University of Würzburg. But Holger knew this was Dirk's chance to escape — and elevate — German basketball. He and Dirk arrived in San Antonio in the evening, during an official banquet for the Hoop Summit, which included Sandro Gamba, the Italian coach of the International Select Team, and his assistant, Donnie Nelson, who was chief aide to his father, Don Nelson, the new head coach of the Dallas Mavericks. Donnie Nelson was headed down to the lobby to escort Dirk and Holger to the banquet when he was stopped by a Nike representative.

"One of the Nike guys says, 'Dirk's welcome, Holger isn't,'" recalled Nelson. This was no way to welcome a visitor after a long overseas trip, Nelson argued. At the same time he understood the rule against agents, because too many of them in America were exploiting young players. "So I take Dirk up and introduce him to the team, get him situated," said Nelson. "And then I slip out, I go down and Holger's sitting there in the frickin' lobby, you know? He's just sitting there. So I say, 'Hey, come on, let's go grab something.' So I buy him a beer, dude, buy him dinner."

Nelson listened to Holger's story. He could not believe at first the point of view to which he was being introduced by Holger.

"It's not some guy that's been to fifty Hubie Brown clinics in Europe and just recites what Hubie has said over the years, you know what I mean?" said Nelson. "A lot of it is just common sense, it's mathematics. And him being this untouched, untainted kind of presence that hasn't been multi-marketed with all of the bull crap that's out there. Because we see a lot of that. The last twenty years the U.S. coaches have been going over to Europe and doing clinics and having exchanges, and it's all good, it's great; but it's the same rehashed stuff. It's like we've taken our philosophies, and they evolve, yes; but very seldom do you run across this culture . . . like a culture that has never been discovered before.

"These are fresh, ingenious, creative — some weird, but a good weird — ideas. And some of the stuff is so aggressive and futuristic that it would blow someone's mind. Even a guy like me that has been around for so long. Now, some of it I don't agree with, candidly, but I'd say 90 percent of it is like, wow, that is a new, ingenious, creative way to teach that, or think about that, and it makes complete, total sense. It was almost like discovering a new star, or a new continent, you know what I mean?"

Holger watched the high school players on the American team warming up for the game in San Antonio as if they were trying to mimic the NBA's arrogance. "They behaved like great stars," said Holger. His instruction to Dirk was to seize the first opportunity: He wanted Dirk to drive the ball on the Americans and slam it down their throats. "I know this American mentality," Holger said. "The thing is they try to scare you the first time, and if you are, it's over."

From the three-point line Dirk flew past one defender and threw down hard with both hands as a second American was whistled for a foul. Dirk walked away muttering in German as if he were the world's toughest guy, as if he were not a suburban kid taught in the isolation of a grade school gym by a sensitive mentor. Dirk would set Hoop Summit records of 33 points and 14 rebounds as a 6-foot 11-inch power forward whose skills were a revelation: He was a big man who dribbled at full speed in the open court; who attacked the basket relentlessly for 23 free throws, making 19 of them smoothly and serenely; who knocked down a pair of three-pointers when his defenders, wary of committing more fouls, backed off.

He was better than Rashard Lewis, Al Harrington, Quentin Richardson and all of the other future NBA players on the American team that lost 104–99 that day. Thirty-six college scholarship offers would come to Dirk based on that performance, but more important was the attendance of forty NBA scouts at the game, and especially the presence of Donnie Nelson, who had already begun conspiring with his father. Two months later, in the middle of the night, a friend from America was telling Holger that Dirk had been chosen with the number nine pick in the NBA draft and then traded immediately to the Mavericks.

"I knew after the first practice," said Nelson of his interest in drafting Dirk.

"After that first practice we didn't need to scout him. Certain people evaluate and project real estate; other people do it with art; we do it with human beings that shoot a little round ball, and we get paid a lot of money for this. And if you don't know your stuff — especially when it's so obvious — you need to find another line of work."

Holger had believed in this day's coming with the faith of a scientist who trusts the conditions of his experiments. They had not yet completed their five-year scheme to lead Dirk to the NBA, though that timeline had been murky because there was so little precedent. "We were very fast in his plan because he was listening," said Holger. "In America everybody plays basketball, but they don't teach kids the details. Everybody learns to create their own shots. They have the bodies but no technique."

When Dirk agreed, tepidly, to join the NBA earlier than expected, Holger made the final preparations. In very little time Dirk was going to be alone in the New World. "I said, 'Dirk, we have to talk about what money means, and what it means to be rich,'" recalled Holger, who explained that Dirk might have a big house with a pool and a membership at the most expensive country club someday. "But that is not being creative anymore — sitting on the money and spending the money."

Holger backed up his point by refusing to accept any payment from Dirk apart from expenses. This arrangement would endure throughout Dirk's career because, as Holger insisted, money was not what their experiment was all about. "I'm having fun," Holger would say. "I get to work with a player who listens to me and learns from me. I'm doing what I want to do in a field I love."

Together they would make a second trip to America. Holger would take Dirk to Las Vegas, to expose him to the excesses. "Dirk showed no interest," said Holger with relief. "Then we went to the southern rim of the Grand Canyon." They hiked down to Phantom Ranch, rested for three hours, and then began the hike back up. Holger used the long climb to explain what lay ahead for Dirk. "Many times you think you are near the top," warned Holger, "but then you get there and find that you still have a long way to go."

"On a game day I get a phone call at five from one of the trainers," Nick Creme said. "He said, 'You need to get over to Dirk's house right away and change his tire. He can't get to the game.'"

Dirk usually carpooled to games in Dallas with his neighbor Steve Nash, but another engagement had forced Nash to drive in separately. By this time Dirk had been in America for three years.

"I'm in my slacks because I work game nights; I'm kind of dressed up," Creme said. "I go over to the house and he says, 'They sent *you*?' So I changed the tire. I got all dirty. I got the spare on in his garage, and he just sat there and watched. He had no idea how to change a tire so he could drive himself to the game. Then he said, 'Give me your cellphone number in case something happens again with this spare.' The next day he calls me because he wants to follow me over to the place to get the tire switched out. He says, 'I don't want to deal with the people by myself.'"

This was how two strangers born six weeks apart became the best of friends. Nick Creme was a 22-year-old former Division III college basketball player, a small guard who had earned an office internship with the Mavericks that led to his new full-time job with the team. Dirk was putting together an All-NBA season with astonishing skills that American basketball had never seen in a 7-footer, and yet the most mundane aspects of his new life were baffling to him. As they grew friendly, Creme would come across old snapshots of Dirk, from his rookie year in Dallas, tucked into a sleeping bag on the couch of Dirk's mostly empty condominium. "He was sleeping on the couch before he had a bed," Creme said. "It was 'What the hell am I doing in this country?'"

Paychecks in enormous amounts would lay uncashed in his TV room. When he did buy a bed, it was a twin, which was much too short for someone his size. An employee of the Mavericks, Lisa Tyner, would help Dirk manage the overwhelming details of daily life. He had never lived away from home, and now he was having to find his own way in a country where so many everyday matters were foreign to him.

The truth was that he hadn't wanted to come to America. The day after the draft, the Nelsons had arrived in Germany on a private plane to convince Dirk to accompany them back to Dallas. International players were rare in the NBA, and most of them, including Patrick Ewing and Hakeem Olajuwon, had been educated in American schools. Drazen Petrovic and Sarunas Marciulionis were among the few who had established themselves in Europe before coming to the NBA. Overall, the world's greatest basketball league was employing only thirty-eight players from outside America. The Mavericks had broken new ground by gambling a high pick in their draft-night trade for a German teenager with no meaningful experience and a counterintuitive style that he and his mentor had invented. The Nelsons couldn't begin to sell their fans on this star of the future if Dirk was unwilling to participate in the present.

In the days preceding the 1998 draft, Holger had attempted to reduce the pressure on Dirk by announcing that he would spend the next two seasons in Europe, where several of the biggest clubs were bidding to sign him for $1 million or more per season. The Mavericks tried to assuage Dirk's fears by arranging for him to play one-on-one in Dallas against their 6-9 power forward Samaki Walker, who himself had been a number nine pick in the 1996 draft after two seasons at the University of Louisville. Winning two of his four games against Walker gave Dirk some small hope that he would not be embarrassed in the NBA. He and Holger sat by Don Nelson's swimming pool until the early morning, talking over the pros and cons before agreeing to give the NBA a try.

From the moment he promised to play for Dallas the next season, Dirk was hoping there would be no season. By the time he had returned home to Würzburg, NBA commissioner David Stern had made good on his threat to lock out the players, leaving Dirk with the vague expectation that the owners' stalled contract negotiations with the players would eat up the entire 1998–99 NBA season. He spent the fall of 1998 playing for the X-Rays, until the surprise announcement of an NBA agreement in January 1999. The Mavericks opened their abbreviated training camp two weeks later, and within four days Dirk's humiliation had begun. He averaged 8.2 points while suffering multiple embarrassments in each of the forty-seven games he played during his truncated rookie season. "Go at him! He's soft!" he would hear the opposing bench yell at whomever he was guarding. After considering the strengths and weaknesses of his teammates, Dirk decided he was indeed the worst player in Dallas.

He thought hard about quitting; true to Holger's preaching, his three-year contract worth $4.7 million held no value for him. Dirk had been happier making $1,000 per month with the X-Rays. Holger would make eight trips to America to console and encourage and work with Dirk privately on the court. "The first year was tough," said Holger. "He was close to going home. I said, 'No, giving up is not an option.'"

At least he wasn't the only one. A lone source of comfort was that Steve Nash was having a hard time too. Yet, paradoxically, it was because of Nash that Dirk was now suffering in Dallas. "We weren't going to take a chance on Dirk unless there was a really, really good reason for it," said Donnie Nelson. "Well, the really, really good reason was Steve Nash."

Donnie Nelson had served as an assistant coach in Phoenix during Nash's first two NBA seasons with the Suns, and he recognized the potential in Nash even as he scrounged for minutes behind the established point guards Jason Kidd, Kevin Johnson and Sam Cassell. After Nelson had been hired by Dallas, he urged his father to trade for Nash. "'In your system I think he's a top-five point guard in the league. I think he's a multiyear All-Star,'" Donnie Nelson recalled telling his father. "I was commuting on my Harley back then, so I was just pulling out and all of a sudden I feel a buzz, and it's Danny Ainge from Phoenix." Nelson pulled over to talk to Ainge, the head coach of the Suns. Ainge told him that Nash would be sent to Dallas in a draft-night trade that would empower the Mavericks to make the other trade for the rights to Dirk.

It is hilarious to look back at the pictures of the two future MVPs being introduced side by side at a press conference in Dallas — 24-year-old Nash with his brightly dyed blond hair and Dirk, nine inches taller and four years his junior, with his own naturally blond hair parted in the middle and hanging in a floppy bowl cut.

Nash had been born in South Africa and raised in British Columbia. His younger brother, Martin, was on his way to becoming a professional soccer player in England and North America while Nash grew up idolizing Isiah Thomas for the creativity and competitive fire that enabled him to overcome his small size. At 6-3 Nash would be a different kind of underdog than Thomas. Midway through high school in Victoria, Nash was sent by his parents to a nearby boarding school so that he could raise his failing grades. He received one American basketball scholarship, from Santa Clara University in the San Francisco Bay Area. The announcement four years later that he had been chosen by Phoenix with its fifteenth pick in the 1996 draft was booed by Suns fans because they knew nothing about him. In his first year with the Mavericks, Nash turned out to be even more disappointing than Dirk. His new coach, Don Nelson, railed at him to shoot more often, while the fans booed him for shooting too much.

Nash and Dirk were a pair of immigrants trying to make sense of their surroundings, with Nash the Canadian looking out for his younger friend from Germany. They lived next door to each other in two-bedroom condos in the emerging Uptown neighborhood of Dallas. At night they would practice together at the side basket of a public gym whose main court was crowded with pickup games. Afterward they would go around the corner to their favorite bar, The Loon, for cans of beer and cheeseburgers.

The Mavericks finished seventh from the bottom of the NBA with a record of 19-31. Dirk returned home to immerse himself in the comfort of hard work. He trained every day with Holger, sleeping in the cellar of his parents' home and then driving an hour each way to the grade school gym in Rattelsdorf, where he would fetch the key from the bakery next door. Throughout his teens, when the NBA had been a magical dream, the workouts had been experiments of theory. Now that Nelson had introduced Dallas to its foreign rookie by comparing Dirk to Larry Bird, the workouts with Holger carried more urgency.

In his second NBA year Dirk averaged 17.5 points per game, more than doubling his rookie output, while the Mavericks went 40-42, more victories than they had earned over the previous two seasons combined. By year three Dirk had moved past team leader Michael Finley to become the leading scorer in Dallas. Not only did the Mavericks qualify for the playoffs for the first time in eleven years, but they also won a first-round series under new owner Mark Cuban, and Dirk became the first Maverick ever to be named to the fifteen-player All-NBA Teams. By year four he and Nash were both All-Stars. Dirk's career was taking off.

The gray linoleum floor is lined in an array of colors to mark off a variety of sports. The German gym is a simple bright box of a room with rows of windows up high and posters of Kobe Bryant and Joe Dumars tacked onto the wooden wall behind one of the baskets.

Dirk starts by shooting jump shots that swish through as Holger passes the ball back out to him, and a casual chat in German bounces back and forth between them.

Dribbling to his right, Dirk takes one exaggerated step before allowing the recoiling momentum to spin him back the other way in a burst toward the basket. Next come the turnaround jump shots. Dirk extends his right foot out and away from the basket, pivots on it like the turning of a screw, and releases the ball just as he squares up to the rim in midair. Holger, standing near the basket, makes the same movements, like a dance instructor. When the ball gets loose, Dirk kicks it, booming, off the end wall and back toward Holger, who traps it with his feet. Soccer is and always will be their first language.

Twenty-five minutes into the workout Dirk does two complete splits of his long straight legs, one in each direction. His bones crack louder than knuckles, and Holger laughs to affirm there is nothing to fear. Then, with one knee down, Dirk grabs the ball off the floor and rises in a single motion to shoot jump shots from the free throw line. He performs variations of this exhausting drill until it is time to put on the vest.

It weighs twenty-two pounds and looks like a flattened, densely packed backpack, and it is meant to prepare Dirk's ankles, knees and spine for the additional weight he will gain in muscle as he matures physically in the years to come. "First he develops the technique he needs in order to carry the weight, and then he will add the weight," Holger says. "In the States they do it the other way: They increase strength without the technique."

Holger believes that the NBA's infatuation with muscle building is responsible for many injuries. Early in Dirk's career, when the priority of NBA teams was to defend the paint, Holger intervened to prevent the Mavericks from transforming him into a bodybuilder. Nelson agreed that Dirk would lift twice as many repetitions of half the usual weight. It wasn't the work that Holger was trying to avoid; it was the consequences.

Dirk wears the vest for forty-two minutes while performing exercises that would be taxing even without the extra weight. He shoots free throws with each hand. He catches the ball and spins 360 degrees on one foot at the foul line before landing squarely on both feet, in order to rise up, balanced and straight, for eleven jump shots, of which he makes ten. Next come ten consecutive dunks with either hand from under the basket, one after another: As quickly as he regains control of the ball, he is back up airborne again. Then more free throws.

A short break for a drink.

Dirk holds the ball while he and Holger cover the length of the court side by side, back and forth, in a dozen exaggerated steps each way. Then Dirk crosses the width of the court in twelve diagonal strides, reaching down to touch the floor with each step.

From the low post he is shoved away from the basket time after time by Holger, as he absorbs the contact to knock down turnaround jump shots from eighteen feet. Back under the basket, he bends deep to grab the ball off the floor with both hands just as he elevates in one motion to dunk ten times, the last five behind his head.

Finally he rips off the vest and flings it out to center court, where it lands with a loud thud. His blue T-shirt is satiny black with sweat.

Dirk was up most of the previous night with a deep toothache. He complains to Holger that his tooth is killing him as he slams the ball in pain. But then he resumes his shooting around the world of the three-point arc, groaning and gasping. "Super," Holger says, encouraging him. Now Dirk is upside down and walking on his hands from the foul line to midcourt as Holger holds his legs up in the air for balance. Two kids watching through the crack of a window opened upstairs whoop and shout in praise of his trick, their shadows visible in the tinted glass.

Dirk then lies down and Holger stretches his legs, bending them in steady fluid movements. He kneads Dirk's back and massages each of Dirk's bare feet like a humble servant in the Bible. "Sit-ups," commands Holger. Dirk groans as he exercises. "Come on," urges Holger. Twenty sit-ups are followed by ten fingertip push-ups.

At last it is over, ninety-three minutes after it started.

What is fascinating to a basketball audience that has never seen anything like this is the monotony for 24-year-old Dirk. He has been performing these movements at the same speed with which they will be performed in an NBA game — a crucial detail — for one-third of his life already. He has done these exercises thousands of times and will do them thousands of times more, again and again and again, in order to make the extraordinary appear effortless and natural.

It is the summer of 2002, and he is approaching the peak years of his career, when the game will tease and hurt him, and reveal the depth of his devotion.

By 2004 Nash had led the Mavericks to wins in four playoff series. He was also moving back to Phoenix as a free agent, because of Mark Cuban's refusal to invest $60 million in a 30-year-old point guard with a history of back trouble. That Dirk responded with anger to the departure of his best friend and teammate was not entirely inspiring to the Mavericks. There was a hint of weakness in his exasperation. In Los Angeles, Kobe and Shaquille O'Neal were fighting over who should be The Man of the Lakers, but Dirk wanted no part of the burdens of stardom and leadership in Dallas.

"I'd make comments to him, kidding him, like, 'You're the franchise player here,'" said Nick Creme. "He'd always say, 'I'm not the franchise player here. This is Finley's team.'"

In 2005 All-Star small forward Michael Finley was waived at age 32 in order to save Cuban more than $50 million under a one-time-only provision of the collective bargaining agreement, and there could be no denying any longer that the Mavericks were Dirk's team. Dirk was 27, and his career was pivoting naturally by way of its own momentum. After seven deferential seasons of turning away from stardom, he was now bursting into prominence whether he liked it or not.

Even now he was benefiting from low expectations. In the absence of Nash and Finley, no one was expecting Dirk to lead the Mavericks to the NBA Finals in 2006 or to be named league MVP the following season. In Game 7 of the second round of the '06 playoffs, Dirk drove for the tying three-point play, forced overtime with a block of Tim Duncan and finished with 37 points to upset the Spurs. The game was played in San Antonio, and its victims included Finley, who had been picked up by the Spurs. Waiting for Dallas in the Western Conference Finals were Phoenix and Steve Nash, the NBA's reigning two-time MVP. Nash's Suns were beaten in six games by Dirk's Mavericks.

Ten days later the Mavericks were five quarters away from becoming the least talented NBA team to win a championship in modern times. Dirk and 31-year-old Jerry Stackhouse were the only players on the 2005–06 Mavericks to have ever been All-Stars, and it had been five years since Stackhouse had played at that high a level. The center was 24-year-old DeSagana Diop, a 7-footer from Senegal, who would average less than 3 points per game in all of his dozen NBA seasons. Joining him in the starting lineup for most of the playoffs was second-year point guard Devin Harris, whose play, like that of many of his teammates, would recede under the pressure of the NBA Finals against the more gifted Miami Heat of Dwyane Wade, Shaquille O'Neal, Gary Payton, Alonzo Mourning and coach Pat Riley, all future Hall of Famers. In the end that championship would be lost because Dirk's teammates and Avery Johnson, the 41-year-old former point guard who was completing his first full season as head coach, simply weren't good enough to earn it.

Don Nelson, who had resigned as coach of the Mavericks in 2005, recognized the pressures that were piling up on his older players, and on Dirk in particular. As the new coach of the Golden State Warriors, Nelson would impose on his former team the most embarrassing upset in the history of the NBA playoffs. Dirk's Mavericks had responded to their 2006 Finals collapse by winning sixty-seven games during the 2006–07 regular season. But in the first round of the playoffs they could win only two of six games against the torrid-shooting Warriors, who followed Nelson's orders to crowd and bump and harass Dirk on their way to becoming the first bottom seed to knock off a number one team in an NBA best-of-seven series.

Cuban would file a lawsuit against Nelson, to be rejected by an arbitrator, alleging that Nelson had used "confidential information" from his years with the Mavericks to plot their defeat, which was obviously true. But it was also true that the Mavericks were vulnerable. What Nelson's Warriors did to Dirk was the same thing Doc Rivers's Celtics would do to LeBron in Cleveland three years later. In the decisive 111–86 loss at Golden State, Dirk converted only 2 of his 13 shots for 8 points, settling for timid jumpers instead of attacking the defense, and generating more turnovers than field goals.

When LeBron was embarrassed by the Celtics in 2010, he behaved as if he couldn't wait to put himself back in front of the cameras, as if *The Decision* would distract him (and his audience) from what had happened. Dirk's reaction was entirely different. His instinct was to vanish overseas, as if the loss to the Warriors had been entirely his fault.

But the league office would not permit him to leave. The NBA told the Mavericks that Dirk needed to stay in Dallas on the likelihood that he would be named MVP after all of the other individual awards for the regular season had been handed out. "Are they even going to want to have a press conference?" asked Dirk, as if the fiasco of his postseason had laid to waste the preceding six months.

"He took losing that series harder than anything he'd taken," Creme said. "He didn't want to leave the house. He said, 'I'm out of here — give the trophy to somebody else.'"

"I don't think I've ever felt worse for someone than when he won the MVP," said Casey Smith, the Mavericks' athletic trainer, who was with Dirk when he received the news of his award. "I think, literally, he didn't want it."

Twelve days after his worst night in basketball, Dirk showed up for the ceremony looking overheated and uncomfortable in a dark pins-striped suit. He was the first European-born winner of basketball's greatest individual award. He had led the NBA's winningest team with 24.6 points and 8.9 rebounds per game. His 3.4 assists were a career best, as were his shooting percentages from the free throw line (90.4), the three-point line (41.6) and the field overall (50.2). He had been hoping to get through the ceremony by cracking self-deprecating jokes, but then Cuban preceded him to the microphone with an emotional speech in which he cried while praising Dirk's commitment.

"You don't have to encourage him to get into the gym; he's the guy you have to lock out," Cuban said. "He's not the guy who you wonder if he cares; he's the guy who hurts so much when things don't go the way you want. That's what makes him an MVP. He's an example that you don't have to fit a certain role, a certain model, but if you work hard enough and care enough, anything is possible."

Dirk was embarking on the most important period of his career. Everything that had happened to him until now had been influenced by the forces of will around him. He had been guided by Holger's curiosity and generosity, Nash's passion and Cuban's ambition, and the currents of their influence in combination with the power of his own oars had swept him along. The ride had been carefree and fun, as he looked back, and nothing like the next phase of his development would be. Now, as never before, he was on his own to decide who he was and why he played and what it was going to amount to in the end. It was time to find the meaning in the blue eyes staring back at him in the mirror, the mask that smiled to hide the loneliness and self-doubt, the artificially bright front teeth anchored in his jaw after so many violent collisions. Dirk, who had eschewed the arrogance presupposed of his talent, had to make a stand on behalf of himself, and he had to do it now.

He had achieved a standard that far exceeded his own expectations eight years earlier when he came to America. He had become the most valuable individual of the world's greatest league. And he realized now, as he held the large trophy in his hands, that it meant nothing to him.

There was no gray area or silver lining to lighten his mood. Other stars of the NBA would have gladly found space for the MVP award within the trophy room of their minds: Kobe would have been able to separate the excellence of his regular season from any shortcomings of the postseason, just as surely as LeBron would be encouraged to rationalize his individual awards despite his team's failures. But Dirk could not. He was an immigrant, and basketball was not his game, nor was the United States his country nor English his first language nor Dallas his hometown. Everywhere he was a guest, always having to prove his worthiness. From the start he and Holger had set out to distance themselves from the other big men, in order to create a new perspective that might enable Dirk to earn the respect that so many American players took for granted. The NBA was a league filled with stars who behaved as if they were entitled to the acclaim and the millions of dollars handed down to them from the era of Michael Jordan.

Dirk was among the exceptions, and his humility made him exceptional in every way. He felt no sense of entitlement because he believed he had to earn his place in this league and this country that had invited him to pursue his faraway dream.

The ceremony celebrating his magnificent achievement filled him with guilt. He gave the large MVP trophy to his parents in Germany, with the understanding that they would appreciate it more than he would.

Meanwhile Dirk, knowing now what he did not want, sought out places in the world where he could figure out what he did want. Holger, who had traveled everywhere, served as his guide. They spent the next five weeks in and around Australia, at the bottom of the earth. They lived in a jeep equipped with bunk beds on the plains of the Outback, sleeping out in the open like frontiersmen. They took in Beethoven at the Sydney Opera House, hiked the canyons of Central Australia, sailed and snorkeled along the Great Barrier Reef. They drove through New Zealand. They rented a house on a Tahitian beach. Almost everywhere he traveled, Dirk went unrecognized. His hair and beard grew unkempt. He drank whiskey from the bottle. He read books in German, slept in the pitch-black of the outdoors and woke with the dawn.

For all that Don Nelson had done in Dallas to define Dirk as a creator of mismatches, it was as coach of the Warriors that he provided his ex-player with the ultimate assessment of his talent. In six playoff games over a dozen days he stripped away from Dirk any sense of comfort and satisfaction for the great distances he had climbed so far, and by the end of that miserable series, Dirk was forced to recognize how much further he had to go.

Over the years to come, the Mavericks' playoff losses would weigh on Dirk like heavy dumbbells in each hand; instead of letting them go, he would lift them incessantly to make himself stronger. A consensus opinion was forming that he lacked the indefinable qualities of an NBA champion. It was to Dirk's credit that these criticisms had no impact on him. What bothered him painfully, however, were the faults that he recognized in himself and that he knew deep down to be real and true. All of the rest of it he could ignore.

Instead of doubting Holger and his methods, Dirk grew ever more committed to their code. He underwent blood tests to determine the foods that would provide the energy he needed. He showed little interest in selling himself commercially, and at the end of each season he continued to donate his playoff share to his fellow Mavericks employees—kicking in more from his own pocket in years of early elimination. The star who was caricatured as soft recovered from injuries quickly and played through pain to a degree that would astonish Casey Smith, who remembered thinking the worst one night when Dirk went down awkwardly and hard. "His leg twisted so much it almost broke the bone," said Smith. "And he missed four games. It's mind-boggling."

Dirk's ankles were perpetually getting sprained. "In Germany they build good cars," Smith once said, "but they don't build good ankles." With each sprain he would be sent home with a bucket of ice bags. "The first twenty-four hours are crucial — you've got to keep it elevated to keep the swelling down, to keep the ice on it — and he won't sleep," said Creme. "He'll be on the couch with NBA TV on, and it's kind of funny because he's sprained them so many times now, but he'll be up all night icing it." The next game Dirk would be running on his heels like an old man, his crooked arms exaggerated like a racewalker's to create momentum and carry him through the opening minutes.

"When you roll your ankle, you tear ligaments every time," explained Dr. Brian McKeon of the Boston Celtics. "Some guys tear it so much that the ligament basically dissolves; they've got nothing there, and bone spurs take over and actually pull it together." Dirk was at that stage. Along the way he was abandoning the wide-open spaces of the three-point line and forcing himself with increasing frequency to play in the low post, like a traditional American big man with his back to the basket. All of the disappointments and pain were deepening his understanding and his hunger. He was learning to see all of the colors, to hear all of the notes.

What he decided at the discouraging end of his greatest season in 2007 was that he had come to the NBA to be a champion. He was going to embrace his greatness in order to win for his team. For the rest of his basketball life every game was going to be important, to a degree he had never imagined in those carefree years when he took neither the game nor himself so seriously.

Whenever Dallas returned to Oakland to play the Golden State Warriors, the Mavericks' communications manager, Scott Tomlin, would stop Dirk in the hallway outside the visitors' locker room and point up high. There was a dent in the drywall made by a large garbage bin that Dirk had thrown in anger after losing in the 2007 playoffs. "Look, it's still there," Tomlin would say as the years went by, and Dirk was strong enough to laugh with him.

Several of Dirk's friends on the Mavericks staff were with him in a restaurant in Denver, across the street from the hotel where they were staying for the second round of the 2009 playoffs, when his cellphone rang. Dirk sat quietly among his friends, listening to someone on the phone, speaking tersely. A short time later the news that his fiancée, Cristal Taylor, who had falsely claimed to be pregnant while living with Dirk, had been arrested at his home in Dallas. Police would identify her by at least eight aliases she had used over the years. A judge in Missouri would sentence her to five years in prison for a parole violation linked to forgery and theft charges.

When Dirk had turned 30 the previous summer, he had gone through a kind of midlife crisis. In fact he was past middle age as an athlete. It had been fourteen years since he had made his leap of faith with Holger, and what did he have to show for it? He had no championship, no wife, no children, no achievement of permanence that he valued.

These were the circumstances that drew him to the mirage of Cristal Taylor. When his friends would visit Dirk, she would stay in the back of the house, out of sight. Dirk's family in Germany worried about him, and Holger did more than worry. He hired a private investigator to research her background, and he was the one who broke the truth of her identity to Dirk. Imagine the risk to their relationship that Holger had taken: How many alliances with an American agent, coach or mentor had ended because the millionaire athlete had fallen for a woman who was no good for him?

The ensuing scandal was the worst of all humiliations for Dirk. Dating back to his arrival in Dallas, he had carried himself in public as if he could afford no mistakes, as if he was forever trying to make a good first impression on America. The scandal amounted to a new depth of failure for him. It also revealed a strength that had been developing over the years without his notice.

Instead of mocking Dirk, the people of Dallas rose up and supported him. Instead of criticizing him or laughing at his expense, they expressed sympathy for him. People calling in to talk shows, letters to newspaper editors and comments posted online combined to create a wellspring of goodwill. They were explaining in all kinds of ways that they had grown to appreciate Dirk's integrity. It was if he was experiencing his version of *It's a Wonderful Life,* in which the hero is overwhelmed by friendships he never knew he had. Dirk had been in Dallas for more than ten years, and not until the worst of all his bad moments occurred would he realize that he had established himself as more than a basketball player for the Mavericks. He was isolated no more in the public sense. His roots, having been tested, were found to be secure. He had become a respected leader of the community, a virtual neighbor to everybody who had been following him for all these years.

The Mavericks would lose that Denver series in five games to Carmelo Anthony's Nuggets, but Dirk, amid the heat of the scandal, would generate an inspired 34.4 points, 11.6 rebounds and 4 assists per game.

He was determined, more than ever, to fight for his new home.

Dirk and Holger were in a gym in Dallas, continuing the work that had consumed and propelled the latter half of Dirk's lifetime. Few words were spoken. The routine had not changed. This was the rhythm of his life, the music of his heart. Sweat bled through his shirt.

It bears repeating: As Ernie Butler had done for Holger, so was Holger doing for Dirk. "It was pretty much the same situation," Holger said, the difference being that Butler had taught what he knew, while Holger was teaching what he believed could be. Dirk maintained his faith in Holger's science in the same way that frontiersmen believed in their code and would not budge from what they knew to be right.

There was no certainty that Dirk would triumph. During that summer of 2010 leading up to *The Decision,* when LeBron, Wade and Chris Bosh were recruited by more suitors than they wanted, Dirk waited in Germany for his phone to ring. And it did not. No NBA team called to show interest in him. He flew into Dallas without fanfare, per his wishes, and late on the eve of his contract negotiations with Cuban, he went online to the Mavericks' website. "They did a thing where all the fans could write a note to me," Dirk said. "I read through some of it, and that was actually really emotional. Some of the fans hit the nail on the head. Yeah, it was great, some of the stuff they said. Obviously some were like, 'Please go.' But most of them were so nice."

This was better than being recruited.

The next day at the owner's mansion, where Dirk and Cuban met alone, it was obvious to both of them that they were stuck with each other. Cuban had been unable to recruit a star like LeBron, leaving him to settle on the imminent trade that the Mavericks would make for Tyson Chandler. Dirk had been ignored by the NBA marketplace. No one believed in him except this billionaire, who had become his partner in basketball and his supportive friend, and who was telling him now, as emotionally as when he had spoken up for Dirk at the MVP ceremony three years earlier, that they were in this together.

As he walked out of Cuban's house, having shaken hands with the owner on his next contract, Dirk realized he had accomplished more than he ever could have envisioned from this adopted way of life. All that was left was to win the championship for Cuban, for the Mavericks and their extended family of fans, for the city of Dallas, for his own family and all of his supportive friends, for Holger and for himself. It was a long list of gratitude for someone who had arrived in America frightened and alone.

Like a tailwind helping Dirk along, the warmth of that summer propelled him through the 2010–11 season and into the opening round of the playoffs against the Trail Blazers. Two nights after their devastating Game 4 loss in Portland, the Mavericks beat the Trail Blazers on their home court in Dallas on 25 points from Dirk. They flew back to Portland, where Dirk scored 33 points to lead them to another win and finish off the series in six games.

As the Mavericks walked off the court, the fans of Brandon Roy were quiet, and neither Dirk nor his teammates were smiling. They were headed for a second-round series against the defending champion Lakers, who were pursuing a third straight title, a fourth successive NBA Finals appearance and the sixth championship for Kobe, to equal Michael Jordan.

Who was Dirk to think that he and his team could beat Kobe and Phil Jackson and the winningest franchise of modern times? Yet Dirk walked on, staring ahead absently, as if not seeing what lay beyond the next workout with Holger.

11

THE CONFLICT

Doc Rivers retired from the Spurs in 1996 and became a TV broadcaster. One year later his large home in San Antonio was burned to the ground by an arsonist incited by racism. The house and all of their possessions were destroyed, their cats and dogs were killed, and it was only by good fortune that Kris and the children had left one day earlier to visit her parents in Wisconsin while Doc was in Seattle for a charity golf tournament.

The Texas Rangers provided Doc and Kris with the names of the teenaged arsonists, even as they admitted there was not enough evidence to prosecute. "The ranger said, 'We're telling you who they are. We know who they are, but there's no way we can get them,'" said Doc. "I remember my wife wanted to hire a private investigator, and undercover people to get in the school and try to befriend them, and get them to eventually confess or start bragging about it. I was like, 'Why?' 'Well, we've got to get these motherfuckers.' I said, 'We know who they are. They've got to live with themselves. I've got to get the insurance done, we have to rebuild a home, my kids are in an apartment. I've got to get to work.' I mean, it bugged her that I didn't give it any more thought. But that happened, and it was done. And, yeah, I would have loved to have seen them in a back alley, I would have beat the shit out of them. But that wasn't going to happen. And if that did happen, then I'd go to jail. So they win again. To me, it was just keep doing your job. Keep doing what you're doing, and so for the first month of that summer, I sat in the apartment, every day, filling out insurance stuff. My job at that point was to get my kids, my family, back to normal.

"I think if we had done it the other way, where we're bitter, we know where these parents are, you end up going to talk to their parents . . . Like that was another thing. They were going to arrange a meeting with their parents. 'I don't want to meet their parents.' She said, 'Why not?' 'I don't want to meet them. Fuck them. Why do I need to meet them? They're going to tell you what you want to hear anyway. If they are good parents, they'll tell their kids what they did was wrong. We don't need that. What is that going to do for us?' 'It'd make me feel better.' 'Well, if you want to have the meeting, we'll have the meeting. But I don't want to have the meeting.'"

They didn't have the meeting.

"What is that going to do for me?" Doc went on. "It's going to make their parents feel better, that's what that was for. That's the way I looked at it. It's going to make them feel better: 'Okay, now they have our blessing and we don't have to feel guilty anymore.' Why would I do that? That was my thinking, and it might have been wrong, but that's how I felt about it. 'Fuck this. I have to fill out these reports and get the insurance money back as soon as I can, so I can buy and build a new home, so my kids can go to school and be normal, instead of us living in a two-bedroom apartment with three dogs and two cats and four kids.' That's how I looked at it."

Another stand he made was to prevent his children from returning to San Antonio until the rubble and other evidence of the fire had all been cleared away from the site. He didn't want them to see the physical scars of what had been their home.

When Doc called Kris that day in 1997 to tell her the house was on fire and it was going to burn to the ground and their animals could not be saved, she collapsed to the floor. Nine-year-old Jeremiah, their eldest, fainted. "He was looking at Mom, he saw her crying, and then he just fell asleep," said Doc. "I'd never heard that part of the story until two days ago. And until I learned about Jeremiah right then, I thought it had the biggest impact on Austin." Austin Rivers was four years old at the time of the fire, and for most of his childhood he didn't like to travel. "To me that's because the last time he left the house to go to Milwaukee, somebody burned his house down," said Doc. "They took his stuff, so he became possessive of everything. He watches people."

By his mid-teens Austin had become an AAU basketball star. In those years he had trouble sleeping if he was alone. He received a scholarship to play for Duke as a 6-foot 4-inch guard destined to become a first-round pick in the NBA draft. "When he moved out to Duke, we looked under his bed — he has three baseball bats, a fucking big kitchen knife, all under his bed," Doc said. "He's good now, but I thought he was affected the most by that event. Definitely made him not trust."

Compared with so many other players in the NBA, Austin was operating from a position of strength because he had been raised by two loving parents.

"Too many kids are growing up without two parents," Doc said. "I don't care if it's two women or two men, I don't give a shit what it is, you need two parents. A lot of these kids are growing up with no supervision, or horrible things done, like the father treats the mother poorly. It's a vicious cycle."

Kevin Garnett and Paul Pierce did not have a relationship with their fathers. The same was true for Rajon Rondo, who was in grade school when he and his two older brothers were abandoned by their father. "That's why I don't trust a lot of people," Rondo, in a rare public admission, told *Sports Illustrated.*

Doc liked to joke that he was a doctor by nickname rather than profession, but this much he knew. "It's a major, major problem in our league," he said. "So many of the players not only don't have a father, some of them didn't have a father or a mother. A lot of them have been raised by grandmothers. First of all the male figure and then the male black figure — very difficult for them to trust, because all through their life that figure let them down, in their mind. It's only one guy, but it manifested itself to all black males. No trust. And then it builds itself as they don't respect authority, because they never had to. Their only authority person in their life is their mom; the male figure, they go back at. And so we get that."

Doc and other NBA coaches tried to earn the respect of young players who were hurting, in spite of their fame and wealth and the hard fronts they put forth.

"I talk to all my players about how they grew up," said Paul Silas, who coached the Cavaliers during LeBron James's first two seasons. "You grow up in a two-parent family, it's just so different. It has an effect on your team when a guy comes and needs psychological help, and a whole lot of these guys do. You get them on your team, you're trying to do the right thing, and it just doesn't work. And you just say, 'That guy right there, he needs therapy.'"

Like Rondo, LeBron was raised by a single mother. But whereas Rondo was introverted and difficult to understand, LeBron was a people person, a pleaser who had many friends.

When LeBron joined the Cavaliers at age 18, he had yet to develop a killer instinct. There was nothing in his background to prepare him for the NBA, much less for the reception by his teammates. "From day one I had some players that were envious of him," Silas said. "LeBron would come to practice and sit over by himself when everybody else was shooting, and that type of thing. And I called him into my office and told him, 'Hey, man, this is the way it is. You've got to go back at these guys — you can't let them do that to you and accept it.' It helped, but it was not really a huge change."

Silas might have been a strong mentor to LeBron — if he had been allowed to stay in Cleveland. He had won three NBA championships in the 1970s — two with the Celtics and another with the Seattle SuperSonics — as a 6-foot-7 All-Star power forward who was named to the NBA's All-Defensive Teams five times. His intimidating presence was set off by his sense of humor and deep baritone voice. Toward the end of LeBron's second year, however, Silas was fired by Dan Gilbert, the new owner of the Cavaliers, who was intent on hiring his own coach. Gilbert's relationship with LeBron was doomed because Gilbert was focused on the end at the expense of the means. Too many times LeBron was given what he wanted at the expense of what he needed. LeBron moved to Miami not only to play with superior teammates but also because he needed the top-to-bottom commitment that was lacking in Cleveland.

Silas was rooting for LeBron to overcome the unique circumstances of his basketball upbringing. "I don't know whether he will ever get that killer instinct or not, because that's just not his nature," said Silas of LeBron midway through the 2010–11 season. "You're talking about a guy that's been at the top of his game throughout his whole career, and he's been better than everybody else, so he hasn't had to fight his way through like a Kobe. When Kobe first got in the league, he had to fight his way."

Kobe, picked number thirteen in the draft, spent the first half of his career trying to prove that he was worthy of jumping straight to the NBA from high school instead of spending a year or two in college. Kobe's success saved LeBron from having to confront those doubts.

"This guy has not had to fight," Silas went on. He was not criticizing LeBron so much as he was sympathizing with him. Nothing in LeBron's brief career had prepared him for the doubts and abuse that followed him everywhere he went. "I asked people when I had him, 'Do you think you can teach somebody how to have a killer instinct?' And they all said, 'No, you either have it or you don't.'"

Other coaches in the NBA raised the same concerns during LeBron's first season in Miami, including those who were plotting his failure. Silas, in the meantime, had been hired at age 67 to coach the young Charlotte Bobcats by their new owner, Michael Jordan. "They don't understand what it really takes to win and win big in this league," he said. "Now a guy like Kobe, he goes out there to kill you, to destroy you, and he's not going to have no buddy-buddy thing. I looked at my guys the other night: One of my players hit somebody, and he fell, and the guy was bending over to make sure he was okay." He shook his head at the idea. "It just happened in the last ten years or so; that's when things became that way."

The main problem, as Doc saw it, was that informal playground basketball had been usurped by the AAU. On the playground players took on all comers and kept the court only as long as they kept winning. In AAU tournaments the outcomes of the games tended to be less important than players' individual performances. Worst of all, as Doc saw it, were the rankings by media companies of the most promising young players. Instead of being humbled by how little they understood and how much they had to learn, the players of LeBron's generation were encouraged to behave like ready-made NBA stars, as if having potential was the same as having achieved something.

"John Thompson once told me, 'Nobody wants to put their reputation on the line anymore,'" said Doc, quoting the retired Georgetown University coach. "Because they get these reputations, and when they're getting their ass kicked they stop playing hard — and then they act like 'I'm not really playing hard.' Because they don't want to put their reputation on the line anymore. Nobody wants to play to win. They don't want to do it. Because of their ranking, their reputation."

Rondo showed that trait at times. If he was shooting badly — his big weakness — during the pregame warmup, he might begin to fool around, as if to pretend he hadn't really been trying. There were other times, however, especially during the biggest games, when his competitive edge was overwhelming. In February 2011, in the fourth quarter of the Celtics' win over the Heat in Boston, Rondo took it upon himself to guard LeBron. He did so without Doc's authority; he told his teammates what he was going to do and then he did it, even though he was seven inches shorter and close to one hundred pounds lighter than LeBron. Rondo wanted that challenge, he wanted to make the big plays, and he was the star of that victory with a triple-double. Along the way he brazenly nosed himself into an impromptu Miami huddle before LeBron shoved him away. Rondo explained later that the Heat hadn't been entitled to privacy because they hadn't called a timeout.

Those efforts separated Rondo from his generation. Unlike most of the young players in the NBA, he had no interest in trying to be friendly with LeBron. "He can't stand anybody else," said Pierce of Rondo.

As far as Pierce could tell, the only non-Celtic in the NBA with whom Rondo appeared to be friends was the Atlanta Hawks' Josh Smith, and that was because they had been teammates in high school. "He cannot stand Chris Paul," said Pierce, who remembered breaking up a fight between the two young stars. "It was right after the game. It was because Chris Paul really said something offensive — like, 'The only reason you're good is because you got Kevin, Ray and Paul.'"

Chris Paul had been accurate with his aim: He knew exactly how to wound Rondo. "Chris was fine with it; Rondo won't let it go," said Doc. "Rondo can get uptight with that shit. I laugh at it: 'Please, you're a gangster? Come on, please. You don't scare anybody.'"

Doc thought it was important to show respect for Rondo by confronting him. Had he looked the other way when Rondo pursued one of his self-destructive agendas, Doc essentially would have been giving up on their relationship. By taking on issues directly with Rondo, as he did repeatedly in private, Doc was trying to show the most sincere form of support. It was the hardest course for him to take, but there was no way forward other than to speak the truth to Rondo.

"The bottom line, at least what I've found, is you treat every single one of them differently," Doc said of his players. "You don't treat them all the same. You've got to treat one with kid gloves, one you've got to ride, one you've got to bring in your office. One of those guys with no father likes to talk, one doesn't."

Danny Ainge and his coach tended to view Rondo from different perspectives. Ainge was influenced by Jon Niednagel, "the Brain Doctor," whereas Doc was skeptical of brain typing.

"Doc doesn't always deal with things the way I deal with them, knowing how Rondo's wired and knowing things about Rondo," said Ainge. "Doc is a guy that is a tough-minded, competitive son of a gun who was raised by a tough cop in Chicago. That's who he is, and I'm happy about that. I think that has helped Rondo. There's no escape from it; you're not going to talk your way out of it, you're not going to get much sympathy from Doc because you're an ISFP. At the same time, he knows how special Rondo is, and he knows how much he needs him, and he knows that he needs him to be a leader. When Rondo doesn't reflect leadership in his play, it gets tough for Doc. So it reminds me very much of my experience with D.J., and my experience with K.J. in Phoenix."

Dennis Johnson, who died of a heart attack in 2007, had been Ainge's Hall of Fame teammate in the Celtics backcourt when they won two championships in the 1980s. Kevin Johnson, who in 2008 was elected mayor of his hometown, Sacramento, had been an All-Star point guard for the Phoenix Suns when Ainge played with and then coached him for six seasons in the 1990s.

"They're all wired the same way and they're all similar in so many ways, and they're all great players that are going to help you win," said Ainge. "But day in and day out, with D.J. you could see why Lenny Wilkens didn't want to keep him, and why Jerry Colangelo traded him away for Rick Robey."

Wilkens, a Hall of Famer as both a player and a coach, coached Dennis Johnson with the Seattle SuperSonics for three seasons. Johnson was MVP of the 1979 NBA Finals one year before he was traded to Phoenix. Jerry Colangelo, the Hall of Fame executive with the Suns, dealt Johnson to the Celtics in 1983.

"You could see those things," Ainge went on about Dennis Johnson, Kevin Johnson and Rondo. "Maybe they're not interested in doing a drill here and a drill there, and 'This morning I don't really feel like playing,' and 'This game is not really that big of a deal' — those are some of the challenges."

Like the two Johnsons, Rondo was unable to control his emotions. That was the context in which Ainge now viewed his point guard.

"They're not consciously choosing to be really lazy," said Ainge. "Rajon doesn't wake up every morning with energy like some people. What Rajon is, is an introvert and a feeler, so a lot of times they aren't going to interact as much. They're not going to have the energy levels that coaches are going to want day in and day out, and teammates are going to want day in and day out. But in the big moments and the big games, he has the ability to get to that level that you want. Whereas someone like me, who wakes up with energy every day, and who goes out and practices hard and plays hard, my energy levels may be too high in those crucial moments. And I didn't really figure that out until later in my career. I had to learn to calm myself and be a little calmer."

The questionable aspect of this comparison was that none other than Larry Bird had referred to Dennis Johnson consistently as the best player he ever played with, whereas none of the current Celtics would ever speak of Rondo in such high terms.

"So the rest of us tried to figure that one out, why Larry would have said that," said Ainge. "I loved D.J., I loved him. But there were times — when he wouldn't pass the ball to Kevin [McHale]; or if I came down the court and I threw it to my left to Larry, and I didn't give it to D.J. on the right for the layin—that he would be really mad and salty and not pass me the ball for a quarter of a game, in a big game. He would react emotionally, thinking or having some sort of paranoia that I was snubbing him or freezing him out. Or just weird stuff.

"But D.J. would always come around. He might hurt our chemistry, and crazy stuff would happen for that game. But then the next day was an apology, and the next day was fun and games. He had a great personality, sense of humor, and it was really easy to get him back. And I would take him on my team. I campaigned for him to be in the Hall of Fame. I think he was a great player."

A thousand miles away in his office in Indianapolis, Larry Bird laughed upon hearing that Ainge had compared Rondo favorably with Dennis Johnson. "D.J., he was nothing like Rondo," said Bird. "Come on, Rondo had problems at Kentucky; Tubby Smith was glad he left. Rondo's a pain in the ass, we all know that. D.J. wasn't a pain in the ass. D.J. was D.J. I mean, him and K.C. [Jones, the Celtics coach] got into it the first couple weeks he was there; I thought they was going to fist-fight. And all of a sudden it was over, I never seen it again."

More often than not, by Bird's recollection, he found himself siding with Johnson during his occasional disagreements with Ainge and McHale. "Yeah," said Bird, "D.J. used to give Danny shit, give Kevin shit—and he was probably right."

Doc wasn't buying Ainge's comparison either.

"Oh, I hate when he goes there. Oh my gosh," said Doc. "He did that at one meeting. I said, 'Danny, listen, we're not going anywhere. That's just some bull-shit. Rondo is nothing like D.J.' I'm like Larry: I didn't know D.J., but I knew enough that he wasn't that. D.J.'s teammates loved him. I don't know that that's true with Rondo. So that's the difference."

Disagreements between the Celtics' president and his coach in regard to the strengths and weaknesses of Rondo or Kendrick Perkins did not mean there were major problems between Ainge and Doc. In fact both men believed their arguments were a constructive sign of how well they worked together. They were trying to hash out the best way to win another championship for the Celtics, and that one goal, which they shared above all else, was greater than their own opinions. The checks and balances of their opposing points of view made the Celtics a stronger organization. Sometimes they would have to agree to disagree, and occasionally leave each other alone if the quarrel grew too heated. But Ainge respected Doc's authority and never told him whom to play, even when Doc began Rondo's rookie season by benching him in order to make him earn his minutes.

"At the end of the day it's amazing how well we get along," said Doc. "Danny is an offensive guy, and the fact that he has allowed me to be a defensive guy just tells you how good he is in a lot of ways."

Ever since the first round of the 2009 playoffs, when Rondo averaged a triple-double of 24.2 points, 10.2 rebounds and 10.2 assists over the first five games against Derrick Rose of the Chicago Bulls, he had been included in the private postgame talks held in the trainers' room by Kevin Garnett, Pierce and Ray Allen. "Kevin will instigate," Pierce said. "We'll be sitting after the game and he'll say, 'What you think?' That's the first thing he'll ask. Then everybody will think about what's going on, and we'll start conversating."

As badly as Rondo wanted more respect in the Celtics hierarchy, he would spend many of those late nights listening and deferring to his elders. But his moods were unpredictable; his teammates could never guess how he was going to react, and that made it difficult for Doc to bestow on him the duties of leadership that Rondo wanted but didn't know how to earn.

In this new era of high-scoring point guards, Rondo was a traditional pass-first point guard reminiscent of Bob Cousy, with enormous hands that enabled him to palm the ball and make outrageous feints. Rondo had been a high school quarterback in Louisville, Kentucky, and under the basket he liked to show bigger defenders the ball, as if faking a handoff, before spinning the other way cleverly for a layup. It was the thinking-man's alternative to the slam dunk.

It had taken Pierce years to realize that Rondo didn't know whether to identify with his own AAU generation or the timeless perspective of his older teammates. "He's kind of like in between both," said Pierce. "He has some of that, and he has some of ours. He's right in the middle . . . and I think we didn't understand that."

Even while driving toward the championship in their first year together, the elder Celtics would see Rondo's anger bubble over when he was accused of being the weak link in their starting lineup. "Definitely he was frustrated," said Pierce. "He wanted things to come a certain way, and it wasn't. But he had to prove himself like all of us did. It's like a lot of great players: Your greatest strength can be your greatest weakness. His was his competitiveness.

"We knew what he was capable of, and we knew he could be great. It was, like, 'We want him to be great so bad — we got a chance to do this.' And I think that was the most frustrating thing for me, because I knew what he was capable of, especially after that one series against Cleveland." Pierce was referring to the 2010

Eastern Conference Finals, which had dispatched LeBron to Miami. "He was un-believable, and it was like, 'Wow, he's ready.' But it has to come on the court and off the court. You have to be willing to be coached, and you have to take criticism when you're trying to be a leader."

Pierce had been raised without a father, and he understood Rondo's issues. "He definitely went into a shell, and you didn't know which Rondo would show up as a person," said Pierce, laughing at his memories. "Some days he didn't speak to anybody. He was more moody than a lot of us. There would be days when he wouldn't say nothing." He laughed again. "It took me a while, from being around him, that 'This is who he is, so I'm not going to be upset if he don't speak to me today, he don't speak to anybody, and he's just more focused on him. That's just who he is.' Definitely we've had our run-ins, but I always try to pick my spots on when to talk to him. It's been tough, it's been a rocky road, me and him, but it's the new generation and it took me a while to understand."

The instant gratification experienced by the AAU generation did them no fa-vors, as far as Pierce was concerned. "I think this generation is a lot more spoiled than we were," Pierce said. "They've been given everything since day one, since they started playing basketball. I wasn't given the shoes, traveled around the country, looked at as a star — even though I was a pretty good AAU player. And so now they get the world. They're treated like NBA players before they make the NBA." He laughed to himself. "These AAU coaches sell the players to wherever, and they get all the sweatsuits and Nikes and everything they wear. I didn't have that growing up. My team was the K-Swiss Pacers: We played in K-Swiss. You see everybody running around in these Nike jumpsuits, which you wish you had, Jordan shoes, and stuff like that. This generation gets it all, and so they feel like they are owed something all the time, you know. And that's the difference."

The irony was that Rondo appeared to be as offended as his older teammates by LeBron's expressions of entitlement. And yet Rondo showed signs of envy as well. The only member of the Celtics who appeared to be oblivious to Rondo's conflict was Rondo himself.

All the same, Pierce believed he was seeing progress in Rondo. Or maybe he was seeing what he wanted to see. The hard truth was that Pierce and his older teammates needed Rondo to lead them past Miami, to help make up for the absence of Perkins and bind the new players from Oklahoma City into the tradi-tional culture of the team. They were counting on him to turn the corner on his issues and make everything right for them after the Perkins trade.

Shaquille O'Neal still had not — and would not — recover from a midseason Achilles tendon injury. Lacking their normal presence in the middle, the Celtics would lose twelve of their last twenty-seven regular-season games. Instead of being drawn closer to his teammates in their moment of need, 25-year-old Rondo was isolated by the departure of Perkins. "It hurt Rondo the most," said Pierce. "You saw it in his play, you saw it in practice, how down he was. They were like Cheech and Chong, like *Dumb and Dumber.*" Pierce chuckled. "They were partners, they were buddies, they went everywhere together."

At the team meeting in the closing weeks of the season, Doc ripped into his players, including Rondo, for mourning the business decision in this business that was paying them all millions of dollars. "He yelled at us, like, 'This is over!'" said Pierce. "He saw we were inconsistent. But that's always the toughest thing, especially when you mess with chemistry. No matter how good a player you bring in here, you're messing with the chemistry, and how are you going to get that in midseason?"

In the eightieth game of the regular season, the Celtics went to Miami and were clobbered 100–77. Absent Perkins, they were outscored 44–26 in the paint, and their lone defeat of the season to the team they hated most dropped them to the number three seed in the Eastern Conference playoffs, behind the number two Heat. And whereas LeBron appeared to be growing more comfortable with his role as the national villain, Rondo was recoiling from leadership.

"Frustration is high on our team right now," said Rivers on the night of that loss in Miami. He hadn't seen the half of it.

"Our principles are sound," Doc said as he sat on a bench in the Celtics' practice facility, surrounded by the old championship banners. "Our execution is not."

He was exasperated with Rondo.

After sweeping Carmelo Anthony's New York Knicks in the first round of the playoffs, the Celtics had gone to Miami and lost both games. Five months of superiority had been squandered in recent weeks. The team had failed to apply the pressure that Doc believed would make LeBron and his teammates crack.

"If you're doing it as hard as you can do it as a team and it's not working," said Doc, "then you know strategically you need a change." But they weren't playing hard. The ball was not moving. He did not see the Celtics committing to the plan that had enabled them to win their first three games against Miami earlier in the season.

Rondo had generated 20 points, 12 assists and 6 rebounds in Game 2 at Miami, but he was not showing leadership defensively. He was not locking in and disrupting the Heat as he loved to do, normally, in the biggest games.

Doc didn't want to hear that Miami was winning because LeBron and Dwyane Wade had learned how to complement each other at the end of their first season together. They had combined for 123 points while seizing their 2–0 series lead over Boston, but Doc was adamant that his team had made the games too easy for Miami's two stars. "As long as I've known basketball, there's only one ball," he said. "You can load to the ball no matter who has the ball, and we haven't done a very good job of that."

There would be one more practice before Game 3. The pressure was building. This was a highly personal series for the elder Celtics and their coach. As they saw it, they were fighting against Miami on behalf of a larger cause, and they needed Rondo.

It happened fast the next morning.

On the eve of their most important game of the year, the Celtics were gathered at the practice facility in their locker room, where Doc stood at the front, near a large TV screen, reviewing the elements they needed to improve in Game 3 against the visiting Heat. His criticism was leaning heavily on Rondo, which signified respect for his young point guard. If Doc had directed the same criticism at Garnett or Pierce — or if Gregg Popovich in San Antonio had happened to criticize Tim Duncan or Manu Ginobili or Tony Parker in the same way before a big game, as he often did — any of those players would have accepted the challenge because they wanted to be challenged. The coach was recognizing their power to influence the game. These were harsh and necessary compliments that they had earned. But Rondo was unable to embrace his own validation.

As the faultfinding wore on him, he yelled back at Doc that he should be criticizing Garnett, Pierce and Allen because they were failing the team more than he was. What Rondo did is known in locker rooms as finger-pointing, and it is one of the most destructive things a leader can do: to blame others instead of himself. As Doc turned his back to cite the video evidence, Rondo threw a plastic pint-sized bottle of Vitaminwater at the screen. It crashed into the TV and splashed on Doc. He turned to face Rondo. The players and assistant coaches jumped up to keep them apart. "Get the fuck out of here!" Doc yelled at Rondo, and Rondo turned and walked out on his teammates

Pierce could not believe what Rondo had done. "That was tough for all of us," he said. "It was like we were putting him in such a high position, and then we got to the point where we're wondering, 'Can he be that guy? Is this a guy that we're going to follow? Is he going to be a leader?' He's got to lead. You've got to take the criticism if you're the leader; you got to swallow it sometimes. That's all part of being a leader, and I just think he didn't understand that yet. You want to be the guy, you want to be the leader, this is a pill you're going to have to swallow sometimes. You're going to have to take criticism. You're going to take more criticism than everybody else. And at that time I don't think he was ready for that."

It wasn't only that Rondo had thrown the bottle at his coach before the team's biggest game. It was also that he had preceded that outburst by blaming teammates who had achieved more in basketball than Rondo was ever likely to accomplish. For the past four years they had been carrying him along, indulging his moodiness, in hopes that he would rise to their standards. When they urged him to take on the leadership for which he had longed, he responded by undermining them. It was true that Doc was harder on Rondo than on the other stars, but that was because Rondo had more to give than they did at this stage of their careers. Rondo had this rare opportunity, which Doc had never experienced in his own playing career, to lead his team to the championship while showing LeBron how it should be done. Doc was trying to help him live out that dream, and it wasn't going to be fulfilled by making nice.

"That's all part of growing and maturing," said Pierce. "And if you don't get it, you blame other people. Make excuses."

Pierce felt betrayed. "We needed him," Pierce said. "It really hurt me that he just walked out like that. It hurt me because our window was short. It was like, 'This is it. We got a great opportunity. We need everybody. It's all hands on deck.'" He laughed to take the edge off the memory, but there was pain in his eyes. "It just really hurt me that that happened that way in one of the most crucial games of the season. If we lose this game, it's over."

If the Celtics hadn't discovered Rondo, if he had slipped into the second round of the 2006 draft and been claimed by a miserable team unable to shroud his weaknesses in shooting and leadership, then he might have spent his first years in the NBA fighting and failing to establish himself. Instead he had been swept up by Pierce, Garnett, Allen and Doc, who had devoted their NBA careers to the pursuit of the championship ring that Rondo had collected in his second year. They could look back and recall how immature they had been at Rondo's age, and remind themselves that his demons had done more harm to him than to them, but their empathy went only so far. Instead of expressing gratitude and a desire to repay them at the end of their run together, Rondo rebelled. He had this once-in-a-lifetime chance to earn the respect he had always wanted. Instead of seizing it, however, he behaved as if to complain that it hadn't been handed to him earlier.

Over the course of the day, when they should have been focusing on Miami, Garnett, Pierce and Allen argued among themselves about whether Rondo deserved the privilege of playing in Game 3. Garnett was most outspoken that Rondo should be welcomed back to the team.

"I was more on the fence; I didn't know," said Pierce. "Doc was on the fence. We were all on the fence, because we knew we needed him — he was the point guard. It was tough. It was definitely a tough situation."

The next day, at the shootaround in the morning, Rondo told his teammates he was sorry. "He didn't cry, but he apologized to us," said Pierce. "I think he was more frustrated at the coaches than us, because he just apologized to us." Defiant to the end.

For the past ten months LeBron had been the adversary who galvanized them, who prompted them to trade Perkins, who wanted what they had without appearing to respect what they stood for. Instead of uniting for their last stand against LeBron, the Celtics were wounded and saddened by this conflict within their own team. Rondo's fellow Celtics could not simply write off his sabotage as an evil act. He was not a villain. They did not hate him. What was so unnerving was that they understood him and the source of his pain. They knew this episode was directed not at them as much as it was drawn from a conflict deep within Rondo that had nothing to do with basketball. What they had not realized was the extent to which they were all at the mercy of his torment. The pain he endured was suffered by all of them. Even for Doc — raised in his safe, loving two-parent home, a survivor of so many incidents worse than this outburst — there was no insulation from Rondo's misfortune. The consequences of whatever had happened to him long ago were now taken on by the entire team. They were all in this together, the healthy and the hurting, from this day to the ending of their world, this band of brothers.

The next incident happened with equal speed and unpredictability. The Celtics were leading 60–50, five minutes into the third quarter of Game 3, when Rondo poked the dribble away from Wade, who spread his arms and legs to box out

Rondo and prevent him from chasing the loose ball. Before Rondo knew what was happening his right arm was hooked with Wade's as Wade turned with a wrestler's angry leverage to throw them both down. Wade bolted back to his feet and stormed away, but Rondo lay behind him on the court, writhing, his left elbow having been bent grotesquely backward when he reached out with his free hand for protection from the fall. "That was disgusting," said Pierce, who was in the game with Rondo. "I thought he broke it."

In the sudden quiet of the TD Garden, as Rondo lay sprawled on his back, a voice could be heard from the Celtics' bench. It might have been one of the assistant coaches.

"The basketball gods are amazing motherfuckers."

Doc came out briefly to see Rondo. Though the play had happened directly in front of him, he had been looking elsewhere as Rondo's left arm was bent backward, and so he assumed that Rondo had banged his funny bone; maybe he had suffered a hard bruise. As Doc returned to the bench, Dr. Brian McKeon, the Celtics' chief medical officer, was holding and pressing the injured arm and talking to Rondo.

"It's called a FOOSH, that's the acronym — a fall on an outstretched hand," said McKeon later. A youthful type A 44-year-old with a medical degree from Georgetown, McKeon was appreciative of the immediacy of the situation. Most patients with an injury like Rondo's are examined hours too late, after the swelling has already locked the elbow out of joint. "By the time they get to the doctor," said McKeon, "you have to have three people pulling there and four people pulling here to get it back in."

In Rondo's case, however, McKeon was able to treat the injury before the elbow could swell. "He was in minimal shock," McKeon said, "but he was screaming, 'Don't touch my elbow, don't touch my elbow.'" McKeon quickly went through the ABCs of trauma care. "'Are you okay? What hurts?' You want to make sure. 'Does the wrist hurt?'" he said. "It's a quick, primary survey before you do something, to make sure you don't screw something else up. 'What about your fingers?' Just basic stuff like that, calming him down, get him to stop dilating, relax a little bit. Then I took him and popped it right back in."

He pulled on the forearm with a turn. He and everyone nearby could hear the elbow pop back into place.

"It was a very audible clunk," McKeon said. "I could feel it in my hands. A joint out of place is very, very painful. It's much more common with shoulders — you see it all the time — and fingers. I remember one of the most traumatic ones was [Houston Rockets center] Yao Ming. Screaming. And his trainer is trying to put [his finger] back in, and he's screaming in words that I can't even understand. Probably Chinese swear words. We got him in a locker room and I crawled on that thing, and if that didn't work, I would have waited another day, let him relax and then put it back in. But you have that little golden minute, so to speak, to put that joint back in, because you can't overpower Yao Ming, not even his finger."

As soon as his elbow had been put back in place, Rondo was helped onto his feet and led off the court, under the stands and down the hallway into the trainers' room adjacent to the Celtics' locker room. "I brought him back here because you've got to get control of the athlete — he's freaking out, screaming, he doesn't know what's going on because it hurts still," said McKeon. "And we got him back in the room, and all he wants to do is keep playing."

"I want to keep playing," Rondo was shouting. "I want to play."

McKeon wasn't sure if Rondo should be allowed back in the game. The decision to let him return would be controversial, as McKeon would realize after the game when he looked at his phone. "I had about forty-five texts from all over the world in about three minutes," he said. "People in France, everywhere — a lot of friends, orthopedic surgeons going, 'What are you doing? Why is he playing?'"

Ainge, team physician Guy Napolitana and athletic trainer Ed Lacerte were in the room with them. McKeon gave Rondo an anti-inflammatory injection of Toradol. He took an X-ray as he manipulated the injured joint. "It was a dynamic X-ray," McKeon said. "Stepped on the pedal and I move the elbow. Make sure there's nothing trapped in it, everything's working, he's got full motion. Ice him down. Give him morphine, which is perfectly legal and not controversial." McKeon would never provide morphine to a player for a number of games in a row, he insisted. "One-time it? No problem," McKeon said. "The doctor's giving it, say no more. I don't think it's too effective. More than any injection, more than morphine, the brain secretes something called endorphins — runner's high and all that. That adrenaline in those endorphins is powerful. They mask all that pain."

Out on the court, as the third quarter of their biggest game of the season was being played out, Doc didn't know what to think. He kept glancing around for an update from Lacerte. "I'm pissed at Eddie because it is taking forever," said Doc. "So he comes out and I say, 'Eddie, where the fuck is Rondo? How fucking long does a fucking elbow take?' And he's looking at me like I'm some fucking nut. He says, 'Doc, Rondo is out for the year.' And I said, 'What?' I had no idea."

The replay was being shown repeatedly on TV, eliciting comparisons to the gruesome compound leg fracture suffered in 1985 by Washington Redskins quarterback Joe Theismann. But Doc had not seen the video.

And then out came Rondo.

The Celtics were holding on to a 72–61 lead at the end of the third quarter when Rondo returned to the court with his left elbow wrapped in a white elastic brace. He had missed only 7 minutes, 2 seconds of the game. He continued past the bench, ignoring his coach, while the fans roared as if they'd seen the second coming of Larry Bird walking through that door. Doc looked over at McKeon, who responded with a thumbs-up.

"I'd say out of every fifty people, two would do that," said McKeon of Rondo's return to the game. "If I didn't get it back so quickly, I would have never let him play. Everybody handles the pain so differently, some more dramatic than others. Rondo's good with pain."

Doc didn't know what to think. From where he sat, a minor bump had turned into a season-ending injury, but now the team doctor was saying that Rondo could play. "Honest to God, if I'd known what actually happened, there's no way I would play him," Doc said. "So the best thing about the whole thing is that I didn't see it. Because I wouldn't have played him."

This was the kind of drama that Rondo was meant to create. His fans had no idea of the harm he had done to his team less than thirty-six hours earlier, and they didn't want to know. They wanted to believe in the story that was being played out on the stage, of Rondo behaving in the finest Celtics tradition as the star who overcomes all. Their energy flowed through Rondo along with his own adrenaline and anger. The fourth quarter was about to begin as he continued his walk across the midcourt line into the Heat's territory, where he stood facing the enemy bench without glaring at the players directly, in the way that a leading man wants to be seen by the villains before he takes them down. Rondo was showing Wade that he could not be knocked out, just as surely as he was encouraging the eighteen thousand fans to show his Celtics teammates and coaches that he was in fact their leader with the full emotional support of his people. Rondo was going to show everyone who he was on his own terms, and he was going to make Miami pay.

He played the entire fourth quarter with his left arm dangling straight down, like a mannequin's, while his right hand did the work of two. Rondo caught passes and rebounds and dribbled and shared the ball and shot at the basket with one hand. He picked up the opposing ballhandler in the backcourt, which was something he didn't particularly like to do when healthy, and he even tried to draw a charge from Wade that flattened Rondo on his back as the building shook with noise. Rondo's play in this game had been erratic before the injury, but now he was focused and disciplined. He began one defensive sequence by deflecting a pass from Chris Bosh before cutting in front of Bosh to intercept the return pass, and he finished the breakaway with a soft right-handed dunk as his left arm hung limp. Rondo's 4 points in the fourth quarter were twice as many as he had scored with both hands previously.

Inexplicably, Miami's defenders were backing away from Rondo now. "I don't know what they were doing," Doc said. "They were never forcing him to his bad arm. I was like, 'What the fuck's going on?'"

The past thirty-six hours had been bizarre in every way. They had revealed Rondo in full—for worse off the court and for better on it. In the meeting room he betrayed his more accomplished teammates and their coach, and in the game he prevailed in spite of an injury that would have done in any number of NBA stars who were usually more reliable than him. Rondo was a player of extremes, and his ability to beat Miami in spite of his mangled arm was not simply a statement of his talent. It also provided insight into his self-destructiveness. By no means had he brought this injury down upon himself, and yet there was a justice to it all the same.

Normally such courage would have set off a rallying cry among his teammates and coaches following their 97–81 victory. But Rondo was no longer capable of such leadership. In their interviews after the game, neither Doc nor Pierce would come close to referring to Rondo as a hero. When Pierce was asked in the locker room what had gone through his mind when he saw Rondo thrown down in agony, he shrugged and replied, "Everybody else needs to step up."

It was the story of Rondo's young career that he was not deserving of the credit he had suffered so greatly to earn. "I just don't believe in the whole hero thing," Doc said. "A hero is not a guy playing injured. Courageous is the kid that has to go to school every day on the bus, with no money, and figure out how he can sneak onto the bus. I played hurt all the time. Why is that courageous? This is what you should do."

• • •

Game 4 in Boston was tied at 86–86. There were 19.5 seconds remaining. Le-Bron had dribbled a turnover off his foot to give the Celtics the final shot at tying the series.

"If we had executed that play and scored and went 2-2, I am positive, Miami is out," Doc said. "The pressure, you could see it. The pressure was eating them alive."

After the series he had a long conversation with the Celtics' principal owner, Wyc Grousbeck, about this opportunity that had been lost. "I said, 'Wyc, you know just as much as me, at the end of the day it comes to supply and break,'" recalled Doc. "I said, 'If you can supply any type of pressure where you become a threat, they're done. Wyc, I'm telling you, you could see it in their faces. The only bulldog they have is Wade. He was trying to win it by himself.'"

There were practical reasons for Wade's dominating role, including the trust he had earned over the past three seasons from Spoelstra. "Dwyane was a much better pick-and-roll player in multiple situations than LeBron was. He just was. Dwyane at that time was quicker off the dribble, et cetera, et cetera, where LeBron was a coast-to-coast driving guy. When it came down to running something that you really needed, I believe at that time Erik felt comfortable in running 'need' plays for Dwyane."

Wade had entered the NBA as an undersized 6-foot-4 shooting guard with none of LeBron's pedigree. He had not been an AAU star in high school on Chicago's South Side, he had received only three college scholarship offers, and he had been sidelined throughout his freshman year at Marquette University for falling short of the NCAA's academic standards. As a junior he had led Marquette to the Final Four, and Riley's Heat had fallen in love with his type A aggression.

LeBron had been "passive" in Game 3, by his own admission, while scoring 15 points. In the crucial third quarter he had missed all three of his shots and surrendered four turnovers, for the thirteenth loss in his last fifteen games in Boston. The following night at dinner, Wade encouraged LeBron to approach the next game as their biggest opportunity in five years, dating back to Wade's 2006 championship run against the Mavericks and LeBron's 2007 breakthrough against the Pistons. LeBron responded with inspired plays down the stretch in Game 4: a game-tying three-pointer over Pierce with two minutes remaining, and a go-ahead layin muscled up from the paint with forty-eight seconds to go.

But then, on the verge of finishing off the Celtics, LeBron gave the ball back to them.

Even with a one-armed Rondo, even with Allen at age 35 and Garnett at 34 and Pierce at 33, even without Kendrick Perkins and in spite of all the Celtics' melodrama, Doc had remained confident that Miami was the more vulnerable team. "I really believe we would have beat them," said Doc; and then he amended his conviction. "Maybe without Rondo it would have been tough." With Rondo handicapped by his useless left arm, the Heat had adapted their defensive game plan against him. "For the first couple of years they'd always guarded him," said Doc. "And people don't realize, the way to stop Rondo is to *not* guard him." The smart play — implemented best by Kobe and the Lakers — was to back away from Rondo defensively, the better to cut off his driving and passing lanes while daring him to shoot. The Heat, however, were guarding him tight through Game 3, which in the counterintuitive world of Rondo enabled his strengths. "I thought it was a big advantage we had," said Doc. But that changed after Rondo's left elbow was injured. "They finally guarded him the way you should guard him," said Doc. "They didn't guard him."

And still the Celtics had this chance, in Game 4, to put a scare into the opponent they most wanted to beat. During the twenty-second timeout, Doc told Rondo to inbound to Pierce, who should wait at the top of the key for Allen and Garnett to approach. But then, as the players walked out of the huddle, Pierce told Rondo in an aside that he was going to pass the ball back to Rondo, who would hold it momentarily before returning it to Pierce.

"Well, Ray didn't know that," said Doc. "So Ray sees Rondo with the ball." Allen was wondering if the original play was being called off, because Rondo wasn't supposed to have the ball. Rondo passed back to Pierce, but now Allen and Garnett didn't know what to do. Were they still supposed to be running their sequence of the play? They looked at each other while Pierce shouted at them to approach. "They fucked the whole timing of it up," said Doc. "Paul made it look like it was somebody else's fault, but it really was Paul's fault." He had taken it upon himself to change the play without informing Garnett and Allen, which left Pierce alone to attempt a long, difficult fallaway jumper that spooned out and enabled LeBron, with 35 points and 14 rebounds in fifty minutes, to come away with a 98–90 victory in overtime.

Even as they began Game 5 in Miami, where Rondo would be limited to 6 points and 3 assists, his ravaged left arm fitted with a funereal black sleeve to match the trim of Boston's green road uniforms, the Celtics continued to behave as if they would reverse their 3–1 series deficit. "Come on, Paul!" shouted lifelong fan and assistant general manager Mike Zarren, his fists raised five rows behind the team bench. The Celtics were ahead 87–81 with 4 minutes, 15 seconds remaining when the Heat scored the final 16 points of the game, the last decade of them coming from LeBron. After he scorched a pair of three-pointers, he stood in place, huffing and puffing in false hyperventilation, as Wade came running over to punch at his chest. The white cloths that covered every seatback in the arena were now being tossed up by the celebrating fans, thousands of them, like confetti in reverse. For the visiting Celtics, it was like a sequel to LeBron's preseason rally. His behavior wasn't genuine, and it wasn't worthy of his talent; it was as if he was still behaving like the star he thought he was supposed to be. "It's hard to watch that shit," muttered one of Boston's coaches in the quiet visitors' locker room afterward.

But the Celtics had lost their chance to do something about it. Their season ended on the score of 97–87, allowing LeBron to advance at the expense of Boston for the first time, and he knelt on the court as if in prayer. The Celtics could not stand the sight of him because of the hard truth that he was reflecting back onto them. LeBron's relief from beating the Celtics was affirmation of his vulnerability. They'd had him where they wanted him, and they had let him get away.

Doc could see that Riley's disciplined culture was beginning to seep in. "The difference between LeBron this year, versus the year before in Cleveland, is we would call 'Slice One' and he would start yelling 'Slice One! Slice One! Slice One!'" said Doc. "And I thought, 'That fucker is doing his homework.' That was impressive. In the playoffs, if you don't know everybody's sets, you're lazy. If you're on the floor and you don't know it and are not yelling it out to everybody, you're not doing your homework. And the fact that LeBron was doing that told me he was in the playbook."

The Heat would move on through the Eastern Conference Finals, finishing off the top-seeded Chicago Bulls in five games. Even so, as he watched LeBron and Wade hugging each other as if their mission was accomplished, Doc couldn't help but wonder if they were ready for the NBA Finals. "That was their championship in some ways; that's how they reacted," he said of their five-game victory over his Celtics. "They were more emotional when they beat us than when they beat Chicago to go to the Finals."

The Celtics had their own worries. Over the final two games of the series,

Pierce, Garnett and Allen had all spent time with Doc in fear that he would no longer want to deal with Rondo. They believed Doc was on the verge of quitting. "The only time I ever thought he would leave was after the thing with Rondo," said Pierce. "I thought that was it for Doc, really."

No sooner had their season ended in Miami, however, than Doc announced at his postgame news conference that he was planning to sign a contract extension with the Celtics. The idea that he would depart because of Rondo was missing the larger point. It was because of players like Rondo that Doc wanted to coach. The priority was to compete for championships, and of course he would insist on a large commensurate salary. But he also recognized the needs of this generation of players, and that the game could help them realize who they were and who they could become.

12

THE TWELFTH STAR

The playoffs were eight days away as Bill Branch watched Kobe Bryant warming up for the seventy-ninth game of the regular season.

"Do you have a good feeling about tonight?" asked a woman in the luxury suite at the Rose Garden arena in Portland, Oregon.

"Never a good feeling," said Branch with a smile of self-effacement. "With other teams I can be optimistic, but with my team, never. Never. Never."

Branch was the assistant general manager of the Portland Trail Blazers. At 5 feet 9 inches he did not look like a basketball lifer. His soft accent and gracious ways connected him to North Carolina, where he had grown up picking the fields in the early summer mornings along Tobacco Road. The franchises that had employed him over the past twenty-three years — the Charlotte Hornets, Denver Nuggets, Oklahoma City Thunder and now the Blazers — had played close to two thousand NBA games, and Branch continued to be obsessed with their outcomes. In his navy sport coat, tie and slacks, he would stand in the back of the suite among the fans and family of Blazers employees who cheered from a perspective entirely different from his.

Kobe pulled up for a ten-foot jump shot, and the scoring was under way. Customers were milling around the suite as Branch leaned left and right in order to see around them. "It's amazing this time of year how every possession is so important," he said. The years of experience and his own sense of decorum had taught Branch to internalize his reactions to the game, as if to mask from these fans how a career in sports can ruin the fun. He and his fellow NBA executives watched their teams with poker faces meant to suppress anguish rather than joy. The most famous example was Jerry West, who as a Lakers Hall of Fame guard was the model for the NBA logo on his way to becoming the general manager who would discover Kobe as a 17-year-old high school senior. West, idolized by millions of daydreaming fans who envied his talent and charisma, could not bear to watch the half-dozen championship teams he constructed for the Lakers. The NBA was a business of joy that generated $4 billion dollars annually, and West's role in building it made him miserable. He was known to drive alone in his car, aimlessly, while his teams played.

"I've done that," Branch said. "And I think everybody misses that juice when they're away from the game. But when you're in it, it's a burden. I know I get too nervous about what is happening."

Kobe was going to make him feel those nerves tonight. In a phenomenal span of 113 seconds he made 4 three-pointers to slash Portland's lead to 53–47 at the end of the second quarter. This was an evening of entertainment for the fans in the luxury suite, who sat watching the peculiar halftime show of a small, sequined woman pedaling a high unicycle as she flipped one empty cereal bowl after another from her toe up into the air to land in a nesting stack on top of her head. For those who saw the NBA as nothing more than another kind of show business, it was absurd for someone like Branch to care as much as he did about the outcome of the games. For Branch and virtually everyone in his line of work, the competition was agonizing because they took every outcome personally. With every loss Branch reacted as if the scoreboard revealed his own shortcomings. He needed to feel that juice, to respect and fear the losses, in order to strive all-out for the victories. This game he was watching was more than a game to him.

"I can't enjoy this," he said with a pained smile, even though Portland's lead had swelled to 74–50 in the third quarter. Moments later Lamar Odom was sinking a three from out top. "See how quickly —" Branch began to say, before he was interrupted by someone pointing to the scoreboard. The Blazers were still up by 19. Branch shook his head and continued, "I'm telling you, though."

His skepticism was borne out. By the end of the third quarter the Blazers' advantage had shrunk to 74–62. "Let's change it up," he said. Branch left the suite and rode an elevator down to the event level. In the long, empty hallway serving the visitors' and home team's locker rooms, he could hear the reactions from the arena, and the roars and groans followed him through a doorway into the vacant sterility of the trainers' room, where he stood watching a small TV screen anchored high above the padded therapy tables. "The broadcast is delayed in here," said Branch. "It's always weird. You can hear the fans cheer or whatever out there, and then you see what happened."

From his pocket Branch pulled out a pair of clippers and began trimming his fingernails over an open trash barrel. It was the nervous equivalent of LeBron biting his nails on the team bench. "How silly do I look," he said, "moving from place to place because things aren't going right?" He tried to explain himself by referring back to a loss in this building two months earlier. "We had them beat, and Kobe came back and got us in overtime," said Branch. Kobe had 37 points that night. "It just crushed us," Branch said, as he threw his wad of chewing gum into the trash.

He could hear the Portland fans chanting the name of forward Gerald Wallace as he walked out through a heavy swinging door into another treatment room built around a small, deep exercise pool designed for the players to run in place against a current produced by the whirlpool's jets. He continued on through another empty room, tiled, with eight showerheads protruding from three walls. "Go to the rim, try to get fouled," Branch muttered to the delayed images of Wallace on the TV now facing him. Odom hit another three. "Fifteen-point game, five minutes left," said Branch, looking away. "That's nothing."

Kobe threw an elbow at Brandon Roy in hopes of drawing a foul before finding Ron Artest for a three-pointer to make it 82–70. "Oh my gosh," Branch said. Kobe drove and dished another three to Artest. 82–73. "Come on, let's go."

Branch's superstition led him back down the hallway into the interview room, where he arrived to see Kobe driving for a layin that he would have dunked in his younger days. 84–75. Kobe drove, hesitated, leaned up for another layin. A 7-point game. Branch was quiet. Two minutes, 9 seconds remained, and this was why a player like Kobe meant everything. Years of work by Branch and his colleagues could be undone by Kobe over the next 129 seconds.

LaMarcus Aldridge of Portland missed the rim with a jump shot, but Nicolas Batum, his quiet young teammate from France, chased down the loose ball and made a wild three-pointer before the shot clock expired. Kobe missed an off-balance three while trying to draw a foul, Wallace drove to the rim to make it a 12-point game, and Branch said, "Let's go."

With newfound authority he strode around the corner and toward the lights of the arena, where he stood in a corner to enjoy the final few seconds of victory. The horn sounded, and Branch withdrew in a hurry back into a darkened corridor beneath the stands. Clearly there was a routine to this, because seven Trail Blazers colleagues arrived to join him there. Without a word they formed a two-sided receiving line of four men on each side to greet the players, coaches and support staff on their way out of the arena to the triumphant locker room. Standing next to Branch in the line was Blaze the Trail Cat, the team's mascot. One after another the players and coaches ran through, high-fiving Branch and then the large, white five-fingered paw of the mascot, his red nose and enormous unblinking eyes nodding in approval. The incongruity of the 45-year-old professional celebrating in coat and tie next to the gigantic cartoon character did not appear to be noticed by Branch as he laughed for the first time all night. It really was amazing how every possession was important at this time of year.

Mitch Kupchak's office as general manager of the Lakers was a small upstairs room with an interior window overlooking the practice court. (It was similar to the view Danny Ainge had from his office in Boston.) The Lakers were downstairs practicing while Kupchak sat at his desk talking about Kobe. "There's nobody like him," Kupchak was saying of Kobe's domineering presence. Kobe gave the Lakers a ruthless weapon that no other team had, and with that weapon came responsibility. Kobe needed to be put to good use. If the Lakers weren't going to use him to win championships, then the weapon was going to be turned against them, which was what happened in the summer of 2007, when Kobe publicly criticized the Lakers while demanding that they trade him to a title contender.

"Going back to the stable factor in this whole thing, Dr. Buss: There was never a chance of him doing something that wasn't in the best interest of the franchise," recalled Kupchak. Jerry Buss, the Lakers' owner, who was 74 at the time, was the one to tell Kobe in 2007 that he wasn't going anywhere. Eight months later the Lakers acquired All-Star power forward Pau Gasol, a skilled 7-footer from Spain, who would enable Kobe to reach the next three Finals and win the two most recent NBA championships.

Kobe was convinced that his trade demand had forced the Lakers to take on Gasol. "No question, I think it helped tremendously," he said. He knew that his outbursts reset the team's priorities, he said, because a key member of the organization had told him so. "I'll keep his name anonymous," Kobe said. "But I don't give a shit. I don't need credit for it. I did what I did; whether people think it was right or wrong, I could care less."

Upstairs in his office Kupchak stiffened at the insinuation that the Lakers ever needed to be coerced by Kobe. "Ownership, [assistant general manager] Ronnie Lester, myself—I think we would take offense to saying we're not competitive, because we are," Kupchak said. "To compare who's more competitive, or to assume that Dr. Buss is not competitive and that Kobe did what he did to get Dr. Buss to do something, that's not true. To believe what you're saying is to believe that I'm not competitive or Dr. Buss is not competitive. And that's not the case at all."

The story of Gasol's acquisition had the ring of truth as Kupchak told it, because it was not a self-serving account. A full year before Gasol was sent to the Lakers, he had requested a trade from the Memphis Grizzlies, who were being managed by Jerry West, Kupchak's former boss. At that time, in February 2007, West told Kupchak that the Grizzlies had no interest in dealing Gasol to the Lakers. Then two things happened. West retired from the Grizzlies at the end of the season and was replaced by Chris Wallace (former general manager of the Celtics). And Andrew Bynum, the 20-year-old center of the Lakers, suffered a knee injury in January 2008.

Bynum was expected to be sidelined for two months, which left Kupchak desperate for a big man. "So we became a little bit more aggressive and we decided to revisit it," said Kupchak of the trade for Gasol. "We probably would not have been as aggressive, we maybe would not have revisited it, if Andrew did not get hurt."

Within three weeks of the injury to Bynum, the Lakers were sending a package of four players and two first-round draft picks to Memphis in exchange for Gasol. The most promising player sent to the Grizzlies appeared to be Javaris Crittenton, an athletic 20-year-old guard who, in 2011, would be charged with murder. Police would allege that Crittenton had become a member of the Crips, a Los Angeles gang, after signing with the Lakers. ("It is not uncommon for individuals involved in professional athletics to go out and join street gangs for protection," Fulton County assistant district attorney and gang prosecutor Gabe Banks told the *Atlanta Journal-Constitution*.) The Grizzlies also received 25-year-old center Kwame Brown, who had been chosen number one overall in the 2001 draft by none other than Michael Jordan on behalf of the Washington Wizards, and had since averaged a thoroughly disappointing 7.6 points and 5.7 rebounds per game.

"What they did in Memphis is beyond comprehension," complained Gregg Popovich, the San Antonio Spurs coach who was contending for championships against the Lakers. "There should be a trade committee that can scratch all trades that make no sense."

But Popovich had it wrong too: The trade would make enormous sense because a throw-in by the Lakers, an apparent afterthought, was Marc Gasol. He was Pau Gasol's younger brother, and after leaving his club in Barcelona, Marc Gasol would sign with the Grizzlies and turn into an All-Star center while earning the NBA's top defensive player award.

While Pau Gasol would elevate his new team into contention, the Lakers and their fans would grow frustrated with Bynum's recurring knee injuries and inattention to basketball. The Lakers coaches would tell Bynum that his two problems were related: He put himself at risk when he lost focus during the game, because he would naturally straighten up out of his ready crouch, and his knees, locked vertically, would be more vulnerable to injury whenever he was bumped off-balance or stepped on an opponent's foot.

And yet Bynum's indifference turned out to be good for the Lakers. As much as the fans would complain about his unfulfilled talent, it was Bynum's most annoying qualities that had enabled Kobe to prevail. For if Bynum had been vigilant and stayed healthy, the Lakers might not have traded for Pau Gasol.

"That's right," said Kupchak.

In a most roundabout way it was because of Bynum's frailty that the Lakers won championships fifteen and sixteen, leaving them one behind the Celtics in the league's most important race.

"That's how it works, really," said Kupchak.

In this counterintuitive world in which he plotted the unforeseeable future of the Lakers, Kupchak knew that neither Kobe nor anyone else could relate to him or Ainge or any of the other general managers who were pursuing the NBA championship. They were like the financial economists in the real world who admitted up front that their formulas were based on relationships and outcomes that defied prediction. Over the past sixteen years the Lakers had owned one pick in the top ten of the NBA draft, which they had used on the injury-prone Bynum, at number ten overall in 2005, and they could thank heaven that he had failed to live up to expectations; because if Bynum had succeeded, the Lakers might not, in this spring of 2011, have been seeking a third straight championship.

"And unless you're in the business, it's hard to understand that," said Kupchak. "In Kobe's defense, he wants to win every game now. He doesn't want to be lectured on what it's like to be in the front office and get a team turned around. My guess is he knows the rules better than anybody — the cap and the tax and how to make trades, et cetera. But in his mind, 'I'll wait a year, but that's it.' In his mind it's mapped out, whatever it is in his life that he wants to accomplish. And my guess is it's at least six NBA championships; and so he'll wait a year. But he's not going to wait three or four years. So I completely get it."

Kupchak, 56, had been around elite players for most of his life. He had grown up on Long Island in New York to become a 6-foot 9-inch All-America at the University of North Carolina, a gold medalist at the 1976 Summer Olympics in Montreal and a 24-year-old NBA champion with the Washington Bullets in 1978 before he signed a long-term contract with the Lakers in 1981. Two months into Kupchak's first season as a Laker, his knee was injured badly. By the time he retired in 1986, he had already begun serving an unofficial apprenticeship to Jerry West in the Lakers' front office.

Kupchak had won four championships since taking control of the Lakers in 2000. But he did not sleep well, and he would warn new general managers like Masai Ujiri of the Nuggets that they would not be able to sleep either. "They call eight months later: 'You told me I'd be starting [work] at three in the morning; how did you know that was going to happen?'" But Kupchak was not complaining. Just the opposite: He was proud to care so deeply, because everywhere he looked, he could see that passion and commitment formed the foundation of success.

"Do you think Phil's relaxed?" Kupchak said of Phil Jackson, who was preparing to retire at the end of the season. "He's the most successful coach ever — he's got eleven rings as a coach, two as a player — but do you think he doesn't feel pressure? He feels it. Obviously this is his last year. Hopefully it's not, but I think it is, and you think he doesn't want to go out a winner? I'll go into the coaches' room after the game, and he'll take his coat off, and he's drenched. People see a guy who's sitting there in a chair, calm, in control; I see a guy, especially after big games, who is visibly shaken — his mind is racing about a play, he's emotional, and you don't see that on the bench."

The only reason Jackson was going to quit was because his 6-foot 8-inch body would not allow him to continue. "If he was ten years younger, I know he wouldn't retire," Kupchak said. "He is handicapped. He's had multiple back surgeries, he's got a knee like my knee, and I know he's contemplated replacement, based on questions he asks me about my knee. I don't think it's something he would do right away, but if he did, then that would mean he's had two back operations — his back is fused — two hip replacements, a knee replacement."

Jackson openly referred to this season as "The Last Stand," and not just because his own end was near. Everyone involved with the Lakers was aware of each game eating away at Kobe's remaining time at the top of the NBA. He was completing his fifteenth season as one of those rare players who proved capable of leading his team to the championship. Basketball, based on its principles of equality and freedom, was a sport of merit, which liberated Kobe to dominate as no quarterback, pitcher or home-run hitter could.

This was why thirty of the NBA's last thirty-one championships, dating back to the arrival of Magic Johnson and Larry Bird, had been hoarded by eleven elite stars. The chronological list was shown to Kupchak on the eve of the 2011 playoffs:

> Magic Johnson (five championships)
> Larry Bird (three)
> Moses Malone (one)
> Isiah Thomas (two)
> Michael Jordan (six)
> Hakeem Olajuwon (two)
> Tim Duncan (four)
> Shaquille O'Neal (four)
> Dwyane Wade (one)
> Kevin Garnett (one)
> Kobe (five)

The exception that proved the rule was the 2004 championship, which was won by the starless Detroit Pistons, who exploited the exhausted Lakers shortly before the divorce of Kobe and O'Neal. Otherwise the rule of the NBA was laid out simply enough: If you didn't have one of those eleven franchise stars, your franchise wouldn't win the championship.

Kupchak was most intrigued by the empty space after Kobe's name. Somebody new was going to join Kobe and the other champions on that list eventually. "It's an interesting one if you're an owner or a G.M. of a team that doesn't have somebody like that," said Kupchak. "But you never know who that next guy is going to be."

After four inconsistent months, Kobe's Lakers had begun to look like championship favorites following the All-Star break, with a run of eight victories, including five against teams headed for the playoffs. They were coming off big wins at Oklahoma City and San Antonio as they arrived in Miami, where they found the Heat reeling amid five straight losses. This was an opportunity for the Lakers to kill Miami's confidence. On the eve of the game Jackson arranged for a team practice in the Miami arena, where he attacked LeBron's vulnerability.

"I enjoy watching the Spurs play," Jackson told a crowd of reporters gathered on Miami's court. "I enjoy watching Boston play; I love the style that they play. I'm not a big fan of the style that Miami plays . . . Their basketball is very much in standing with Xbox games, or whatever those games are when you play one-on-one."

Jackson was piling on with the critics who suggested that LeBron's self-absorption off the court was making him play selfishly on the court. It was true that the Heat relied heavily on isolation plays, but that was because they were still learning how to engage with one another.

"I like to see everybody involved in the game, so I think that's really important in basketball," Jackson went on. "That's what I try to preach as a basketball coach, even though we have a guy that dominates the ball in Kobe."

Riley believed that he was the target of Jackson's remarks, more so than LeBron. "Coaching against him, especially in New York and Miami, he took offense to almost anything I ever did. I'm probably one of his favorite people to take a jab at — which I care less about, by the way," Riley said. "Coaches that talk that way, I think, are wrong, because they don't realize just how much pressure they have put on their team to live up to their words, or how much they might have motivated the other team. I would never, ever say anything like that prior to a game, unless I really wanted to threaten somebody — and the wording would be a lot more violent than the soft words that he would lay on us. You learn over Phil's career that what he was directing at me at that time, or at LeBron or at the Big Three, is that with Big Chief Triangle, it's 'Unless they play the game the way it's supposed to be played — like I coach it — then they're never going to really be anything.'"

The next night Riley watched from his usual aisle seat near the court, and for this particular game he invited his former star Magic Johnson to sit beside him. "He came as a friend and a former player that I coached," Riley said. "He didn't go back into the locker room after, he didn't talk to the players. He came and he left. But LeBron and Dwyane and Chris knew he was there. They'd look over at him."

Riley was diagonally across from Jackson as the game played itself out between them. With two minutes remaining, Kobe was isolated against Dwyane Wade and the score was tied. It was a renewal of the showdown that Kobe had instigated two weeks earlier at the All-Star Game in Los Angeles. He faked and was dribbling free when he felt Wade reaching back to knock the ball loose. Gasol was on the verge of regaining possession, but he was blocked off smartly by the Heat's Mike Bibby, which freed Wade to pick up the ball and pass it ahead to LeBron for a breakaway dunk. Kobe came right back at him again, and Wade blocked his three-point shot. The Heat's 94–88 victory left them undefeated in two games against the defending champions—and much more, it broke their losing streak and rescued their season.

Kobe had played forty minutes and scored 24 points in the 1,275th game of an NBA career that had consumed almost half his life. After leaving Miami his Lakers would win their next eight games, including two against the Mavericks. They were in the midst of a forty-four-day run of seventeen wins in eighteen games. But all of that perspective was irrelevant to Kobe. He could not accept the outcome of this loss. "Foots, go get me two balls," he said to the Miami locker room attendant, Parron Outing, who was nicknamed for his size-16 feet. "We're going back out there on the court."

Kobe explained that he needed to work on his form after missing 12 of his last 15 shots against the Heat. "It's my job," he told the reporters who lined the court watching him. "I've got to work at it. This is what you're supposed to do."

But there was more to it than that. Kobe, dressed in a gray T-shirt and black sweatpants, practiced his shooting for close to an hour immediately after his loss to LeBron. "If you go to *Webster's* and get the definition of 'diabolical,' that was diabolical," said Riley, who noted that Kobe could have just as easily worked on his shooting in the privacy of the Heat's practice gym down the hall. "He was definitely laying down territory like a big dog, lifting his leg and saying, 'I'll be back.'"

Kobe was establishing the rules of the championship race and informing LeBron and Wade that their game-winning sequence changed nothing. He was Kobe Bryant, owner of two successive championships, three straight trips to the NBA Finals and a career of stubborn excellence to back up this larger point he was making as the workers deployed their noisy vacuums to floss around the arena seats surrounding him. Kobe was in charge of the NBA, even when he lost, and wherever he played, the court belonged to him, be it in Los Angeles or Miami, until someone else proved otherwise.

"Of all the players that I've ever coached against, there's no doubt from the time he was a rookie that he was one of the most competitive, kick-ass-with-no-mercy kind of guys in this league," Riley said. "In all the years I coached against him, I don't think he ever once said a word to me. I never sought it out, and he never offered it up, because he knew what I was doing, the same way Michael knew and Larry Bird knew. I was teaching my players to attack in any way I could — double-team him, knock him down — they knew those instructions were being given by me. He had that streak in him, maybe even more so than Michael — a mean streak when it came to playing the game."

"Oh, no question," Kobe was saying on the day before the playoffs.

The question was whether the NBA was more competitive now than it had been earlier in his career, when he was winning his first three championships alongside O'Neal.

"I don't think you can even make a sound argument against that," Kobe said. "If you look at today, there's a lot of young guns in their prime years, two of them being on the same team." He was referring to LeBron and Wade in Miami. "And there's Dwight and the younger, younger guys in Rose and Westbrook and Durant." Dwight Howard had led the Orlando Magic to a fourth straight year of fifty-two or more wins; Derrick Rose, with his top-seeded Bulls in Chicago, was about to be named league MVP; and Russell Westbrook and Kevin Durant had driven Oklahoma City within two games of Kobe's Lakers, who were entering the playoffs as the number two seed in the West. "And you've got the vets in ourselves and Boston and San Antonio," Kobe went on. "It's a very interesting time right now, very interesting time."

His rivals were all generational sons and grandsons of Jordan. Kobe had been the first in line among them, and now he was nearing the end.

When Kobe had blurted out his demand to be traded in 2007, it was a cry for help. "You think about it, I get up every morning, I train before practice, I practice hard, I work after practice, I go out, I play my heart out with the team that I had, scoring damn near 40 points a night trying to win, just to get blasted and criticized for it, saying, 'You can't win without Shaq,' and all this other stuff," he said. "I just wasn't going for it. I was terrified having the second half of my career be like a — no disrespect — a Dominique Wilkins, or all these other great scorers who never won. I was never going to accept that."

His trade demand had created a brief uproar, like a smaller version of *The Decision*, but Kobe was able to draw strength from one person in particular. "I spoke with Michael," he said. "I spoke with Michael, and he gave me some great advice that I'd never share, the advice that he gives me. Because I view it as sacred."

Jordan was unable to relate to LeBron's point of view as a free agent. In 2007, however, he was fully supportive of Kobe.

"As competitive as he is, he completely understood where I was coming from," Kobe said of Jordan. "Michael, in Chicago, they used to criticize him for shooting the ball too much. And he said he got tired of it. He said, 'Fuck it. If you don't like it? Trade me.' Oh yeah."

Kobe would be accused of acting irresponsibly by lashing out at the Lakers. But from his point of view, he was upholding a responsibility that had been passed down by Jordan, who had spent much of his own playing career second-guessing Bulls management and insisting that he be outfitted with a stronger "supporting cast." (Later, when Jordan became responsible for acquiring players for the Washington Wizards or his own franchise in Charlotte, he learned there was more to managing an NBA roster than he had realized.)

"I could understand where they were coming from," Kobe said of the Lakers. "But at the same time these are my years, physically, and I'm not going to waste them going out there every night scoring 40, 50 points, breaking my back to help us win, and in essence just feel like it's a show — 'Let's go watch Kobe score 40, 50 points and lose, and we'll generate revenue.' And I wasn't cool with that. And I was going to say something about it."

An NBA franchise star like Kobe was held responsible for virtually every aspect of his team — for winning the game at the end, obviously, but also for defining his team's attitude and its style of play, for channeling the directions of the coach, for recognizing the strengths and weaknesses of teammates while creating a winning environment in the locker room, for setting the example for teammates, for showing leadership at both ends of the floor, for never showing weakness . . .

The list of duties went on and on, and it was why so many great players would appear to collapse under the weight of their responsibilities in the crucial moments of the biggest games. There was so much for them to take on in basketball — more than a quarterback in football or a pitcher in baseball, both of whom would sit for large portions of each game — because every sequence at both ends of the court ran through them, and sometimes they would shut down like a network overwhelmed by requests. It had happened to Kobe in the playoffs after

O'Neal was gone; and it had happened to LeBron in 2010 at Boston. LeBron had yet to show that he could make sense of all these obligations, and he had multiplied his burdens by turning the world against him with *The Decision*. Kobe, however, had passed the ultimate test in Game 7 against the Celtics, which was why he was so damned arrogant.

In the years before free agency the NBA's biggest stars held no leverage over their teams. By 2007, when the demand for champions far exceeded the supply, Kobe was able to insist that his franchise make a priority of winning. The harm done to his reputation was a small price to pay for his two most recent championships, as he saw it.

By email, on the morning of each Lakers game, Kobe received an individualized scouting report to help him prepare for that night. "I have a standard form, a template," said Mike Procopio, the supplier of Kobe's information. His email would begin with details of the three matchups that Kobe was likely to face — the starting player, his backup and another player who might be assigned to Kobe.

"And then I say how the team is going to be defending him, what they're most susceptible against, what he can do to really mess them up," Procopio said.

A subsequent email would come from Procopio at 2 p.m. by Kobe's watch. "About two or three hours before he's getting to the arena, I'll throw him some more thoughts — that I think they'll play this way, based on information I got from other people that saw them play recently," Procopio said. "And I'm going to reiterate what I said before, and try to really instill confidence that he's going into the game knowing as much as possible about his opponent. I want him to know that he's got every possible bit of relevant information. I see all these guys that try to advise players, and they give all this bullshit, all this stuff that's irrelevant to his game, irrelevant to what's going to happen. I try to cut all that shit out. And then every email is going to be ended with 'You've got this.'"

You've got this, Procopio would insist, because he understood the pressures taken on by Kobe night after night.

"This is your game, you own this, you dominate this, this is you," Procopio said, explaining his pep-talk conclusion. "Again, in a team concept."

Instead of easing toward retirement and leaning on his experiences and reputation to see him through, Kobe was driving himself harder at the end of his career. He was not acting as if he had all the answers. By reading these emails every game day, Kobe was admitting that he didn't know everything. He was responding to his success with humility, which would elicit scoffing from the long list of those who had been subjected to his arrogance. But in his devotion to the game, he was humble, affording himself no break and pushing himself like an undrafted rookie trying to make the team.

Procopio, 35, was the ultimate merit hire. It was not for his experience as a player that Kobe sought out Procopio, who was 5 foot 7 inches tall and overweight, with a shaved head. Nor did Procopio profess loyalty for the Lakers, because his accent betrayed his smart-ass upbringing in the blue-collar Boston suburb of Revere. Money was not the source of his ambition either, because for all of his detailed work for Kobe, Procopio was not being paid.

"I told him I don't want money," said Procopio. "He's asked me on twenty occasions, 'What do I owe you? What can I do for you?' Not one dime, and I never asked."

Kobe had sent him a championship ring after the Game 7 victory against the Celtics, for which Procopio was accused by friends in Boston of becoming Benedict Arnold. "Lock and fucking key, I'll tell you that," he said of the ring's hiding place.

Procopio had been working in Chicago for Kobe's famed personal trainer, Tim Grover, who had made his name by training Michael Jordan in the 1990s. Impressed by their conversations, Kobe began reaching out to Procopio. The first time Kobe asked for advice, in 2008, Procopio let him have it. "I said, 'You need to look more to your teammates as far as drawing double-teams and kicking. You don't do enough of that. You try to win games by yourself. You can't do it that way.'" Procopio's introductory email went on to detail why and how Kobe should be creating open jumpers in the corner for one of his new teammates, Trevor Ariza, as well as opportunities on the elbow for the other newcomer, Pau Gasol. "'You've got to play off your teammates better,'" Procopio said of his message to Kobe. "'And it's not just giving it up. Penetrate, draw the defense and then kick.'"

He realized that he was risking an end to their relationship before it even started. "I was a little worried," admitted Procopio, "but you know what, if you're not going to tell a player the truth, what good are you? You might as well be one of those guys in an entourage that comes around, gets money off the guy, steals off the guy and lives off that guy. Some guys like to be harsh on players like Kobe just to show people, 'I was harsh on Kobe Bryant. I'm going to show them who's boss.' Life's too fucking short. Just get the job done. For the most part players want to be coached and they want to be held accountable, but you've got to have the balls to do it."

Twenty minutes after Procopio sent his email, Kobe replied. "It was 'I see your point,'" recalled Procopio. "And then we went back and forth."

Kobe called Procopio his Jack Bauer, after the counterterrorism TV drama *24*. His friends in Boston, and virtually everyone else who knew him in the NBA, referred to Procopio as "Sweetchuck," a character in the Police Academy movies. That nickname had been given to him in Revere, where he had scored 4 points as a high school player, and it was spread throughout the basketball world by Leo Papile, the long-haired head scout of the Celtics, who was arguably the most eccentric character in the NBA.

Papile was the son of a cop in Quincy, south of Boston, and he ran one of the nation's top AAU programs, the Boston Amateur Basketball Club. Papile was not one of the AAU exploiters. He was well established already within the NBA and independently wealthy by way of real estate investments. He was an intense, no-nonsense coach whose AAU players — all of them — earned college basketball scholarships, and some of them moved on to the NBA.

Procopio had been working the scorers' table and refereeing local AAU games in 1994 when Papile agreed to hire him in the parking lot of the Wonderland dog-racing track in Revere, where Papile had arrived in a blue Cadillac. "Leo said, 'I don't want you around here to know how long their pricks are, right? I want you here to coach them,'" Procopio recalled. Over the years he learned how to coach by watching, listening and asking pointed questions whenever he had the chance.

Procopio tutored himself while working at Michael Jordan's basketball camp every summer. "I'd always want to try to get questions off him, like footwork stuff; like 'Where do you put the ball?'; 'Why do you put it there?'; and 'In this situation what would you do to score?' And he's pretty fucking good when he knows you're not trying to get something off of him," Procopio said of Jordan. "Same thing with Kobe. I don't ask him what the fucking weather is; I don't ask him what his favorite movie is; I want to ask him basketball stuff."

What Procopio had with Kobe was an impersonal version of Holger Geschwindner's relationship with Dirk Nowitzki. The absence of money changing hands enabled them to trust each other and focus on the larger goal that drew them together. The 2010–11 season was the first year Procopio delivered reports to Kobe before every game, and the work was exhausting. "It was a long, long year," he said as he looked back on it. "I was through the ups, I was through the downs, I was through this whole playoff turmoil thing, and it was tough. It was a very, very hard season. It was tough to watch. It was weird, just how good they are, and they just never clicked."

As Kobe approached the finish line of the 2011 playoffs, Procopio could see the Lakers losing their way. "I like the triangle and I'm a fan of it," Procopio said, "but for that team I think there should have been some changes made within the triangle, to get some more action out of pick-and-roll coming off screens. They needed some help. You're not going to isolate with the triangle. You have to create your own opportunities, and that wears you out a little bit."

The rest of the league was using pick-and-roll plays to create instant mismatches that sprung players open for three-point shots or drives to the basket. "The triangle works best when you're cutting off post players and there's constant movement," Procopio said. "But when the ball is caught on the perimeter and you're not setting screens, it's a tough thing."

He would see positive results the few times they switched into the pick-and-roll to salvage a possession. "I'd say, 'Kobe, why don't you try this?' He'd say, 'Mike, it's not in our system,'" said Procopio. "He was very, very respectful of Phil."

The Lakers would be pushed to six tiring games in their opening-round series against New Orleans, despite the absence of the Hornets' second-best player, All-Star forward David West, who had suffered a devastating knee injury one month earlier. But hungry young point guard Chris Paul was able to drive the Hornets to a split of the first four games.

Little more than an hour before the decisive game in New Orleans, Kobe lay on a training table in the visitors' locker room, a therapist turning and flipping him and kneading deep into the tissue, as if trying to resuscitate the old muscles and joints. It was a form of pregame torture that would enable him to score the 24 points his team would need from him that night.

Several days earlier, during the Game 4 loss in New Orleans, Kobe had rolled his left ankle badly and left the arena on crutches. But he refused to undergo an X-ray or MRI to diagnose the injury because he didn't want to know the result. "He won't let them deal with it," said Jackson. "We're trying to convince him that it might be a good idea."

Kobe played, his team won the next two games, and Jackson's confidence was renewed as he looked ahead to the second round against the Mavericks, who had lost ten of thirteen games to the Lakers since the arrival of Gasol in Los Angeles. This group, insisted Jackson, has the "potential to be as good as any team I've coached with the Lakers."

The late-day workouts with Holger continued in Los Angeles, on the girls' court at a high school not far from the old Forum, where Magic Johnson had played in the 1980s against Larry Bird, Isiah Thomas and Michael Jordan. The girls' gym was a small, simple space not unlike many where Dirk had worked out in Germany. "We couldn't get the men's gym because they had practice or something," said Casey Smith, the Mavericks' athletic trainer, who snapped pictures with his cellphone of Dirk the underdog training humbly, like Rocky Balboa throwing punches in a meat locker. The surroundings added urgency to their sessions, Smith said: "We had to leave when it was getting dark."

Holger would be with the team for more than two months. It made for a grueling schedule for Dirk, who worked each night with Holger in addition to attending the team's practice earlier in the day. Every day, in between their sessions, Holger wore the same black leather jacket, regardless of the heat, and he seemed to wear the same few clothes underneath. Dirk's teammates would taunt Holger by begging Dirk to start paying him.

In Game 1 of the Western Conference Semifinals, the Lakers straddled halftime with an extended run to stretch their lead to 60–44 early in the third quarter. The Mavericks responded by benching DeShawn Stevenson, who had committed two straight turnovers, and replacing him with 25-year-old Corey Brewer, a skinny 6-foot-9 swingman who had won two national championships at the University of Florida. Brewer's impact was immediate: He missed a layup, but he and his teammates kept attacking the glass and recovering the rebound until Dirk was able to curl around a screen for a traditional three-point play. Tyson Chandler finished a lob from Jason Kidd, Dirk fed Shawn Marion for a layup, and Kidd drilled a three to slice the deficit in half.

It was tight the rest of the way, but the Lakers refused to surrender the lead on their home floor. One minute remained when Kobe pulled up from ten feet for the last of his 36 points to keep the Lakers ahead, 94–91. Dirk replied in kind with a move straight out of his workouts, driving left and planting hard on his left leg to sink a fallaway jump shot that no one else would have dared attempt. As he and his Mavericks retreated back to their basket, the change in their character was becoming apparent: Each was taking up his exaggerated defensive posture, and they looked nothing like their old selves. They were serious as never before, with all thanks to Chandler, the leader of their defense, who slid over to cut off Kobe's drive and force him to kick out to the three-point line, where the ball was intercepted by Jason Terry. When Gasol committed a panicky foul during the ensuing inbounds play, Dirk made both free throws to steal the lead for the first time in the second half.

Needing a basket, the Lakers committed another turnover when a handoff from Gasol to Kobe was blitzed by Kidd, who made one free throw with 3.1 seconds remaining. A timeout was called. The ball was inbounded at midcourt. Kobe, trailing by 2 points, sprinted out and around a Bynum screen that left Kidd far behind the play. Kobe grabbed the pass and went up straight with a three-pointer. It bounced hard off the back rim, a few inches long from twenty-six feet.

The Mavericks followed the 96–94 victory with another one, two days later, 93–81. This time in the visitors' locker room Dirk knew what to say. "I've been up 2-0," he said casually to his teammates. "I've been down 2-0. It doesn't matter, because they're going to bring it Game 3, and we've got to be ready."

Nothing more needed to be said because his teammates knew that Dirk was right. They knew who they were and that they could not take anything for granted, not even the fact that only three NBA teams had ever recovered from an 0-2 deficit at home in a best-of-seven series. Most relevant to the Mavericks was their respect for the Lakers. All that Dirk and Mark Cuban and the other Mavericks wanted was to win one championship, and here they were trying to upend a coach who had won eleven of them, an owner who had won ten, and the most accomplished player in the game, who was desperate to win his sixth.

"I might be sick in the head or crazy," said Kobe after his Lakers had lost Game 3 98–92 in Dallas, "because I think we're still going to win the series. Win on Sunday, go back home, and see if they can win in L.A."

Kobe, deviously, wanted to confront Dirk's Mavericks with the reputations they were trying to undo: theirs as losers, and Kobe's as the ultimate winner. Win Game 4, as Kobe was planning, watch the Mavericks choke away Game 5 in Los Angeles, and then come back to Dallas and hold them accountable for the disappointments of their recent past. Make them relive their losses of the past five years, as if that was who they were and all they would ever be.

No offense was taken by Dirk, whose past had become a source of his newfound strength. The old playoff collapses didn't worry him as much as they encouraged him to appreciate the confidence that he could feel growing within him and radiating among his teammates. The Lakers were slowing the tempo, which was inviting his Mavericks to play faster and more instinctively, as opposed to dwelling on the unlikeliness of their 3–0 series lead.

The Mavericks had been knocked down and counted out so many times that the fear of failure, which used to preside over them, had been replaced by a healthy respect for the first punch and the power derived by throwing it. Each game had helped them realize their own strength, and by Game 4 in Dallas they could not wait to put that strength to use. Their lead was 24 points at halftime, and it was 94–68 when Lamar Odom was ejected for blindsiding Dirk with a hard shoulder early in the fourth quarter.

A review of their shocking seven days against the defending NBA champions helped the Mavericks make sense of their own transformation. They were the older team, but their play was more upbeat and confident. They had built up their front line around their 7-footers, Dirk and Chandler and Brendan Haywood, in hopes of nullifying Gasol, Bynum and 6-foot-10 Odom. But the crucial difference emerged on the perimeter, where their pick-and-roll game gave them an advantage that Jackson's triangle could not match.

Dirk, Cuban, coach Rick Carlisle and the rest of the Mavericks looked up to the Lakers in much the same way that Miami emulated Boston. As the series approached an ugly end, it was as if the Mavericks were turning into the Lakers, and the Lakers, vice versa, were expressing the frustrations that had defined Dirk and his team for the previous five years. Ron Artest had been ejected for clotheslining J. J. Barea in Game 2, Jackson had lost his temper with Gasol in Game 3, and now Andrew Bynum was being ejected for another cheap shot against Barea in the fourth quarter of Game 4, stripping off his shirt disrespectfully as he crossed the court on his way to the locker room.

After their 122–86 victory had finished off the Lakers in four games and Phil Jackson had hobbled out of the arena, apparently for the final time as coach of an NBA team, the Mavericks did not know what to do with themselves. The Lakers had driven them to play better than they imagined they could. But there were two rounds still to play and nothing yet to celebrate.

Kobe didn't know how to react either. He was still keeping his eyes on the goal of a sixth championship, but the window had closed. The coach who had escorted him and Jordan to all of their championships was gone. Kobe's knee was degrading, his teammates were receding, and Jerry Buss's health was failing.

Kobe would take no solace in this, but he had fulfilled his higher calling. He had upheld the competitive standard that Jordan had passed on to him a dozen years earlier. Now that responsibility was being taken up by Dirk, of all people. Dirk, the immigrant, was all that stood between LeBron and the championship.

13

THE FINALS

Scene of the crime," Mark Cuban was whispering to himself, just loud enough to be heard, like an actor musing for his audience.

It had been five years since Cuban's previous visit to Miami for the NBA Finals. He was hunched over on one of the black padded chairs that formed the visiting team's bench in the AmericanAirlines Arena. Bordering the court was a large milling pack of reporters, NBA employees and on-air talent. The swarm of TV cameras and equipment and technicians, as well as their cables lying all over, made every step a potential hazard. The court itself seemed smaller as a few players warmed up uncomfortably around the two baskets. Game 1 of the 2011 NBA Finals was less than two hours away.

The return of Cuban's Mavericks to this venue had seemed unlikely two months earlier. Chandler was criticizing his teammates' inattention defensively and the hollow commitment it revealed. In the final week of the regular season, the Mavericks appeared to be on their way to a fifth straight loss when Jason Terry launched into a tirade against J. J. Barea, their tiny young point guard, while trailing by 14 points to the visiting Clippers. Terry was angry that Barea was dribbling instead of feeding passes to him at the three-point line. Coach Rick Carlisle regained control by meeting privately with Terry after the game. "He said, 'Don't worry about what your teammates can't do,'" Terry recalled. "'Focus on the positive things this guy does for us, because he doesn't just fuck up—he does some great things for us.'"

Carlisle's advice would be affirmed weeks later when Barea's dribbling helped sweep Kobe Bryant's Lakers. "If you look at our Laker series, we wanted to use penetration to break the defense down," said Terry. "The shooters began to become wide-open, and if he wasn't dribbling as much then, we wouldn't have got those open shots."

"A big, big moment," said Dirk Nowitzki, as he recalled stepping in with his teammates and the assistant coaches to suppress the incident, even as Carlisle screamed at Terry and pointed, like a headmaster, for him to sit at the end of the bench, where he was drawn aside by Cuban for a heart-to-heart. Terry was late returning to the court from the locker room after halftime, and he sat watching glumly as his teammates recovered to end the losing streak without him. "The next day they all apologized, and Jet for the rest of the season was very positive and wanted to work every day," Dirk said. "It was something that needed to happen, and it kept everybody honest."

Terry, 33, had arrived at training camp that season with a new tattoo of the championship trophy on his right biceps as an expression of his commitment. In the final days before the 2011 playoffs, he accepted responsibility for his earlier actions. "That negative energy that I was having out there, the guys fed off that," said Terry. "They look to my body language, to my energy, and it was negative at that time—and so that was the way we played. Negative. Once that energy turned all positive, it was magic."

The surprise was that Terry's point of view had been refined by Carlisle, who was more intellectual tactician than inspirational leader. "I would never say he's a people kind of guy," said Dirk, who had seen Carlisle rely on assistant coaches Dwane Casey, Terry Stotts and Tim Grgurich, as well as team psychologist Don Kalkstein, to strengthen the personal connections within the team. "They got good relationships with the players, where they can come up at any time and talk about stuff," said Dirk. "Where that might not be Rick's strong suit."

Carlisle, calculating as he was, was able to recognize his own weaknesses. Most retired players become coaches because of their magnetism, as if it is in their nature to lead, but Carlisle did not have that particular strength going for him. Early in his career, when he was trying to become an NBA head coach for the first time, he would acknowledge to prospective employers that his technical mastery of the Xs and Os amounted to only 10 percent of the job, and that the other 90 percent involved building relationships. "I'm always working on that," he admitted years later as coach of the Mavericks.

He was fired from his first head-coaching job in Detroit, where he was known to treat employees terribly. When Larry Bird was hired as team president of the Indiana Pacers, one of his first suggestions was to replace coach Isiah Thomas with Carlisle, who one year later would hold the Pacers together following the league-mandated suspensions resulting from their 2004 brawl in Detroit. Even now in Dallas, the 51-year-old coach was routinely lost in his own deep thoughts and unaware of the impressions he made. "Yeah, I've improved for sure," he said. "But, I mean, I'll never be all the way there."

He fed on good ideas and didn't care who came up with them. Early in the season Dirk and Jason Kidd asked Carlisle to promote 6-foot 5-inch shooting guard DeShawn Stevenson to the starting lineup, in order to strengthen the Mavericks defensively and make Terry more dangerous coming off the bench. The Mavericks won twenty-one of their next twenty-four games before Carlisle demoted Stevenson in order to experiment with Rodrigue Beaubois, a young 6-foot shooting guard from Guadeloupe, who was the most explosive athlete on the roster. By the final week of the season Dirk and Kidd were back in front of Carlisle, convincing him to reinsert Stevenson into the starting backcourt, and it was by no coincidence that the Mavericks then went 12-3 in the playoffs before entering the Finals.

Carlisle's biggest move involved his fractured relationship with Kidd, who had been acquired in 2008. The Mavericks had lost three of their next four playoff series as he and Carlisle clashed over control of the offense. Instead of siding with the player and firing the coach, or vice versa, Cuban's response had been to invest in a better relationship between these two strong-willed men. He rehired Kalkstein to work year-round with the Mavericks, and the psychologist enabled Kidd to vent his frustrations while eventually recognizing Carlisle's strengths as a tactician. Carlisle, in turn, was empowered to hire one of his coaching mentors in Grgurich. The Mavericks were back in the NBA Finals because they had learned to talk out their problems even though their three leaders — Dirk, Kidd and Carlisle — were introverts.

"It was Coach Carlisle falling back and saying, 'You know what, Jason, you run the offense. You do that,'" said Terry. "'I'll manage the guys, I'll manage the minutes, and whatever we do offensively is on you. You got it.'"

The Mavericks' fluid style had defined this surprising postseason run. Neither Carlisle nor Kidd was shouting out the call of the next play, which prevented opponents from anticipating where the ball was headed. The Mavericks were brimming with scorers whose experience enabled them to read the defense and make plays for one another without a word being spoken.

During the 2010 postseason Dallas had swooned in the opening round because Kidd had been worn down by an ear infection in addition to the big minutes he had absorbed. But now Kidd was refreshed because, in advance of training camp, trainer Casey Smith had approached Carlisle with a plan to trim three minutes off the thirty-six per game that Kidd had averaged during the previous regular season.

"You say it's only three minutes a game," said Smith, but then he did the math: The total savings was equal to sidelining Kidd for six entire games. In addition to averaging 33.2 minutes per game in 2010–11, the Mavericks gave Kidd a full six days off by benching him for two games in early April, less than a week before the playoffs. Those were the only games he missed.

"We let him sleep a lot," Smith said. "No early mornings." The first game without Kidd turned into the fourth straight loss for the Mavericks, but Smith was adamant. "We lost that game against Denver, and everyone's freaking out," Smith said. "I'm like, 'No, he's still sitting out the next game.' 'But we need to win.' 'I know we need to win, but we need *him*.'"

Over the past two regular seasons the Mavericks had gone 34-18 in games decided by 5 points or less because Kidd was at his best in those moments, coming up with scrambling, unscripted plays that few stars had the instincts to make. No player in the Miami Heat's playoff rotation was within five years of Kidd's age, and yet throughout the NBA Finals they would be unable to turn his age into a weakness. Instead, at 6 feet 4 inches tall and 205 pounds, Kidd took turns guarding LeBron James and Dwyane Wade, who together were twenty-one years younger. Kidd's ability to take on the most difficult assignments gave Carlisle the freedom to adapt in other ways.

"We lacked a little bit of what Jason Kidd could give their team because he didn't have to be a scorer," said Heat president Pat Riley. "He just had to be a leader and an organizer and a tough defender and a playmaker and all that. I thought Jason Kidd was integral to that whole situation."

Like Dirk and Terry, Kidd was hungry to make up for previous disappointments: He had lost two NBA Finals with the New Jersey Nets in 2002 and 2003, and each time the same lesson came through. "They were never in distress," Kidd said of his Lakers and Spurs opponents who won those two championships. "You could always see them with composure, being able to find a way, always just staying the course."

It was with that lesson in mind that Kidd and Dirk approached Cuban during the season with a variety of proposals to scale back his outspoken behavior. "Let's just try skipping a game or two on the road," said Kidd of his ongoing requests for Cuban to tone himself down. When they found themselves winning under these quieter circumstances, Kidd then asked Cuban to consider staying away from road trips entirely. That suggestion was a nonstarter.

"We had plenty of little discussions about him not sitting on the floor, about him talking to the media and always throwing stuff out there," said Dirk, recalling Cuban's inflammatory responses during the 2006 NBA Finals that had escalated his team's collapse. "But he's our number one fan and he's doing this 100 percent and he's behind us, so I understand some of it."

There was a time when Dirk had been more than understanding about Cuban's behavior. In his youth he had been happy to defer to Cuban as public leader of the Mavericks. Yet neither Dirk nor Kidd could see the good any longer in Cuban's tirades, and in particular his focus on refereeing, which too often distracted his team at times when composure was essential. Cuban had long reflected the mood of his team — happy when times were good, lacking in composure otherwise — but what the Mavericks needed now was a poker face.

In the early going of their series with the Lakers, Cuban declined to give interviews. It was as if he had stopped in mid-sentence, and the longer Cuban held his tongue, the deeper his team moved through the playoffs. "It helped him understand what we've been trying to tell him," said Kidd. They weren't winning because he had shut up; rather his silence became an expression of their focus and determination. He was offering his sacrifice to a team that was winning because of the adaptations that players, coaches and staffers had made on behalf of one another.

In the Western Conference Finals the elderly Mavericks were up against the Oklahoma City Thunder of Serge Ibaka, James Harden, Russell Westbrook and Kevin Durant, all 22 or younger. Durant, listed at 6-9 but closer to 7 feet, was a 2.0 version of Dirk, with an evolved athleticism to complement his explosive three-point range, and his 24 points in Game 2 shot the Thunder to an upset win in Dallas. But Durant had yet to develop Dirk's cleverness or resolve, and while Dirk was leading the visitors back from a 15-point deficit in the final five minutes of Game 4, Durant could not muster a reply. Dirk would finish with 40 points in the overtime victory that provided Dallas with a 3–1 series lead, while Durant was going 0 for 6 with 2 turnovers in the last ten minutes.

After their requisite victory in Game 5 in Dallas, a brief ceremony was held in the locker room to present the Mavericks with their trophy as champions of the

Western Conference. What happened next is in dispute. Several members of the organization remember Dirk saying, "We've already got one of those," and then dropping the trophy into a laundry bin.

"No, that's not true," Dirk said. "I just lifted the thing real quick and then I left, because I didn't really want to celebrate. I knew we had four rounds to win and we had won three. In 2006 we were just so happy to be there, and I wanted to make sure that we're not — we're there to win one more round."

So here sat Cuban, back in Miami, five years since his last NBA Finals, the loudmouth no more.

"Scene of the crime," he whispered with a grin. "It's déjà vu all over again."

Yet it was more than revenge that Cuban was seeking.

The Heat looked like champions-to-be, and Cuban knew very well that virtually everyone was picking LeBron to roll to his first of many titles. But Cuban also knew that his team would not surrender to appearances. There was no pretense to his Mavericks. In the minutes before this unexpected chance at redemption, he was at peace and uncharacteristically quiet.

Cuban's smile did not last. His Mavericks were throttled defensively by Miami in Game 1, losing 92–84.

And now, in the fourth quarter of Game 2, the déjà vu was close enough for him to reach out and grab. There in front of Cuban was Dwyane Wade, the hero of '06, splashing down a three-pointer from the corner as his fallaway momentum carried him into the Mavericks' bench near the owner's seat to seize an 88–73 advantage for Miami. Cuban glared at the celebrations of Wade and LeBron as they skipped their way back across the court, the short span of 7 minutes, 15 seconds separating them from their anticipated 2–0 series lead.

Dirk was watching too.

"For me going into the fourth quarter, I know it's winning time," LeBron had bragged after helping Miami pull away in the closing minutes of Game 1. "That's when the game is won."

More than six weeks earlier, on the eve of the Heat's first playoff game together, Wade had interrupted a team dinner by bringing out his 2006 championship ring — the reward he had earned at Dirk's expense. The gaudy ring made his hand look smaller as he reminded LeBron, Chris Bosh and his other teammates that this was why they had come together.

They had gone on to win twelve of their fifteen playoff games against the Philadelphia 76ers, Celtics and Bulls. Their half-court offense had been clunky, dependent too often on one-on-one isolations, but defensively they were as aggressive and quick to the ball as an NFL secondary.

"In a lot of ways it was a joyous year," Riley said. "A lot of parties, a lot of fun and laughter." He remembered the annual Christmas party, held at his house for the Heat players and staff and their families. During the Yankee swap of gifts, LeBron's presents were stripped from him time after time. "Now I know how it works here in Miami," he proclaimed to the roars of his new teammates and colleagues. "It's hazing."

On the night before Game 1 of the NBA Finals, Wade, LeBron and Bosh reunited on the court of their arena in Miami, where eleven months earlier they had guaranteed an easy run of multiple championships. The hard year they had created for themselves was almost behind them, with their dignity still intact. Not once had any of them—LeBron in particular—lost his temper in public, in spite of the jeering hatred that relentlessly greeted them away from Miami. "I think about how strong a shell LeBron has," Riley said. "Even though he's a sensitive man, he took everything pretty much in stride. I never saw him crack."

LeBron had shown impressive progress over the second half of the season. Instead of getting bogged down amid the criticism and scrutiny, he had emerged as Miami's best player, leading his new team with 26.7 points and 7.0 assists per game to go with his 7.5 rebounds. Neither he nor Wade, who had generated 25.5 points per game, had ranked among the top two candidates for Most Valuable Player (which had been awarded to Derrick Rose of the Chicago Bulls, with Dwight Howard of the Orlando Magic as runner-up), and that slight had bound them more closely together during the playoffs. A mutual understanding between Wade and LeBron had been forged over recent weeks: LeBron was more productive by dint of his superior talent, but Wade was still the leader.

"I went through a lot, signing to be here and the way it panned out," LeBron had said of *The Decision* during a postgame news conference after finishing off the Celtics. "I apologize for the way it happened, but I knew that this opportunity was once in a lifetime."

It had been his first such apology, and it wasn't much. He was hinting that a championship would ultimately validate his behavior: as if the triumph of his talent on the court would prove, retroactively, that the reaction to his show had been all about nothing.

And yet the hatred for LeBron was diminishing, slightly, by way of the respect that was building for him. He was winning the big playoff games in spite of the public protests. He was still detested nationally, but there was hope in Miami that a championship would enable him to claim the high ground.

With their victory in Game 1 of the NBA Finals, LeBron and his teammates were on a 28-6 tear dating back to the visit by Kobe three months earlier that turned their season around. They had become the NBA's hottest team thanks to mean defense and the overwhelming talent of three stars in their prime. They had turned their nightmarish year inside out, forcing the rest of the NBA to question how LeBron, Wade and Bosh could be stopped simultaneously. In Game 1 against the Mavericks, LeBron sank four of his five three-pointers while generating an efficient 24 points with 9 rebounds, 5 assists and 1 turnover, and his throttling defense kept Terry scoreless in the fourth quarter.

For Dirk's Mavericks, their positive momentum had been reversed with discouraging familiarity. The fourteen consecutive regular-season games that Dallas had won against Miami were suddenly irrelevant; all that mattered was this fifth straight Finals loss to the Heat dating back to 2006. The bad news built up quickly in Game 1: Backup center Brendan Haywood incurred a hip injury that would limit him to eleven minutes for the remainder of the series. Terry sustained a bone bruise on his right wrist while trying to dunk. And fears that backup forward Peja Stojakovic would be unable to keep up had been confirmed by his fifteen scoreless minutes in the opener.

Most worrisome was the injury suffered by Dirk in the fourth quarter as he tried to strip the ball from Bosh. A torn tendon in the last joint of his left middle finger had rendered the tip of the finger useless. It was not his shooting hand —he could be grateful for that—but Dirk was struggling nonetheless in Game 2. He was an ineffective 6 for 17 with 5 turnovers through the first forty-five minutes.

The worst thing any team could do was turn the ball over to Miami in the open floor. Throughout the Celtics' nine games against the Heat that season, Doc Rivers had implored his team to carry the ball out-of-bounds rather than surrender it to LeBron or Wade for a fast-break dunk that could energize the Heat. But the Mavericks were showing little such discipline in Game 2. Midway through the fourth quarter, the Heat had already scored a franchise playoff record 31 points off 20 Dallas turnovers. Five of those turnovers happened in a span of three devastating minutes as Wade attacked relentlessly for a dunk, four free throws and what appeared to be the clinching three-pointer from the corner. Cuban could see the past coming to life directly in front of him as Wade ran to his spot near the Mavericks' bench as passes on the run from LeBron to Mario Chalmers circulated like a double play around the infield to find Wade for his shot, which he sank while falling away out-of-bounds. Even as he struggled to maintain his balance, he kept his long right arm outstretched and his wrist cocked down, as if channeling the last shot of Michael Jordan.

Wade had 36 points already. In the eleven previous playoff games in which he had scored 35 or more, including the last four games of the 2006 Finals, Miami had won every time. Now he stood at the end of the Mavericks' bench like a five-year-old statue, his shooting arm extended for Dirk's consideration.

Dirk had been fascinated by his injury on the eve of Game 2. With the fingertips of his right hand, he kept toying with the end of his left middle finger, flipping it back and forth like a light switch. He was amazed to be feeling so little pain. Casey Smith spent the day fitting him with a variety of splints while his teammates offered advice.

"You need to go Ronnie Lott with that thing," Brian Cardinal said to Dirk. "You need to take it off at the knuckle."

Cardinal was referring to the San Francisco 49ers safety who, after suffering a crushed left pinky finger in 1985, famously decided to have the tip of the finger amputated because surgery to fix the finger would have prevented him from rejoining his team on time for the following season.

Dirk appeared to have no idea who Ronnie Lott was, never mind what had become of his finger.

"He couldn't do that," replied Kidd, shaking his head with disappointment. "He's not that tough."

"It's not like he ever uses his left hand anyway," Cardinal said.

Dirk wasn't thinking about his injury the following night as he walked toward his team's bench, which moments earlier had been hijacked by Wade. Dirk had been insisting that he held no grudge against Wade, even if it was impossible to forget what had happened between them. The complaints by Cuban of one-sided officiating in 2006, as well as Dirk's need to assume the blame for his team's collapse, had been seen by Wade, understandably, as a refusal by the Mavericks to recognize his phenomenal performances five years ago: He had averaged 34.7 points, 7.8 rebounds and 2.7 steals in those NBA Finals to lead Miami to the championship. Dirk, by comparison, had generated 22.8 points, shot 39 percent and missed a tying free throw that could have forced overtime in Game 3.

"Dirk says they gave us the championship last year," Wade had said in 2007. "But he's the reason they lost the championship, because he wasn't the leader that he's supposed to be in the closing moments. That's because of great defense by us, but also he wasn't assertive enough as a leader is supposed to be."

When Dirk and Wade reunited at the NBA All-Star Game in Las Vegas a few days after Wade made those comments, they refused to greet each other, even as they hugged, shook hands with or bumped fists with all their other opponents and teammates.

As Wade vacated the Mavericks' bench after his big three-pointer, his fans already celebrating their next championship, he was met on the court by Le-Bron, who was backstepping away from Wade while throwing a flurry of shadow punches at Wade's chest. Within a few nationally televised seconds, LeBron was emptying the cache of goodwill he had been accumulating over the past few months. This scene reminded millions of fans why they had been against him. If LeBron was already drawing attention to himself at this premature stage of the Finals, imagine how insufferably he would behave if he were to actually win the championship in another two or three games.

Riley, sitting with his wife in their usual seats near the court, didn't like what he was seeing. "He over-celebrated at that time, instead of being the lethal assassin and just looking down at him [Wade] and giving him a nod," Riley said of LeBron. "I actually thought what he did was so natural, but it also motivated the crowd to act the way they acted."

The fans stood and threw their white seatback covers up in the air by the hundreds.

"They were throwing them on the court like we had won the game," Riley said. "I actually stood up, telling them to calm down, waving my hands [as if to say] 'It's not over.' The arena was like the celebration [in July] when we got the three of them. And I'm saying to Chris, 'My God, there's seven minutes to go.'"

For Dirk, the sideshow reactions of LeBron were nothing compared with his own memories of Wade's triumphant leadership. Trailing by 15 points, Dirk had 7 minutes, 14 seconds in which to escape the gravitational pull of 2006. In their team huddle Terry was shouting, "Nobody likes a show-off!" Which was rich, coming from him. But Dirk was oblivious to the irony. His expression was blank.

"There's no way we're going out like this," Terry said to Dirk, but Dirk didn't need to hear it. He was vanishing, receding, not in weakness, but to a place of strength.

Terry generated the first 6 points after the timeout. He was able to score because LeBron, inexplicably, was no longer guarding him. Bosh missed a three-pointer at the end of the shot clock, and in response Dirk spun to feed Shawn Marion for a runner. Now it was 88–81. More than four minutes remained. "Let's go, Heat!" the fans chanted miserably. As LeBron answered with a pair of free throws, the mechanical bell of a cash register was broadcast from the arena loudspeakers, a special effect that was not helpful: LeBron was not money. And he knew he was not money.

This was the winning time that LeBron had said would be easy — the time to make good on his promises, to begin paying off his championship IOUs. He watched Dirk feeding Kidd for an uncontested three-pointer and then saw them fist-bumping each other as they headed back downcourt.

In reply LeBron dribbled away a few seconds hopelessly before missing a fallaway jumper off the front rim. Dirk, double-teamed, relayed the ball out to Kidd, who sent it on to Terry for a contested midrange jumper that brought Dallas within four, 90–86, as Miami called a timeout with 3 minutes, 11 seconds to go.

The next day at practice coach Erik Spoelstra would accept the blame for these final minutes by telling his players that he had taken his foot off the gas. Of course it wasn't as simple as that.

"I've watched my team blow a 15-point lead in a playoff game in the fourth quarter, so I know what I would have done," said Riley, referring to the timeout when they led by 15 points, LeBron was celebrating early, and the staff was clearing the white seatback covers off the court. "I would not have let LeBron go from the end of the court to sprint over and chest-bump [Wade] in front of their bench. I would have stopped him, grabbed him, got him to the huddle. Would've had Udonis [Haslem] grab Wade, get him down here real quick into the huddle. Because we just don't do that.

"At those times it's what I call landing the plane: no celebrating, no tipping of the wings. I wanted to run out on the court and get them from where my seat was. Give them nothing, give the opponent nothing, because it does fire a team up."

Kidd almost stripped Wade of the ball just before a jumper by Udonis Haslem was no good. This was followed, next time down, by an errant three by LeBron. The rebound was kept alive by Wade out to Bosh, enabling Miami to dribble down the clock again, leaving it to LeBron to settle for another three, which he missed again. That rebound was chased down by Haslem, who fumbled it before trying, inexplicably, to save the possession by flinging a blind pass over his shoulder to the frontcourt. The ball was run down by the Mavericks for a three-on-one fast break that was finished, left-handed, by Dirk around Haslem to even the game at 90–90 with 57.6 seconds to go.

As he watched the Heat's collapse, Riley was reminded of his own helpless feelings as a 39-year-old coach, one year younger than Spoelstra. "I felt that way in 1984, in Game 2," said Riley of his first NBA Finals against Larry Bird's Celtics. Riley's Lakers had run away with the opener and were leading Game 2 in Boston by 2 points in the final seconds. "Instead of advancing the ball to the half-court, I took it out in the backcourt," Riley said. "Made a substitution I shouldn't have made. I took out Jamaal Wilkes, who had the best hands in the league, and I put the rookie in, Byron Scott. Inbounded the ball to James Worthy. I told James exactly what was going to happen. I said, 'You're going to get trapped off the ball. Throw it right back to Magic and we're fine.' And he got the ball, he got trapped off of Magic, threw the ball across the court. I saw Gerald Henderson, I said, 'Oh my God.' It was almost like I was saying to myself, 'If Byron would go after this ball like he's a wide receiver, we'll be fine.' But he never went after the ball. He just sort of stood there and watched Henderson go right in front of him and lay it up. To me, that was a strategy mistake. I should've taken the ball at half-court, and we wouldn't have had that problem."

Instead of going up 2–0 and returning to Los Angeles with the likelihood of sweeping those Finals, the Lakers would lose Game 7 in Boston.

The problem this time was not strategy as much as it was discipline.

"You see players acting that way and pre-celebrating, which is a norm in the NBA now," Riley said. "If you go back and look at video of the Dallas Mavericks' bench, I can bet that half of those players were watching how we were behaving at that time. You're just firing them up even more: 'These guys think they've got this won,' then boom! Jumper, jumper, jumper, 9 points, 7 points, 6 points. That's what starts the choke. That's what starts the pressure, when you start giving away something that you worked so hard to get, and then you start to feel tight, under pressure, not playing the game normally. That's what happens. It happens. It changes, like, in an instant. One bad decision. One bad pass. The whole tenor of a series can change."

With thirty-six seconds remaining, Wade missed a three-pointer.

Ten seconds later, Dirk made his.

The Mavericks were ahead 93–90 inside of the final half minute when LeBron made what would be his finest play of the series. Inbounding from the sideline following a timeout, he two-handed a long chest pass across the court that found Chalmers alone in the distant corner for the tying basket.

"Jet decides to take a snooze in the possession, and we give up a wide-open three," Dirk would say later. "I mean, there was nobody even in reaching distance."

Terry, having failed to chase Chalmers to the corner, knew what he was going to hear as he saw Dirk removing his mouth guard. Dirk yelled at Terry on the court, in full view of everyone, and again on the bench during the Mavericks' timeout with 24.5 seconds to go. And then, like steam, the anger vanished. Dirk moved on from the mistake. His expression was instantly tranquil as he listened to Carlisle diagram the final shot for him.

The pressure should have been overwhelming for Dirk, his thick blond hair sweated through to a darker shade, as he waited for Kidd to dribble away ten seconds following that timeout. For the past five years Dirk had been driven to earn another chance at fulfilling his lifetime of professional devotion, and these NBA Finals—this game, unwound now to a few remaining dribbles—were all that was left of his last reasonable chance, given his age and the ages of his teammates. And yet Dirk was unburdened as he darted toward Kidd to receive a short bounce pass at the left elbow of the three-point line.

His defender for the last shot was Bosh and not Haslem, who had guarded Dirk so effectively five years earlier. "I expected Haslem to be on me," Dirk said. "But it really didn't matter because I tried to go early."

Dirk knew that Miami had not committed all its allotted fouls for the fourth quarter, and so he took for granted that Bosh would foul him before he could shoot, in order to disrupt the play and force the Mavericks to inbound the ball with little time remaining.

"I thought for sure they were going to take a foul once I dribbled," said Dirk, "and then we were going to take it out and run some play to get a quick shot."

Facing the basket as calmly as if no one were in front of him, Dirk raised the ball high with both hands to the right of his head, frozen there like a martial artist poised before the attack. He swung the ball left and then right again, as his dribble followed his momentum around to his right. There was an ungainly dancer's pause before he spun back again the other way. He was ducking under past Bosh when it occurred to him, with liberating clarity, that Bosh was not going to foul him after all. The effect of Miami's failure to commit the simplest of plays was astonishing: The pressures that Dirk had been carrying for all these years, the disappointments and the doubts, were transferred away from him and onto his opponents, like a handoff between the two sides, a zero-sum exchange.

After years of humiliation, Dirk was no longer worrying about the outcome so much as he was focused on his craft, as if in a quiet German gym. The fulfillment of everything he had ever wanted was hanging not on some miraculous shot, but rather on this move that he had performed thousands and thousands of times in practice with Holger. In that frozen moment before Dirk launched his drive, Bosh appeared to be mesmerized by the distant, vacant look he saw in his opponent's eyes. Dirk was not driven by insecurity. He had earned the right to make the shot he was about to take. He was thousands of miles away, his instincts owning his movements, leaving him with the time to think his way through his life's climax — to own this chance, instead of being owned by it.

"I spun," he would recall, "and what happened in the other games when I spun, they were coming from some direction — they were coming." Since they weren't fouling him early, Dirk figured that a second Miami defender would be arriving any time now from the blind side to corral him. So, too, did Joey Crawford, the lead referee on top of the play.

"When you saw him go," said Crawford of Dirk, "it's almost like you're waiting for someone to come over from the weak side. Because that's our system of trying to get the play right." Crawford was trying to anticipate what would come next so that he would not be surprised. "And nobody came," Crawford said. "I was surprised that somebody didn't come from the other side."

This second crucial failure by Miami — not to send the extra defender — made Dirk's one-on-one drive simpler for Crawford to judge. "If they contest it, that's a hard play," Crawford said, "because you've got verticality and the whole nine yards."

It turned out to be not a hard play at all for the referee, and it could not have felt simpler for Dirk, even though his entire career was riding on its outcome. "I turned around and there was nobody there," Dirk said. "So I just thought, 'Now it's time to take the lane,' and I was able to get all the way to the basket."

Dirk was galloping hard when he noticed LeBron to his left, turning to face him, but LeBron couldn't leave Terry alone in the corner. Then Haslem came lunging out from the far side of the lane, but his fingertips were just short of reaching the ball. By now Dirk, seeing Haslem coming, had released his layup early and high with a gentle scooping of his left hand, the ball kissed free by the splinted tip of his middle finger. Off the glass softly and through the net it fell.

On his way back downcourt Dirk watched Wade miss a frantic runner from thirty feet to give the Mavericks the 95–93 win.

"We probably should have put LeBron on him," Riley said of Dirk's winning drive. "LeBron should take all those moments on those kinds of guys. He went by Chris, but he never would have gotten by LeBron."

What Miami had done to Dirk in '06, so Dirk had done to Miami now. The Heat's attacking athletes had settled for threes that were beyond their range, while Dirk, the extraordinary shooter of his generation, had beaten them with a drive. He had outscored them 9–3 down the stretch. In those final minutes the Heat had had but one meaningful run at the basket, and it had been taken by LeBron. The lane had opened up for him, the basket had been his, and he had left his layup on the front of the rim, like a frightened golfer who leaves a two-footer short of the hole.

Back home in the Dallas locker room on the morning of Game 3, the Mavericks' psychologist, Don Kalkstein, was handing out his game-day quiz to the younger players. At this late stage of the season, the quiz was mainly intended to help Ian Mahinmi, a 24-year-old from France, who had become the first center off the bench after Haywood was injured.

There were three parts to the quiz: First was a review of the strategy for the game that night, with the questions prepared by Terry Stotts in hopes that the players would talk among themselves to come up with the answers. Next were questions about the rules and regulations of the NBA in general. Third was a section on NBA history.

"The idea was I've got an opportunity to teach young players the philosophical approach to being a professional basketball player," Kalkstein said. "Knowing the trade is a big part. Not only should you be skilled, but — in my opinion — you should know how far the three-point line is, how far the free throw line is. A lot of players don't know the actual distance."

The history questions might focus on the opponent for that night by asking, for example, which players' numbers had been retired by the Miami Heat (a trick question, based on Pat Riley's honoring of Michael Jordan) while also focusing in general terms on the players who had established the highest standards of excellence over the years.

Not long after Kalkstein started passing out the quizzes to the younger Mavericks, the older players took an interest in them. "What do you got there?" asked Dirk, who agonized over the historical questions. Soon Kidd was asking Kalkstein to drop a quiz at his locker. Cardinal would look up information and share it with the rest of the class. Even Casey Smith would submit to the quizzes. "Casey would joke around, 'I can score higher than you and I didn't go to shootaround,'" Kalkstein said. "It was exactly where we were trying to go by building team chemistry and creating dialogue."

Wade had his own method for building team chemistry. During the Heat's practice on the eve of Game 3, he was attacking the basket and hounding his teammates defensively in hopes of restoring the aggressive mood that had been squandered in the final minutes two nights before. "My teammates seen it," Wade would say after Game 3. "They can tell I wanted this game."

Tensions were rising, and Wade's response was to provide the leadership that was not forthcoming from LeBron. In Game 3 LeBron would not attempt his first shot until the seventh minute, on his way to 17 points overall and 4 free throw attempts — revelations of his passivity. If LeBron didn't know how to lead, then Wade was not going to defer, not now. Wade would finish with 29 points and 11 rebounds on his way to driving Miami to a 14-point advantage in the second quarter. His post-up move into the lane put Miami ahead 81–74 midway through the fourth quarter, in advance of the anticipated Mavericks comeback.

Down the stretch Dirk outscored Miami 12–7. He and Wade exchanged jump shots to keep the score tied into the final minute, when LeBron backhanded a pass to Bosh deep near the left baseline. Bosh looked worse than he felt as he faced up to the basket. His left eyelid was swollen after being poked by Kidd in the first quarter, an accident that had dropped Bosh to the floor for a long while before he hopped up and was led to the bench for treatment.

Bosh had been born in Dallas and raised in a stable two-parent home. He attended Lincoln High School, ten minutes away from the mammoth redbrick AmericanAirlines Center, which opened during his senior year, when he was honored as the nation's top high school player. Bosh's NBA teams had played in this new arena eight times, and he had lost every game. In Game 3, with his family and friends in the stands, he had missed 12 of his 17 shots, including his last 2 jumpers.

His left eye was seeping and his vision still blurry as the Mavericks' 7-foot center, Tyson Chandler, charged out from the basket at LeBron, daring him to send the ball to Bosh. ("I don't care if he missed 15 in a row," said LeBron after the game. "He was wide-open and that's his sweet spot.") Without hesitation Bosh was rising off the floor to shoot with 42 seconds to be played, relying not so much on the skewed vision of his one good eye as on his years of practice and feel. His elbows were bent to either side, his toes pigeoned in as the ball flicked forth from his left hand, and he settled back down to wait that long second for the reaction of his hometown. The arena went quiet, and he was ecstatic.

So now Game 3 came down to Dirk, the adopted son of Dallas, and he had two chances to reply. First, he passed the ball out-of-bounds in a misunderstanding with Shawn Marion. Then, with 4.4 seconds remaining and Haslem driving him out farther from the basket than he would have liked, Dirk's fallaway jumper clanged off the back of the rim.

Chris Bosh had come home to score the final basket of Miami's 88–86 victory.

The Mavericks were in trouble again. Not only had they yielded the home court advantage back to Miami, but they had been outplayed for all but a few stretches of the first three games, while Wade had emerged as the most valuable player of the Finals — better than Dirk so far. Dirk in turn was warning his teammates, and Terry in particular, that he could not be asked to provide all of the scoring. "If we have the open looks, we just got to make them," Dirk told reporters after the Game 3 loss. "We haven't made enough of them. If we're going to keep shooting in the low 40s, it's going to be tough to win."

One reason they had converted only 43 percent of their shots through the first three games was because they had played predictably. "We have to force the game," Marion had said after Game 1. "We were calling so many sets, it just kind of took the rhythm out of everything we normally do. When we're out there freelancing and playing the game and making it up as we go, we're one of the best to do it."

Carlisle was dealing with all of these issues. In this era of endless data, he was the NBA's best at translating all of the facts and impressions into a single common language, then dismissing most of it as irrelevant, setting aside other bits for future consideration and focusing on the parts that mattered right now. He was a ruthless processor.

His distinctiveness was a good thing for the Mavericks, because few coaches would have done what Carlisle was about to do: Three games into the NBA Finals he was planning to make wholesale changes to the rotation that had carried Dallas to the brink of the championship. "I was thinking about doing it before we lost Game 3," he said. "I just felt like, over time, if you can't score 96 points or more, you're not going to beat Miami enough. We weren't going to score enough with Stevenson because we didn't have the playmaking."

He was referring to 6-5 DeShawn Stevenson, who had been starting at shooting guard at the request of Dirk and Kidd.

"We were getting in a slugfest the first six minutes, and we tried to come out of that even," Carlisle went on. "And then all of a sudden we were into bad matchups all over the court when we got our second group in."

Instead of trying to stay close in the early going, Carlisle recognized that his team needed to take the game to Miami. They had to stop playing cautiously and start attacking. At practice on the eve of Game 4, he told Cardinal, who had played only sixty-seven seconds in the Finals, that he would be receiving Stojakovic's minutes as the first forward off the bench. The next day at shootaround Carlisle made the bigger announcement: He would be starting J. J. Barea in the backcourt alongside Kidd and demoting Stevenson to the bench.

Barea was listed at 6 feet but was noticeably shorter. Born and raised in Puerto Rico, he had moved to Miami at 17 and played four years at Northeastern University in Boston before arriving in Dallas as an undrafted point guard. "He's a big-heart guy, and he's a ballbuster competitor," Carlisle said. "Starting Barea was something that I felt was the right thing, but I also felt, for it to be most effective, we had to keep it quiet."

While surfing online in the afternoon, Carlisle came across a breaking-news item. He read that Barea would be starting that night in Game 4 for Dallas. "I'm like, 'All right, what the fuck is going on here?'" he said. "People don't understand how something like that can throw a game haywire. Because now all of a sudden before the game there's a crowd of people running to Stevenson: 'Why aren't you starting?' There's a crowd of people running to Barea: 'What do you think about starting the game tonight?' And then it can become a churning mess."

When Carlisle arrived at the arena, he asked a Mavericks staffer to find out who had leaked the story. He was not surprised to hear that it had been Jason Terry. "He always talks," said Carlisle. "I was about to go talk to the press pregame, and this is as big of a story as there's been in the Finals, other than the comeback in Game 2. You make a lineup change like this and start a 5-foot-10 guy, instead of a guy that's been guarding LeBron James, that's kind of a big deal."

Carlisle refused to confirm or deny the lineup change to reporters before the game. "In a lot of those situations," he said, "I ask myself, 'Okay, what would Chuck Daly do?'" Daly, who had died two years earlier, was the LeBron of charm: He was the king of schmooze, so charismatic and confident as coach of the Detroit Pistons in the 1980s that he was able to implement the harsh defenses that pummeled Michael Jordan — and then turn around and not only coach Jordan with the Dream Team in 1992 but also play golf with him in Spain on game days.

"That thing really pissed me off," said Carlisle, but he decided he wasn't going to make an issue of it with his players. "Even though in the morning I had basically said to the team, 'Look, we have got to keep this quiet, because it's the right thing.' But Jet just can't help himself."

That night Barea's unpredictable penetrations into the paint were buttressed by the second-unit play of Stevenson and Cardinal and especially Terry, who was back to attacking offensively. "He didn't start playing good until he started shooting his mouth off," said Carlisle of Terry, who scored 17 points.

Several Mavericks would be proud of their contributions to the 86–83 victory in Game 4: Marion, Chandler and Stevenson each scored in double figures to keep Dallas alive, while Dirk missed 13 of his 18 shots entering the final tight minute.

Dirk was ill. He had felt something coming on the night before Game 4, and by the next day his fever had spiked up to 102 degrees. He would play thirty-nine minutes in Game 4, and during his brief times on the bench he sat, enervated, in his warmup clothes with towels wrapped around his head and neck. Wade was throwing another 32 points at the Mavericks, but LeBron was having his most passive night yet — 8 points on 3-for-11 shooting with 4 turnovers. As the importance of each game was growing, he was shrinking.

After Wade missed a free throw to leave Miami in an 82–81 hole, he and LeBron watched as Dirk, in spite of his miserable condition, generated a spinning drive — this time to his right. With 14.9 seconds to go, he shouldered past

Haslem and squeezed the decisive layup hard and low off the glass to prevent Wade from blocking the shot. Of Dirk's 21 points overall in Game 4, 10 came in the final quarter during the Mavericks' 21–9 game-ending run.

LeBron, by comparison, attempted one failed shot in the fourth quarter, and he played no role in Miami's final possession, in the final 6.7 seconds, which was fumbled by Wade. "I've got to do a better job of being more assertive offensively," LeBron acknowledged after Miami's 86–83 loss, as if repeating a mantra.

The last three games had been decided by 7 points in all, and if LeBron had been attacking the rim, he might have won his championship by now. That the series was even at 2-2 was an indictment of his self-enforced inertia.

The drama of the Mavericks was never ending. With the series even at 2-2, Carlisle was looking ahead to Game 5 when he heard that Stevenson had gone on a TV talk show and criticized LeBron. It wasn't much — Stevenson said that LeBron had "checked out" in Game 4 — but it was enough to create more hysteria, given the intensity of attention paid to all things LeBron.

Stevenson wasn't at all concerned that his words would incite LeBron to awaken from his slump, because LeBron was no Kobe. "That's something I would never in my life say about Kobe," Stevenson said. "Never. If somebody asked me that about Kobe, I would totally change the whole subject." While he was certain that Kobe would have attacked and punished him for any perceived criticism, Stevenson believed that LeBron didn't have the killer instinct to hold a grudge. "I don't think he is like Kobe," Stevenson said. "No disrespect toward LeBron, but I don't think he has that type of mentality of them guys like Magic Johnson and Larry Bird, Kobe Bryant, Michael Jordan — guys that would take that and try to destroy you every possession."

All the same, Carlisle felt it necessary to bring up Stevenson's comment among the Mavericks players. On the morning of Game 5 Carlisle said, "You guys go on the radio and start saying things, or whatever, and I'm listening to this whole thing with Stevenson yesterday —"

Stevenson tried to interrupt him, but Carlisle held up a hand.

"Just hold on a second," he said to Stevenson, and then he faced the team. "If you guys are going to talk shit, will you please talk some shit and not tap-dance? Because the kind of game we're getting into tonight, you'd better be ready not only to talk shit but go out there and back it up.

"Once the ball goes in the air," Carlisle went on, "it's all out the window anyway. But you better get your minds ready to go out there like you have talked some real shit, and not this bullshit."

And then in the locker room he showed them a three-minute video of hockey highlights from the ongoing Stanley Cup Playoffs that he had asked his staff to piece together. The Boston Bruins, having lost two tight games to open the finals, had clobbered the Vancouver Canucks by a combined 12–1 in Games 3 and 4. "The sound of guys hitting the boards and crashing and stuff like that — our guys are going, 'Whoa! Holy Jesus!' It was great," said Carlisle. "We had watched so much basketball video during the playoffs that it was just something else to get us on the same sort of concept, but seeing it in a different sport."

The video drove home Carlisle's message in an emotional and inspirational way. "They wore them down," he said of the Bruins, who would go on to win the Stanley Cup. "We're not a big, physical team, but we have enough quickness and know-how to position ourselves where we're up and into somebody. And we could do it against those guys, because they didn't have a classic point guard, and we wanted to pressure LeBron. I mean, just make it hard on him."

Riley sat in the hotel with his coaches until three or four in the morning as they reviewed their fourth-quarter difficulties in advance of Game 5, to be played later that night in Dallas. "Sit there, have a couple glasses of wine, watch them coming up with their principles," he said. "Spo does a great job of managing his staff. And the fact they're doing it all on computers rather than on blue stock — it's fun for me to sit there and watch them operate."

It was a far different experience for LeBron, in his room searching for inspiration. His pursuit had led him online. He stayed up most of the night reading reports by journalists that detailed all of his recent failures. At 2:27 a.m. he posted a message on Twitter that was both revealing and redundant:

Now or Never!!

"It was just a personal message to myself," he told reporters later that morning as he stood in the hallway outside the visitors' locker room in Dallas. "It has nothing to do with anyone else besides myself. I was just in the zone at that point."

"I was not aware of him doing that," said Riley, "and if I was aware I would have told him to shut off his device and go to bed, or just watch games, or something."

Was LeBron surfing through his own negative reviews in hopes of re-creating the conditions that had driven him to respond so aggressively at Cleveland seven months earlier? After an extended year of trying to ignore the draining environment, of numbing himself to the booing and jeering, he was now engaging with the outside world in search of the inspiration he could not find within himself.

The Mavericks had been shuffling a variety of lead defenders onto LeBron —from Shawn Marion to DeShawn Stevenson to Jason Kidd to Brian Cardinal —while also switching to zone defenses for short, disruptive bursts in each game. They wanted to remind LeBron of what he had seen one year earlier in Boston: a blockade of several opponents between him and the basket. Their plan was wise and well executed, but all the same the Mavericks had not been expecting LeBron to be so easily deterred.

"Back in the '70s or '80s there were other distractions, but there was nothing like this," Riley said. "When you rolled out of bed in the morning, you got dressed. You read the newspaper, maybe you had a cup of coffee or something, you went to practice. And now, before they even get dressed, they're answering emails, calls, texts, getting back to people, making appointments, checking out what's being written about them. I just think that there's so much more today. I don't say it's bad. I say it's normal, to the extent that this is the world they are operating in. But there are just so many more things that can distract a player, that can depress a player, and it's all right there every day set up in a menu for them."

This was another new reality that never occurred to Michael Jordan. In his day interviews were arranged at specific times, and communication with his fans was limited to the one-way street of TV. He filmed his commercial messages, they watched, and no one had any idea what he was doing at 2:27 in the morning. LeBron, by comparison, was transparent and accessible. He was continuing to reveal his weaknesses and vulnerabilities in ways that Jordan never let show. On top of everything else that he was struggling to manage on the court, LeBron was still learning how to negotiate this two-way interactive street.

"It's an alone world," Riley said. "I learned this from being around Jerry West for five years, a guy so celebrated and beloved in L.A., and he was alone a lot of the time. At the end of the night, when you put your head on the pillow and stare at the ceiling, you're alone. That's something that superstars and people who really care about what they're doing take on."

That night LeBron walked into the visitors' locker room to find a dozen journalists from North America and around the world waiting for him in front of his locker. All of them were aiming video cameras in his direction. They weren't expecting him to give an interview. All they sought was content of him pulling on his black undershirt with horizontal stripes of padding around the rib cage. He pulled on his black Heat jersey.

"No photos in the locker room — it's only video," announced a Heat staffer. "It's an NBA rule. If you take any photos, you'll be asked to leave the locker room."

LeBron sat oblivious to his zoo. How was it to be watched always, to be aware that everything you did would be dissected and scrutinized like so many clues? He was wearing headphones and singing along with the lyrics out loud, including the profanities.

14

THE SHERIFF

The first four games of the 2011 NBA Finals were decided by a total of 15 points. It was the tightest start to the championship round in more than forty years, with three of the games coming down to last-minute shots by Dirk Nowitzki and Chris Bosh. In Game 5, however, the point of view changed. The crucial play happened in the opening minutes, to the regret of lead referee Joey Crawford and his fellow NBA officials, who were working the game that night in Dallas.

"It's a hard play there," said Crawford months after the pivotal game. He was wearing a golf shirt and slacks in a corner office at NBA headquarters high above Manhattan, where he was facing a wall loaded with digital video recorders and flat-screen televisions. The NBA supervised its referees from this large room, heavily air-conditioned for the sake of the high-tech equipment. The frigid climate somehow accentuated the vinegary warmth of the aftershave that rose like steam from Crawford's freshly shaven head. At age 60 he was the best referee in basketball, which was to say that he knew his own faults better than anyone else.

Crawford stared at the biggest TV on the wall as Dwayne Wade was shown driving to the basket in a slow-motion close-up. He saw Wade leaping head-on into the chest of Brian Cardinal. A foul was called instantly by one of Crawford's partners, longtime NBA referee Mike "Duke" Callahan. He ruled that Cardinal had illegally blocked Wade's path to the basket. Cardinal's foul resulted in two free throws for Wade.

After the game, in his hotel suite in Dallas, Crawford had been joined by Callahan and Bill Kennedy, the third referee for Game 5, as well as their families, friends, and colleagues from the NBA refereeing department, for an informal party that lasted into the morning, while they relived the game again and again via a loop of the TV broadcast. When they saw Cardinal being bowled over by Wade, Callahan's fellow referees — Crawford in particular — did not shy away from asking him about his call. "We kept busting Duke's balls that night, saying, 'Duke, did you like it?'" recalled Crawford with a thin smile. "He said, 'No, I don't like it, I don't like it, I don't like it.'"

Among the three major professional leagues in America, the games of the NBA were surely the hardest to officiate, based on the speed and unpredictability of basketball and the varying interpretations of its rule book. NBA referees faced criticism and accusations far more often than the NFL's game officials or MLB's umpires. Instead of protecting one another when a mistake was made, NBA referees were more likely to respond to public controversies by piling on. "They'll say, 'Hey, asshole, what did you do on that play?'" Crawford said of the innumerable times colleagues called out his blunders. In turn, when Crawford saw an embarrassing error being made on national TV, he would enjoy leaving a voicemail for the referee to hear after the game: "I'll call somebody and I'll go, 'Wowwww. What a great call on that play at ten minutes in the first quarter. Great job!'"

NBA officials didn't spare one another's feelings because the truth was the truth. The best referees spoke with one another the way that cops often do.

"You've got to have a little asshole in you to be a referee," said Joe Borgia, the NBA's vice president of referee operations, who was led into the business by his father, the legendary NBA referee Sid Borgia. "It's such an anti-, negative business. I try to tell young refs, I say, 'They don't really hate you — it's the uniform.'" At one time Borgia tried to help his son become a referee. "I said, 'You got to start reffing intramurals.' He says, 'Dad, I don't like people yelling at me.' I said okay. He could never be a referee. We're different. We're a different breed of people. I mean, I hate to say that. But you've got to be fucked-up to be a ref."

I had asked Crawford to review Game 5 with me to better understand how he, his fellow referees and their supervisors managed in this new era that had been influenced by the broadsides of Mark Cuban. Our interview turned into a daylong investigation that was also attended by Borgia; Steven Angel, the NBA's senior vice president of league operations and officiating (a job title created amid the gambling scandal of NBA referee Tim Donaghy); and not one but two NBA communications staffers, who were there to manage the NBA's ongoing transition from secrecy to transparency in refereeing.

Borgia sat at a control panel, manipulating the replays of Wade's collision with Cardinal back and forth, holding it and then letting it go slowly, like a fisherman patiently reeling in a big fish. "What happens is, Dwyane doesn't clear him," said Borgia, blessed with a naturally loud voice that rarely needs a microphone. "This was an offensive foul."

"Yeah," Crawford admitted. "It's an offensive foul."

"Cardinal doesn't move," Borgia went on, as he reeled in the play one last time. "His shoulders never move sideways, and the contact's more than marginal. That should be offensive, just looking at it from there."

"It was a tough play," Crawford said.

As Borgia released the controls and the ESPN broadcast of the game continued, further examples of Cardinal's harassing style appeared on-screen. "You're seeing a little bit of a bump — what we call extracurricular activities — going on in the game," Crawford said. "Why he's doing it? I don't know."

"He's like a disrupter right now," Borgia said.

"I don't know why he's doing it. I don't care," said Crawford, his voice rising slightly. "If he keeps disrupting, you're going to start calling fouls, as simple as that."

The two of them were discussing Cardinal's reputation when the broadcast shifted to a scene of Wade limping dramatically to his team's bench, where he collapsed. The training staff scrambled to treat his left hip, which had been bruised moments earlier in the collision with Cardinal. There were close-ups of Wade scowling in pain and then hobbling away to the locker room with three minutes remaining in the first quarter. He was going to miss the next six minutes of the game.

"I didn't even know he went off the court," said Crawford, staring blankly at the TV. "How about that? I had no idea that that man went off the court."

"Good game awareness," Borgia responded sarcastically.

"I swear to God I had no idea," insisted Crawford.

"Dwyane left the building!" Borgia shouted.

For tens of millions of fans around the world, a narrative triangle had developed over the preceding four games between 7-foot Dirk Nowitzki, who would lead the scoring in Game 5 with 29 points; LeBron James, who would generate a triple-double yet continue to fall short of providing the offense his team needed; and Wade, who had snatched the championship from Dirk in 2006 and was determined to do so again. Wade's hip injury, which would limit him for the remainder of the Finals, was a crucial twist in the plot: It would shine the light ever more harshly on LeBron and his unfulfilled promises.

Crawford wasn't focused on the theater of the NBA Finals because it had little to do with his job. It was irrelevant to him that LeBron and Dirk were approaching each other from opposite ends of the basketball world—the American and the immigrant, the CHOSEN-1 and the underdog—in pursuit of the championship that would make sense of each of their life's work. That story was the macro. Crawford was obsessed with the micro.

"There's been numerous times somebody will walk in the locker room and say, 'Somebody had 40-some points,' and I didn't even know he had 4," Crawford said. "You go in that locker room, all you care about is you got the plays right, and that down the stretch you didn't cause the team to lose a game. You don't give a shit who scored 58 points or 60 points. You don't care."

There was a reason the sound was turned down to a whisper on the Game 5 telecast that Crawford and Borgia were reviewing months after the fact. The reason was that two parallel narratives were being played out. There was the game that was accessible to everyone around the world—the unexpected showdown of Dirk versus LeBron, with Wade conspiring to sway the balance. And then there was this other game, the one that Crawford had been trying to get right for all of his life.

The biggest playoff games tended to be low-scoring defensive struggles, as typified by Game 7 in 2010 between the Lakers and Celtics, which Crawford had also worked. Three times in the past eighteen years there had been a seventh game in the NBA Finals, and Crawford had been assigned to all three. (He had been told that he would be refereeing Game 7 in Miami if the series went that far.) "It was like this aura, this angst, where everybody was subdued," Crawford said of the Los Angeles–Boston showdown one year earlier. "I don't know whether it was because the players felt that history, but it was a real mystique, a weird, weird feeling."

Instead of being mired in the past, Game 5 in Dallas went the other way. Both teams generated at least 100 points for the only time in the 2011 NBA Finals. The scoring-challenged Heat made 52.9 percent of their 70 shots, while the increasingly confident Mavericks went 13 for 19 from the three-point line. Together they were previewing the future of the NBA: In years to come the league would renew the enlightened narrative of teamwork and speed that had been set forth by the Boston Celtics in the 1950s and '60s.

Crawford loved the working conditions of Game 5. "When you have a slow game, when they're just banging it into the post, you've got to worry about the kicking, the big guys, the screens," he said. "But when they're up and down, man, it's the best. Because everything's just wide-open. You see everything. And I never worry about the running aspect of it. Darell Garretson used to say he used to hate it, and I said, 'It's because you couldn't run.' That's why he didn't like it. He'd tell me, 'Fuck you.'"

"Put him in the leper crew," Borgia said.

The leper crew received the worst assignments from Garretson, who served as supervisor of officials for eighteen years until 1998.

"Yeah, exactly, put me in the leper," said Crawford, laughing. "But that's what you want every game. You want the ball to go in."

"Ball to go in!" Borgia shouted.

"The game is a piece of cake when that ball goes in," Crawford went on. "Players aren't pissed off . . . We all want the same thing. Because you're going down the stretch of a game and that ball's shot and you got a 2-point game, 1-point —you're saying to yourself, 'GO IN! GO IN!' And now down at the other end you're going, 'GO IN!'"

The NBA's younger referees tended to blend into the background of the game, as if they preferred to work in its camouflage. But Crawford was incapable of blending. To anyone who didn't know him personally, he looked mean and exacting. He had slits for eyes that hid their whites and a hunched neck feeding the bald helmet of his head. During the games he leaned forward, with his hands up defensively like a boxer, which he had never been, in spite of his technique of sliding his black sneakers from side to side in search of the perfect view. The whistle dangled from his lips like an unlit cigarette.

He was the face of authority in basketball, with a scowl that was both provocative and comforting. He was never going to allow himself to be shoved around, not even in a game as big as this. The question, for much of his thirty-four-year career in the NBA, was whether he would shove back.

One of Crawford's partners in Game 5, Bill Kennedy, was known among his colleagues as "Billy Dee Williams," based on the theatrical flourish with which he acted out his calls. Along those lines, Crawford had come to understand how he came across, and so when players approached to question one of his calls, he tried to stand at ease, with his hands behind his back, to signal his newfound open-mindedness. Even his partners refused to confront him during Game 5 unless they approached him together.

"Billy wouldn't come to me without Duke," Crawford said. "They were afraid that I was going to snap on them because they were going to change my call. When we were back at the hotel, I said, 'You two jerk-offs.'"

"You would have snapped if *one* of them came — you would have," Borgia said. "Be honest. Face up. You would have changed [the call], but you would have snapped."

"I said to them [at the hotel], 'I don't know if I would have went to Jake O'Donnell or Earl Strom, to be honest with you,'" Crawford said of the NBA's leading referees from the 1970s and '80s. "And I started laughing, I said, 'It makes me feel good that you came to me.' Fuck me. I was wrong, okay? So my partners came to me."

It was important to project strength and confidence when he was refereeing, to not only uphold the laws but also sell himself as trustworthy. That was why Crawford practiced his officiating signals routinely in his home in Philadelphia. When he passed by a mirror, he would pause and watch himself in order to see what everyone else saw when his whistle stopped the game. He might be on his way to the kitchen when he would pirouette and point smoothly in the opposite direction (his understated gesture for offensive fouls, which he had borrowed from the baseball umpire Joe West), or jab the fingertips of one hand into the flattened palm of the other (for a technical foul), or helicopter his short, thick arms to bring the game to a halt. "I still walk around the house like that, calling plays," he said in his raspy Philadelphia accent. "And my wife looks at me and says, 'You are a jerk-off.'"

"I went to a guy," said Crawford. "You know, a sports psychologist. We started talking about different stuff, and he'd say, 'How was your father?' I'd say, 'He was nuts.' It was how he approached situations. He approached situations with force, and that was the way in that day." But there was no physical violence, Crawford insisted.

His father, Shag Crawford, was a Major League Baseball umpire for twenty years. One afternoon when Crawford was 10 he was waiting by the umpires' room for his father to finish work at the old Connie Mack Stadium in Philadelphia. "You knew the game got over because you could hear the clicks coming up," he said. As the rattling footsteps of the spikes grew louder, they were accompanied by voices: "Shag, you no-good motherfucker!" And then Crawford heard the voice of his father: "Fuck you! Fuck you!" The clicking and the arguing grew louder until his father, who was being held back by men in baseball uniforms, saw his son and yelled, "Get in the room!"

An older brother, Jerry Crawford, also umpired in the major leagues from 1977 until his retirement in 2010. Joey Crawford diverged into basketball. He was an exceptionally talented 26-year-old referee — quick-minded, tough and needing to prove himself night after night — when he broke in with the NBA in 1977. His elders approached their work with the same force as his father. In those days very few NBA games were televised nationally; every arena was an outpost disconnected from the others, and it was the responsibility of the referee to assert law and order as he saw fit. Strom, O'Donnell, Richie Powers, Joe Gushue — each was like a sheriff meting out his own version of justice.

"If I refereed one night with Richie Powers — we're talking '77 — I had to do it the way Richie did it," said Crawford. "Two nights later if I went with Earl Strom, I had to do it the way he did it. Or they would chastise the shit out of you."

Instead of deferring, Crawford learned from them to indulge in his competitive anger. "Strom one night in Kansas City was going to kill me," Crawford said. "I threw Phil Johnson out, threw him out real early in the game, and Earl got me in the locker room and said, 'You fucking motherfucker. You fucking do something like that again I'm going to kick your fucking ass.' Because I threw him out real quick. It was one of these — bang! He said, like, 'You fucking asshole!' Bang! And then I hit him again."

In trying to be like his role models, Crawford was being led astray. They intervened in fear that Crawford was someday going to get himself thrown out of the league.

"I went in the locker room one time, put my two hands up like this," he said, grabbing his own head where his hair used to be. "Because I kept throwing coaches out of the game and I was distraught. And I called my idol, Joe Gushue, and thought I was going to get a pat on the back. And he told me that it was my fault."

In the 1980s, while Commissioner David Stern was rescuing the NBA by marrying it to television, Garretson was demanding that his fellow referees call the game by the book, murky as it was with so many rules subject to interpretation. A uniform perspective of right and wrong was being enforced for the first time, and Crawford was having trouble keeping up with the evolving point of view. He was continuing to throw out players and coaches at a rate that was becoming noticeable in the newly interconnected world. The TV cameras were focusing on him too often. He was becoming the story at the expense of the game.

Crawford bottomed out in Game 2 of the 2003 Western Conference Finals in Dallas when he ejected Mavericks coach Don Nelson for glaring at him during a timeout. A half minute later Crawford was also throwing out Nelson's lead assistant, Del Harris, who, strangely, had asked to be tossed.

Summoned to New York for his comeuppance, Crawford tried to explain that Nelson had been asking for it by way of his body language. "When I got into the office, I was a little concerned, not a lot concerned," he said of his private meeting with Stern, because Crawford was convinced he had done nothing wrong. "I looked at him and I said, 'What did you want me to do: Wait until he called me a no-good motherfucker?' And he said, 'Yeah! Because that way I can defend you.' When Commissioner Stern fined me over the Nelson thing, he told me, 'Don't do anything like that again.'"

Four years later Crawford did worse when he noticed Tim Duncan of the Spurs laughing at him from the bench. He lost his temper and ejected Duncan, who would complain that Crawford had dared him to a fight. "I knew when I did it I was done," Crawford said. "I didn't know if I was going to have a job. I knew that I totally screwed up."

After halftime, with Miami trailing 60–57, Wade stayed in the locker room until midway into the third quarter, which added to LeBron's burden. LeBron would eventually generate 17 points, 10 assists and 10 rebounds, but what the Heat needed was prolific scoring. They were desperate for the most talented player on the planet to wrest command of the game from Dirk.

"Now they're picking up their intensity on Dirk," Crawford said. "We know that they think he's soft and they're going to beat him up and all that shit. That's your job. You're refereeing."

It was none of his business to get into anyone's personal biography. But if Brian Cardinal or Udonis Haslem was plotting to break the rules, for whatever reason, Crawford needed to be on top of it.

"Plus you got a smaller guy on [Dirk] in Haslem," said Borgia, picking up on Crawford's observation.

"Very good point by Joe," Crawford agreed. "You see he's giving up that [size]. He's got to do something."

Haslem, in spite of being 4 inches shorter than the 7-foot Dirk, had guarded him successfully in 2006 by crowding and hassling him. Five years later, however, Dirk had learned to overcome bullying defenders. In Game 5 he was extending his influence far beyond the final stretch of the fourth quarter. He was proving to be the most important player throughout the season's biggest game.

With 9 minutes, 40 seconds remaining and the Mavericks leading 90–85, Dirk posted up Haslem and dribbled laterally into the lane, where his turnaround jumper was blocked from the weak side by Wade. None of the three referees, who had spaced themselves to form a triangle of sight lines around the half-court, called a foul.

"They want Dirk not to come to the basket, but Dirk's so good he'll fade away and shoot it," Crawford said. Even now, with the hindsight of television replays, he wasn't sure whether a foul should have been called. "Three of us got bad angles: I'm looking at his ass, Duke's got players in front of him, and Billy's looking through the off guy. So the three of us are in no-man's-land. The best thing there is exactly what happened. Nothing. Because we're not guessing."

They had followed procedure. No guessing. No assuming that a foul or violation had been committed unless it was actually seen. This bottom line also applied to traveling calls, which were missed so often by NBA referees.

"Watch Dirk's right foot," Borgia said, while dwelling on another replay earlier in Game 5. "Does he move it? Technically he moved it in. We could get literally every travel, and never miss one. But we're going to have to have the referee stare at the pivot foot. And if we do that, what are we going to miss? Dirk might get smacked in the face."

Violations, including traveling calls, were the equivalent of misdemeanors. Fouls, such as Dirk being smacked in the face, were like felonies. The referees worried more about felonies than misdemeanors, which was why they tended to focus their attention up high, away from the sliding feet that were so infuriating to fans, who complained that NBA stars were allowed to travel as they pleased. "If we could take one eyeball down here and one over there, we would be damn good," Borgia said.

Another complaint was that the NBA applied a different standard to fouls involving the biggest stars, but that was because they were more difficult to gauge, Borgia explained. "With a lot of hand-check, body-check, we use rhythm," Borgia said of the defensive tactics employed against the NBA's explosive scorers.

"Does it affect the player's rhythm, speed, quickness, balance? What's hard with a player like Dirk, some of his natural moves are off-balance. So it's hard to tell."

"We were talking about this yesterday," Crawford said. "People that are tough to referee. Shaq. Him. LeBron."

The difference between LeBron and Dirk was that Dirk scored without outrageous athleticism. He was like the rare character actor who shared top billing with Hollywood's more charismatic stars.

"This guy's a freak," Borgia said. "I mean, 7-footers just don't do this shit: off-balance, fallaway 29-footer. We were in a meeting one time, talking about possibly making the interpretation that you have to take a 'normal' shot. And I was like, 'Oh-oh-oh, hold on.' I said, 'Then what's Dirk?' Fifty percent of his shots you would consider not normal."

The question at the league office had been whether to award free throws to players who tossed up impossible shots cynically, for no purpose other than to draw a foul.

"We were discussing continuation-type things, and if he's falling away from the basket off-balance," Borgia said. "But Dirk does that. That's normal for Dirk. So you can't define 'normal.' He's one of those freaky players that's just absolutely amazing."

Dirk's loss in the 2006 NBA Finals had incited him to deal with his weaknesses. LeBron was just beginning to learn a similar lesson. In the years to come, LeBron would be known for his deep array of skills, but he was not yet proficient as a midrange shooter, a post-up scorer or a pick-and-roll playmaker. For now, at age 26, he was known for his passing, his defense and above all his athleticism.

"I told people, I said, 'There's some players you need to see live to appreciate them,'" Borgia continued. "LeBron's one of them, because you can't see the explosiveness on TV."

That explosiveness wasn't being seen so much in Game 5, however. Wade was limping between plays and not able to assert himself as he had for much of the Finals. LeBron, having not yet learned the fine details of leadership, was unable to take over. And so this game took on the personality of the underdog at the expense of the CHOSEN-1.

In 2007, three months into Crawford's open-ended suspension for his treatment of Duncan, news broke of the NBA's worst gambling scandal. Tim Donaghy, a longtime referee, acknowledged that he had been betting on NBA games since 2003 and had been providing insider information to his gambling partners about the NBA's officiating crews and how they were likely to influence games since 2006. He served fifteen months in prison after pleading guilty in August 2007 to conspiring with gamblers.

"No one thought anybody would do that," said Crawford. "And he did it. He did it. You know what, he was a pretty talented referee. But money was his god. Very dangerous, as far as I'm concerned, when you see people like that. They're very dangerous people to me. And money was his god."

By the 2010–11 season the catcall references to Donaghy were heard only rarely during NBA games. "I hear of it more in Philly because I live there and he lived there," said Crawford. "He lived at one point maybe five miles from me. And the same people that he was dealing with, you're seeing these people. You go to a football game — my grandson plays football — and all of a sudden the guy says, 'Hey, Joe, somebody says so-and-so is over there.' Fuck him. I don't give a shit who's over there. But you're being asked these questions about Donaghy all the time simply because we're from the same area."

What did he think of Donaghy? That was the question Crawford was asked most often.

"My wife, she gets really, really nervous when somebody asks me," Crawford said. "Because I don't answer it properly. I answer them, 'I hope he's dead.'"

He laughed.

"When somebody says it, she knows what's coming," Crawford said. "Because it ends the conversation. It ends it."

And then, after the questioner walked away, Mary Crawford would confront her husband and say, "Do you have to do that?"

"Yes," Crawford would answer. "I do."

Donaghy's case had influenced the NBA to deepen its background checks on referees, while demanding that officiating crews stay in the same hotel before games and steer clear of gambling environments year-round. A big part of Steven Angel's newly created job was to study the movement in point spreads in order to discover whether the spread changed before or after information about an injury or trade was made public. "We have a screen that we've developed which includes a whole number of different game-by-game and then multiple-game statistics to compare against the lines and see what's happening," Angel said. "We monitor it very closely."

In the past the NBA's oversight of referees had focused, haphazardly, on improving their performance. Those efforts had grown more coherent and mindful of the sinister. "Now we're looking for things a little bit differently," said Angel. "We're very much on top of it, and I talk to the guys in Las Vegas regularly."

When Crawford was reinstated by Stern for the 2007–08 season, he was no longer focused on staking out his own territory against his adversaries on the sidelines and in the stands. With his profession endangered by Donaghy, Crawford couldn't afford to indulge himself at the expense of the league.

"And it hit me: There's more to it than me," said Crawford. "You look back on it, it's the macho bullshit, and that's all it is. Because I think when you're starting, you're trying to prove to everybody that you can do this at the top level, and you can give me whatever you can give me. You want to call me a motherfucker? You're gone. Asshole? Okay, you're gone. Believe me, I did it that way, and the way I'm doing it today works a thousand times — my father's rolling over in his grave — it works a thousand times better. It's not only better for you as the individual, but it's better for the game."

During Crawford's suspension from the playoffs, which prevented him from working the NBA Finals for the first time in twenty-two years, he met with the dean of adult studies at Neumann College (now University) in suburban Philadelphia about pursuing a degree in liberal studies. "I was sweating in my armpits like when I was called up to see Stern," Crawford said. "Everybody in my family was involved with the milk and bread unions, and they all drove trucks. And nobody in my family ever got educated, because one of my uncles was a big union rep for bread and milk. So nobody said, 'Joe, study.' Because your uncle was going to get you a job. There wasn't an education mentality . . . I just wanted to prove that I could do that — prove to me that I wasn't dumb."

He was like so many players who had sold themselves short by focusing on basketball at the expense of their education. "I'm the only guy in my family that ever went to college," he said. He got up and walked across the room for a box of tissues. "What was funny," he said, drying his eyes, "they made you do a Power-Point and a huge term paper. I stayed away from sports on every subject because I didn't want to do it — because I wanted to broaden my horizons, I guess. But I did my last one on the Dominican Republic's effect on Major League Baseball. The only Dominican in the Hall of Fame is Juan Marichal. So I'm doing the Pow-erPoint, and Juan Marichal is the guy with the bat."

Crawford was showing his class a violent photograph from 1965 of the San Francisco Giants pitcher swinging a bat down on the skull of Los Angeles Dodgers catcher John Roseboro, as an umpire steps in too late to separate them.

"I'm standing there, I said to the class, 'Now, see this guy right here with the mask and that blue uniform?' I said, 'That's my father.'"

Crawford was still holding the tissue between his fingers.

"But that was my proudest moment, getting my degree, to answer your question," he said. "See, you made me cry now. Now you're going to say Joe is a pussy."

"They're playing harder," Borgia said dramatically, as if he hadn't seen Game 5 several times already.

A 9–0 run by Miami, culminating in a three-pointer by Wade, put the Heat ahead 99–95 with 4 minutes, 38 seconds remaining. A little more than one minute later, Jason Terry tied the game with a three-pointer.

"All you care about right now is this twenty-four seconds," said Crawford, staring at the TV as if the game were live and he was back there all over again. "Twenty-four seconds. You're thinking, 'All right, on the slot, this is what I'm looking at.' 'I'm the lead, this is what I'm looking at.' There's nothing else in your repertoire. You're done. That's it. It's those twenty-four seconds. Everything else is out of your fucking head. Everything."

LeBron received the ball on the left side, where he found himself isolated against Jason Kidd. LeBron took his time. He turned to face Kidd before settling for an errant jump shot from eighteen feet. At the other end of the court Dirk caught a pass in the same spot, attacked instantly and dunked softly to push Dallas ahead 102–100 with less than three minutes to go.

"It's the ultimate in officiating at our level, the highest level in the world, I don't care what anybody says," Crawford said. "And you get done, this kind of game, you walk in the locker room. And nobody's beating down your door? It's for us the greatest feeling. I hate to tell my wife that."

"Ecstasy!" Borgia shouted.

"It's the greatest feeling in the world because you just did something with two other people that was just out of sight," said Crawford. "There is nothing can compare to that."

LeBron drove the baseline for a would-be layup that was transformed into an offensive foul, thanks to the defense of Tyson Chandler. There was a frantic back-and-forth sequence of the ball being stripped cleanly from Wade, of Le-

Bron swatting a breakaway layup by Shawn Marion, of Chandler blocking Wade's pull-up jumper.

Terry drove to the basket, collapsed the defense and backhanded a pass to Kidd for a three-pointer. Dallas was up 105–100 with eighty-six seconds left.

"I never got to this level," Borgia said as he nodded at the TV screen, which he had frozen at the pivotal moment of the season. Borgia had refereed professionally for twenty-one years, with the last decade spent in the NBA, and he had never done what Crawford was doing here. "It's not that they just ran seven miles," Borgia said. "It's that for three freaking hours it's just their mind, the focus, and when you focus on something that long it's exhausting."

"Well," Crawford said, "you don't want to fuck it up, to put it to you bluntly."

"To put it nicely, you'd want to get every play right," Borgia responded while laughing hoarsely. They were both emotional and keyed up all these months later.

"You want to get every play right," Crawford continued. "You think that I understand what this means to these two franchises? All of us do. Sixty of us know that. This is our league too; we don't want to do anything that's going to look bad about our league. We love the NBA just as much as anybody does."

Then Dallas went up by 8 points with 33.8 seconds remaining after Terry hit a three-pointer over LeBron.

"There you go!" Crawford shouted. "That's it. Now you're saying, right now you're just sitting there; for thirty-some seconds the three of us are going . . ."

"'Phew,'" said Borgia, finishing the thought. "'Thank you.'"

"'Thank you,'" Crawford agreed. "And it all now just went . . ." He made a sound like a freshly punctured tire. "Now all we got to do is just discipline the game now."

"Because now it's not going to come down to your call," Borgia added.

By now Crawford was comfortable with all the oversight and second-guessing. NBA supervisors graded every decision that he and his colleagues made, and in so doing eliminated the concept of "makeup" calls, by which referees used to atone for their mistakes by punishing the other team. Crawford didn't mind taking an extra moment to slow the play down in his mind before putting air in the whistle. "Because everybody's judging us," he said, nodding toward the high-tech wall. If only they could have invented the video equipment sooner.

The new imagery not only helped him grasp the minute details. It also enabled him to see the bigger picture and his role in it. As Crawford watched himself in miniature, sliding and hopping and turning to run from one end of the court to the other and then back again, he was recognizing a larger story playing out on the screen.

In 1999 an immigrant had arrived to compete in the American game among the greatest Americans. One dozen years later, in Game 5 of the 2011 NBA Finals, Dirk Nowitzki had turned out to have the same chance to fulfill his dream as LeBron James and everyone else on the court. Crawford, Kennedy and Callahan, in spite of their own flaws and insecurities and the vaguely written rule book they were honor-bound to enforce, had enabled the spirit of basketball to prevail. They hadn't cared about the final tally of points. Their objective had been to safeguard, as best they could, the fundamental ideal that all players — the native-born Americans and the foreigners, the blacks and the whites, the explosive athletes and those who were less-gifted — had the opportunity to compete on an equal playing field, and may the best man win.

"These kinds of games, when you're done and the three of you walk in, you know," Crawford said. "You know. You know. You just grab one another because you understand what you just did."

Sometime in the days ahead, there was going to be an internationally televised celebration of the new NBA champions, replete with trophies and bottles of expensive champagne. On the night following Game 5, Joey Crawford threw another kind of party in his hotel suite in Dallas. He ordered in cold cuts and filled the bathtub with ice to chill the beer, and the relieved, triumphant voices of his friends and him could be heard down the hallway into the morning. Theirs was a celebration of fairness.

15

THE TRIUMPH

On the morning of Game 5 LeBron James was pleasant and smiling as he spoke quietly with the reporters who gathered around him outside the visitors' locker room in Dallas. A short time later he was walking down the hallway behind Dwyane Wade as a camera faced them with every step.

"Did y'all hear me cough?" said Wade on his long walk out of the building. He was dressed in his team's black outfit of shorts, T-shirt and a large Finals cap. "I think I'm sick," Wade said, and he coughed into his fist with a grin as he looked back over his shoulder to glance at LeBron walking along behind him. LeBron lifted up the collar of his own black T-shirt and coughed into it.

"This weather, man," said LeBron after he had coughed again.

They were mocking Dirk Nowitzki's fever from two nights before.

"This weather's crazy," said Wade with a big smile as the cameraman continued to retreat in front of him.

"It's hard to go from 85-degree weather and then go to 90," said LeBron as Wade coughed again.

Wade was one of those stars who paid a physical tax on the sensational plays he made. More often than any NBA star of his era, his drives to the basket landed him hard, as if he had been thrown violently from a car crash. He would flip and tumble out-of-bounds into the photographers so routinely that the Celtics had learned to work his accidents into their game plan, with Doc Rivers urging his players to count on pushing the ball hard the other way whenever Wade started to drive — make or miss — because he was unlikely to get back up in time to recover defensively. Wade was usually injured in some way or other, though he rarely discussed his pain. His knees were aging prematurely, he was receiving treatment on his surgically repaired shoulder, and yet all the same he had pushed through his misery to average 30 points over the first four games against Dallas. He had to be frustrated that his suffering had not been rewarded with a commanding 3–1 lead in the Finals, if not the championship already.

But there was more to LeBron and Wade's little outburst. There was annoyance that they, the greater stars, were being neutralized by the Mavericks. There were also the hard feelings from 2006 that neither Wade nor Dirk had forgotten. And then there had to be an air of resentment, too, that Dirk was being lauded for playing with the sniffles, as Wade and LeBron appeared to see it, while Wade, asking for no sympathy and receiving none, gritted through his ailments.

That night, after Miami's loss in Game 5, Wade was asked about his bruised hip. "I don't talk about injuries," he said.

Could anyone have blamed them for questioning whether the difference in coverage — the veneration of Dirk versus their demonization for having joined together in pursuit of teamwork and championships in Miami — was influenced by race?

It would have been entirely natural for there to be resentment that the legend of Michael Jordan's "flu game," in which he overcame illness to win Game 5 of the 1997 NBA Finals with 38 points, was being invoked not only on behalf of a white foreigner but also at the expense of LeBron and Wade, two African Americans who ranked among the league's most valuable stars.

During the 2006 NBA Finals, after his Miami Heat had won three straight games at home, coach Pat Riley had instructed his players to pack for the trip to Dallas as if they would be staying for one game only.

Five years later the Mavericks were doing the same. They were ahead 3–2, and as they prepared to travel back to Miami for Game 6, they packed light, as if a seventh game would not be necessary. And then they added their own twist: They would arrive at the arena for Game 6 wearing black coats or suits, which had been their fashion for close-out games throughout the playoffs. Their goal was to preside over Miami's "funeral."

The Mavericks were angered by Wade and LeBron's mocking of Dirk, which Dirk himself denounced as "a little childish, a little ignorant." He said, "I've been in this league for thirteen years. I've never faked an injury or illness." And yet the Mavericks had no interest in enabling Miami to change the agenda by knocking Dirk back on his heels. The only response that mattered would be to win Game 6.

There were thousands of blue-shirted Mavericks fans in the stands that night in Miami as Dirk, the German, stood with his hand over his heart for "The Star-Spangled Banner." "That's something that we started as a franchise after 9/11," he said. "I still keep doing it to honor the country that has been taking me in, that has been so good to me for a long, long time."

Keith Grant, the assistant general manager who had worked for the Mavericks for all thirty-one of their NBA seasons, was sitting in the lower bowl of the Miami arena, a dozen rising rows above the team's bench. He looked down to find his 18-year-old son, Brian, sitting in the second row next to Mark Cuban. To Grant's right was Dirk's mentor, Holger Geschwindner, in his standard black leather jacket. As the game wore on, Grant could see Holger sending signals whenever Dirk looked up from the court — the V to keep his fingers spread, or the slow flicking of the wrist to suggest a higher arc for the ball, or a rotisserie movement of the hands that might have had something to do with rhythm and pace.

"Holger," said Grant during Game 6, "if there's something you need to tell Dirk, get out of the seat and go down and tell him. If it's that important and it helps Dirk, then get down there."

"Oh, no, no," said Holger, shaking his head.

At one point Dirk stood on the court staring up at Holger, who stared back down at him motionless. It was as if they were communicating by telepathy.

Dirk was 1 for 12 at halftime.

There was a sense among the Mavericks that if they were ever going to win the championship, the final steps would be drawn-out, as if in slow motion. But it was not happening that way at all. The shots were coming quickly to Dirk — too quickly — and he was missing them, one after another. All nine of his attempts in the second quarter were off target. On his way back to the bench for a timeout he was met on the court by Cardinal, who was high-fiving and shouting, "I love it! I love it!"

"What are you talking about?" Dirk said.

"Not making a shot in the first half! I love it!" said Cardinal, nodding his head wildly. "Save all your bullets for the second half — don't make a shot!"

"You are crazy," muttered Dirk as he brushed by.

Dirk's strength was failing him at the worst time, and yet the Mavericks were leading 53–51 because Terry was scoring in rhythm with his trash-talking for 19 points in seventeen minutes. To prime himself on the night before the game, he had slept in Heat shorts. The preseason tattoo of the championship trophy on his right biceps bulged with each jump shot, and he celebrated his three-pointers by crouching to zoom away with his arms extended. He was a show-off through and through, and nobody at the Miami end of the floor liked it.

Dirk, Terry and all their teammates were bonded more tightly than ever in this game. The lineup improvements had reinforced their strengths and encouraged them to play as if finishing one another's sentences. Barea was getting to the basket, Stevenson made as many threes in the first half as Terry, Marion was defending LeBron and attacking at the other end, and Cardinal's efforts would provide him with a photograph that he would frame and hang in his home in Indiana: After drawing a defensive charge, he is shown being helped back onto his feet by Dirk and Kidd, the players he used to torment before he joined the Mavericks.

It was becoming obvious that LeBron's affliction had spread to Wade. LeBron would score an efficient but unsatisfactory 21 points on 15 shots, while Wade — slowed by his sore knees and injuries to his hip and shoulder — would be limited to a 6-of-16 night from the field for 17 points. He and LeBron would combine for 11 turnovers.

A jump shot by Ian Mahinmi at the third-quarter buzzer edged the Mavericks' lead to 81–72. The relatively tight score, however, did not reflect the distance that had grown between the team that was bonding and the one that was splintering.

The Mavericks' advantage swelled to a dozen points when Barea pierced inside for a finger-rolling layup midway through the fourth, and by now Dirk was back in rhythm. He made a couple of jump shots that seemed smooth and easygoing, in comparison with the frantic actions of the Miami stars. The Heat fans were beginning to walk up the stairs and out the exits, abandoning their arena to its occupiers in blue.

LeBron missed a pair of agitated three-pointers, and Wade missed one too. At the other end the Mavericks were running their offense naturally against the once frightening Miami defense. The Heat, in surrender, were not even bothering to foul. With a half minute to go, Dirk laid the ball off the glass with LeBron in chase to make it 103–92. His shot went down and through the net while Dirk turned and ran back with one fist, and then two, raised overhead.

So began the stages of his withdrawal. As he watched Terry strip free another Miami turnover, he reached up and around to grab the back of his head with both hands as if he had been arrested. Everyone on his sideline was celebrating in one way or another. His teammates on the court looked as if they could not believe what was happening. But Dirk's reaction was of a kind all his own. He wore a look of stunned panic. He ran his long fingers through his wet hair, away from his face, as if in distress.

"At that moment I was absolutely furious," Riley said. "We allowed them to take the game from us. We allowed them to take this championship from us. Could we have won it? Yes, but we allowed them in some way, shape or form—lack of concentration, overconfidence or fearfulness. We sort of almost choked that thing away."

Until just then, Riley had viewed the Mavericks as being vulnerable. "They were great in the sixth game," Riley said. "They were absolutely great. When they smelled title, they came and just took that from us."

The details became part of Riley's enduring basketball memory. He would be haunted by the Heat's ongoing inability to deal with Barea; by the shotmaking of Terry and Stevenson in the first half; by the series of pick-and-rolls they ran successfully for Dirk, Terry and Kidd (who, as Riley saw it, was the second-best player in the series after Dirk); and especially by the 8-for-15 performance of Dirk in the second half. He scored 10 points in the fourth quarter to finish them off.

"He was a great player, right in his prime," Riley said. "But when it came to Dirk in the fourth quarter, if we had to do it over again, we would have defended him differently, or with different people. Instead we sort of let him play. We let him get into his comfort zone, and it only took three or four possessions where he could just play—and then you're down 7 or 8 points. And then in Game 6 he was dominant. Once he smelled the opportunity to win a championship, he had full steam ahead."

Dirk had long been appreciated throughout the NBA for his skills, the mismatches he created and his pioneering role as a big man with three-point range. But his performances on this stage won him new respect.

"He hit one off-balance shot, going away from the basket, off the wrong foot, and he banked it in," said Larry Bird, who was watching the NBA Finals with some of his oldest friends in Indiana. "We was watching the game and I said,

'Boys, at that level, to do that is incredible.' Going away from the basket, what he was doing—off his right foot, reaching back and banking off the spot on the backboard he was aiming at—was just incredible."

The contrast between the fourth quarters of Dirk and LeBron was especially galling to Riley. By no means, though, did he believe that LeBron's failure to produce offensively was all-defining.

"I never mentioned one word to him—or even to Erik—about his fourth-quarter play. I didn't blame him for anything," Riley said of LeBron. "I recall in 2006, once we got to Game 6 down in Dallas, that even though Dwyane ended up with 36 points, the five crucial plays in the fourth quarter to allow us to win were made by James Posey, twice, Haslem, twice, and Antoine Walker. They simply double-teamed Wade every single time down the court. But when the other guys got open, they delivered.

"You can't just go to a guy, and all of a sudden it's on him: 'I've got to dunk it, I've got to hit threes, I've got to hit layups, I've got to make every play.' We had seen that a tremendous amount of times with LeBron in the past, and that always led to him losing, never winning. So when I looked at the fourth quarters, he wasn't just standing around, not doing anything. Maybe he should have been more assertive, more selfish, all of those things. But that would have been going against the game plan. And those games that we lost down there—Games 3 and 5—were very, very close games.

"A guy's killer instinct can only be as good as the guy who's next to you and their killer instinct," insisted Riley. "How many of your four teammates on the court are going to make two or three crucial non-scoring plays that will define the difference between winning and losing in a close game? Does LeBron have to do everything? Does he have to make every rebound? Every block? Every steal? Every dunk? Every jump shot that he takes? Everybody's got to accuse something, especially with somebody as great as him."

Riley was reminded again of the 1984 NBA Finals and how he felt after his Lakers had let their advantages slip away while losing in seven games to the Celtics. That loss would strengthen them. They would develop the backbone and cohesion necessary to win their next two Finals against the Celtics.

He recognized that losing now might help LeBron, Wade and Bosh win later. "We looked tight and stressed, and all of that I think came with the expectations," he said. "I knew we were going to have these guys for at least three more years. I was trying to make the best of it."

But thinking ahead to the years to come was beyond his vision as he sat waiting for the final seconds to expire.

"I was not saying to myself, 'This is going to be good for us,'" he said. "I don't believe losing any championship is good for you. That championship was decided with six minutes remaining in the fourth quarter of Game 2. It doesn't take much, and when that little thing happens, the other team smells it — they smell it. I do think if we'd won Game 2, we'd have won the championship.

"I think that our team was better than their team, that if we could've held it together and didn't make those mistakes and stayed fairly fundamental, then we would have beaten that team. But they were good enough, and they had world championship material and experience. And if you didn't do the right things, they were going to get you."

The Heat called a timeout with 18.8 seconds remaining to prepare for their defeat. Enough self-inflicted harm had been done, and they wanted to react with integrity. Security guards were ringing the court, connected to one another by a flimsy rope that they would tighten in order to hold off fans at the buzzer. As Dirk came out of his huddle, he looked up and raised a fist to Holger.

In the seat next to Holger, Keith Grant was grinning proudly at the sight of his son with Cuban, who was jumping up and down and grabbing Brian Grant and everyone else nearby. When Dirk made his layup, Grant knew they had won the championship. He moved toward the aisle and looked over his shoulder.

"You coming?" he asked Holger.

Holger shook his head no. His eyes were wet.

The majority of the fans remaining in the building were cheering for Dallas. These final minutes before the presentation of the trophies would be hectic. Workers carrying the pieces of a temporary stage hurried into the arena, waiting for the final buzzer that would permit its assembly on the court for the televised championship celebration. The players in the game were already congratulating one another as the horn sounded on the Mavericks' 105–95 victory. Cuban — screaming and crying and laughing — grabbed Carlisle and one Mavericks player after another. LeBron congratulated a few of his opponents until he could take no more of it and left the court. Bosh broke down in tears in the hallway and needed to be helped to the locker room. Wade searched the crowded floor for Dirk. He couldn't find him.

· · ·

In those last moments before the horn, Dirk was hopping over the scorers' table and vanishing inside the long backstage hallway beneath the stands.

Tim Frank, the NBA's senior vice president of basketball communications, was three steps behind as he followed the newest champion toward the visitors' locker room. "Dirk!" he yelled, but there was no stopping him.

An NBA colleague who was in charge of the imminent trophy presentation approached Frank to remind him, frantically, that the show could not go on without Dirk. "I said, 'You stay here and let me handle him,'" recalled Frank. "The worst thing would have been somebody bombarding him and not being sensitive about it."

Frank went into the visitors' locker room. Dirk wasn't there. He continued on through the room and into the shower, and there was Dirk sprawled out on his back on a wooden bench against the wall, his knees up high, a towel over his face.

Frank leaned over him. "This is awesome," said Frank in a low voice. "I am so happy for you. But listen, I've got to get you out there."

"I can't, I can't, I can't," cried Dirk, his throaty voice muffled through the towel.

"Listen, take a minute," said Frank. "This is a big deal for you to come out there."

Just then Scott Tomlin entered the locker room. He was one of the Mavericks' media relations representatives. He was also one of Dirk's best friends. Since 2003, when he joined the Mavericks, Tomlin had been part of the group that would go out to dinner with Dirk on the road or meet at his house to watch games on TV. Frank stepped away from Dirk and told Tomlin, "I don't know if we're going to get him back out on the court."

Tomlin moved into the shower area as Frank looked out the locker room door to see another NBA colleague pointing furiously at his watch. Frank waved him away.

"So I walk back there," recalled Tomlin, "and Dirk is sitting up on that bench, his head in a towel, and he's sobbing. Just bawling. It was a very visceral reaction to what had just happened. It was really something to see. I put my arm around him and I go, 'Hey, let's get back out there. You've got to accept your trophy.' And he said, 'I can't go back out there.' And he's crying, he's kind of shaking."

He did not want to be seen like that.

"I go, 'Hey, you've got to get back out there. You've got to go back out there because you earned this,'" Tomlin said. "I'm trying to reason with him, but at the same time I'm thinking, 'This is a cool moment.' I said, 'You've got to get out there to accept what's yours. Your teammates are getting ready to accept the Larry O'Brien Trophy. You've got to be out there for that.'

"And he says: 'I just need thirty minutes.'"

Tomlin laughed as he recalled that part.

"I said, 'Thirty minutes!' I said, 'Look, you have three minutes. Maybe.'"

Here was the difference, fundamentally, between the two opposing stars. One year earlier Commissioner David Stern had been pleading with LeBron not to go on television, because he had nothing yet to sell. Now the NBA was begging Dirk to show his face, and he wanted to hide.

"There was a time when I didn't know if he was going to get up," recalled Tomlin, and what he said next to Dirk was firmer in tone. It was said in friendship. "I said to him, 'If you're not out there when they accept that trophy, you're going to look back and you're going to regret it. You want to be out there.'

"And then there was another pause — and it was probably only five seconds, but it felt like five minutes — where I wasn't sure if he was going to get up. And just out of nowhere, he didn't say anything, he just stood up and walked out of the locker room, and we all walked out there together."

As Dirk raised himself up, Tomlin was struck anew by the size of his friend. He was a giant.

After the game LeBron sat next to Wade in a makeshift interview room and answered questions.

"Obviously you've dealt with so much criticism for the last year that wasn't at all to do with basketball," a reporter asked. "When you're getting criticized for what's happening on the court, does that bother you?"

LeBron had produced his requisite 7.2 rebounds, 6.8 assists and 1.7 steals per game during the NBA Finals, which was an array that few other stars could equal. But he had averaged a scant 17.8 points in the Finals (one-third fewer than he scored during the season), he had let down his teammates and himself, and it was because of his failure to score, to deliver as he had promised, that he was now being criticized.

"No, that doesn't bother me," LeBron said. "I understand this is a huge stage, and you want to perform well for nobody else besides your teammates. That's ultimately what it's about for me. If I can play well for my teammates, help my teammates win basketball games, then I'm always satisfied with that. It hurts me, and I get on myself when I'm not able to play well and help my teammates win."

That was the basketball side of LeBron talking.

Then the next question: "Does it bother you that so many people are happy to see you fail?"

"Absolutely not," he said, and now the off-the-court side of LeBron was showing its face. "Because at the end of the day, all the people that was rooting on me to fail, at the end of the day they have to wake up tomorrow and have the same life that they had before they woke up today." He was speaking to the millions of fans who had campaigned for his defeat. "They have the same personal problems they had today," he went on. "I'm going to continue to live the way I want to live and continue to do the things that I want to do with me and my family and be happy with that." It was as if he was reliving the night of *The Decision* all over again. "They can get a few days or a few months or whatever the case may be on being happy about not only myself but the Miami Heat not accomplishing their goal, but they have to get back to the real world at some point."

And that was the last that would be seen of that side of LeBron. In the future he would be wary of exploiting his own best qualities again.

Down the hallway in Miami, in the visitors' locker room, the Mavericks would celebrate more quietly than any championship team in recent memory. Champagne was being sprayed amid the laughter and embraces, but there was nothing contrived in their response. They could not believe it was over — that there would be no practice tomorrow and no more opponents to beat.

"We were all celebrating in our own little way," said Brian Cardinal, "but at the same time we were such a confident group that we didn't want it to end. We all enjoyed each other so much, and we all got along, and we were all able to harass each other and screw around and nothing was untouchable. There were so many battles that players have gone through on the court."

And now many of those battles had been resolved.

"I'm sure it was to the point where a lot of guys were really, really excited," said Cardinal, "but at the same time just privately, in their own mind, thinking, 'Man, this is unbelievable.'"

In the midst of the Mavericks' euphoric reflections arrived Riley, who came by to shake hands with Carlisle and congratulate him on the championship that probably could not have been wrung from this team by any other coach.

Holger visited the locker room and stayed for a time, and then he was gone.

That night there were two parties. The coaches and executive staff and their families met in a ballroom at the team's hotel for a quiet celebration. In the meantime Cuban, his players, the support staff and anyone else who wanted to join in went straight to the enormous nightclub LIV at the Fontainebleau hotel in Miami Beach, where they danced and drank and posed with the trophy they had won. Fans of the team were invited to join them. Word spread by text message. "It was loud; you couldn't talk," said Dirk's friend Nick Creme. "It was pure bliss."

"I should have waited for about a week, ten days, and then met with them," said Riley. "Especially with the veterans. They were the shortest exit meetings I ever had with players."

It was two days after their Game 6 loss. Bosh was in Riley's office for their year-end chat. An aide told Riley that LeBron had arrived for his 3 p.m. meeting. LeBron was asked if he would like to take a seat outside while Bosh was finishing. LeBron wasn't interested in sitting.

"He was walking back and forth in front of me," said Riley, who could see LeBron outside. "Finally, at 3:03, he came into my office. He walks right over to the window and he looks out. And he says to me, 'You're late.' And Chris smiles, because he got it."

"Coach, we can finish this later," Bosh said as he excused himself from the room.

"He paced for a minute and a half, walking in front of my desk and looking at me and out at the water," Riley said of LeBron. "I just stared at him. Then he sat down and he just leaned back and he stared at me. I said, 'You know, you can go if you want. We don't have to have this meeting. There's nothing really to talk about, unless you really want to talk about something. We can talk about it later.'

"I said, 'Look, you had a great year. We've got a lot in front of us.' I can't even remember the exact words; I have it written down in my diary somewhere. He just shook his head the whole time. He didn't want to say why we lost. He didn't ask any questions about what we were going to do. He just wanted to go home, I think. Just get out of the office and get out of there and go home. And he does the same thing that I'd do when I was coaching. He goes into his man cave, or wherever he goes — into that hole we all go into after a loss like that. Then one day we come out. It's usually about a week later, and you come out of it.

"We didn't talk much. If we talked, it was 'How you doing? Appreciate what you've done this year.' There was no instruction from me. A guy like that, there are times that they don't even want somebody else's solace. They don't want somebody to give them empathy. They want to take the pain: 'Don't try to make me feel good. Don't say something — that's bullshit. I'm hurting, I'm painful, I lost again. I tried to bring the Big Three together.' Even though he wouldn't admit it, deep down inside he was probably taking it all on himself: 'I fucked this up.' He might have been saying that to himself. He didn't say that to me, but he might have been feeling that: 'I know how I should play; I didn't play that way; it was so strange.'"

LeBron had almost won the championship in spite of himself. For one agonizing year he had enabled himself to be defined negatively, and against his own instincts he had fought to defend his new discouraging identity, even though he hadn't believed in it. He had been conflicted and strung out, his self-doubts revealed by his passive fourth quarters against Dallas — and still he had almost prevailed.

If he had triumphed in 2011, would his breakthrough title have convinced him to fully embrace the villainous persona? Would he have gone on to lead the NBA down a cynical path? No one will ever know, because LeBron had been stopped — and arguably saved — by Dirk in the final moments of the crucial games.

"He had gone through a tumultuous year," Riley said. "Whatever his thoughts were, he didn't express them to me. I'm just speaking out of what he might have been feeling — that he was taking the brunt of this loss, didn't want to talk about it, didn't want anyone to feel sorry for him, wanted to go home and take a long one-week LeBron James bath. Then I saw him ten days later, and he was fine. He got it. He got over it."

Four days after the Finals came the championship parade through downtown Dallas, which Cuban paid for out of his own pocket. "You're looking at the best basketball team on the planet," Carlisle told a full house of fans inside the AmericanAirlines Center before the team set out on the parade route. "Also, the best basketball player on the planet, Dirk Nowitzki."

Dirk rubbed tears from his eyes after hearing the compliment from his coach, and again when he saw that Cuban was too overcome by his own emotions to speak. This was nothing like the day four years earlier when he had received his MVP award. Many tributes were coming his way, and Dirk had earned them by his own high standards.

"I'd like to say one thing, and I mentioned this to my players the other day," Carlisle said to the fans as Cuban stood, crying, on the stage of his arena. "There is a big difference in this world between success and fulfillment. And Mark has had obviously unbelievable success in business and in his life. But the thing you all must understand is, for him, it never mattered the cost. It was being able to bring this moment to you that has brought him this fulfillment."

One week after he won the championship, Dirk turned 33. A surprise birthday party was held in his honor at a restaurant in Dallas. It was organized by Holger and Dirk's girlfriend, Jessica Olsson, whom he would marry one year later. "Dinner for 41," the evening was titled, in honor of Dirk's uniform number. The usual suspects were there — Donnie Nelson, Brian Cardinal and Dirk's closest American friends.

The Dallas Symphony Orchestra string quartet provided the music. Dirk sat at the head of the table, with forty guests on either side of him, including Mike Modano, who had led the Dallas Stars to the National Hockey League championship in 1999. Scott Tomlin stood to make the introductions. Among them were Dr. Eric Olson, who had won the Lefoulon-Delalande Grand Prize from the French Academy of Sciences in 2009; Dr. Alfred G. Gilman, who had been awarded the Nobel Prize in Physiology or Medicine in 1994; and Dr. Johann Deisenhofer, who had received the Nobel Prize in Chemistry in 1988.

"All of a sudden it went quiet," said Holger. Many of Dirk's friends were uncomfortable. They had not expected to be joined by guests from beyond their small sporting community, but this was the point that Holger had made long ago, when he had first asked Dirk if he was willing to commit to excellence. This was not about the degree of loft required for the perfect shot, and it was not about the money he had earn, and it was not even about the trophy the Mavericks had won.

"I just wanted to make sure Dirk knows that 'Hey, you guys are now highlighted guys,'" said Holger of his protégé, the new champion of the NBA. "'But there is a bigger world. There are other feats. There are the smart guys.' And the funniest thing was, nobody was talking to them because they were scared." The winners of the sporting world were intimidated at first, but then the wine was poured, the conversation flowed, and their similarities drew them together. They were dreamers all. "And those guys had so much fun," said Holger, with the brightest of smiles as he thought of Dirk and the scientists. "It was a really great party."

Dirk's focus on the basket had never been meant to close him off from everything else. Now he was realizing, in his fulfillment, that the game was a bridge to a new world.

• • •

In the NBA season of *The Decision,* there were many such bridges.

Kobe Bryant built a bridge from the Jordan era, fighting for the sanctity of competition on the court.

Doc Rivers built a bridge from the Celtics dynasty of the 1960s, upholding their original values and reframing traditions for this new world.

More bridges were built by Isiah Thomas, who showed that the meanest streets could be survived; by Gregg Popovich, who constructed a basketball wonderland in San Antonio based on the ideals of the game's overseas frontier; by Joey Crawford, who insisted on fair competition based on the fairness he struggled so hard to establish within himself; by Larry Bird, who saw what LeBron James could become; by Pat Riley, who would help LeBron get there; and by LeBron himself. He had inherited a world of wealth and fame from Michael Jordan. With no small thanks to lessons learned during his first-year season away from home, LeBron would earn his own place atop that world. The 2010–11 season had been his pivot. He had taken a step back in order to burst forth.

The conflict between the game and its rewards that had resulted in *The Decision* would, in the years to come, be transformed by him. His championship play on the court would be reflected off the court in the learned wisdom of his interviews, in the stands he would make on behalf of social causes, and in his return to the Cavaliers, with whom he would bring the championship to Cleveland.

On his way to that outcome, LeBron crossed a bridge that had been constructed by the surprise champion of the 2011 NBA Finals, with the help of his architect, Holger Geschwindner. His long foreign journey to the championship proved that the NBA was indeed a theater in which the values of America were meant to be thrashed out. The immigrant, whose triumph measured the strength of his humility, provided the game of freedom, equality and merit with a higher calling worthy of those values.

Basketball, thanks to Dirk Nowitzki, had grown up at long last to become the sport of the American Dream.

EPILOGUE: THE WAY FORWARD

Shortly after his Celtics were beaten in the 2011 playoffs by Miami, Doc Rivers underwent surgery on his throat, which had been the plan from the beginning of the season. "The doctor was almost positive that it was a noncancerous polyp," said Doc, whose father-in-law had died of throat cancer. "For my wife and my mother-in-law, they were not on board with me going through the season. They were 100 percent not on board. They wanted to fuck the season: 'You got to go now.'"

The reason he was aware of his need for surgery was because he had received repeated calls from the most unlikely source: someone who hardly knew Doc but took it upon himself to warn him after having an episode of his own. "He was saying, 'I tell all coaches that they've got to go because they use their voices all the time,'" said Doc. "And one time, two times, three times he badgered me. He actually called me and said, 'Doc, have you set up an appointment?' I said, 'No, man. What the fuck?' My voice was fine. And he said, 'Call Dick Vitale.' And then I get a text from Dick Vitale, who says, 'I can hear it in your voice.'"

So he had gone to see a doctor, who discovered a spot on Doc's throat, and it was all because of this intervention. "Do you know who it was?" asked Doc. "This is going to shock you: It was World Wide Wes, who I don't even really know." William "World Wide Wes" Wesley, a power broker of AAU basketball and a close adviser to LeBron and many stars of his generation, had been the one to call Doc again and again, and then to reach out to the TV announcer Dick Vitale, until Doc had been convinced to take care of himself. Karma is like the Celtic Way itself. Those who are true to their values will be rewarded in abundance.

One dozen days after Miami's loss to the Mavericks in the 2011 NBA Finals, Heat president Pat Riley was pleased to see that LeBron James was back to normal.

"When I did see him again, he said, 'Hey, man, who are we going after?'" Riley recalled. "I gave him numbers to Shane Battier and all of these other free agents, and he was on the phone, calling these guys. He got perked up again because I was going to get him another couple of players. I remember him calling Shane and Shane calling us. And so LeBron got right back into helping the team become better."

Time was short. The lockout would be declared by Commissioner David Stern on July 1, 2011.

The lockout would stretch on for 161 uninspiring, soul-draining days. By the terms of the previous collective bargaining agreement, the players had been guaranteed 57 percent of the NBA's annual revenues. Under the new agreement, as settled in December 2011, they accepted a lesser share that would range between 49 and 51.2 percent. In addition, Stern and his deputy commissioner, Adam Silver, succeeded in negotiating an imperfect but progressive agreement among the owners by which the more successful franchises would pass a share of their revenues on to the less rich teams. The mediation with the players turned out to be less devitalizing than the in-house haggling among the owners. "If you only knew . . ." said Stern with a sigh.

In addition to the bickering over money, the owners also wanted to create a hard salary cap, which would limit the money they could offer players, as well as a hard luxury tax, which would punish a team like Miami for hoarding the biggest stars. "The NBA owners came in and taxed teams punitively for trying to become great — for taking on big contracts," Riley said. "We were the test case, as soon as we signed those three guys."

There were two immediate casualties of the lockout. The first was Kobe Bryant, who believed the Lakers would be trading for 26-year-old Chris Paul. The All-NBA point guard had made it clear to the New Orleans Hornets that he would not be signing a new contract with them. As a result the Hornets had sought to trade their best player before losing him to free agency for nothing in return.

The Hornets franchise was undermined by the same financial issues that had resulted in the lockout. The owner, George Shinn, had been unable to make ends meet in the small media market of New Orleans. But instead of allowing Shinn to sell the Hornets to a new ownership group that would likely move the franchise to a larger market in the wake of Hurricane Katrina, the 2005 disaster that had devastated New Orleans, Stern had insisted that the NBA buy the Hornets for $300 million and operate the team until a permanent buyer could be found.

This arrangement put Stern in charge of managing the Hornets' affairs while he was also overseeing the league. His temporary conflict of interest wounded Stern when he decided that the Hornets were taking on too much salary in the proposed trade that would send Paul to the Lakers. He instructed the Hornets' front office to search for a deal that would reduce costs — thus enabling the franchise to find a buyer — and they wound up sending Paul to the Los Angeles Clippers instead. Neil Olshey, the general manager of the Clippers, believed that his presentation to LeBron in 2010, six days before *The Decision,* had ultimately influenced Paul's choice to go to the Clippers. LeBron's agent in that meeting had been Leon Rose, who also happened to be Chris Paul's agent. "Leon had been through the process with us," Olshey said. "He knew all about the young talent we had." As a result, Kobe was left stranded in L.A.

Stern was the other casualty of the lockout. He would be accused of "vetoing" the trade of Chris Paul to the Lakers, furthering complaints that he had amassed too much power as commissioner.

A young, established star like Chris Paul might have revitalized the Lakers. Without him, they floundered. Mike Brown, who had coached LeBron in Cleveland, lasted one season and not quite two weeks as the initial replacement for Phil Jackson. The Lakers fired Brown impulsively after a 1-4 start in 2012–13.

The Lakers spoke briefly with Jackson about returning as coach before they turned abruptly to Mike D'Antoni, in hopes that his fast-twitch offense would lead them back into contention with center Dwight Howard and point guard Steve Nash, who had won two MVP awards while playing for D'Antoni in Phoenix. But Nash was 38 and breaking down, Howard was unhealthy and unhappy, and Kobe declined to go along with D'Antoni's offense.

The dynasty was disintegrating fast. Jerry Buss, who had won ten championships as owner of the Lakers, died in 2013 at age 80. Kobe suffered a torn Achilles tendon at the end of the 2012–13 season and a variety of injuries over the next two years. Nonetheless, he received a two-year contract extension worth $48.5 million in recognition of all that he meant to the Lakers. He was their only draw.

In 2015–16, his final season, they went 17-65, and yet in his farewell game at age 37 he scored 60 points at home (while taking 50 shots) to beat the Utah Jazz 101–96. Kobe outscored Utah 23–21 in the fourth quarter, and no player in the league had a higher-scoring game that season. He was true to himself to the end.

In Dallas the harsh luxury tax of the new collective bargaining agreement convinced Mavericks owner Mark Cuban that he would be setting back his team by re-signing center Tyson Chandler, whose defensive leadership had been crucial to their recent championship. Chandler would move on to the Knicks as a free agent, and Cuban would later admit to regretting his decision. Over their next half-dozen seasons, the Mavericks would win fifty games once, miss the playoffs twice and fail to win a postseason series.

The season following the lockout was truncated to sixty-six games. The Mavericks received their championship rings on Christmas Day and then trailed by as many as 35 points in an opening-day rematch with the Heat in which LeBron generated 37 points, 10 rebounds and 6 assists. "We came to Dallas and that was it, man," said Riley. "I knew the team was different that year."

And yet there they were again, trailing 3–2 to the Celtics in the 2012 Eastern Conference Finals and needing to win Game 6 in Boston in order to stay alive.

The Celtics had won Game 5 at Miami on a long last-minute jumper by Paul Pierce. "He hit a three-point shot in LeBron's face, which beat us, and I remember LeBron walking back to the bench with his head down, his shoulders slumped over," Riley said. "I was thinking, 'Why would he give him so much space? Do what you're supposed to do to contain him.' Then Paul turned his head on him, and as he was going back to the bench, he was shaking his head and mouthing something that was mocking LeBron. And then we went on to Boston and LeBron got 45."

LeBron's performance in Game 6 — he shot 19 of 26 from the floor with 15 rebounds and 5 assists — was the greatest show Boston had seen since Michael Jordan scored 63 points against Larry Bird's champions in the 1986 playoffs. "He exorcised himself," Riley said.

The resilience and poise that carried LeBron's team through their sea-change 98–79 victory could be traced back to the lessons he had drawn from the 2011 Finals. "It took me to go all the way to the top and then hit rock-bottom, to realize what I needed to do as a professional athlete and as a person," LeBron would say weeks later, after he won his breakthrough NBA championship. "I just got back to being myself, and I didn't care too much about what anyone said about me. I kind of made my own path, but did it the right way."

In the 2012 Finals the Heat lost the opener at Oklahoma City before recovering to win Game 2. "That was probably the most important game in that Big Three's tenure," said Riley. "I remember LeBron just taking over in the fourth quarter. There was a different thing. He was taking tough shots and making them."

LeBron had taken leadership of the Heat that season with Dwyane Wade's blessing. When Chris Bosh went down with an abdominal strain in the opening half of the 2012 playoffs, LeBron came running over. "Get up! Get up!" he yelled, before realizing the severity of the injury. Bosh would miss nine playoff games, but LeBron would compensate with 30.3 points and 9.7 rebounds per game while averaging 42.7 minutes in the postseason.

When he knew the championship was on the way in the closing minutes of Game 5 against the Thunder, there was none of the over-the-top celebrating that had disgusted the Celtics one year earlier. He was authentic and focused and no longer playing the grandstanding role that had so clearly been foreign to him. "If LeBron says that losing that Finals was the best thing that ever happened to him, and if he really did learn a lesson — what lesson is that?" said Riley. "If I watch him now, he very rarely ever celebrates. He's like, 'Let's just finish the goddamn game.' If something great happens, he might pat somebody on the head. But he's not going to put on a demonstration. He's just clinical, get it done, let's finish this thing, and he keeps his focus."

That first championship summer would conclude with LeBron leading his undersized U.S. team to the gold medal at the 2012 Olympic Games in London. Months later he was named Sportsman of the Year by *Sports Illustrated*.

"I was playing to prove people wrong last year," LeBron said after he had been named Finals MVP on the night of his first championship. "People would say I was selfish, and that got to me. That got to me a lot because I know that this is a team game. All last year I tried to prove people wrong, and it wasn't me. I was basically fighting against myself."

He was never again going to predict that winning would be easy. "It was the hardest thing I've ever done as a basketball player," he said of the championship he had won. All of the advantages he appeared to have inherited from Michael Jordan — the instant endorsements, the certainty of his potential — had turned out to be obstacles that had made it more difficult for him to find his way.

"He was now, finally, what was tattooed across his back," Riley said. "He was that guy."

"Everything that went along with me being a high school prodigy when I was 16 and on the cover of *Sports Illustrated*, to being drafted and having to be the face of a franchise, everything that came with it, I had to deal with and I had to learn through it," LeBron said. "No one had went through that journey, so I had to learn on my own. All the ups and downs, everything that came along with it, I had to basically figure it out on my own. I'm happy now that nine years later I can finally say that I'm a champion. And I did it the right way. I didn't shortcut anything. I put a lot of hard work and dedication in it, and hard work pays off."

In that summer of 2012 Ray Allen infuriated the Celtics. He left Boston to sign with LeBron in Miami.

"For him to go there—all of us feel disrespected by it," Pierce said three months later. "Kevin is pissed, I'm pissed, Rondo's pissed, Doc's pissed. I mean it's genuine hate for them now. That's equivalent to me saying, 'Okay, I'm going to sign with the Lakers now'—which I would never. I would never do that. We're taking it like a smack in the face."

Allen would explain that he had been tired of hearing his name involved in trade rumors. "I was in the trade rumors last year—I was," said Pierce, who was approaching his fifteenth year with the Celtics. "And I told Danny just send me somewhere warm if it's going to happen."

That was going to happen, but he wasn't going anywhere warm. After winning 41 games and losing 4–2 in the opening round of the playoffs to Carmelo Anthony's Knicks, the Celtics turned over their roster in 2013. Coach Doc Rivers, who had no interest in a painful, years-long rebuild, was essentially traded to the Clippers for a first-round draft pick. Pierce, Kevin Garnett and Jason Terry—who had left Dallas one year earlier as a free agent—were dealt to the Brooklyn Nets, who were desperate to contend for the championship. Pierce was 36, Garnett was 37, and the Nets would go no further than the second round with them.

In return Danny Ainge received four unprotected first-round draft picks from Brooklyn, making the trade one of the great swindles of modern times. Ainge would replace Doc with Brad Stevens, a terrific young coach from Butler University, who—despite having no NBA experience—would return Boston to the playoffs in 2015 and the Eastern Conference Finals in 2017.

Along the way Ainge would give up very little to acquire the 5-foot 9-inch point guard Isaiah Thomas (who had been named after the Pistons champion when his father, a Lakers fan, lost a bet). Thomas would turn into an All-NBA star for the Celtics. In a separate deal, Ainge would trade Rajon Rondo to Dallas, where the point guard would clash publicly with coach Rick Carlisle. Controversy would follow Rondo to Sacramento for one season, and then to Chicago and New Orleans, where his coaches would rave about him as a mentor to younger teammates.

In Miami the Heat were surviving their own seventh game in the 2013 Eastern Conference Finals against Larry Bird's Indiana Pacers. In 2012 Bird had been named NBA Executive of the Year, making him the only person in league history to receive the awards for best executive, best coach and MVP. From 2012 through 2014 the Pacers would threaten the Heat annually in the latter rounds of the playoffs while taking every series to at least six games. But LeBron, in fulfillment of Bird's expectations, always came through.

The prospects were not so promising for Miami in Game 6 of the 2013 Finals. The visiting Spurs held a 95–92 lead and were seconds away from closing out their fifth championship when LeBron missed a three-pointer. The long rebound was relayed by Chris Bosh to Ray Allen, who backpedaled frantically into the corner before smoothly forcing overtime. The Heat survived, 103–100, on LeBron's 32-point triple-double, and then he scored 37 as Miami pulled away at the end of Game 7 to win 95–88.

By now LeBron had turned himself into one of the NBA's most efficient shooters from midrange and one of the most effective playmakers with his back to the basket in the post — two lost arts in the modern game. As he stood on the victory podium with his second championship trophy, he was asked how he had learned to withstand the scrutiny that had followed him since *The Decision*. His answer surely made Isiah Thomas proud. "I can't worry about what everybody say about me," he said. "I'm LeBron James, from Akron, Ohio, from the inner city. I'm not even supposed to be here."

In the preseason of his first year with the Clippers, known for many years as the worst franchise in sports, Doc was at the team's charity golf tournament at Trump National Golf Club in Los Angeles when Donald Sterling, the 80-year-old owner of the team, introduced him to V. Stiviano. She was Sterling's mistress.

"The first thing she says is 'Are you going to trade DeAndre Jordan?'" recalled

Doc, who listened to her rant about the hopelessness of the Clippers center, who would lead the NBA in rebounding that season. "And I said, 'Well, number one, clearly you don't know anything about basketball. And number two, that's my job, not yours, and that's none of your business.' Donald looked at me and didn't say a word. That's not the best way to come into a new job, when you're getting into an argument with the boss's girlfriend, and there were other people standing there. So from that point on, I never heard a word from her."

The following April, with Stiviano's blessing, a recording of her private conversation with Sterling, in which the Clippers' owner expressed irritation that she had posted a photo of herself with Magic Johnson, was made public.

"Don't put him on an Instagram for the world to have to see so they have to call me," Sterling said in the recording. "And don't bring him to my games. Yeah, it bothers me a lot that you want to promo, broadcast that you're associating with black people. Do you have to?

"You can sleep with them. You can bring them in, you can do whatever you want . . ." Sterling went on. "The little I ask you is . . . not to bring them to my games."

Of his own players, the majority of whom were African American, Sterling said, "I support them and give them food and clothes and cars and houses. Who gives it to them? Does someone else give it to them?"

The Clippers were in the midst of their opening-round series in the 2014 playoffs against the Golden State Warriors when team president Andy Roeser told Doc that a tape involving Sterling might be coming out. "I assumed it was a sex tape," Doc said. "So I didn't think much of it." Five days later another staffer brought the tape to Doc. "My fucking heart dropped," he said. "I could not believe it. Within an hour it was out."

He was with his team in Oakland preparing for Game 4 against the Warriors the next day. "I'm trying to figure out what to do," Doc said. "Literally, what to do. What to say. How to act. I took forever to put my gear on. I didn't know if I wanted to put a Clipper shirt on for a minute. I went back and forth. I put on a Nike shirt, Clipper shirt, Nike shirt — I went back and forth because you have to think of everything when you get in front of your players, how you want to look. Do you want to look a part of it, or do you want to distance yourself from it?"

He reminded himself that it had been his decision to join the Clippers as their coach and senior vice president with control over the front office. "I knew there would be risk when I decided," he said of Sterling's reputation as an unreliable owner. "Most rational people told me I was nuts."

He walked into the meeting with his players to find them all on their cellphones. "I'm thinking, 'Oh my God, social media,'" Doc said. "That was my first big thing with social media. 'They're reading everything, they're getting advice — we're being separated right now by social media.'"

He was used to being prepared, down to writing out his speeches by hand before every game, but for the most important meeting of his career he had no notes. There had been no time. And his players were angry.

"I didn't know what I was going to say," he said. "Everybody was sitting there with their arms folded. That's a sign that they're not hearing me, they're not letting me in right now. I'm the guy standing in front of them with the Clippers shirt on, and they're pissed at me too. Finally, what I thought broke the ice, I said: 'Let me stop here, guys. I want to tell you. My name is Glenn Rivers. I'm from Maywood, Illinois. And I'm black.'"

They started laughing. He repeated the introduction.

"I said, 'I'm a black guy, and I am pissed off by this whole thing.' I told them why I was pissed. I told them about all the things that have happened to me racially. I also said, 'And I don't care if you're black or white, this is not a racial thing. This is something that is unjust, and you should be pissed.'"

J. J. Redick, who is white, said, "I'm just as pissed as you guys."

"So I told them, 'I'm standing here as your microphone. I'm going to do whatever you guys want to do. If you guys don't want to play, we're done. I think that's a bad decision, but I'm going to honor what you guys want to do.' And then I said, 'I know this. I know when I grew up in the backyard and I played basketball by myself and I was making those fake crowd noises like every kid does, Donald Sterling was never in my dreams. He never entered into my thoughts. I didn't say I wanted to win a world championship for Donald Sterling.' And I said, 'So if you allow him to be the reason you don't win, then shame on us.'"

They had put their phones aside. They were staring back at him.

"I said, 'This is what I know. We have to have one voice. We cannot have more than one voice. I would like to be the speaker for you guys. If you'd like to have someone else speak for you, I'm good with that. But it can only be one voice, one thought, one way. The one thing I know about this, and I'm looking at all you guys, looking at all this crap on social media and all these people trying to tell you what to do or how to act — they don't have any skin in the game. What's going to happen is one of you guys is going to say something stupid and you're going to be the story. If you can trust me, I will represent you and I will try my best to say the right thing. I guarantee I'm going to screw some stuff up. But just trust me. It's coming from the right place. Let it be one voice.'"

Then it was onto the bus for practice. They were up 2–1 in the series, and it had gone without saying, before the release of the tape, that nothing could be more important than seizing control with a win the next day.

"Going to practice, I was naïve," Doc said. "I knew it was a big deal, but I didn't think it was a national deal. When we pulled up, there were TV trucks and there were hundreds of media people, and this was no longer sports." The only members of the organization to make statements were Doc, on behalf of the Clippers, and point guard Chris Paul, on behalf of the National Basketball Players Association.

"I had to make some really tough decisions," Doc said. "I'm getting calls from Jesse Jackson, Al Sharpton and everyone. I didn't take anyone's call because I didn't need any more voices in my head.

"The other thing, and I wish I could remember who told me, but he basically said, 'I've been a civil rights guy my whole life, and if I learned anything, it's that the people who are persecuted are the people who are left having to answer. It's never the person who does it. So don't say something dumb while everyone's waiting for your answer, because you didn't do anything.'

"That really helped me because it's so true. Donald Sterling's the one who said all of the stupid stuff. Matt Barnes didn't say anything stupid, and neither did De-Andre Jordan and neither did Chris Paul. It was the guy who said it that should have responded. Yet we're always the ones left. The ones persecuted are the ones having to show people how they're going to react. And not only that, but you're judged on how you react. You didn't do anything, but all of a sudden people are calling you names. Like if you play, you're a sellout. If you don't play, then you're stupid."

He wasn't surprised that his team lost 118–97. Before the game Doc told his assistants, "We're going to get the fucking shit beat out of us tonight." He was on the team bus heading to the arena when he learned that Sterling and his wife, Shelly, were planning to attend the game. Doc was screaming at Roeser over the phone when a couple of his players asked, "Everything good, Coach?"

"I said, 'Everything's good; this is something else,'" Doc said. "They knew it was full of shit, but what else are you going to say?"

Donald Sterling was convinced to leave the arena, but Shelly Sterling sat courtside across from the Clippers' bench as they ceremonially removed their warmup jerseys and prepared for the game with their red shirts on inside out. Afterward she rode on the team bus and plane back to Los Angeles with Doc's permission. "That was a mistake, and I'd told the guys I'd make some," Doc said. "I had some compassion for her. She didn't do anything either. But when guys saw she was on the bus, they went to the other bus or they walked right by her. And I thought, 'Oof, this was not a good decision.'"

Back in Los Angeles, on the morning of Game 5, Doc took a 6 a.m. call from Human Resources. "He says, 'Hey, man, I hate to do this to you, but you have to come down here. You have to talk to our employees. There's a chance we're not going to have employees by the end of the day. We're having a bad day here,'" Doc said. "I went downtown, and it is still emotional to this day, because there were literally employees crying. There were people answering the phones about season tickets and getting screamed at, calling them racists or Uncle Toms, and you could see they were emotionally beat-up. I told them, 'This is the start of a new organization.' I said, 'We are going to be the best organization in basketball someday, and you're going to be a part of it. I have no idea how the hell we're going to get there. But we are going to get there, and I guarantee you that.'"

Rivers was working closely with Adam Silver, who was facing his first crisis in his third month as NBA commissioner, following Stern's retirement after thirty years in charge. "I saw a tough side, an emotional side, of Adam that you rarely see," Doc said. "Adam was pissed. He said, 'Doc, you just trust me. You've been dealt a wrong, and we're going to right this for you. We're going to get this right, and everyone that is responsible will be dealt with immediately.' And when he said that, you knew, 'All right, we're good.'"

Before Game 5 Silver announced a lifetime ban and a $2.5 million fine for Sterling. He also promised to force the sale of the Clippers, which would result one month later in former Microsoft CEO Steve Ballmer's purchase of the team for $2 billion. In the meantime Rivers was still trying to beat the Warriors, even as he was having to make decisions on the business side. "Before Game 7 they were running by me what they should put on the fucking T-shirt," Doc said. "That was the one time that I got frustrated, and I called Adam and said, 'Hey, what the fuck? I'm trying to coach a Game 7, and I need somebody here.'" Within the week Silver had appointed Dick Parsons, the former CEO of Time Warner, to be the Clippers' interim CEO.

The Clippers won Game 7 at home, 126–121. They went on to lose to Oklahoma City in the second round, and in future postseasons they would advance no further than that. Doc, who had never presided over an NBA front office, had been charged with transforming the Clippers into title contenders while learning on the job.

He had thought the rebuild in Boston would be too painful. By 2016 Doc's Clippers were losing in the first round, while the young Celtics were reaching the Eastern conference finals.

In San Antonio, Gregg Popovich was sitting for a TV interview at the Spurs' practice facility with local TV reporter Don Harris.

"Last question," said Harris. "I called the Basketball Hall of Fame. I prepared a major case for Gregg Popovich —"

"Are there going to be questions after this?" said Popovich.

"No," said Harris.

Popovich wrenched himself up out of the chair with a comical wince as he unhooked the tiny microphone near his collar. He was ending the interview.

"Oh come on now, wait!" said Harris. "You've got to hear my question."

"You know by now it's not about me," said Popovich as he walked past Harris and sat in another chair, away from the TV news camera.

Harris said, "I was going to ask you a question."

"I know you were," said Popovich. "The Hall of Fame is for Larry Brown or Larry Bird and Magic Johnson and Red Auerbach and guys like that who are real coaches and players. I just happen to be here."

"You're a Hall of Famer, Pop."

"I just happen to be here," Popovich insisted. The interview had ended and they were arguing in private. "It's like being in a tsunami and you just happen to be there. I was here. Good to see you though."

Harris ignored the dismissal to inform Popovich that there was a long tradition of celebrated players and coaches who embraced their candidacy for the Hall of Fame.

"Well," said Popovich, "I know who I am. I'm a Pomona-Pitzer fucking Division III asshole who was 2-22 his first year. That's who I am."

"You're going in, Pop," said Harris. "My question is, why wouldn't you go ahead and go in now? That's what I was going to ask."

"What are you asking me for? What do I know? I can't even get out of the first round."

They were arguing weeks after the elbow injury to Manu Ginobili had knocked the Spurs out of the 2011 playoffs.

"When I nominated you, they said —"

"You nominated me?" Popovich looked horrified.

"I tried to nominate you, and they said —"

"Is that how it happens?" Popovich said. "People nominate you?"

"Yeah," said Harris. "I wrote you a nomination letter, and they told me thanks but Pop has made it clear that he doesn't want to go in while he's still coaching."

"Well," answered Popovich, "that would presume I think I'm going in and I deserve to go in. So I would tell that guy that he doesn't know what he's talking about. He's talking for me instead of me talking for myself."

Tom James, the Spurs' director of media services, asked Popovich to step outside for a moment because one of his assistant coaches needed a word. As Popovich was leaving, Harris shouted at him with mocking dejection: "I'm never going to nominate you again, that's for sure."

"Why would you?" said Popovich over his shoulder. "I'm an asshole."

The exchange helped explain the Spurs' response to their collapse in the final two games of the 2013 NBA Finals at Miami. They were able to recover from those traumatic losses because none of them — starting with Popovich and 37-year-old Tim Duncan — had assumed they were entitled to win those games.

Duncan, who appeared to be on the way out in 2011, had recovered his form, remarkably. Tony Parker had emerged as the leader of the Spurs' revamped perimeter-based offense. Ginobili was still imposing off the bench. And Kawhi Leonard — a 22-year-old small forward whose 2011 draft rights had been acquired from the Pacers — was on track to become the best two-way player in the NBA. The Spurs won sixty-two games, earned a rematch with the Heat and then left nothing to chance while scorching Miami by 57 points over the last three games of the 2014 NBA Finals. "We ran into one of the greatest performances by a team in the history of the NBA," said Riley of the Spurs, who won in five games by way of their teamwork, exquisite ball movement and 46.6 percent shooting from the three-point line.

Popovich was humbled by that championship. "A day didn't go by where I didn't think about Game 6," he said of the previous year's Finals. "For the group to have the fortitude that they showed to get back to this spot speaks volumes about how they're constituted and what kind of fiber they have."

"Miami, for me, has been almost like college for other kids," LeBron said in a 2014 *Sports Illustrated* essay co-written with Lee Jenkins. "These past four years helped raise me into who I am. I became a better player and a better man. I learned from a franchise that had been where I wanted to go."

Instead of going on TV, LeBron was announcing his departure as a free agent in a magazine. He was leaving Miami to reclaim his home.

"People there have seen me grow up," LeBron said. "My relationship with Northeast Ohio is bigger than basketball. I didn't realize that four years ago. I do now."

Riley had seen the signs of departure in LeBron's final days. "But there was no feeling of that until after the season," he said. "After the season, it started to get dicey. I was assured by people close to LeBron that everything was fine. But it wasn't. I should have talked to the man myself. I never broached it. I had a chance to do that at Mike Mancias's wedding."

Mancias, James's longtime trainer in Cleveland, had been working for the Heat for the past four years. At the wedding Riley spent time with LeBron's mother. "I spoke to Gloria for a half hour at the bar — we were laughing and singing — but I never brought it up with her either," Riley said. "Then I started hearing rumors of moving vans. Once he left, everybody was gone. They had leases to condos, they had bought cars — and they were gone. Everybody had planned to leave, at least that's what I heard. I didn't go overboard investigating what happened. I just said, 'This was something that had been in the works probably for a while.'"

The plan was to add talent around the Big Three and extend Miami's run to five straight NBA Finals and three championships. The key acquisition in 2014 would have been Kobe's championship teammate Pau Gasol. "He took the meeting with me because he wanted to play with LeBron," Riley said. "I gave the number of Pau to [LeBron's agent] Rich Paul and texted also to LeBron, 'Could you call him?' I said, 'This is for our team.'" Riley heard bad news from Gasol's agent, Arn Tellem. "Arn told me that LeBron had called Pau: 'I'd love to play with you, wherever I may be.' Then Arn called me on the phone and said, 'I think you have a problem.' I said, 'I know I have a problem.'"

Riley was invited to Las Vegas to make his pitch to re-sign LeBron, but Maverick Carter wasn't at the meeting, and LeBron kept glancing at the World Cup final on TV. "I should not have made the trip," Riley said. "It was like I was intruding on something."

At least he heard the final word from LeBron himself. "He was cordial," Riley said. "The first four words were 'I want to thank,' and I said to myself, 'Oh shit.' I just said, 'Good luck.' I didn't say one other word."

Riley felt as if he'd been played. "Was I naïve or just so hopeful?" he said. "I wasn't naïve. But I was so hopeful because I didn't want this to end. We were a good pairing as an organization and a superstar. Just a heads-up, and it would have been secret. Give me a heads-up, and I'm going to be sworn to secrecy, and I would have started the work of getting players. Micky [Arison] and I and the team deserved a heads-up. That's the only thing that angered me after he left. That is the only thing."

Riley was aware that he would be accused of hypocrisy — that after benefiting from LeBron's decision-making style in 2010, he was decrying the same behavior four years later. "We had reached understandings during the [free-agency] moratorium with Chris and Dwyane on salaries, that LeBron was going to get the max, and those two guys would get less, and then we would get Luol Deng to come in with them. He would have been a great addition, and he was willing to take less money to get in there.

"Did we deserve more than Cleveland got from him? What we did get was the same treatment. He was consistent. He didn't let anybody know. Cleveland got *The Decision*. We got the letter from *SI*."

"I had two to three days of tremendous anger. I was absolutely livid, which I expressed to myself and my closest friends," Riley said. Then, over the weeks and months to come, he came to see the move to Cleveland from LeBron's point of view. "My beautiful plan all of a sudden came crashing down," he said. "That team in ten years could have won five or six championships. But I get it. I get the whole chronicle of his life.

"While there may have been some carnage always left behind when he made these kinds of moves, in Cleveland and also in Miami, he did the right thing," Riley went on. "I just finally came to accept the realization that he and his family said, 'You'll never, ever be accepted back in your hometown if you don't go back to try to win a title. Otherwise someday you'll go back there and have the scarlet letter on your back. You'll be the greatest player in the history of mankind, but back there, nobody's really going to accept you.'"

Riley watched LeBron's abandoned fans in Cleveland embrace the return of their prodigal son, who went back to wearing his Cavaliers uniform with Jordan's number 23. LeBron dumped his trademark headband, but he continued the pre-game ritual of handshakes that had once been ridiculed by the Celtics (and had since spread throughout the league). Along the way Riley realized how far his former player had come. Miami, which had gone 224-88 on its way to four NBA Finals with him, dropped out of the playoffs the year he left. Cleveland went from losing forty-nine games to winning fifty-three and reaching the NBA Finals in his first year back. The questioning of his killer instinct had become laughable as LeBron produced 35.8 points, 13.3 rebounds and 8.8 assists in 45.7 exhausting, do-everything minutes for his depleted Cavaliers in their 2015 Finals defeat to the Warriors.

"He's unbelievable in how he has grown to this point," Riley said. "He has so much confidence now, because he's conquered that world of doubt. And there's no doubt that he had doubt. They can say whatever they want to say back in 2010 when they said, 'We're not afraid of anything.' But they had doubt. They wouldn't have left if they didn't have doubt that they could win anymore in Cleveland.

"I felt he was the best player of all time when he was playing for us, especially in the back-to-back championship years. I know what somebody had to do to coach a player who is one of the best of all time and also try to stop a player that's the best of all time. We're seeing him emerge right now as that player. I see a no-nonsense guy now. He may be one of the highest-IQ players in the game ever. As we speak today, he has emerged physically and spiritually, and has total control of his environment, both on the court and off the court."

In 2016 Riley watched as LeBron baited Draymond Green of the Warriors to punch him in the groin, earning Green a one-game suspension that enabled the Cavaliers to recover from their 3–1 deficit in the NBA Finals and force Game 7. "The worst thing that a man can do to another man, especially in the NBA: You don't ever step over a man on the floor. It's like you're pissing on him. It is one thing players in this league will not tolerate. Did he bait Draymond into that? Did he say, 'I'm going to step over him and maybe he'll kick me in the nuts, and maybe he'll get suspended'? I wouldn't be surprised if he knew what he was do-ing, because he's so smart. It reminded me of Kevin McHale taking down Kurt

Rambis," said Riley of the incident that enabled the Celtics to overcome his Lakers in the 1984 NBA Finals.

On the night of the seventh game in Oakland, Riley broke his silence. "I didn't want to send him anything that he could read before he hit the floor," he said. "As soon as he hit the floor, I sent a text to him. I said, 'Win this and be free.'" He never got back to me with a response. In fact he said something after the game," Riley said with a laugh.

After LeBron won his championship for Cleveland, he told ESPN's Dave McMenamin: "When I decided to leave Miami — I'm not going to name any names, I can't do that — but there were some people that I trusted and built relationships with in those four years [who] told me I was making the biggest mistake of my career. And that shit hurt me. And I know it was an emotional time that they told me that because I was leaving. They just told me it was the biggest mistake I was making in my career. And that right there was my motivation."

"It wasn't me," Riley said. "I never said anything to him." He couldn't account for others in his organization who might have lashed out. "That's one of LeBron's greatest traits," continued Riley, "that somewhere in him there's such a competitive thing that he's going to find something to motivate himself to win." Michael Jordan had the same trait.

When Jordan was the NBA's leader in the 1990s, he was criticized for rarely taking a stand on social issues. In that era, when the NBA was obsessed with achieving financial stability, Jordan had his hands full breaking through commercially as the star of the "black sport."

The next generation of stars, liberated financially by Jordan, has taken on the responsibility of speaking out. LeBron has served as their leader — alongside Carmelo Anthony, Dwyane Wade, Chris Paul and others — as he has expressed points of view on issues of all kinds that affect African Americans and other groups. In 2017 he received the J. Walter Kennedy Citizenship Award in a vote by the Professional Basketball Writers Association, which recognized the LeBron James Family Foundation for its work in motivating children in Akron to stay in school and attend college.

"I really enjoy listening to him now," said Gregg Popovich, who himself has taken on a greater role in social activism. "Because he's a grown man, and he knows what he thinks. In the beginning this guy was telling him to say this, this guy's telling him to do this, you know — because he has people around him — but he's saying what he thinks now. And what he believes. He's gotten to that point."

Crucial to LeBron's development off the court has been his insistence on retaining his team of advisers, in spite of the mess they created for him in 2010 by steering him to put on *The Decision*. Instead of firing them, he ensured their loyalty by standing by them. And they, having known him since high school, have helped him to fulfill a public identity that was true to his beliefs. Together they created their own business model from the ground up.

Not quite two years after his exit from the Heat, there was still pain on both sides as Riley watched LeBron in the 2016 NBA Finals. Riley is close friends with Peter Guber, an owner of the Warriors, and he had mixed feelings about LeBron winning a championship away from Miami. "As I was sitting there watching, I was indifferent to it," Riley said. "But towards the end, when they got close, I said, 'I want to get this over with. I want to get it over with and win that damn thing so the guy doesn't have to be put up on a damn cross every year. I'd like to get this over with and get on to normalcy in this league.'"

He found himself cheering when LeBron covered the full court to block a breakaway layup by Golden State's Andre Iguodala. "That was one of the greatest single plays I've ever seen," Riley said. "When he came flying out of the corner on the fast break, I thought, 'Why didn't Klay Thompson step in front of him?' He was right in front of LeBron. If he would have, he could have changed the game. But once LeBron took off at the free throw line, as he was flying through the air, he was going to get it on the right side of the board if it was a right-handed layup, or if Iguodala had gone up and under, to use the rim to protect him, he was going to get it with his left hand. But there was no way that that ball was going to go in the basket. To me, that was his 'Thank God, I'm free at last.'"

In the final minute LeBron fed Kyrie Irving for the championship-winning three-pointer, securing the Cavaliers' 93–89 victory and the first championship for a Cleveland team since 1964. "Winning two championships with us gave him that supreme confidence that he can do it," Riley said. "Then the guts to leave and go back home: 'Now I'm going to bring this back to you, Cleveland, to the Rust Belt, to Akron.' It was just him saying, 'I have total control of my life.'"

In Miami they were all gone. Bosh was waived by the Heat in 2017, following the development of persistent blood clots over a period of three years. Wade moved back home to Chicago in 2016 for one lucrative season with the Bulls. The following year, as a 35-year-old free agent, he signed a relatively small contract with Cleveland in order to reunite with his good friend. This time there would be no doubt that LeBron was the leader.

"That will really motivate Dwyane," Riley said. "LeBron is the one guy who can get to Dwyane and tell him, 'Get your ass in shape and go play harder.' He can get the greatness out of Dwyane. He did the same with Ray Allen. He goes right after them. The only way you can lead that way is you have to be above and beyond reproach, and he is above and beyond because of the way he trains and performs night in, night out. He knows what drives the LeBron phenomenon, and that's winning. He won't tolerate mediocrity."

LeBron, with three NBA titles amid his ongoing run of seven NBA Finals, was liberated. And so, too, in a sense, was Riley, whose organization had helped transform the potential of the NBA's most talented star into reality — even if only for four years. Someday LeBron's number would be retired in Miami alongside Jordan's. By then, Riley knew, the circumstances of LeBron's departure would mean very little in comparison with all that he had achieved.

"I'm a good Irishman," Riley said. "I don't hold a grudge. Only the drunks do — and the Celtics. But not me."

In the TD Garden in Boston, Dirk is running as if his ankles are dead. He's not pushing off them so much as they are being carried along while his arms, shoulders and hips swing him forward in their exaggerated way. He is advancing, stiffly, from spot to spot, catching passes and making shots in between. "Aaagh!" he groans after a rare miss from the corner.

"You got to give me that shit," urges Mike "Sweetchuck" Procopio, Kobe's former adviser. One day in 2012 Kobe stopped asking for advice and responding to Procopio's emails. That was how Procopio knew they were no longer working together, and he is not the type to suffer hurt feelings. One year later the Mavericks hired him to be their player development coach, for which he did insist on a salary.

As Procopio dribbles, Dirk sets the screen, separates, catches, spins and shoots.

"I want you to get on your knees and fucking beg like the worm that you are," Procopio says.

"Where did we find this guy?" Dirk asks his teammate Devin Harris.

"Chicago," Harris says.

"No," says Dirk, "he's *Bahstan*."

"I was with a mob guy," says Procopio, whose accent betrays his Boston roots, actually the suburb of Revere. "He was talking about breaking your legs. He said he thought we broke your legs five years ago the way you're walking."

It is November 2016, and the league is turning over. Joey Crawford, the referee, has been retired for half a year because of a bad knee. Larry Bird is going to be stepping down from the Pacers at the end of the season. Isiah Thomas is back in New York—running the Women's National Basketball Association (WNBA) team. Kobe has been long gone from the Lakers, who in three months are going to hire Magic Johnson to be their team president.

Phil Jackson will be on his way out as president of the failing Knicks, three years after he was hired to restore them to contention with the triangle offense; Anthony is going to follow him out the door in a trade to Oklahoma City. The Thunder will ask Anthony to help offset the 2016 free-agency departure of Kevin Durant to Golden State. After enduring echoes of the criticism that LeBron had absorbed five years earlier, Durant and two-time MVP Stephen Curry led the Warriors to their second championship in three seasons at the expense of LeBron's Cavaliers.

Chris Paul will be dealt by the Clippers to join with James Harden in Houston, Paul George will be moved by the Pacers to Oklahoma City, and Kyrie Irving, in emulation of Kobe's divorce with Shaquille O'Neal, will ask for a trade out of Cleveland to separate him from LeBron. In the summer of 2017 the Cavaliers will deal him to Boston in a blockbuster exchange for Isiah Thomas—thus renewing LeBron's personal rivalry with the Celtics.

While so many rival teams are loading up with A-list talents, LeBron at age 32 will be recast as an elder star, charged with staving off the younger generation of Curry and Durant—shooters modeled after Dirk—while holding them to the highest standards. It will be his turn to play the same noble role that was fulfilled in 2010–11 by the likes of Dirk, Kobe, Paul Pierce, Tim Duncan and so many of the others who were committed to beating LeBron and thereby enabled his progress.

And so the recycling will continue. In 2018 LeBron will be expected to opt out of his contract and become a free agent nearing the end of his career, a decision to be made under entirely different circumstances than *The Decision*.

Dirk, 38 years old, is the mainstay. In his nineteenth season with Dallas, he is refusing to give in to the sore Achilles that has been sidelining him. The Mavericks are in Boston for their game against the Celtics tonight. Dirk isn't ready to play just yet. The best he can do is survive this late-morning workout and the abuse from Procopio that comes with it.

"Enjoy it right now," he says to Dirk, while feeding him shot after shot. "Because this is the last time you'll be relevant in Boston."

"If you didn't have a sense of humor, you'd be fucked," Dirk says.

"We tend to not like people on our roster who know exactly where they were when Kennedy got shot," Procopio replies.

Dirk misses one from the top of the three-point line.

"You're shooting as bad as Brian Cardinal," Procopio says, and he nods toward a janitor. "The custodian just asked if we traded for him."

Kevin Garnett and Ray Allen are retired already, and Paul Pierce, finishing his career with the Clippers, is on his way out; soon he will be patching up his relationship with Allen. Tim Duncan is gone, but Popovich, true to his word, has kept the program going in San Antonio. Holger Geschwindner is still Dirk's mentor, though he is back home in Germany at the moment. Procopio has taken his place as a kind of substitute teacher who remembers very well that Rick Pitino dreamed of drafting Dirk in the first round for the Celtics in 1998.

"Dirty, you would have been back in Germany after eighteen months if you'd fucking played for Pitino," Procopio says. "You would have been in the fetal position leaving here."

His sarcasm appears to be contagious. When Procopio calls for another drill, Dirk turns to Harris and says, "What are you doing? I need you out here."

"You want picks?" says Harris. "You never use them in the game. I don't see why you want them now."

The ball is flying in an oddly shaped circuit, from Procopio to Dirk, in a loop through the basket, then back to Procopio, around and around and around as Procopio makes light of the points milestone Dirk will be achieving later in the season.

"You think I get to 30,000 by luck?" Dirk asks.

"Yeah, because here you'd be at 1,800," Procopio answers. "Dude, you'd be running pick-and-pops with Stephon Marbury in China if you'd played here."

The shots are being made, one after another, as casually as if Dirk were washing windows or grilling hamburgers or merely flipping a coin and catching it, flipping and catching, up and down.

"Thirty thousand points, 1,100 rebounds," Procopio announces derisively.

The ball keeps finding its way through the basket.

"Thirty thousand points, 1,100 rebounds and 400 good things to say about your teammates," Procopio amends.

"And 270 '*What the fuck is he doing?*'" adds Harris in a bad German accent.

There are now 113 players in the NBA from outside the United States. Altogether they account for 25 percent of the league, and Dirk is their role model. Back home in Dallas, his wife, Jessica, has recently given birth to their third child. All of his dreams are coming true.

Shooting his way has never been as easy as Dirk has made it look, and never so demanding as to make him give it up. At the end of this season, Dirk is going to agree to another two-year contract — seasons twenty and twenty-one for him — at the extreme bargain of $5 million annually. For him, it really has never been about the money, and throughout this late autumn morning he has not stopped grinning at Sweetchuck.

ACKNOWLEDGMENTS

It took six years to pull this book together, mainly because I set out to write it before the story had emerged. When Susan Canavan of Houghton Mifflin Harcourt invited me in February 2011 to write a book about the NBA in the wake of LeBron James's controversial move to Miami, my response was somewhat vague. I told her that I was interested in getting at the symbolism and meaning of the NBA and basketball in general, which had been a huge blind spot for the league and the sport.

The Decision created an opportunity for this discussion to occur. What was it about LeBron's TV show that struck a nerve? Why were so many millions of Americans frustrated and angry with him and his league? By understanding the causes and effects of *The Decision,* maybe this book could close in on the larger question of basketball and its importance in America and around the world.

Any conclusions that I reached would have to be supported by the story. And that story kept changing as LeBron, by his own admission, continued to develop and mature over the years. His defining victory with Cleveland in the 2016 NBA Finals helped me realize what had been achieved five years earlier by Dirk Nowitzki — LeBron was affirming the revelation set forth by Dirk that basketball is the sport of the American Dream — and then I knew that this story was ready to be told.

As I write this in 2017, the American sports landscape is shifting. Baseball, the game of summer, is losing popularity because it is slow. Football, the game of war, is endangered because it is violent, according to brain-injury research that links long-term neurological damage to the collisions that are inherent in the sport. And so the NFL and MLB find themselves struggling to change their fundamental identities. It's as if those two Old World leagues don't know what they're supposed to be anymore — whereas LeBron, his league and its sport have all come of age.

I am indebted to all who are quoted in this book, as well as to the scores of NBA sources, named and unnamed, who have taken me into their confidence over the years so that I may benefit from their insight. The relationships I've developed with you have been the best part of my job.

Thanks to John Vinocur, the legendary editor of the *International Herald Tribune*, who in 1992 hired me as the sportswriter for the world's largest international daily newspaper. My six years in Europe — three in Paris, three in London — provided the perspective and ambition I needed to pursue this story.

Thanks to Vince Doria, who as editor of the *Boston Globe* assigned me to all three of the Larry Bird–Magic Johnson NBA Finals in the 1980s while enabling me to write about the NBA's greatest generation. Vince also read an early draft of this book and helped me understand what it could be.

Thanks to Hank Hersch, who was my first and finest NBA editor at *Sports Illustrated*, and to Brad Weinstein, who ran the NBA coverage for SI.com but was of the old school — dedicated to getting things right while protecting his writers and their writing the way the best editors do.

Thanks to Steve Quintana, Scooter Vertino, Eric Jackson and everyone at NBA.com. And likewise to Joe Sullivan of the *Boston Globe*, for whom I will always be grateful.

I doubt whether I could have finished this book without the advice and support of Steve Fainaru, who read through a late draft and spent hours discussing the story with me. Throughout the years of this project Jackie MacMullan was, as always, the sister I never had. I am lucky to know her.

I am grateful for the support of friends like Mark Linehan, Leigh Montville and Don Skwar. The same goes for Bob Ryan and Dan Shaughnessy, NBA mentors who have become lifelong friends. Thanks to Joe Amorosino, Steve Bulpett, Shaun Clancy, Morry Levine, Nate Long, Terry Lyons, Steve Marantz, Tom McLaughlin, Ken Powtak, Liz Robbins, Frank Shorr and Willie Weinbaum.

Ed Kleven, I miss you dearly.

Thanks to David Black, for keeping my spirits up and always looking out for me, and to Susan Canavan, Jenny Xu, Barbara Jatkola, Laura Brady, Phyllis De-Blanche, Megan Wilson and the crew at Houghton Mifflin Harcourt.

Thanks to Chris Thomsen for the development of IanThomsen.com, and to him, his sister Jacqueline Thomsen, and Ben Cormier for their journalistic input and marketing strategies in this new media era.

Thanks to Marguerite Schropp Lucarelli, Greg Payne and Suzanne Wright.

Thanks to Tim Frank, Brian McIntyre, Michael Bass, Maureen Coyle, Mark Broussard, Peter Lagiovane, Joanna Shapiro, Peter Steber, Michael Perrelli, John Acunto, Amanda Thorn George, Mike Wade, Rachel Walsh and their colleagues at NBA Communications.

Thanks to the facilitators who helped me with the teams featured in this book: Jeff Twiss, Christian Megliola, Heather Walker and Brian Olive of the Celtics; Tad Carper, Garin Narain, B. J. Evans, Jeff Schaefer and Amanda Petrak of the Cavaliers; Sarah Melton and Alan Rakowski of the Mavericks; John Black, Alison Bogli, Calder Hynes, Josh Rupprecht and Nick Mazzella of the Lakers; Tim Donovan, Rob Wilson, Michael Lissack and Nick Maiorana of the Heat; David Benner and Krissy Myers of the Pacers; Tim Gelt, Teri Washington, Tomago Collins, Dan Tolzman and Nick O'Hayre of the Nuggets; and Tom James and his staff of the Spurs.

A special thanks to Scott Tomlin of the Mavericks. Thanks also to Ed Markey, Ben Cafardo and Dan Wasserman, as well as to Brian Magoffin at Springfield College.

Thanks to Jerry Colangelo and his team at USA Basketball, including Jim Tooley, Sean Ford, Craig Miller, Caroline Williams and Jenny Maag.

Thanks to Mike Gorman, Tom Heinsohn, Sean Grande, Cedric Maxwell, Abby Chin, Brian Scalabrine, Greg Dickerson, Donny Marshall, Gary Tanguay, Michael Felger and Paul Lucey; to Chuck Cooperstein, Mark Followill, Brad Davis, Bob Ortegel and Jeff Wade; to Eric Reid, Tony Fiorentino, Jason Jackson, Mike Inglis and John Crotty; and to Mark Boyle, Quinn Buckner and Clark Kellogg.

Special thanks to Kenny Grant, Ernie Butler and Elke Clausen.

Thanks to Josh Robbins at the Professional Basketball Writers Association, which champions the NBA's finest storytellers, who in spite of all obstacles continue to hold the NBA and other leagues accountable to the values of the sport.

Thanks to former colleagues Jack McCallum, Lee Jenkins, Chris Ballard, Phil Taylor, Chris Mannix, Sam Amick, Scott Price, Steve Rushin, Rick Reilly, Alexander Wolff and Paul Forrester; and to David Aldridge, Steve Aschburner, John Schuhmann, Sekou Smith, Scott Howard-Cooper, Shaun Powell, Lang Whitaker and Fran Blinebury.

I owe much to the work of so many NBA writers over the years, including Adrian Wojnarowski, Brian Windhorst, Jeff Zillgitt, Mike Monroe, Marc Spears and Mark Murphy. Thanks also to Henry Abbott, Jonathan Abrams, J. A. Adande, Mitch Albom, Harvey Araton, Kevin Arnovitz, Bruce Arthur, Rod Beard, Howard Beck, Ian Begley, Jerry Bembry, Julian Benbow, Ken Berger, Marc Berman, A. Sherrod Blakely, Ben Bolch, Stefan Bondy, Rick Bonnell, Tim Bontemps, Rachel Brady, Mike Bresnahan, Chris Broussard, Ric Bucher, Candace Buckner, Bill Burt, Scott Cacciola, Geoff Calkins, Jessica Camerato, Mike Carey, Janis Carr, Shams Charania, Anthony Chiang, Ben Cohen, Paul Coro, Ryan Cortes, Greg Cote, Joe Cowley, Tim Cowlishaw, Tom D'Angelo, Frank Dell'Apa, Chris Dempsey, Nick DePaula, Sean Deveney, Kevin Ding, Bradford Doolittle, Gregg Doyel, Bill Doyle, Bill Dwyre, Kerry Eggers, Amin Elhassan, Helene Elliott, Vince Ellis, Tom Enlund, Perry Farrell, Jonathan Feigen, John Feinstein, Jim Fenton, Dave Feschuk, Mike Fine, Mike Finger, Bob Finnan, Chad Ford, Chris Forsberg, Joe Freeman, Nick Friedell, Randy Galloway, Tania Ganguli, Mike Ganter, Art Garcia, Jonathan Givony, Joseph Godman, Jimmy Golen, Ben Golliver, Vincent Goodwill, Rick Gosselin, Michael Grange, Sean Gregory, Israel Gutierrez, Tom Haberstroh, Alan Hahn, Buck Harvey, Mark Heisler, Kurt Helin, Chris Herring, Adam Himmelsbach, Benjamin Hochman, Richard Hoffer, John Hollinger, Baxter Holmes, Johnette Howard, Jan Hubbard, Jill Hudson, David Hyde, Jesse Hyde, Al Iannazzone, Frank Isola, Barry Jackson, John Jackson, Dwight Jaynes, Sally Jenkins, K. C. Johnson, Adi Joseph, Cathal Kelly, Fred Kerber, Adam Kilgore, Jay King, Bob Kravitz, Jon Krawczynski, Doug Krikorian, Matt Langone, Mitch Lawrence, Dan Le Batard, Armel LeBescon, Gil LeBreton, Arnaud Lecomte, Michael Lee, Robert Lee, Josh Lewenberg, Bill Livingston, Jason Lloyd, John Lombardo, Aaron Lopez, Zach Lowe, Brian Mahoney, Rob Mahoney, Bobby Marks, Jeff McDonald, Mike McGraw, Tim McMahon, Aaron McMann, Dave McMenamin, Kevin McNamara, Mark Medina, Len Megliola, Mike Monroe, Gordon Monson, Mark Monteith, Matt Moore, Michael Muldoon, Liz Mullen, Manny Navarro, Ian O'Connor, Bill Oram, Massimo Oriani, Kevin Pelton, Chris Perkins, Dan Peterson, Mike Pina, Bill Plaschke, Terry Pluto, Steve Popper, Dwain Price, Diane Pucin, Jason Quick, Scott Raab, Tom Reed, Bill Reiter, Bill Reynolds, Tim Reynolds, Shandel Richardson, Brian Robb, Darren Rovell, Richard Sandomir, Mary Schmitt Boyer, Brian Schmitz, Mike Schmitz, Eddie Sefko, Andrew Sharp, Drew Sharp, Bud Shaw, Ramona Shelburne, Chris Sheridan, Kevin Sherrington, T. J. Simers, Bill Simmons, Ethan Skolnick, Doug Smith, Sam Smith, Earl K. Sneed,

Scott Soshnick, Scott Souza, Marc Stein, Ethan Sherwood Strauss, Elliott Teaford, Rich Thompson, David Thorpe, Ronald Tillery, Justin Tinsley, Chris Tomasson, Pablo S. Torre, Brad Townsend, Broderick Turner, Jodie Valade, Joe Vardon, George Vecsey, Peter Vecsey, Ailene Voisin, Michael Wallace, Gary Washburn, Mike Wells, Mark Whicker, Jason Whitlock, Michael Wilbon, Ira Winderman, Mike Wise, Tom Withers, Gery Woelfel, Branson Wright, Ohm Youngmisuk, Mark Zeigler and Jerry Zgoda.

All my love to Maureen, Jacqueline and Chris Thomsen and to Gabriel Golden; to Elizabeth, Eigild and Glenn Thomsen; and to Maureen and Donald Ford and their large, loving family. I am more grateful for your support than you can ever know.

INDEX